THE DEVELOPMENT OF
AMERICAN ROMANCE

MICHAEL DAVITT BELL

THE DEVELOPMENT OF AMERICAN ROMANCE

The Sacrifice of Relation

THE UNIVERSITY OF CHICAGO PRESS
Chicago and London

The University of Chicago Press, Chicago 60637
The University of Chicago Press, Ltd., London

Library of Congress Cataloging in Publication Data

Bell, Michael Davitt.
   The development of American romance.

   Bibliography: p.
   Includes index.
   1. American fiction—19th century—History and
criticism. 2. Romanticism—United States. I. Title.
PS377.B4   813'.2'09   80-12241
ISBN 0-226-04211-1 (cloth)
        0-226-04213-8 (paper)

The balloon of experience is in fact of course tied to the earth, and under that necessity we swing, thanks to a rope of remarkable length, in the more or less commodious car of the imagination; but it is by the rope we know where we are, and from the moment that cable is cut we are at large and unrelated. . . . The art of the romancer is, "for the fun of it," insidiously to cut the cable, to cut it without our detecting him."

HENRY JAMES, Preface to *The American*

It is with fiction as with religion: it should present another world, and yet one to which we feel the tie.

HERMAN MELVILLE, *The Confidence-Man*

CONTENTS

PART THREE
A WORLD OF WORDS

ACKNOWLEDGMENTS

IT HAS TAKEN ME EIGHT YEARS TO RESEARCH, WRITE, AND REVISE THIS study. During that period I have received help from many quarters, which it is now my pleasure to acknowledge. Many ideas were first tested on (and refined by) my students at Williams College and Princeton University. A fellowship from the American Council of Learned Societies, in 1974–75, gave me a chance to devote full attention to the project. I have received generous assistance from the staffs of the Williams College Library, the Princeton University Library, the New York Public Library, the Harvard University Library, and the Boston Atheneum.

Lawrence Graver, Robert Merill, John Reichert, and Robert E. Streeter read the book in typescript; I thank them for their many helpful suggestions. I am especially grateful to Don Gifford for his reading of an earlier version of the study. In countless places he helped me clarify the details of my argument, and his overall thoughtfulness renewed and enlarged my understanding of what I was up to. My thanks also go to Claudia Bell, Peter Berek, Robert Dalzell, Ann Douglas, David Langston, and Frederick Rudolph for reading individual chapters and helping me to improve them. My special debt to William Hedges, for his detailed comments on an earlier version of chapter 4, is acknowledged in the footnotes to that chapter. And I am grateful to the editors of *Early American Literature* for permission to reprint chapter 3, an earlier version of which appeared in that journal.

At various points I have received assistance from the Williams College Class of 1900 Research Fund. Nadene Lane cheerfully and rapidly typed chapter 8 after I inadvertently cropped a finger tip with an electric lawn trimmer, and Shannon Gilligan caught and corrected inaccuracies in my quotations. I am particularly grateful to my cousin, Hester Bell McCoy, who, in the midst of a vacation in northern Ontario, devoted many hours to helping me with the proofreading.

There is unfortunately no space to thank all those whose friendship has sustained me, and hence my work, over the past eight years. Many of their names appear above, in other capacities. The book is dedicated to the two friends who have helped the most.

INTRODUCTION

THIS IS A BOOK ABOUT AMERICAN ROMANCE. MORE PRECISELY, IT CONSIDERS the development of a particular tradition of romance in American fiction—an experimental tradition, emerging in the 1790s and 1820s in the work of Charles Brockden Brown and Washington Irving and culminating in the 1840s and 1850s in the great tales and romances of Poe, Hawthorne, and Melville. Since the idea that America's fictional tradition is one of "romance" is neither new nor universally accepted, it seems appropriate to begin by suggesting the particular nature of my inquiry.

In 1948 Lionel Trilling argued that "the novel"—concerned with "reality" and "manners," characterized by "social texture"— "never really established itself in America.... American writers of genius have not turned their minds to society." Their fictions have thus been, not "novels," but "romances."[1] This argument was taken up, and expanded or transformed, by various critics in the 1950s, notably by Richard Chase and Perry Miller. In subsequent decades the distinction between American "romance" and British "novel" has become something of a critical commonplace, even a cliché.[2]

This cliché has had, nevertheless, plenty of detractors, especially recently. The actual differences between American "romance" and British "novel," it is argued, have been greatly exaggerated.[3] We are told that Trilling's notion of "reality," on which his definition of "novel" depends, is naive.[4] It is urged that, in any case, distinctions between the "romance" and the "novel" are only spuriously distinctions of genre, resting more on matters of theme or subject than on differences of style, mode, or form.[5] Since the idea of American romance seems on the one hand a commonplace and on the other a matter of controversy and confusion, it might appear that a student of nineteenth-century American fiction would be wise to avoid the term "romance" altogether.

Whether wisely or not, I have chosen to emphasize and retain this term, for one all-important reason: whatever our present argument over its meaning, "romance" is the word that Brown, Irving, Poe, Hawthorne, and Melville used to describe what they at least thought they were doing. Rather than reject the word, it has seemed to me more responsible to investigate what these writers and their contemporaries meant in using it. Only then can we assess its historical importance and its usefulness in describing or understanding whatever tradition may be embodied in their work. In Part One, therefore, I present the various and often contradictory meanings given to "romance" in nineteenth-century critical discourse, and in chapters 3 through 6 I turn in more detail to the effect these various meanings had on the thought and work of Brown, Irving, Poe, Hawthorne, and Melville.

Perhaps I might clarify my approach, and its relation to earlier discussions of American romance, by specifying some things I am *not* doing. I am not repeating the argument that American romance is distinguished by a lack of "social texture" (in fact I have doubts about the truth and the meaning of this generalization), for I am more interested in continuities of style and form, or in the recurrence of certain attitudes toward style and form. Nor am I concerned to revive or redefine the distinction between "romance" and "novel," for the truth is that in nineteenth-century discourse this distinction is far less important than the more general distinction between *all* fiction and what conventional thought took to be "fact." Indeed, the novel/romance distinction was often used to obscure the larger dichotomy. The avowed "romancer" admitted or proclaimed what the "novelist" strove to conceal or deny: that his fiction was a figment of imagination.

Finally, and what is most important, this study is in no sense an attempt at theoretical definition of the genre "romance." I am not looking for a category into which to fit the work of my five writers. I am attempting, rather, to understand *their* categories in order to approach the experience mediated by these categories and the fiction that grew, in part, out of this mediation. There may be a single meaning of "romance" that would describe *Moby-Dick*, Shakespeare's last plays, and *The Romance of the Rose*, but that is not the sort of meaning I am after. "My *instinct*," Melville wrote to his British publisher in 1848, discussing his shift of purpose while writing *Mardi*, "is to out with [that is, to openly reveal] the Romance" (*Letters*, 71).[6] I simply want to know what a statement like that meant to a writer like Melville and how his understanding of "romance" informed what he wrote.

Leo Marx has written of the cultural historian's approach to works of American literature that it

> has developed considerable skill in relating individual products of mind . . . to large collective mental formations—myth, ethos, ideology, world view, and the like. But, until we can apprehend these formations as they are related to a concept of social structure and its operation, they will continue to seem unmoored—a ghostly, free-floating cloud of abstractions only distantly related, like the casting of a shadow, to the actual struggles of everyday life.[7]

We are unsure of what it meant, in sociological terms, to "be a romancer" in nineteenth-century America, yet this is the question we must ask if we would understand not only the "actual struggles" of those who chose to "out with the Romance" but the relationship their works, "collective mental formations" and all, bore to the culture of their America. Who and what, in that complex process of interaction that constitutes a whole culture, were they struggling for—and as? My intention in chapters 1 through 6 is thus not simply to investigate the theory and practice of romance in the works of Brown, Irving, Poe, Hawthorne, and Melville but to consider what seems equally important: the connection between this theory and practice and the five writers' actual experience, as "romancers," of their culture.

The emphasis in the last two chapters, which deal primarily with Hawthorne and Melville, is somewhat different. The experimental tradition under discussion grew out of concrete social or cultural circumstances—notably, the status of the identity "romancer" in the early nineteenth century and the ways in which these five writers accepted or manipulated this status in their lives and in their work—but it also drew on the conscious exploitation, by some of our romancers, of a seeming affinity between certain formal problems of fictional narrative and what they saw as a "formal" problem of nineteenth-century American national culture. "American romance" meant many different things to many different people, but in what seems to me its most interesting aspect in the work of the five writers here considered it was a highly self-conscious experimental fictional tradition that transcended solipsism by exploiting and investigatiing an analogous self-consciousness in the national experiment of which it was a part.

A good deal of modern and "postmodern" literature is similarly self-conscious and experimental, turning in on itself to explore such matters as the nature and validity of linguistic statement and fictional representation.[8] These matters were central to the romances of Brown, Irving, and Poe, but Hawthorne and Melville went one step farther. They openly advertised the apparent congruence between the specific problem of form and validity in fiction and the more general problem of form and validity in their new national culture and, ultimately, in any culture. In such terms, the romancer's formal experiments, his fear of the artifice and insincerity of forms, took on, by analogy, a specifically cultural or social dimension.

Hawthorne and Melville recognized that, like the romance, the new nation required the embodiment of strange new truths in forms—forms of behavior and belief, of character and institution, of literary fiction. In such a view, all visible culture seemed a kind of fictional language, a species of romance, a fabric of artificial formalism uneasily concealing the anarchic energy that had produced it.

PART ONE

"TO OUT WITH THE ROMANCE"

My instinct *is to out with the Romance, & let me say that instincts are prophetic, & better than acquired wisdom.*

MELVILLE to John Murray (1848)

Do not meddle much with works of the imagination—Your imagination needs no feeding, indeed it is a mental quality that always takes care of itself; and is too apt to interfere with the others. Strengthen your judgment; cultivate habits of close thinking, and in all your reading let KNOWLEDGE *be the great object.*

IRVING TO HIS NEPHEW, PIERRE P. IRVING (1824)

PROLOGUE

AMERICANS BEGAN TO WRITE PROSE FICTION IN EARNEST DURING THE FINAL decade of the eighteenth century. There was fiction in America earlier, but its appearance was sporadic, its intention occasional, its purpose so propagandistic or blatantly allegorical as to call into serious question its status as fiction, let alone as art. Beginning in 1789, however, with the publication of William Hill Brown's *The Power of Sympathy*, the American fictional roster reflects, if not consistent excellence, at least a fairly consistent engagement.[1] From 1789 on, fiction-writing was an activity in which a significant and ever-growing number of Americans participated.

There are various reasons for this sudden increase in fiction-writing. Financial rewards were not high; indeed, of all American romancers and novelists before 1850, only Cooper was able to support himself wholly by writing.[2] But the influx of popular British fiction suggested at least the possibility of success, and the exoticism or outright escapism of much that was popular made the prospect attractive. Even the drawn-out suffering of Clarissa offered relief to those caught in a more mundane domestic drudgery, and many a fledgling lawyer—one thinks particularly of Brown and Irving—found in the charms of fancy potential release from the boredom of provincial respectability.

It is also important that our first real decade of fiction-writing coincided with the first decade of our national life. As British provinces, the colonies could easily make do with what came from England and was popular; but as a distinct nation, so the nationalist argument ran, we needed a literature of our own, with native settings and native themes. It is always hard to assess the effect of nationalist propaganda on actual works of literature, but it is clear that nationhood provided an added incentive to would-be native geniuses. The fact that *The Power of Sympathy* appeared in the year

3

of Washington's first inauguration may be mere coincidence, but it is a significant coincidence all the same.

Yet, however strongly the stick of nationalism may have been applied, the carrot of an "American" fiction remained elusive. The models for emulation, in a country with no native tradition of prose fiction, were still European, mainly British. In the 1790s the strongest influence remained the sentimental novel of seduction. Could Clarissa not languish in Connecticut? The impressive popularity of Susanna Rowson's *Charlotte Temple* (1791) suggested an affirmative answer, as did a host of other Richardsonian imitations. Some writers, most notably Hugh Henry Brackenridge in *Modern Chivalry* (1792–1815), turned to the picaresque novel, developed in England mainly by Fielding and Smollett, as a vehicle for social and political satire. Anne Radcliffe's addition of gothic terror to the seduction novel, threatening the heroine's mind as well as her body, had an enduring impact in America. And the vogue of Sir Walter Scott and historical romance, beginning in the second decade of the nineteenth century, was especially opportune for the literary needs of the new nation. Scott's emphasis on national history and local color, as Cooper and a host of other "American Scotts" soon learned, provided the perfect formula for advertising a distinctively "national" literature.

The story of British influence on American fiction is fascinating and important, but it is not the whole story. What seems even more fascinating—to me, as it has to many others—is the story of how British models were transformed, transmuted, or regenerated by American conditions. It seems important at the outset to ask two questions about these conditions and their influence. First: As Americans began to write fiction, how were they disposed to regard what they were doing? If what emerged in America, as we have so often been told, was a tradition of "romance," what did the term "romance" mean to Americans at our first turn of century? This question is the subject of chapter 1. Second: What did it mean, for those who chose so to identify themselves, to *be* "romancers"? What were the attractions, or risks, of this form of social identification? And how did those who embraced, or flirted with, this role, deal with it? These questions are the subject of chapter 2.

4

ONE

When this poison infects the mind, it destroys its tone and revolts it against whole-some reading. Reason and fact, plain and unadorned, are rejected. Nothing can engage attention unless dressed in all the figments of fancy, and nothing so bedecked comes amiss. The result is a bloated imagination, sickly judgment, and disgust towards all the real businesses of life.

THOMAS JEFFERSON to Nathaniel Burwell (1818),
on "the inordinate passion prevalent for novels."

LOOMINGS

"WHEN A WRITER CALLS HIS WORK A ROMANCE," DECLARED NATHANIEL Hawthorne in his preface to *The House of the Seven Gables* (1851), "it need hardly be observed that he wishes to claim a certain latitude, both as to its fashion and material" (1). Most of Hawthorne's contemporaries associated "romance" with "latitude," with freedom of invention, but they were far from agreement as to the precise nature and purpose of this freedom. "Romance" has many meanings in nineteenth-century American discourse—meanings often mutually contradictory. After Hawthorne's *Seven Gables* preface, the best-known American definition of "romance" is probably that of Henry James, in his preface to the New York edition of *The American* (1909). Both definitions are important, and we should recognize that they are quite different.

In Hawthorne's view, romance is fundamentally an integrative mode. While it allows "latitude" in presenting "circumstances, to a great extent, of the writer's own choosing," such imaginative play is strictly controlled by what one might call a higher moral realism. The romancer is free to depart from the novelist's obligation of "very minute fidelity, not merely to the possible, but to the probable and ordinary course of man's experience," but he is admonished to make only "a very moderate use" of these imaginative "privileges." The romance "as a work of art . . . must rigidly subject itself to laws, and [it] sins unpardonably, so far as it may swerve aside from the truth of the human heart" (1). For Hawthorne the domain of romance is a world of balance or reconciliation—what he describes in "The Custom-House" (in *The Scarlet Letter*) as "a neutral territory, somewhere between the real world and fairy-land, where the Actual and the Imaginary may meet, and each imbue itself with the nature of the other" (36).

James, on the other hand, characterizes romance in terms of a radical lack of integration between the actual and the imaginary. "The only *general* attribute of projected romance that I can see," he writes, "is the fact of the kind of experience with which it deals—experience liberated, so to speak; experience disengaged, disembroiled, disencumbered, exempt from the conditions that we usually know to attach to it."[1] We must pay attention to what is being said here. "Romance," for James, is less the label of a form or genre than of a kind of experience. Its central "latitude" is psychological.

Like Hawthorne, James cautions against overindulgence of fantasy, but he bases his advice not on the assumption of a higher moral realism (implying a symbolic or metaphorical connection between "fiction" and "truth") but on a concern for the aesthetic or psychological effectiveness of fantasy itself. "The greatest intensity," he argues, "may be so arrived at evidently—when the sacrifice of community, of the 'related' sides of situations, has not been too rash. [Romance] must to this end not flagrantly betray itself; we must even be kept if possible, *for our illusion* [my emphasis], from suspecting any sacrifice at all."[2] The Jamesian romancer may wish to conceal his "sacrifice . . . of the 'related' sides of situations," but it is this "sacrifice," rather than a "meeting" of the actual and the imaginary, that qualifies his work as a "romance." James continues his account with a now-famous metaphor:

> The balloon of experience is in fact of course tied to the earth, and under that necessity we swing, thanks to a rope of remarkable length, in the more or less commodious car of the imagination; but it is by the rope we know where we are, and from the moment that cable is cut we are at large and unrelated. . . . The art of the romancer is, "for the fun of it," insidiously to cut the cable, to cut it without our detecting him.

For James, then, the essence of romance lies in its moral irresponsibility, its severing of those connections or "relations" between imagination and actuality that characterize the mode for Hawthorne. In Hawthorne's view, romance is controlled, serious, moral, and conservative. For James it is an art of pure (if "insidiously" disguised) fantasy, which "more or less successfully palms off on us" a spurious facsimile of experience, "disconnected and uncontrolled."[3]

Modern critics seeking a sense of what American Romantics meant by "romance" have generally turned to the conservative theory of Hawthorne. This theory, discussed in the final section of the present chapter, was important and influential. But it is James—despite the fact that he wrote in the first decade of the twentieth century—who comes closest to the primary meaning of the term in British and American discourse before the Civil War, and one suspects that it was an important function of the conservative theory of romance to obscure this primary meaning. In other words, in spite of the efforts of Hawthorne and others to legitimize the mode through an apologetic of moral symbolism ("relating" illusion to truth, the imaginary to the actual), "romance" meant, first of all, fiction as opposed to fact, the spurious and possibly dangerous as opposed to the genuine.

ROMANCE AND RATIONAL ORTHODOXY

William Congreve and Clara Reeve, among others in England, gave currency to the "generic" distinction between romance and novel, in terms similar to those Hawthorne used in the *Seven Gables* preface;[4] but English writers generally defined romance in psychological or ethical rather than aesthetic terms, and they went far beyond the formal discrimination of genres to raise questions of intention and effect. As J. M. S. Tompkins describes prevailing British opinion at the end of the eighteenth century:

> "Romance" implied a seductive delusion, pathetic or ludicrous, according to the quality of the victim and the angle of the commentator. . . . To be romantic [was] to prefer the satisfactions of imagination to those of reason.

"Romance" was the term for *any* tale or novel that acknowledged itself to be a work of invention rather than imitation, of "fancy" rather than "reason." "We now use the term *romance*," wrote Sir Walter Scott in 1827, "as synonymous with fictitious composition."[5]

The same primary connotations obtained in contemporaneous American usage. In 1824, for instance, General William Sullivan declared the facts and scenes of the Revolution "so strange and heroic that they resemble ingenious fables, or the dreams of romance, rather than the realities of authentic history." Or there is the account of the persecution of his sect by the Mormon saint, Parley P. Pratt: "would to God it were a dream—a novel, a romance that had no existence save in the wild regions of fancy." For Pratt, clearly, "novel" and "romance" are virtually synonymous; generic distinction is subordinate to a more basic discrimination between all fiction and actuality. In the same vein, in 1800, Charles Brockden Brown distinguished romance not from the novel but from history. Romance, for him, was not one kind of fiction as opposed to another but all fiction as opposed to fact.[6]

This is the most prevalent distinction in nineteenth-century critical terminology. In an 1836 review of Bulwer's *Rienzi*, Poe discriminated carefully between the author's "scrupulous fidelity to all the main events in the *public* life of his hero" and "the relief afforded through the personages of pure romance which form the filling in of the picture" (7:236). In

1857 Irving informed a correspondent who had inquired about the truth of the personal portions of *The Alhambra:* "Everything in the work relating to myself, and to the actual inhabitants of the Alhambra, is unexaggerated fact. It was only in the legends that I indulged in *romancing.*" Of his campaign biography of Franklin Pierce, Hawthorne wrote nervously in 1852: "though the story is true, yet it took a romancer to do it."[7] And in Melville's *Confidence-Man* the Cosmopolitan replies to Charlie Noble's question about whether the story of Charlemont is "true":

> "Of course not; it is a story which I told with the purpose of every story-teller—to amuse. Hence, if it seem strange to you, that strangeness is the romance; it is what contrasts it with real life; it is the invention, in brief, the fiction as opposed to the fact." [160]

The fundamental property of romance, then, was conceived to be its departure from "truth," from "fact," its cutting of the Jamesian cable tying imagination to "reality." To describe romance in this way was not, finally, to distinguish it from realism or mimesis, for the general run of nineteenth-century comments on romance distinguish it not from *realism* but from *reality*—and this point is crucial. Romance was not an abstract or symbolic representation of objective reality; as we shall see, it was involved with objective representation only when "mingled" with history. Furthermore, even "purely" aesthetic descriptions of romance, defining it in terms of liberated formal experiment, do not quite coincide with nineteenth-century discussions of the mode. American critics and commentators, at least before Poe, were far less concerned with form itself, with "beauty," than with the sources of imaginative fictional utterance. For them the "unreality" of romance was above all psychological. In Irving's *Tales of a Traveller*, following the burlesque "Adventure of the Popkins Family," a skeptical Englishman condemns the tale as "a mere piece of romance, originating in the heated brain of the narrator" (376). What matters most, then, in nineteenth-century discussions of romance, is neither content nor form but psychological motive and effect.

At the heart of this theory of romance, radically dualistic in its separation of fancy and reason, imagination and actuality, was a profound concern with the origins of fictional (as opposed to historical) rhetoric—origins perhaps masked, "for our illusion," by historical "mingling," but origins nevertheless intensely there. "My *instinct*," as Melville wrote to his British publisher, John Murray, in 1848, "is to out with the Romance, & let me say that instincts are prophetic, & better than acquired wisdom" (70). To "out with the Romance" was first of all to substitute "instinct" for "acquired wisdom," fantasy for reason. This was the context in which Brown, Irving, Poe, Hawthorne, and Melville chose to become "romancers." To "out with the Romance" was, to paraphrase James, to sacrifice the "relation" between the car of imagination and the reality of earth. Romance emanated from, and appealed to, the unfettered imagination, the "heated brain," of narrator or reader. It was therefore both deeply fascinating and deeply subversive.

It was inevitable that the theory of romance should turn, at least initially, on questions of psychology and morality. Well into the nineteenth century it was the consensus of American ministers, moralists, and critics that the writing or reading of imaginative fiction was at best frivolous and usually dangerous. As Thomas Jefferson wrote of what he called "the inordinate passion prevalent for novels":

> When this poison infects the mind, it destroys its tone and revolts it against wholesome reading. Reason and fact, plain and unadorned, are rejected. Nothing can engage attention unless dressed in all the figments of fancy, and nothing so bedecked comes amiss. The result is a bloated imagination, sickly judgment, and disgust towards all the real businesses of life.

Similarly, in a chapter on "Romances and Novels" in his *Brief Retrospect of the Eighteenth Century* (1803), the Reverend Samuel Miller complained that fiction-reading has "a tendency too much to engross the mind, to fill it with artificial views, and to diminish the taste for more solid reading." "To fill the mind with unreal and delusive pictures of life," he insisted, "is, in the end, to beguile it from sober duty, and to cheat it of substantial enjoyment." Fiction and imagination, according to received opinion, were antithetical to and subversive of a whole series of American values: "reason and fact," "the real businesses of life," "sober duty." They were thus regarded with open hostility.[8]

To be sure, this hostility was not uniquely American.[9] Still, historical circumstance and intellectual tradition conspired to make it especially acute in the new nation. When British fiction emerged at the beginning of the eighteenth century, England already had a long and distinguished heritage of nonutilitarian literature, a heritage notably lacking in the colonies; and by the late 1780s, when Americans were beginning to write novels and romances in significant numbers, England boasted an achieved tradition in fiction in the works of Defoe, Richardson, Fielding, Smollett, Sterne, and their contemporaries. These writers were frequently attacked in England for immorality, although Richardson was largely protected by his alleged concern for promoting and rewarding virtue. But whatever the protests lodged against their works, these men had succeeded; they had established a precedent. Before Cooper and Irving, there were no such exemplary careers in America, with the brief and hardly encouraging exception of Charles Brockden Brown's.

Orthodox American opinion, religious or secular, confronted the aspiring romancer with a set of rationalist axioms—aesthetic, metaphysical, political, and ultimately psychological. Rhetoric was inferior to meaning, possibility to actuality, stimulation to stability, imagination to reason or judgment. Imagination, if not strictly controlled, posed a threat both to individual happiness and to social cohesion. These assumptions, generally pervasive in Colonial America, were particularly so in Puritan New England,[10] and they were reinforced by the spread of Scottish Common Sense philosophy in the late eighteenth and early nineteenth century.[11]

Terence Martin has detailed the terms in which Scottish thought denounced fiction, but they are worth summarizing here, since they were also the terms used to discuss fiction in America before the Civil War. Imagination, the Scottish writers agreed, was "naturally" subordinate to judgment or reason, but it was all too easy, as Dugald Stewart warned in 1792, "by long habits of solitary reflection to reverse this order of things, and to weaken the attention to sensible objects to so great a degree, as to leave the conduct almost wholly under the influence of imagination." As an antidote, Stewart recommended—in terms consistently echoed by Irving, Hawthorne, and others—"*mingling* [my emphasis] gradually in the business and amusements of the world." Imagination, Stewart admitted, was the source of sensibility, sympathy, and genius. Unchecked, however, it led the mind into melancholy and even insanity. "To a man of an ill-regulated imagination," he wrote, "external circumstances only serve as hints to excite his own thoughts, and the conduct he pursues has in general far less reference to his real situation, than to some imaginary one in which he conceives himself to be placed." Given these dangerous tendencies, literary encouragement of fantasy was clearly folly. For "those intellectual and moral habits, which ought to be formed by actual experience of the world, may be gradually so accommodated to the dreams of poetry and romance as to disqualify us for the scene in which we are destined to act."[12]

A threat to individual happiness, imagination was also deeply dangerous to social order. "The imagination," wrote Hugh Blair, whose *Lectures on Rhetoric and Belles Lettres* (1783) were widely influential in America, "is most vigorous and predominant in youth; with advancing years, [it] cools, and the understanding ripens." More characteristic of youth than of stable maturity, imaginative literature was also more typical of primitive than of modern societies and partook, therefore, of the other salient quality of youth and barbarism: "In the infancy of all societies," according to Blair, "men are much under the dominion of imagination and passion." "Imagination and passion." That this equation was by 1783 a commonplace does not diminish its importance. There was, as yet, no explicit identification of fantasy with sublimated eroticism, although the idea is implicit in most Scottish-influenced writing and would come very close to the surface in the works of American romancers. But the Scottish philosophers and their American pupils were mainly interested in effects and results, and these, to them, were perfectly clear. "Poetry," in Blair's definition, was "the language of passion, or of enlivened imagination." It was on "understanding" that society had to rely for order and stability. Hence the hysterical fears of orthodox ministers and moralists in the aftermath of the French Revolution. The American Samuel Miller saw the corrupting tendencies of imaginative fiction thus:

> Every opportunity is taken to attack some principle of morality under the title of a "prejudice;" to ridicule the duties of domestic life, as flowing from "contracted" and "slavish" views; to deny the sober pursuits of upright industry as "dull" and "spiritless;" and, in a word, to frame an apology for suicide, adultery, prostitution, and the indulgence of every propensity for which a corrupt heart can plead an inclination.[13]

It is significant that Blair and his contemporaries associated imagination with the very state of society to which Rousseau and his followers appealed for the sanction of their revolutionary doctrines.

One should be cautious in discussing the "influence" of Scottish philosophy in America. It did not so much introduce new attitudes as provide a new and conveniently secular means of supporting what were already firm convictions. For this very reason, the vocabulary it contributed took hold in the United States with extraordinary tenacity, and—what matters here—our writers of fiction were firmly locked in its grasp. Brown expressed his enthusiasm for Blair's *Rhetoric* as early as 1787. Poe, we are told, "knew at first hand Hugh Blair's *Lectures on Rhetoric and Belles Lettres*, Lord Kames's *Elements of Criticism*, the critical writings of Archibald Alison, Thomas Reid, and especially Dugald Stewart." At Bowdoin, during Hawthorne's undergraduate years, freshmen studied Blair's *Rhetoric* in the third trimester; in the first two terms of the senior year they read through Stewart's *Philosophy*.[14]

It is more difficult to discover the extent of Irving's and Melville's reading in Common Sense philosophy and aesthetics, but the influence of at least the attitudes conveyed by Scottish thought is clear in both.[15] In 1824, for instance, Irving warned a nephew against entering "the seductive but treacherous paths of literature" in thoroughly conventional terms:

> Do not meddle much with works of the imagination—Your imagination needs no feeding, indeed it is a mental quality that always takes

care of itself; and is too apt to interfere with the others. Strengthen your judgment; cultivate habits of close thinking, and in all your reading let KNOWLEDGE be the great object.[16]

As for Melville, orthodox condemnation of fiction provided him with one of his major themes. In 1810 the Reverend James Gray, educated in Scotland and very much under the influence of Common Sense thought, warned a young Philadelphia audience against the dangers of fiction:

Permit me to caution you against ever making the characters of romance a standard by which to judge of character in real life. For . . . perhaps it may be found that no persons are more apt to err and blunder, when introduced on the stage of real life than those whose imaginations have been deeply impressed with the characters of fictitious composition.[17]

Strikingly similar sentiments are expressed briefly by Melville in the guidebook episode in *Redburn* and at length in *Pierre*, in the hero's discovery, after trying to live his life according to literary models, that a work of art, "though a thing of life, was, after all, but a thing of breath, evoked by the wanton magic of a creative hand" (169). Especially close to Gray—although Melville had surely never read his address—is the narrator's question in *The Confidence-Man*, whether "after poring over the best novels professing to portray human nature, the studious youth will still run the risk of being too often at fault upon actually entering the world" (60). It matters not at all, in the final analysis, whether Melville read Gray, or Stewart, or any of the Scottish writers. Their ideas permeated his literary culture; they were inescapable. Romance, first of all, was "fiction" opposed to "fact."

It seems clear, then, that Brown, Irving, Poe, Hawthorne, and Melville turned to "romance" in a hostile climate, a climate in which the fictionality of fiction was accentuated and condemned. It is thus not surprising that the primary nineteenth-century meaning of "romance," as pure and dangerous fantasy, played an important part in their thinking about their chosen mode. How, precisely, this climate affected them, how it influenced their choice of vocation and the works they produced, is a complicated matter, to which I shall turn in the next chapter. First, however, it may be useful to consider some other meanings of "romance" in nineteenth-century discourse. These coalesced into what we might call the "conservative" theory of romance, a theory often used to cover up the primary and subversive implications of the term.

The Conservative Theory of Romance

As we have already seen in Hawthorne's preface to *The House of the Seven Gables*, nineteenth-century descriptions of "romance" do not always observe the radical distinction between "fiction" and "fact," but the dualism was overcome only through a deliberate and rather duplicitous defensive strategy. In much nineteenth-century usage the term "romance" is not literary at all but vaguely emotional. Poe, for instance, could speak of the "romance" of Sarah Helen Whitman's character or of the "generous romance of soul" of the mother of Lucretia Maria Davidson (*Letters*, 370; *Works*, 10:222). One attributed (or "related") romance to reality by claiming to find in "real" objects, scenes, or actions qualities associated with literary romance, especially the air of imaginative susceptibility induced or recalled by romantic literature. "Romance," in this sense, was frequently linked with "poetry" which could also be abstracted from its literal context to connote a vaguely imaginative species of experience. In this vein Irving wrote of a youthful visit to Ogdensburg, New York, fifty years after the fact: "It was all a scene of romance to me, for I was then a mere stripling, and everything was strange, and full of poetry."[18] The same notion lies behind Melville's justification, in the 1848 letter to John Murray, of his decision "to out with the Romance" in *Mardi*. "I have long thought," he wrote, "that Polynisia furnished a great deal of rich poetical material that has never been employed hitherto in works of fancy" (*Letters*, 70).

By attributing to reality itself the "romantic" or "poetic" qualities of subjective imagination, American writers, influenced by associationist aesthetics and by the example of Scott, attempted to bridge the chasm between fantasy and experience, fiction and fact. It is in this sense that we should understand the vogues of historical romance and romantic history. They offered an apparent mode of reconciliation; they provided a rationale for what I have been calling the conservative theory of romance by viewing "romance" as a "historical" or "realistic" mode whose "reality" just happened, luckily, to be "poetic" or "romantic." Poe parrots this conventional argument in an 1835 review of Theodore Irving's *Conquest of Florida:*

> There is so much of romance in the details of Spanish conquests in America, that a history of any one of the numerous expeditions for discovery and conquest, possesses the charm of the most elaborate fiction, even while it bears the marks of general truth. [8:37]

Such apparent reconciliation of historical "fact" and romantic "fiction" could be achieved, however, only in what nineteenth-century writers repeatedly referred to as the "misty past." The more recent past or the present, by their insistent "reality," reopened the chasm between fact and fancy, revealing once again the primary fictionality of romance. Hence Hawthorne's apology in the *Seven Gables* preface for the contemporary setting of his work: "It exposes the Romance to an inflexible and exceedingly dangerous species of criticism, by bringing [the author's] fancy-pictures almost into positive contact with the realities of the moment" (3). That is to say, it revealed the "neutral territory" for what it really was—a moral or psychological battlefield. But for those who stuck with the "misty past," so the argument went, and blamed the "romance" of their method on their material, there was at least the apparent promise of a permanent cease-fire.

It is at this point that the conservative theory of romance intersects with the debate over the prospects for a national literature. There was a wide variety of opinion about what, precisely, would render our literature national,[19] but the most prevalent conviction regarding literary "Americanism" was that it should and could be based on American materials. As William Gilmore Simms wrote in the preface to his best-known work of fiction: "'The Yemassee' is proposed as an *American* romance. It is so styled as much of the material could have been furnished by no other country."[20] Thus Melville turned, in his masterpiece, to the American whale fishery. Irving mined the past and present of Dutch New York, Hawthorne the past and present of Puritan New England. Cooper chose upstate New York and the wilderness. Already in 1798, at the beginning of his brief career as a romancer, Charles Brockden Brown insisted that "to the story-telling moralist the United States is a new and untrodden field" ("Advertisement for *Sky-Walk*," 135), and a year later, in his preface to *Edgar Huntly*, he declared that "the field of investigation, opened to us by our own country, should differ essentially from those which exist in Europe" (3).

One of the earliest and most influential organs of American literary nationalism was Boston's *North American Review*, established in 1815. "We have in the way of subjects," William Tudor wrote in the first number, "a rich and various mine that has hardly been opened." He proceeded to list these subjects in the kind of catalogue that would become an almost obligatory feature of the nationalist manifesto, from the *North American* in 1815 to *Leaves of Grass* in 1855. Materials are not themselves art, and these lists are often little more than exercises in defensive chauvinism, insisting that, if we did not have big writers, we at least had big waterfalls. However, the influx of associationist aesthetics during the second decade of the nineteenth century provided a new vocabulary for relating "poetic" qualities to artistic subject matter. Beauty, the associationists argued, is not an absolute; it derives, rather, from the association (especially the traditional,

16

time-honored association) of particular ideas either with each other or with particular objects. The terminology of associationism had become thoroughly commonplace by 1825, when Longfellow proclaimed to his fellow Bowdoin seniors, including Nathaniel Hawthorne, that "whatever is noble and attractive in our national character will one day be associated with the sweet magic of Poetry."[21]

Still, Longfellow's future tense was ominous. The assumptions of associationism were as often used to demonstrate the hopelessness as the hope of a literature based on American materials. At the beginning of *The Sketch-Book* Irving distinguished Europe as the realm of "storied and poetical association" (17). Earlier, in an 1810 essay on Thomas Campbell, the Scottish poet, he explained the problem with America:

> Among the lesser evils, incident to the infant state of our country, we have to lament its almost total deficiency in those local associations produced by history and moral fiction. . . . Our lofty mountains and stupendous cataracts awaken no poetical associations, and our majestic rivers roll their waters unheeded, because unsung. [160–61]

Such complaints were widespread and of long duration. In 1860, in his preface to *The Marble Faun*, Hawthorne was still making the same objection to American materials.

Associationism thus revealed what was wrong with America, but it also suggested a clear procedure for remedying our deficiencies: one might work up native materials by *providing* them with "poetical" associations. One might, as Irving described his intention in the 1848 preface to *Knickerbocker's History of New York*, "clothe home scenes and places and familiar names with those imaginative and whimsical associations so seldom met with in our new country, but which live like charms and spells about the cities of the old world" (4). One might, this is to say, Europeanize America. It may be true, as William Hedges argues, that this alleged motive was more important to the Irving of 1848 than to the Irving who wrote the *History*, forty years before; but the cultivation or invention of national associations undoubtedly played a part in his original scheme as well, and there is surely a sense, as Hedges writes, "in which such stories as 'Rip Van Winkle' and 'The Legend of Sleepy Hollow,' though largely Germanic in origin, are attempts by Irving to equip the American landscape with a kind of mythology."[22] Indeed, the Germanic origin seems part of the point, as if European associations might simply be pasted or grafted onto American scenes.

It was in such terms, in any case, that Irving's American tales and sketches were consistently praised by his contemporaries. Will America, Longfellow asked in 1825, "one day be rich in romantic associations? Will poetry . . . [render] every spot classical?" In the same year, James Kirke

Paulding wrote to his friend Iving: "your own country . . . is proud of you, and the most obscure recesses of the land, even old Sleepy Hollow, are becoming almost classical, in consequence of the notice you have taken of them." Or, as Edward Everett wrote ten years later, reviewing Irving's *Tour on the Prairies:* "We thank [the author] for turning these poor barbarous *steppes* into classical land." Associationism was thus crucial to literary nationalism. It provided an aesthetic justification and method for the exploitation of national materials, not only for Irving but for many of his contemporaries and successors, notably Hawthorne.[23]

While the associationist program seemed to validate a literature based on national materials, it did not propose a literature otherwise radically different from the literature of Europe—different, that is to say, in kind or form. This is why Irving's admirers praised him for making "barbarous" America "classical." American materials were to be made amenable to the literary imagination, but that imagination was not, in itself, conceived in distinctly "American" terms. In a society nervous about "art," associationist aesthetics allowed the skittish to talk about materials rather than about the creative process. It was in this sense that associationism served to rationalize the theory of American fiction.

If associationist thought was crucial to the theory of nationalism, it was equally crucial to the conservative theory of romance—the theory that attempted to make peace with rational orthodoxy by denying the more insidious implications of romancing. By connecting or "mingling" imaginary ideas with "real" materials, associationist aesthetics promised simultaneously to validate those materials for literature and to overcome the essential disrelation of romance. American writers, by attributing to reality itself the "charms" of "romance and poetry," seemed able to overcome romance's primary sacrifice of relation. They seemed able to bridge the chasm between fantasy and "real" experience, between fiction and fact. Thus an "American romance"—a romance based, through association, on American materials—would be safe and conservative, firmly anchored to the rock of "solid and substantial" native reality. Even as it endowed America with "poetical associations," it would, as Hawthorne put it again and again, reconcile the "Imaginary" and the "Actual."

This conservative rationale for national romance was widespread in American critical discourse in the first half of the nineteenth century. It appears regularly in prefaces to romantic histories and historical romances and in reviews of such works. In purely quantitative terms it should probably be considered *the* theory of American romance, but as a theory of romantic fiction it was not really tenable, at least not for those who kept in mind the primary meaning of "romance" in the nineteenth century. The problem was that fictions based so firmly on native materials might be national but would hardly be romances.

James Kirke Paulding, in his 1820 essay on "National Literature," argued for the possibility of "romantic fiction" in America based solidly on native "materials for romantic adventure," but his definition smacks far more of what his contemporaries called the "novel" than it does of the "romance":

> The best and most perfect works of imagination appear to me to be those which are founded upon a combination of such characters as every generation of men exhibits, and such events as have often taken place in the world and will again. Such works are only fictions because the tissue of events which they record never perhaps happened in precisely the same train and to the same number of persons as are exhibited and associated in the relation.[24]

It is surely difficult to distinguish Paulding's confinement of the *romancer* to "such characters as every generation of men exhibits, and such events as have often taken place in the world and will again," from Hawthorne's limitation of the *novelist*, in the *Seven Gables* preface, "not merely to the possible, but to the probable and ordinary course of man's experience" (1).

The point to be stressed about Paulding's deemphasis of fictionality is not that he was a realist before his time but that for him a literature based on national materials was necessarily realistic, being based not on unfettered imagination but on a rational judgment of the typical and representative. What Paulding ignores, in following the logical implications of conservative nationalism, is that radical meaning of "romance" that pervades the warnings of critics and moralists at the beginning of the century. And it is hard to fault Paulding's logic. If national romance grew out of native materials, it was no longer primarily the product of the author's "over-heated imagination." For all its overtones of imaginative coloring and sentiment, the theory of conservative romance, based on associationist aesthetics and ultimately on American "reality," was finally a theory of realism, of rational mimesis.

Many commentators agreed with Paulding about the necessity of realism in American romance, but they were far less happy about it than he was. They saw this realism as a major problem—a problem traceable to the alleged deficiency of our literary materials. In 1827 an anonymous writer in the *American Quarterly Review* gave utterance to one of the staple complaints of nineteenth-century American criticism:

> Strictly speaking, there has been no dark or romantic age, in this country, *connected* [my emphasis] with its European race. The adventures, the sufferings, the conflicts, of our forefathers, besides being of a recent date, all partook of severe reality....
>
> Our history and tradition consequently connect themselves but

19

awkwardly with every thing supernatural, or out of the ordinary course of nature.[25]

There is a logical fallacy in this complaint. "Novelistic" qualities of "severe reality" or allegiance to "the ordinary course of nature"—which would result from *any* method that bases art on the materials of art—are here attributed not to the method but to the materials. This fallacy was widespread in American critical discourse. The problem was not just the absence, in American scenery and history, of "storied and poetical association." More generally, America was seen as lacking the sort of relation that conservative romance required—and that European "reality" supposedly possessed—between material circumstance and imaginative experience. In America, to put it bluntly, one couldn't blame one's "fiction" on one's "facts."

The consequences of this situation for the American romancer, as critics and commentators outlined them, were quite contradictory, and this may explain why twentieth-century critics have trouble deciding whether romancers thought American conditions made romance inevitable or impossible.[26] On the one hand, many writers complained that romance-writing in America was, if not quite impossible, then at least extremely difficult. This is what Hawthorne means in his preface to *The Marble Faun* when he laments that "it will be very long . . . before romance-writers may find congenial and easily handled themes either in the annals of our stalwart Republic, or in any characteristic and probable events of our individual lives" (3). What he means is that conservative romance—the sort of integrative, "related" romance linked with Europe—will be impossible in America. We don't yet have enough "reality" that is already "romantic."

On the other hand, in its primary sense of fiction as opposed to fact, "romance" was perhaps made inevitable by the supposed dissociation of imagination and actuality in America. After all, the primary sense of "romance" grew out of that dissociation in the first place. Perhaps the inevitable corollary of barren American "reality"—bereft of all association—was the romancer's imagination, unanchored, floating "at large and unrelated." This is the conclusion reached by the anonymous writer in the *American Quarterly Review* in his pessimistic comment on the favorite associational strategy of conservative romancers:

> The infusion of romance into history, cannot, we think, but have a bad effect on the reader, by rendering the dull matter of fact of the latter, tasteless and spiritless, in comparison with the piquant extravagance of the adulterated mass, and weakening at the same time that salutary distinction, which the mind should always preserve between truth and falsehood. The imagination ought not to be pampered thus, at the expense of the other faculties.[27]

The passage is intriguing in its assumption that a radically divided sensibility is a sign of mental health. But this assumption was widespread. The reviewer's "salutary distinction" is, of course, the distinction upon which Common Sense psychology insisted, and it lay at the heart of the primary definition of "romance" as fiction as opposed to fact. Indeed, the reviewer's second sentence precisely echoes the warnings of ministers and moralists against the dangers of fiction and fantasy. Conservative romancers loved to complain about the barrenness of American materials, but their real problem, it would seem, lay not in the nature of American "reality" but in the way they were disposed to see the relation—or lack of relation—between *all* "reality" and the imagination.

Most popular or conventional national romance in pre–Civil War America was written on the explicit or implicit assumption that the sacrifice of relation could be overcome or evaded because certain native materials were already imbued with "storied and poetical association" or could be so imbued. To ignore this body of American romance would be to ignore a major portion of our literary history: Cooper, Simms, Sedgwick, and a host of others. Furthermore, the program of those who based the hope of American literature on national materials was quite antithetical to the primary implications of "romance"—the implications surveyed in the first section of this chapter. Nevertheless, in the failures and contradictions of the conservative program lurked the very sense of "romance" that the program seemed designed to evade. If "European" romance was finally impossible in America, perhaps only the sort of romance against which moralists inveighed could be truly "American."

Washington Irving, whose very lack of critical originality makes him a valuable index of conventional thought, meticulously cultivated the interface between romance and history. If he sometimes anticipates Hawthorne's idea of the "neutral territory," we should not be surprised; for like Hawthorne, he, too, sought relation in literature. Thus he wrote to John Murray (his English publisher and the father of Melville's) about his desire, in *The Conquest of Granada*, "to assume a greater freedom & latitude in the execution of the work, and to mingle a tinge of romance and satire with the grave historical details."[28] Just as often, he attributed such "mingling" not to the author but to his material. Thus Geoffrey Crayon, in "Westminster Abbey" (in *The Sketch-Book*), describes a crusader's tomb, musing on "those military enthusiasts, who so strangely mingled religion and romance, and whose exploits form the connecting link between fact and fiction; between the history and the fairy tale" (137).

But there is an important difference between Irving and the Hawthorne of "The Custom-House" and the *Seven Gables* preface. For the former, romance is not itself the neutral territory but one of the forces contesting the field—the fiction or "fairy tale" as opposed to the fact or history. Even as he sought modes of reconciliation, Irving always kept the fictionality of romance in view; and in this he is closer than Hawthorne to the primary meaning of "romance" in nineteenth-century America—a meaning still very much alive at mid-century. "Proceeding in my narrative of *facts*," Melville wrote to *his* John Murray in 1848, explaining his new purpose in *Mardi*, "I began to feel an incurible distaste for the same; & a longing to plume my pinions for a flight, & felt irked cramped & fettered by plodding along with dull common places,—So suddenly [abandoning] the thing alltogether, I went to work heart & soul at a romance." Which, he assures his less than delighted publisher, "shall afford the strongest presumptive evidence of the truth of Typee & Omoo by the sheer force of contrast" (70).

TWO

Oh, reader, list! I've chartless voyaged. With compass and the lead, we had not found these Mardian Isles. Those who boldly launch, cast off all cables; and turning from the common breeze, that's fair for all, with their own breath, fill their own sails. Hug the shore, naught new is seen; and "Land ho!" at last was sung, when a new world was sought.

MELVILLE, *Mardi*

CASTING OFF

THE FIRST AMERICAN FICTION WRITERS DID NOT, BY AND LARGE, CONTEST the prevailing hostile attitudes toward fiction. Far from proclaiming the validity of imagination, they made a point of accepting and even advertising the corrupting influence of most fiction in order to promote their own works as rare exceptions that proved the rule. To the moralists' charge of unreality they replied that their own stories, as countless subtitles proclaimed, were "Tales of Truth" or "Founded on Fact." To the charge of immorality they just as consistently replied, in defensive prefaces, that their own tales were carefully arranged to point a moral and thereby instruct the reader. Their own fictions were solidly on the side of "judgment" and "virtue." The immediate effect of orthodox suspicion of fiction was thus to force aspiring novelists into postures of extreme realism and extreme didacticism.[1] For many of their successors, as we have seen, literary nationalism and associationist aesthetics provided a more sophisticated but equally defensive means of evading the opprobrium of "romancing." The breakdown of these postures marks the true beginning of self-conscious romance in America, and hints of this beginning can be glimpsed in a number of our earliest works of fiction.

BEGINNINGS

Our first fiction writers did not confine realistic and didactic apologetics to subtitles and prefaces. Often the novels themselves warned against the dangers of novel-reading. This is the whole point of Tabitha Tenney's *Female Quixotism* (1801), in which we witness the dire fate (in this case spinsterhood) of a woman who fed her expectations on the illusions offered by fiction instead of basing them on solid experience and judgment. A

25

similar point is made more melodramatically at the conclusion of William Hill Brown's *The Power of Sympathy* (1789): the hero is found dead by his own hand, an open copy of *The Sorrows of Young Werther* by his side. So much for the influence of fiction!

Earlier in the same work, a conversation about the dangers of novel-reading leads Brown to introduce an authorial footnote describing the seduction and death of Elizabeth Whitman, a real-life story on which, eight years later, Hannah Foster would base *The Coquette*. The moral of Miss Whitman's story is clear. "She was a great reader of novels and romances," Brown writes, "and having imbibed her ideas of *the characters of men*, from these fallacious sources, became vain and coquettish, and rejected several offers of marriage, in expectation of receiving one more agreeable to her fanciful idea."[2]

The great subject of early American fiction, reflecting the abiding influence of Richardson, was the tale of seduction. While suitably sensational, it was ideally geared to the obligatory didactic emphasis, warning young readers of the dangers of allowing passion to overcome reason and judgment. But the conflict between judgment and passion had larger implications. Orthodox opinion equated passion with imagination, the source of fiction itself, and it is this equation that dominates William Hill Brown's moralizing on the seduction of Elizabeth Whitman:

> WITH a good heart she possessed a poetical imagination, and an unbounded thirst for novelty; but these airy talents, not counterpoised with judgment, or perhaps serious reflection, instead of adding to her happiness, were the cause of her ruin.[3]

Following the conventional logic of the time, American novels of seduction, because they dealt with the dangers of passion, often pointed to the dangers and terrors of "poetical imagination" as well. In doing so they involved themselves in an insoluble contradiction, implicit in any effort to attack imagination in a work of imagination and here compounded by the attempt to be "moral" and "true to nature" at the same time; for fictional "truth," as even the most sympathetic of the Scottish critics admitted, inevitably goes beyond the simple perceptions or conceptions of fact described by Thomas Reid. As Blair, Stewart, and Alison recognized, *all* literary expression, whatever the author's protests to the contrary, involves an appeal to the reader's imagination; and what the Scottish philosophers asserted, American novelists bore out in their practice.

For instance, in *Charlotte Temple: A Tale of Truth* (1791), the most popular of all early American novels, Susanna Rowson's didactic control is seriously undermined by her effort to communicate the truth of her tale. On the one hand, her heroine, seduced and abandoned, has a clear function in the novel's didactic pattern. She is a fallen woman, "by thoughtless passion led astray." She knows not "the deceitfulness of her own heart," and she exemplifies the dangers of love "when operating in a young heart glowing with sensibility." On the other hand, Mrs. Rowson is concerned, if only to make her moral more affecting, to present Charlotte in a sympathetic light. Thus, in spite of her moralistic warnings against "sensibility" and the "heart," she urges the reader to respond to Charlotte's plight with "a heart of sensibility." Toward the end of the novel Charlotte condemns herself, for sound didactic reasons: "We both," she moralizes to the licentious Mrs. Crayton, "too easily followed the impulse of our treacherous hearts." But Mrs. Crayton is condemned by the author for apparently quite contradictory reasons: "The kneeling figure of Charlotte in her affecting situation," writes Mrs. Rowson, "might have moved the heart of a stoic to compassion; but Mrs. Crayton remained inflexible."[4] This uncertainty of intention in *Charlotte Temple*, its wavering between appeals to judgment and sympathy, is in large part ethical, but it is also at least implicitly aesthetic, reflecting antithetical conceptions of the nature and purpose of literature. As a moral tale the novel attempts to bypass conventional hostility toward fiction by appealing to the reader's judgment, but as a "tale of truth" its appeal is inevitably to the reader's sympathy, sensibility, and imagination—the very qualities which, as a moral tale, it condemns.

The same radical confusion informs other novels of the period. In Brown's *The Power of Sympathy*, after the hero's Wertheresque suicide, his friend Worthy laments: "thou wast possessed of a too nice sensibility"; yet, in the same paragraph, Worthy has already declared, in connection with his own reaction to his friend's death: "Indeed a man without sensibility exhibits no sign of a soul."[5] Particularly fascinating, in this respect, is Hannah Foster's *The Coquette* (1797). Eliza Wharton, the heroine, is courted by a minister, Boyer, whose "love" conforms perfectly to the dictates of Common Sense conservatism. "I am in no danger...," he writes to a friend, "of becoming an enthusiastic devotee. No, I mean to act on just and rational principles." The issue could not be stated more clearly. Eliza rejects him, explaining to a friend who had urged her acceptance: "My reason and judgment entirely coincide with your opinion; but my fancy claims some share in the decision."[6]

The reader, put off as much as Eliza by Boyer's cold rationalism, cannot help sympathizing with her decision; but Eliza is punished severely for choosing "fancy" over "reason and judgment"—this is still, after all, a moral tale. Seduced by the villain, Sanford, she finally expires in exemplary contrition, with the didactic Mrs. Foster in hot pursuit. "May my unhappy story," Eliza exclaims toward the close, "serve as a beacon to warn the American fair." Yet, while Mrs. Foster may intend to demonstrate the superiority of reason to fancy, she is clearly aware, on some level, of the ways her novel's sentimental appeal, itself imaginative, threatens to undermine the whole moral house of cards. Eliza herself may, with Clarissa-like masochism, accept and encourage didactic judgment. "Alas," she laments, "tears are vain; and vain is my bitter repentance! It cannot obliterate my crime, nor restore me to innocence and peace!" But didactic control has already been contradicted, in almost exactly the same words, by Eliza's friend Julia, who writes: "In my breast, you are fully acquitted. Your penitential tears have obliterated your guilt, and blotted out your errors with your Julia."[7]

Now the confusion indicated by these examples is in no sense especially American, for the sentimental secularization of the great Calvinist debate between Justice and Mercy—the reduction of it to an ambiguous psychological conflict between Head and Heart—is a pervasive feature of the increasingly bourgeois culture of eighteenth-century Europe and England, and the sentimental confusion we have noted in the early American novels is present in eighteenth-century British fiction as well; it lies at the heart of Richardson's appeal in particular. Moreover, a writer's material always has a tendency to liberate itself from the ordered pattern of meaning he attempts to impose upon it.

Still, for early American writers of fiction, the conflict between didacticism and sensibility was particularly intense because, even while it raised questions that were clearly and directly relevant to their own ambiguous position as imaginative writers in a hostile culture, they could not openly acknowledge this relevance. Since fiction was, by official definition, dangerous, "truth to life" had to be conceived in narrowly moral and realistic terms. These writers could not admit that sympathetic realism was itself necessarily imaginative, appealing not to Common Sense but to passionate sensibility. Thus the liberation of sympathetic imagination from formal control is always, in their novels, incomplete and clandestine. Incapable of being overtly declared, it is forced underground or is sublimated into the novels' plots or into characters' comments on these plots. This is why so many heroines are seduced by novel-reading or by "poetical imagination." In the last analysis the overtly didactic struggle between reason and passion expresses, even as it strives to conceal, a deeper struggle between didacticism itself—the agent of reason—and the power of sympathy. In spite of their intentions, and although their works are nominally "novels" rather than "romances," these fiction writers were forced to bear out, or at least bear witness to, the insidious implications of the romancer's art.

TO "BE" A "ROMANCER"

Analyzing the moral and aesthetic confusions of our earliest fiction has, admittedly, some similarity to the beating of dead horses. William Hill Brown, Susanna Rowson, and Hannah Foster are largely forgotten, and they were succeeded within fifty years by some of the most powerful writers America has known. It is tempting to see in the emergence of a major fictional tradition in the first half of the nineteenth century, and in the "American Renaissance" generally, a dramatic rejection of orthodox American attitudes toward literature and imagination. The growing acceptance and cultivation of romance in the decades following the turn of the century represents, in this view, an abandonment of the narrow realism and didacticism of the earlier period.[8]

It is no doubt true, as Terence Martin has argued, that the romance helped "liberate the American imagination from the essentially anti-fictive context of its society," but he surely goes too far in arguing further that the rise of romance marked a "breaking away from the implications of Scottish metaphysics" and that, as a result, "one who created fiction in the mode of romance assumed the validity of imaginative experience."[9] Surely, few writers of fiction before the Civil War "assumed" with anything like full conviction "the validity of imaginative experience." Brown, Irving, and Hawthorne often painfully denigrated not only the order of imaginative experience but their own status as writers of fiction. The "conservative" theory of romance, best articulated by Irving and Hawthorne, was no effort to break away from rational orthodoxy. It was, rather, an effort to reconcile fiction with Scottish thought—to "mingle" (or, in James's term, to "relate") the imaginary and the actual. It was simply a more sophisticated version of the abject apologetics of our first fiction writers. Poe and Melville were more openly defiant, and this quality gives them a special attractiveness to modern readers; but the very terms of their defiance took shape from the ideas and attitudes against which they rebelled, and the guilt attendant on their declarations of allegiance to imagination constitutes no small part of the history of their careers.

What distinguishes Brown, Irving, Poe, Hawthorne, and Melville from their less able predecessors and contemporaries is not that they overcame earlier problems but that they faced them with far more awareness. They continually return in their fiction to doubts and questions about their medium, about the source of its power and its place in society. They most assuredly indicated a place for imagination in America, but that place was often small and inconspicuous, not to say uncomfortable. What is far more important, the imagination whose place they indicated was in many respects precisely the sort of imagination against which American moralists had inveighed for nearly two centuries.

If Poe and Melville—and, to a lesser extent, Brown, Irving and Hawthorne—turned against the assumptions of their culture, they nevertheless did so in the context of that culture, as members and products of it. To choose the role of romancer in a society that equated romance with insanity and subversion and seldom granted its authors an enduring financial reward was to embrace what sociologists call a "deviant career." What sociologists tell us about the implications of such a choice is very instructive. As Kai Erikson remarks:

> Every human community has its own special set of boundaries, its own unique identity, and so we may presume that every community also has its own characteristic styles of deviant behavior.... In the first place, any community which feels jeopardized by a particular form of behavior will impose more severe sanctions against it and devote more time and energy to the task of rooting it out. At the same time, however, the very fact that a group expresses its concern about a given set of values often seems to draw a deviant response from certain of its members. There are people in any society who appear to "choose" a deviant style exactly *because* it offends an important value of the group—some of them because they have an inner need to challenge this value in a direct test, and some of them... because they clumsily violate a norm in their very eagerness to abide by it.[10]

While it may seem extreme to regard writers as deviants, doing so at least reminds us that they wrote in a social context; it makes us aware that culture, for them, was more than a set of intellectual-historical counters and that to embrace the imagination was to cross the boundaries of official nineteenth-century orthodoxy. We must pay attention, then, to what it meant for Brown, Irving, Poe, Hawthorne, and Melville to become "romancers" in a hostile society. The deviant model also reminds us that the "reality" from which romance departed was less a defensible philosophical conception of objective substance than a social norm: "solid and substantial enjoyment," "the real businesses of life," and the like.[11]

Erikson has another and even more important point to make about deviance in relation to its cultural context. Whether he chooses his deviance deliberately or inadvertently, Erikson argues,

> the deviant and his more conventional counterpart live in much the same world of symbol and meaning, sharing a similar set of interests in the universe around them. The thief and his victim share a common respect for the value of property; the heretic and the inquisitor speak much the same language and are keyed to the same religious mysteries; the traitor and the patriot act in reference to the same political institutions, often use the same methods, and for that matter

are sometimes the same person. . . . The deviant and the conformist, then, are creatures of the same culture.[12]

Erikson's cultural sense of deviance helps us to understand the irony of history by which the very stringency of rational orthodoxy forced on our truly imaginative writers a conception of imagination very like that held by the Common Sense moralists—one far more radical, that is, than would have been required of them in a more permissive cultural climate. For the romancer as for his orthodox antagonist, the root meaning of "romance" in America remained fiction as opposed to fact, deviant imagination as opposed to normative actuality, subversive delusion as opposed to sober truth. The theory of romance, even for our most radically rebellious romancers, was always fundamentally dualistic. "To out with the Romance" was still, for Melville in 1848, to follow "instinct" rather than "acquired wisdom"—to cut the Jamesian cable relating the car of imagination to the reality of earth. In its heart, as our romancers learned well from their culture, fiction was irresponsible and dangerous, threatening to psychological, social, moral, even formal literary order. Why or how, then, did they choose to *become* "romancers"? And what, for them, were the implications and consequences of this choice?

The sociology of deviance, especially the "labeling" or "interactionist" theory developed and elaborated by Edwin Lemert, Howard Becker, Kai Erikson, and others, proposes a theory of culture highly suggestive to anyone interested in the general status and identity of American writers and, more specifically, in what it meant, in nineteenth-century America, to "be" a "romancer." "Labeling" theory understands both "normalcy" and "deviance" as counters in an ongoing game rather than as absolutes. "Deviance," it insists, should be viewed not as an isolated, pathological aberration but as a phenomenon involving the whole culture, deviant and conformist alike. As Becker writes in his best-known sentence: "Deviant behavior is behavior that people so label." "Deviance," he elaborates, "is not a quality that lies in behavior itself, but in the interaction between the person who commits an act and those who respond to it."[13]

In *Outsiders: Studies in the Sociology of Deviance*, Howard Becker has proposed a "sequential model" for the deviant career, detailing the step-by-step process through which an individual's deviance is socially and psychologically confirmed. Whatever its general validity as a paradigm for all deviant experience, this model is of great value to anyone interested in the motives and consequences of the decision to become a "romancer" in nineteenth-century America. The point of applying it to romancers is not simply to belabor their, or their society's, perception of their peculiarity. The point, rather, is to understand their careers and writings in terms of

31

their interaction with the values, both "normal" and "deviant," current in their cultural setting.

We must also recognize that the comparison of Becker's paradigm to the careers of romancers is most interesting when it fails to work—when the pattern of literary vocation, on the part of our romancers, does not conform to his model. Whatever its "deviant" connotations, "being a romancer" often conferred positive status as well. For all the melodrama of such moralists as the Reverend Samuel Miller, the label "romancer" was clearly more ambiguous than, say, the label "prostitute." Romancers, consequently, were freer than most deviants to manipulate—to confirm or to neutralize—their deviant identity. This ambiguity and manipulation were central to the experience and the products of "being a romancer" in nineteenth-century America.

Becker's model consists, loosely, of four stages.[14] First, an individual must engage, or be thought to have engaged, in a socially proscribed or peculiar action. Next, and perhaps most important, the individual must be caught and certified or labeled "deviant," often in some sort of symbolic degradation ceremony. Next, provided that the individual continues or is continued in the career, he or she joins a deviant group, a deviant subculture providing the support of association with like-minded outcasts. Finally, and often in conjunction with membership in this subculture, the deviant forms or subscribes to a deviant rationale, an ideology justifying the proscribed activity as being somehow superior to what his society considers "normal."

At the beginning of the nineteenth century the practical difficulties facing the professional imaginative writer were enormous—so much so as to raise the question of why anyone turned to the profession of imaginative writing.[15] The personal or psychological difficulties of being such a writer, and especially of being a "romancer," were even greater. It is not simply that society branded the romancer as a deviant, for deviance very likely had a good deal to do with his choice of the identification in the first place. Charles Brockden Brown and Washington Irving, among our first professional romancers, pretty clearly turned to writing as an escape from, even a defiance of, the "real" legal business for which they were being trained. That Irving's escape from the law was facilitated by the death of his fiancée, Matilda Hoffman, only deepens the psychological complexity of his commitment to literature by broadening the field of responsibility which he apparently hoped, like Rip Van Winkle, to escape. Yet Brown abandoned fiction-writing after only a few years. Irving prospered, but after 1824 he presented himself not as a "romancer" but as a "biographer" or "historian." Neither of these men, that is to say, held consistently or for long to the antisocial implications of his first decision. In this sense their careers hint at the basic tension animating what we might call the sociol-ogy of literary vocation in nineteenth-century America—a tension be-tween writers or romancers and "normal" society and, ultimately, within writers themselves.

For Becker a deviant career begins, except in cases of false accusation, when an individual engages in a socially proscribed or peculiar action. The act may be deliberate—a willful embrace of the label—or unwitting: "I *thought* it was just a cigarette!" With romancers this last distinction may seem meaningless. You don't become a "romancer" without intending to. But Melville, we recall, only meant to record in *Typee* an adventure his friends had enjoyed, a good-natured social "yarn." It was only later, when his *"instinct* . . . to out with the Romance" (71) caught him while writing *Mardi*, that he became a "romancer" in the full sense.[16]

Next, in Becker's model, the individual must be caught and certified or labeled "deviant." With romancers this seems a fairly simple step. The root of "publication" is "public"; you can't publish in a closet. Except that you can. Hence, for instance, the nineteenth-century cults of anonymous or pseudonymous publication. Moreover, there were many ways of pub-lishing in one's own name without getting "caught." Literature was taught in colleges; it had long been the adornment of the accomplished lady or gentleman. It had snob appeal. It was a means of self-realization and upward mobility for the socially or educationally deprived—notably, in the nineteenth century, for women. The trick was to write "respectable" or "responsible" fiction—didactic tales, for instance, or "tales of truth," or "national romances" illustrating the poetic potential of American mate-rials. Melville wrote two "true" narratives of adventure, *Typee* and *Omoo*, with little risk and indeed a great deal of aggrandizement of his status. With the "romance" of *Mardi* he was "caught." But he was forgiven on the basis of *Redburn* and *White-Jacket*. With *Moby-Dick* and, especially, with *Pierre*, he was "caught" for good. His "normal" critics and in-laws kept urging him to return to the "realistic' social mode of *Typee*.

Melville, by the time of *Pierre* and undoubtedly long before, pretty clearly wanted to be "caught," but most romancers, as we have seen, sought to avoid being labeled. This effort lies at the heart of their "theoretical" pronouncements about the "mingling" of fact and fiction, the actual and the imaginary. Sociology, here, has an important hint for the literary historian: that authors' generalizations about literary *kinds* or *genres* may often be understood most fruitfully as social gestures, efforts to evade or embrace being "caught." John Cotton, in his preface to the *Bay Psalm Book* (1640), announced the translators' adherence to "fidelity rather then poetry" in their versification of the Psalms.[17] While smiling at Mather's quaint attempt to dissociate his own "poetry" from the "poetic," one may suspect that the conservative theory of romance, as a "realistic" mode dealing with "romantic" materials, often stemmed from an analogous desire to dissociate its proponents' social identity from the pejorative connotations of the label "romancer."

The last two stages of Becker's model of the deviant career have a special fascination for the student of American literary vocation, for, by and large, at least until after the Civil War, our writers failed to conform to them. First is the formation or joining of a deviant group, a deviant subculture. Until recently, America—as opposed, say, to France—has not nurtured literary "schools"—writers grouped together *as writers*, engaged in and identified by a common endeavor. To be sure, there have been many literary "gatherings," notably the famous Berkshire picnics of 1850–51, when Hawthorne, Melville, Holmes, Duyckinck, and their friends carried baskets of champagne into the mountains. But much of this "literary" society—one thinks of Boston's Saturday Club—involved a concerted effort at social normalcy. The keynote of the Saturday Club was not shared deviant identity but "good fellowship."[18] Melville, in his review of Hawthorne's *Mosses from an Old Manse*, speaks of the "shock of recognition" (415) among fellow geniuses. Yet his own literary friendship with Hawthorne soon cooled. Many explanations have been offered for this cooling, but it was enough, I would hazard, for Melville to have asked Hawthorne (and this is what the great letters are about) to be a "fellow genius." In terms of adherence to imagination there was still more shock than recognition, even in 1850, in the idea of a shared antisocial "literary" identity.

The final stage of Becker's sequential model is the formation of a deviant rationale. The deviant justifies his activity as more genuine than alleged "normalcy" and becomes involved, consequently, in "a general repudiation of conventional moral rules, conventional institutions, and the entire conventional world."[19] In the enforced conviction of his own superiority, the deviant labels *society* "deviant." For the nineteenth-century romancer, a rationale of this kind is not hard to outline: "What I imagine," he would insist, "is far more real than that paltry fiction *you* call 'reality.'" Poe's criticism, when he deigns to consider "you" at all, follows this pattern. So does Melville's. Thus the philosopher Babbalanja, in *Mardi*, asserts that "what are vulgarly called fictions are as much realities" as gross matter; "for things visible are but conceits of the eye: things imaginative, conceits of the fancy" (283–84). After *Mardi*, however, Melville's criticism is increasingly characterized by doubts about the superiority of the romancer and the truth of "things imaginative," and it is in these doubts that he expresses his deepest kinship with his predecessors and contemporaries.

Charles Brockden Brown's deviance, for instance, did not survive the experiment of trying it out. In the ten years of his life after he abandoned fiction he became "normal" with a vengeance, and in this he set the pattern for the great majority of our fiction writers before the Civil War, who tended either to join in "normal" society's devaluation of their calling or to present that calling, conversely, as if it were simply a "normal" career. Cooper, for example, consistently described his writing as a business enterprise, even demanding payment for the onerous task of rereading his own books.[20] Irving's mode is customarily that of apologetic, even guilty, self-deprecation. Hawthorne, in his letters and prefaces, falls all over himself in his effort to distance his own social identity from that of the author of his peculiar work. As he wrote to James T. Fields in 1860, concerning his expectations for *The Marble Faun:* "My own individual taste is for quite another class of works than those which I myself am able to write. If I were to meet with such books as mine, by another writer, I don't believe I should be able to get through them."[21] In Hawthorne's prefaces the "romancer" is more often than not some curiosity whom the "normal" Hawthorne is describing. A similar narrative stance dominates much of Hawthorne's fiction and most of Melville's short fiction in the 1850s, notably "Bartleby." It is essential to recognize the psychological ambivalence, the social predicament, lying behind narrative strategies of this kind.

This excursion into social psychology may seem out of place in a study of the development of a literary mode, but it is of the utmost importance. For the actual people who identified themselves as "romancers"—or who recoiled from such identification—what James called the "sacrifice of relation" was, first of all, a sacrifice, as they saw it, of their relation to society, to social normalcy. Moreover, this social sacrifice would seem to have been part of the attraction of "being a romancer." For the five writers with whom I am dealing there is strong evidence that a sense of alienation preceded their choice of a literary career. Brown and Irving fled the law. Poe, Hawthorne, and Melville all lost their fathers early, and they clearly felt the guilt and resentment normally experienced by children in this situation, not to mention the outcast's sense of dependence on relatives or foster parents. Might not such people have chosen the deviant label "romancer" in part precisely *because* it could validate, or at least give substance to, their sense of alienation? If one could find no secure place inside society, one could at least choose the relative security of a well-defined place outside it. In the deviant status of "romancer" an alienated young man could find, as it were, an objective correlative for the outcast's rage against society.[22]

Still, for most of these writers—Poe is an exception, Melville a partial exception—the risk of identifying completely with the antisocial implications of their status was apparently too great, and to evade or neutralize them was not necessarily difficult. As I have already suggested, there were many strategies for accomplishing this: claims of "realism," of moral intention; contentions that writing is, after all, a business like any other. The conservative theory of romance offered the excuse that the "romance" emanated not from the writer but from his material, and most of our romancers, whatever alienation may have lain behind their initial choice of fiction-writing as a career or emerged from their experience of engaging in it, set out to imbue that career with "normalcy." They were thus caught between absolutely contradictory imperatives, between internalizations of socially defined oppositions. The romance, they were compelled to insist, was "just a cigarette." But that was not, one reasonably suspects, why they smoked it. Seen in these terms, the theory and practice of romance in nineteenth-century America were founded for the most part less on a rationale, in Becker's sense, than on a rationalization.

"Being a romancer" in nineteenth-century America often involved not just an effort to reconcile "imagination" and "reality" but a delicate psychological balancing act between cries of isolated rage and cries for love and attention. The territory was far from neutral. Behind the fiction of Brown, Irving, Poe, Hawthorne, and Melville, and behind their theoretical ruminations on "romance" as a genre, lay the complex and contradictory experience of "being a romancer" in a hostile culture. "Dollars damn me," Melville wrote to Hawthorne in 1851. "What I feel most moved to write, that is banned,—it will not pay. Yet, altogether write the *other* way I cannot. So the product is a final hash, and all my books are botches" (128). At the time he penned this protest, Melville was finishing *Moby-Dick*.

PART TWO

MYSTERIES AND MASKS

A person, who has been burrowing, to his utmost ability, into the depths of our common nature, for the purposes of psychological romance,—and who pursues his researches in that dusky region, as he needs must, as well by the tact of sympathy as by the light of observation,—will smile at incurring such an imputation [of egotism] in virtue of a little preliminary talk about his external habits, his abode, his casual associates, and other matters entirely upon the surface. These things hide the man, instead of displaying him. You must make quite another kind of inquest, and look through the whole range of his fictitious characters, good and evil, in order to detect any of his essential traits.

HAWTHORNE, Preface to *The Snow-Image*

"You admit, then, that the absence of spasmodic movement was phenomenal."
"It was phenomenal, Mr. Purser, in the sense that it was an appearance the cause of which is not immediately to be assigned."

MELVILLE, *Billy Budd*

PROLOGUE

THE JAMESIAN SACRIFICE OF RELATION, I HAVE ARGUED, LIES AT THE heart of nineteenth-century American romance. Whether as a liberation to be sought or as an unpleasant fact to be evaded or obscured, this sacrifice was central both to the definition of "romance" and to the experience of "being a romancer." Nineteenth-century American romance had its roots in intellectual culture—in the body of ideas, beliefs, and assumptions inherited from Puritanism and reinforced by the spread of Scottish Common Sense thought—and it had its basis in the sort of cultural interaction described by sociology. With these two statements the cultural historian might rest, having seen how "theoretical" ruminations on the definition and discrimination of genres grew out of social experience and social interaction.

But the literary historian is obliged to raise a different sort of question, or set of questions. How, exactly, did such cultural conditions influence the formation and perpetuation of a literary tradition? How did the romancers' sense of the sacrifice of relation and their ambivalent reactions to this sacrifice inform the actual romances that they produced? How were the social or psychological dilemmas and strategies of the romancer transformed into the aesthetic dilemmas and strategies of the romance? How, that is to say, was the disrelation of the "deviant" romancer from his "normal" society transformed into the fundamental disrelation of romance as a form of literary expression—a disjunction of sincerity from artifice, of nonverbal meaning from linguistic statement, of mysterious impulse from the mask of ordered expression? It is with these questions in mind that the following four chapters approach the fiction of Brown, Irving, Poe, Hawthorne, and Melville.

THREE

Yet am I sure that even now my perturbations are sufficiently stilled for an employment like this? That the incidents I am going to relate can be recalled and arranged without indistinctness and confusion? That emotions will not be re-awakened by my narrative, incompatible with order and coherence? Yet when I shall be better qualified for this task I know not. Time may take away these headlong energies, and give me back my ancient sobriety; but this change will only be effected by weakening my remembrance of these events. In proportion as I gain power over words, shall I lose dominion over sentiments.

BROWN, *Edgar Huntly*

SENTIMENTS AND WORDS
Charles Brockden Brown

THE REAL HISTORY OF AMERICAN FICTION, THE HISTORY OF ITS DEVELOP-
ment as a serious form of literary art, begins with the six romances of
Charles Brockden Brown: *Wieland* (1798), *Ormond* (1799), *Edgar Huntly*
(1799), *Arthur Mervyn* (1799, 1800), *Clara Howard* (1801), and *Jane Talbot*
(1801). Hastily, even furiously, written, they exhibit glaring defects; but,
for all their flaws, they possess, especially the first four, originality, intelligence, and power. They received the praise of such later writers as
Hazlitt, Shelley, Poe, Hawthorne, and Margaret Fuller, and they de-
served it. As a precursor of American Romanticism, Brown probed central questions about politics, psychology, and literary expression, and, as
the first American romancer to respond seriously and profoundly to the
antifictional hysteria of his culture, he produced a body of work prophetic
of much of the later development of the theory and practice of the American romance.

Scattered through Brown's novels and prefaces and through the three
periodicals he edited between 1799 and 1810 are many statements about
the nature and purpose of fiction.[1] At times they resemble the conventional apologetics of his contemporaries, the claims of strict, normative
"realism" and didactic intention. For instance, in the prefatory letter to
Ormond, the narrator, Sophia Courtland, writes: "You are desirous of
hearing an authentic, and not a fictitious tale." Ormond, she writes, "is
not a creature of fancy" (3). *Wieland*, Brown writes in his preface, "aims at
the illustration of some important branches of the moral constitution of
man" (3). Of novels generally he writes, in the 1798 Advertisement for *Sky
Walk* (a work completed but never published): "The value of such works
lies without doubt in their moral tendency" (136).[2]

These claims of truth to nature and "moral" intention are not, however, as conventional as they at first seem. Sophia's claims of accuracy are curiously clinical in their emphasis on literal factuality. Ormond need not embody generally understood conceptions of human nature; he need only to have occurred in fact. In a similar vein, Brown declares, to justify his portrayal of Theodore Wieland's bizarre dementia, that "if history furnishes one parallel fact, it is a sufficient vindication of the Writer" (4).

The comments on the "moral" purpose of fiction are even more unusual. The "moral tendency" of the *Sky Walk* Advertisement is hardly didactic at all, involving, rather, such things as "lofty eloquence" and "the exhibition of powerful motives." "The world is governed," the Advertisement declares,

> not by the simpleton, but by the man of soaring passions and intellectual energy. By the display of such only can we hope to enchain the attention and ravish the souls of those who study and reflect. . . . A contexture of facts capable of suspending the faculties of every soul in curiosity, may be joined with depth of views into human nature and all the subtleties of reasoning. [136]

In the contexts of the didactic seduction novel or of the orthodox reaction against the enthusiasm of the Great Awakening or the French Revolution, such phrases as "soaring passions" and "ravish the souls" had, clearly, a threatening significance—of which their author was by no means unaware. What makes Brown fascinating is that he was willing, at least in theory, to identify himself with the insidious forces of passion and eloquence. The real affinities of the *Sky Walk* Advertisement are thus with a writer like Poe rather than with Susanna Rowson or Hannah Foster.

When Brown writes of *Wieland* that it "aims at the illustration of the moral constitution of man," "moral" means "psychological" rather than "didactic." Fiction exhibits the play of "powerful motives," not the stabilizing precepts of rational religion and virtue. Which is to say that, for Brown, in his critical writings, the sympathetic portrayal of character on its own terms is the principal goal of fiction. In theory he rejects both the attack on fiction and imagination and the evasive responses contemporary novelists made to that attack. He openly, even defiantly, champions the writer's eloquence and imaginative power in an age and land intensely suspicious of both. Here, surely, is our American Byron, appearing years before Poe or Melville—and even before Byron!

The image is appealing, but it needs qualification. First, for all his grandly theatrical defiance, Brown conceives imaginative power in terms remarkably similar to those employed by the harshest opponents of fiction. Like them he sees fictive eloquence, operating independently of social morality, as inherently threatening to the control of society and judgment, "suspending the faculties of every soul." There is, in the idealistic enthusiasm of Brown's early writings, as in his turning to literature and radicalism from the "respectable" pursuit of legal studies, a good deal of the desire to outrage solid normalcy.[3] One recalls Kai Erikson's comment about those "who appear to 'choose' a deviant style exactly *because* it offends an important value of the group . . . because they have an inner need to challenge this value in a direct test." The threatening quality of the imagination, as Brown portrays it, recalls Erikson's other point: that "the deviant and his more conventional counterpart live in much the same world of symbol and meaning."[4]

Furthermore, Brown's espousal of imaginative power is *theoretical*, and this, in the context of his thought, is a most important qualification; for while he could be idealistic in theory, he was notably skeptical in practice. Indeed, the movement from defiant idealism to pragmatic skepticism constitutes not only the major subject of his fiction but the most basic pattern of his own intellectual career. Again and again his novels follow a theoretical idealist to the logical and disastrous extremes of his ideals and theories; finally, in *Jane Talbot*, the hero renounces his idealism in order to achieve social acceptance and personal happiness. This last novel was a kind of personal testament; by 1801 Brown himself had renounced the deviant, theoretical radicalism of his youth in favor of the skeptical and pragmatic Federalism of his last years.

Brown's political transformation is a significant if minor episode in the history of American intellectual culture at the turn of the century. It matters here because, for Brown, the renunciation of radical theory was accompanied by the renunciation of fiction. *Jane Talbot* was his last novel. By 1803 he could declare of his earlier writings: "I should enjoy a larger share of my own respect, at the present moment, if nothing had ever flowed from my pen, the production of which could be traced to me."[5] It is perhaps unfair to read Brown's novels in the light of this subsequent disavowal of them, but the novels themselves justify such an approach, for they contain the seeds of their author's later conversion, including his renunciation of the ravishing power of fiction. Brown's theory of fiction was not so much a rationale for his practice as it was a *donnée* or hypothesis that the novels themselves subject to logical scrutiny. Skepticism about theoretical ideals, including his own ideals of the power and purpose of fiction, characterized Brown's thought from the beginning of his career. He might wait until 1803 to disown eloquence and imagination, but the thought and feelings behind that act were already implicit in the plots and narrative strategies of his four best novels: *Wieland, Ormond, Edgar Huntly,* and *Arthur Mervyn.*

IMAGINATION, SINCERITY, AND DUPLICITY

The gothic plots of these novels turn on a contest between two recurring figures: a virtuous but inexperienced protagonist—Clara Wieland, Constantia Dudley, Edgar Huntly, Arthur Mervyn—and an antagonist—Carwin, Ormond, Clithero Edny, Welbeck—whose attitudes and actions threaten the protagonist's conceptions of virtue and order. At the center of these novels is a dialectic between innocence and experience or, to use the terms Brown himself preferred, between "sincerity" and "duplicity." The novels' plots develop the difficulties of practicing honesty and idealism, difficulties Brown had already noted in the early 1790s:

> I think it may safely be asserted that of all the virtues mankind is most universally deficient in sincerity.... How many motives are there for concealing our real sentiment, for counterfeiting approbation and conviction? And how many occasions are there, on which, if its immediate and temporary effects only be considered, sincerity is criminal, and when a strict adherence to it would be, not only an infraction of politeness but a deviation from rectitude?[6]

We see, here, the curiously hypothetical reasoning from principle to complication that characterizes Brown's novels. They present, in the figure of the antagonist, the logical, duplicitous, and deviant or "criminal" extreme of the sincerity by which, for his part, the protagonist attempts to live. It is in such terms that the central struggle of the novels must be understood.

The meaning of this struggle may, however, be approached in various ways. Brown's enthusiasm for Godwin's *Political Justice*, which discusses sincerity largely in political terms, has led some readers to emphasize the political side of his thought. To be sure, political ideas were important to Brown. His conversion to Federalist conservatism involved a movement from belief in absolute sincerity in social relations to a recognition of the inevitable role played by intervening and complicating circumstance, and some of the antagonists in his novels—notably, Carwin and Ormond—are linked with the excesses of the Revolution in France. It might be objected with some justice that Carwin and Ormond have little real "political" substance, that in his portrayal of them Brown substituted melodramatic stereotype for serious political analysis. It should be noted in his defense, however, that melodrama was a staple of contemporary political discourse; Timothy Dwight, for instance, could declare of the secret Order of the Illuminati, founded in Bavaria and popularly supposed to have caused the French Revolution and to be plotting similar disasters for America: "ADULTERY, assassination, poisoning, and other crimes of the like infernal nature, were taught [by them] as lawful, and even as virtuous actions."[7]

Nonetheless, the threat to the equanimity of Brown's protagonists is more fundamentally psychological than political. As many readers have noted, Brown is centrally concerned with the forces that threatened eighteenth-century ideas of psychological order, as codified in Locke's *Essay Concerning Human Understanding*. In *Wieland*, for example, Clara Wieland tells the story of her brother Theodore's growing insanity. At the behest of what he takes to be supernatural voices, Theodore murders his wife and children and attempts to kill Clara. She attributes these voices to the ventriloquist-villain, Carwin. Her Lockean sense of psychological order, based on the assumption that all ideas and resulting motives derive from sense impressions, is thus seriously undermined. Carwin's ventriloquism reveals the complexity and unreliability of the sensory apparatus upon which all else depends, and when Wieland's insanity turns out to have arisen from his own mind, and not from Carwin's suggestions, Clara is faced with a process of idea-formation quite outside Locke's model of the mind. In psychological terms, *Wieland* potrays the contest between Lockean rationalism and the power of the irrational.[8] It taps the vein of fascination with irrationalism and insanity that inevitably lay beneath the surface of the "Age of Reason."

The Wielands' idyllic American community is destroyed by the force of imagination, by voices heard and visions seen in dreams. Wieland's insanity represents, in fact, almost a case study of those dangers of an "ill-regulated imagination" against which Dugald Stewart warned in 1792. Stewart, whether or not Brown knew his work, is relevant in other ways as well, for irrationality has specific literary connotations in the novel: the Wieland family, we are told, is related to "the modern poet of the same name." Their grandfather devoted his youth "to literature and music" and might be regarded, as Clara writes, "as the founder of the German Theatre" (7). While Theodore's delusions are literally religious, these aspects of the Wieland family background suggest that among the irrational forces threatening Clara's sense of order may be the force of literary art and literary imagination. If imagination, threatening the control of sober judgment, lay at the root of insanity, did it not also form the basis of literary eloquence?

The Artist as Villain

That Brown, in spite of his pre-Romantic defiance, shared his contemporaries' fear of fiction and imagination is clear in a story he published in 1798, "A Lesson on Sensibility." This tale concerns one Archibald, "a youth of lively parts," but one whose "sensibility had become diseased by an assiduous study of those Romancers and Poets, who make love the basis of their fictions."[9] He suffers, that is to say, from the same disease that afflicts William Hill Brown's Elizabeth Whitman or the heroine of Tabitha

Tenney's *Female Quixotism*. Through a process too involved to relate here, Archibald's diseased sensibility leads to a gruesome disappointment in love (involving the premature burial and starvation of his beloved), and he becomes a raving maniac. "He has remained for some years," the female narrator moralizes, "an example of the fatal effects of addicting the undisciplined mind to books, in which Nature is so fantastically and egregiously belied."[10]

The point is made even more forcefully, and in a way that ironically undermines the very narrative in which the point is being made, in a revised version of the story published in Joseph Dennie's *Port Folio* in 1809 as "Insanity: A Fragment." In this version, the narrator's husband intrudes at the close to reveal that the experience to which Archibald attributes his insanity was itself fictional, deriving solely from the effect of books on his sensibility: "the whole existed only in his own imagination: . . . the whole is a dream, regarded by him indeed as unquestionable reality, but having not the slightest foundation in truth."[11] Such, for Brown as for his more conventional contemporaries, were the dangers of exposing the mind to unreal and delusive pictures of life.

These same dangers lie behind the disastrous events of *Wieland*, which also culminates in delusion and insanity. At the close of her story, still believing that Carwin's ventriloquism produced Theodore's "supernatural" voices, Clara moralizes: "If Wieland had framed juster notions of moral duty, and of the divine attributes; or if I had been gifted with ordinary equanimity or foresight, the double-tongued deceiver would have been baffled and repelled" (273). Carwin is only indirectly responsible for Wieland's madness: his vocal deceptions merely unsettle Theodore's ability to distinguish between fact and fiction, leading him to accept the reality of voices produced by his own imagination. But this is precisely the sense in which moralists feared that fiction would unsettle the mental balance of novel-readers.

There is much else in Brown's novel to link Carwin's ventriloquism with the art of the fiction writer. In the *Sky Walk* Advertisement, Brown wrote that the purpose of the novelist's "lofty eloquence" is to "enchain the attention and ravish the souls of those who study and reflect" (136). On first meeting Carwin, Clara has a clearly sexual reaction to the power of his voice:

> The voice was not only mellifluent and clear, but the emphasis was so just, and the modulation so impassioned, that it seemed as if an heart of stone could not fail of being moved by it. It imparted to me an emotion altogether involuntary and incontroulable. When he uttered the words, "for charity's sweet sake," I dropped the cloth that I held

in my hand, my heart overflowed with sympathy and my eyes with unbidden tears. [59]

Here is a power comparable to fiction's passionate eloquence, uncontrollable in its appeal, irrational in its effects. Clara is "ravished" by this power, described in highly suggestive metaphorical language. Moreover, Carwin himself is literally a teller of tales, a romancer: "His narratives," Clara writes, "were constructed with so much skill, and rehearsed with so much energy, that all the effects of a dramatic exhibition were frequently produced by them" (84).

Carwin is a special sort of artist. Clara assures us repeatedly that her own tale is true, that she is disguising nothing. Not so with Carwin: "His tale is a lie, and his nature devilish" (243). "It would be vain," Clara is told by her suspicious lover, Pleyel, "to call upon Carwin for an avowal of his deeds. It was better to know nothing, than to be deceived by an artful tale" (145). In Clara's version of her contest with Carwin, then, the conflict between sincerity and duplicity acquires a specifically literary dimension. In *The Rhapsodist* (1789), Brown's first published work of literature, Brown had his persona insist that "the sincerity of my character shall be the principal characteristic of these papers" (1). Yet even the Rhapsodist feared that his literary performance might be considered but "an artful contrivance, designed to show the skill and ingenuity, rather than the fidelity, of the author's pencil" (9). If Clara represents the Rhapsodist's claim of absolute literary sincerity, then Carwin represents his fear that all literary expression, being "artful," leads inevitably to artificiality and deception.

Such fears were elaborated in 1800 in a series of essays, very probably by Brown, entitled *The Speculatist*. In one of these essays a friend of the Speculatist wonders whether even the man of benevolent sincerity may be but "performing a part in order to obtain [the world's] good opinion." If so, he concludes, "life appears like one great masquerade, at which every object is decked in false colours, and the attention of observers diverted from an useful analysis of the genuine character, by the vagaries of the one which is assumed."[12] It is fitting that Carwin's eloquence should find its expression in ventriloquism, a vocal masquerade. An essayist in Brown's *Literary Magazine* wrote in 1803 that the artist gains his ends, "not by imitating the works of nature, but by assuming her power."[13] Such ideas particularly alarmed moral and religious critics of fiction; for was not the artist, in his manipulations of reality, usurping the power of God?[14] Poe would base *Eureka*, his cosmological prose poem, on this analogy. In *Wieland* Clara implores the "double-tongued deceiver": "Thou art the author of these horrors! . . . I adjure thee, by that God whose voice thou hast dared to counterfeit, to save my life!" (255). Carwin, "*author* of these

47

horrors," masquerades as God, and in doing so he sets forward a chain of circumstances leading to Wieland's illusory and destructive visions of divinity.[15]

At the close, Clara assures us that Carwin "saw, when too late, the danger of imposture" (267). She claims to have avoided this danger herself by adhering to an art based on sincerity, but her claims in this regard are at least open to suspicion. A tale-teller herself, she has a strong stake in the disavowal of duplicity; in this sense, Carwin acts for her as a kind of scapegoat. As will be more explicitly the case with Arthur Mervyn, self-exoneration has its place among Clara's narrative motives. Moreover, if Carwin's eloquence reveals the artificial "effects of a dramatic exhibition," it is Clara's grandfather who founded the "German Theatre." In any case, Clara's protestations of sincerity are seriously undermined by the conclusion of her story. When Theodore's imaginary voices turn him against her, Clara appeals to Carwin, the impostor, for protection. He responds by counterfeiting the divine voice that has urged Wieland on and by having that voice—like the voice of Twain's Satan in *The Mysterious Stranger*— attest to the "truth" of its own nonexistence.

This ruse, while successful, is doubly ironic: to communicate the truth, Carwin must resort to imposture, and his "truth" destroys Wieland just as surely as illusion destroyed his wife and children. "Now finally restored to the perception of truth," writes the increasingly baffled Clara, "Wieland was transformed at once into the *man of sorrows!* " (258). Sincerity is once again corrupted by "artful" duplicity, in ways that now corrupt the purity of Clara's own narrative purpose. Her true story has been opposed all along to Carwin's imposture. At the end, however, she can only declare to her remembered brother, who has committed suicide in his despair: "Oh that thy phrenzy had never been cured! that thy madness, with its blissful visions, would return!" (259). Even Clara turns at last from "truth" to the "blissful vision" of imagination and insanity. Her antifictional sincerity crumbles in a general welter of moral and artistic confusion. We must distinguish this confusion, however, from that of such writers as Susanna Rowson or Hannah Foster, also torn between "truth" and imaginative sympathy. It is Clara who is confused here, not Brown. Her confusion is his subject.

The same confusion permeates the world of Brown's *Ormond*. Constantia Dudley, another sympathetic female figure of sincerity and virtue, confronts the trials of poverty, of pestilence, and ultimately of the villainous advances of Ormond, who announces at their first interview: "I will put your sincerity to the test" (128). Ormond is Brown's fullest representation of a character's descent from idealism to "philanthropic" villainy. Ormond rigidly separates his high ideals from his base, but theoretically justifiable, practical actions. He is also, of all Brown's characters, the most sexually aggressive and the most clearly linked to the ideals and excesses of the French Revolution. All of these forces—depraved idealism, sexual aggression, and political radicalism—are brought to bear against Constantia's virtue, against both her virginity and the ideals by which she tries to live.

But Ormond has another attribute, one that seems inexplicable in terms of his function in the novel: "In early youth," writes the narrator, Sophia Courtland, "he discovered in himself a remarkable facility in imitating the voice and gestures of others" (95). We are told at some length of the steps by which this facility became habitual. Yet, after his first visit to Constantia, in the guise of a chimney-sweep, Ormond's love of disguise, so elaborately introduced, has no function in the plot.

On the symbolic level, however, his "remarkable facility" is quite appropriate. His abilities, we are told, "would have rendered his career, in the theatrical profession, illustrious" (95). The same comment, interestingly, is frequently made about Zenobia in Hawthorne's *Blithedale Romance.* In *Ormond,* Sophia writes of the title character that he "blended in his own person the functions of poet and actor, and his dramas were not fictitious but real." For Ormond, the goal of such "real" drama is power:

> Ormond aspired to nothing more ardently than to hold the reins of opinion—to exercise absolute power over the conduct of others, not by constraining their limbs or by exacting obedience to his authority, but in a way of which his subjects should be scarcely conscious. [147]

It is in this sense that his "remarkable facility" is turned on Constantia:

> By explaining his plans, opportunity was furnished to lead and to confine her meditations to the desirable track. By adding fictitious embellishments, he adapted it with more exactness to this purpose. By piecemeal and imperfect disclosures her curiosity was kept alive. [147]

In the *Sky Walk* Advertisement, Brown had characterized the novel as "a contexture of facts capable of suspending the faculties of every soul in curiosity" (136). Like Carwin, then, Ormond acts in a sense the role of the artist as master of eloquent duplicity.

Halfway through *Ormond,* Sophia introduces her title character, and she begins by confessing her difficulties:

> I know no task more arduous than a just delineation of the character of Ormond. To scrutinize and ascertain our own principles are abundantly difficult. To exhibit those principles to the world with absolute sincerity can scarcely be expected. We are prompted to conceal and to feign by a thousand motives; but truly to portray the motives and relate the actions of another appears utterly impossible. [92]

Sophia's confession suggests that her own narrative, like Clara's, may fall short of absolute sincerity, and it indicates that, for Brown, the problem of fictional portrayal of character was analogous to the more general problem of literary sincerity, since both presented the writer with the final impossibility of knowing and expressing the truth. Whether in presenting himself or in ascribing motives to another, the writer was tempted into artfulness; and since he could establish patterns of motivation only through conjecture, he was forced to rely on imagination. One thinks in this connection of Melville's tortuous analysis of Claggart's "natural depravity" in *Billy Budd*.

In his Preface to the *Lyrical Ballads* Wordsworth announces what M. H. Abrams has called "the expressive theory of art," the theory that, somewhere around the turn of the century, displaced the "mimetic and pragmatic" as the dominant force in English criticism. "The central tendency of the expressive theory," Abrams writes, "may be summarized in this way: A work of art is essentially the internal made external."[16] At the heart of this fundamental Romantic idea is the notion that subjective states can become "objects," as it were, of mimesis. One might be tempted to see this subjective mimesis, or realization of hidden motive, as the essential project of the romance, although Poe, Hawthorne, and Melville subsume it in the larger project of what we might call "spiritual mimesis."[17] But Brown's comments on the mimesis of subjective states, like those of most of his American successors, are mainly concerned with the near impossibility of the project or, conversely, with its real danger should it chance to succeed.

In his 1800 essay on "The Difference between History and Romance," Brown identifies the novelist's analysis of motive with "romance," with fiction,[18] and a few months after publishing *Ormond* he admitted, in "Walstein's School of History," the difficulty of placing reliance on conjecture: "no situation can be imagined perfectly similar to that of an actual being" (154). For such reasons, Sophia Courtland, in spite of her prefatory claim that Ormond "is not a creature of fancy" (3), is finally forced to admit that her portrayal of him is nevertheless a work of imagination.

What happens in Sophia's story is that the imaginary quality of her *delineation* of Ormond becomes embodied in the *character* of Ormond as he acts in the novel. In the *Sky Walk* Advertisement, Brown wrote that the writer's "eloquence" finds its fit object in "the man of soaring passions and intellectual energy" (136). In Brown's novels this man emerges again and again as not only the object but the objective correlative of this eloquent "energy" and its terrors. In *The Rhapsodist* and in his portrayal of Carwin, Brown reveals his fear that such energy will inevitably be falsified by the effort to communicate it—by the effort to make the internal external.

The outcome of *Ormond* suggests that Brown feared equally what would

50

happen if sincere expression were successful. What if orthodox moralists were right about the essential demonism of the imagination, of the buried self? Toward the close, Ormond begins to set aside his habit of imposture, much to the terror of the sincere narrator, Sophia. "The veil that shrouded this formidable being," she writes, "was lifted high enough to make him be regarded with inexplicable horror" (231). Ormond's principal boast, Sophia writes earlier, "was his sincerity" (94). In his final interview with Constantia this figure of revolutionary sincerity and imaginative power finally emerges in his true form—as the conventional villain of the seduction novel. All else failing, he determines to rape the fair protagonist. He thus reveals the purpose, the energy, at the heart of his elaborate masquerade even as he opts for the open revelation of truth: "My avowals of love were sincere; my passion was vehement and undisguised" (233). Confronted with this figure of "soaring passions," Constantia has no choice. She kills him.

Carwin and Ormond, men of "soaring passions and intellectual energy," become, at last, figures of the artist trapped between a possibly dangerous sincerity and a perhaps inevitable imposture, between literary energy and the artfulness of literary order. To say this is not to reduce Brown's first two novels to the status of allegorical portraits of the artist, for in these novels the artistic conflict between sincerity and duplicity emerges as only one aspect of a more general opposition—literary, psychological, and political—between energy and order. That is to say, Brown's villains are *simultaneously* seducers, revolutionaries, and artists. As such, they embody a whole complex of related forces allied against orthodox conceptions of stability. Brown was hardly original in perceiving the similarity between the passion that overthrows the understanding and the revolutionary doctrines that threaten to overthrow settled societies, nor was he unique in perceiving the relationship of revolutionary passion to the artistic imagination. In portraying these forces acting in concert, he was only expressing in fictional form the conventional wisdom of his age.

What distinguishes Brown is the self-consciousness with which he made the conventional fear of fiction an overt preoccupation of works of fiction, making finally explicit the tensions implicit in the works of his more conventional fiction-writing contemporaries. In this self-consciousness he seems quite modern. The energy of a Carwin or an Ormond threatens not only the order of the mind and the community but the order of the work of art as well. If these figures represent the disastrous practical consequences of the doctrines of sincerity by which Clara and Constantia attempt to live, they also represent the hazards of that literary sincerity by which Brown was attempting to write. They thus foreshadow Hawthorne's odd proposition, in "Fancy's Show Box," that "a novel-writer, or a dramatist,

51

in creating a villain of romance, and fitting him with evil deeds, and the villain of actual life, in projecting crimes that will be perpetrated, may almost meet each other, half-way between reality and fancy" (225–26). As Brown himself put it in the early 1790s, there are "many occasions . . . , on which, if its immediate and temporary effects only be considered, sincerity is criminal."[19] *Wieland* and *Ormond* provided their author with such occasions. In them the "novel-writer" and the "villain of romance" do meet in a morally ambiguous neutral territory, "half-way between reality and fancy."

Masks of Words

In *Wieland* and *Ormond* Brown's fears about the motives and effects of fiction are embodied mainly in the figures of the villains; their importance, that is to say, is mainly thematic. Such fears do have a tendency, particularly in *Wieland*, to raise questions about the narrators' own sincerity of purpose—about the masks of language in which they clothe their own "truths"; but by projecting their doubts onto the villains of their stories, Clara and Sophia are freed—and, through them, perhaps Brown as well—of at least the conscious obligation to explore their own possibly duplicitous motives and strategies as tale-tellers. In *Edgar Huntly* and *Arthur Mervyn*, however, Brown embodies his fears of fiction directly in the narrative structures of his novels. Perhaps the shift from female to male narrators is crucial. In any case, Edgar and Arthur tell their own stories, and the eloquence that threatens them is consequently their own.

In *Edgar Huntly* Brown is concerned with neither revolution nor the impostures of idealism. As the narrator of his own tale, however, Edgar *is* concerned with the conflict between sincerity and duplicity, literary energy and literary order, imagination and the language that gives it expression. Edgar believes in the need for "order and coherence" in narrative, and yet he fears that such coherence may be irreconcilable with the emotional "truth" of his adventures:

> Time may take away these headlong energies, and give me back my ancient sobriety; but this change will only be effected by weakening my remembrance of these events. In proportion as I gain power over words, shall I lose dominion over sentiments. [5]

This problem is central to Edgar's narrative. His story turns on the implications of telling and hearing tales and on the ways in which rational forms of expressive order ("words") obscure or repress the irrational sources of artistic energy ("sentiments"). In the narrative structure of *Edgar Huntly* Brown explores the means by which certain kinds of literary

52

expression and response attempt to reverse or overcome the demonic revolutionary impulses revealed in *Wieland* and *Ormond*.

At the beginning of his story Edgar is seeking the murderer of his friend Waldegrave. He comes to suspect a mysterious somnambulist, Clithero Edny, and follows him into the wilderness to extort a confession. When Clithero does confess, however, it is to a quite different crime. *His* story, nested within Edgar's, tells of his having been raised by a Mrs. Lorimer, a benevolent woman persecuted by her villainous brother, Arthur Wiatte. In spite of Wiatte's treachery, Mrs. Lorimer was persuaded (and the ambiguous "salvations" of Clara and Constantia may suggest her reasons) that her own survival depended on his continued existence. One night Clithero killed a thief in self-defense, only to discover to his horror that the assailant was Wiatte. Overwhelmed by guilt—irrational in view of his blameless motives—Clithero succumbed to a compulsion to "save" Mrs. Lorimer from knowledge of her brother's death by killing her, too. His attempt failed, but she collapsed from shock. Clithero then fled, convinced that his actions had led to her death. Tormented by his "inexpiable guilt," he has come to the American wilderness.

As soon as he finishes his tale, which occupies six chapters of Brown's novel, Clithero vanishes into the forest. Edgar is deeply moved by what he has heard. "I had communed," he writes, "with romancers and historians, but the impression made upon me by this incident was unexampled in my experience" (86–87). From here on, the novel's action concerns Edgar's response to Clithero's narrative.

Consciously, he is filled with compassion, with a sympathy that overwhelms moral judgment—which is to say that, on the conscious level, he reacts like a good reader of sentimental fiction or like Brown's earlier feminine narrators, substituting charity for censure. He sets out to exonerate Clithero and thus to "save" him. "It must at least be said," he reasons, "that his will was not concerned in this transaction. He acted in obedience to an impulse which he could not control or resist. Shall we impute guilt where there is no design?" (87). This is the question the novel sets out to answer, and its implications are as much literary as psychological, for narrative, too, may move as much by "impulse" as by "design."

Unconsciously, Edgar reacts to Clithero's story with a very different sort of sympathy. "My judgment," he confesses, "was, for a time, sunk into imbecility and confusion. My mind was full of the images unavoidably suggested by this tale, but they existed in a kind of chaos" (87). Just as Clithero acted against Mrs. Lorimer "in obedience to an impulse which he could not control nor resist," and just as Clara Wieland's reaction to Carwin's voice was "altogether involuntary and incontroulable" (59), so Edgar is propelled "unavoidably" into a "kind of chaos." Archibald Alison wrote in 1790 that "we feel the sublimity or beauty [of

53

works of art], when our imaginations are kindled by their power, when we lose ourselves amid the number of images that pass before our minds, and when we waken at last from this play of fancy, as from the charm of a romantic dream."[20] There is no evidence that Brown had read Alison, but he did not need to; Alison was simply expressing a widely accepted conception of aesthetic experience, of the imaginative response to works of art. This same conception governs the events of *Edgar Huntly*. Edgar's mind is filled with a "chaos" of "images," a condition of irrational imaginative excitement, arising in response to a tale.

Thus, even as he consciously dismisses the importance of Clithero's irrational behavior, Edgar unconsciously begins to imitate it. He is himself transformed into a somnambulist, thereby manifesting a guilt that is, in some obscure way, comparable to Clithero's. He follows Clithero into a wilderness clearly symbolic of the unconscious mind (the woodland grave, perhaps, of his friend "Waldegrave");[21] and his new life, described as a "hideous dream," becomes at last quite literally dreamlike. After retiring to sleep in his uncle's house, he awakens in a cave, from which he emerges to battle Indians and panthers and to make hundred-foot leaps into the Delaware River. As he notes himself, these fantastic adventures must seem to the reader "the vision of fancy, rather than the lesson of truth" (185).

Edgar's response to Clithero's story hints at a profound unconscious sympathy between artist and audience. Many details, both of the story and of Edgar's response, hint further at the mechanism by which such irrational sympathy operates. For instance, Clithero remarks, almost casually, of his killing of Wiatte: "I was impelled by an unconscious necessity. Had the assailant been my father, the consequence would have been the same" (70). Edgar pursues, and yet becomes curiously identified with, Indians who years before killed *his* father. He uses a rifle given to him by his paternal teacher, Saresfield. At the beginning of his dream adventure he finds this rifle in the possession of one of his Indian victims; he learns later that it had just been used to kill his uncle, who adopted him after his father's death; and, near the close, he "unwittingly" turns this rifle on his last remaining father figure, Saresfield, who had given him the weapon in the first place. Both Edgar and Clithero, it would seem, are plagued by unconscious urges to slay figures of paternal authority and by the "irrational" or "inexplicable" guilt consequent on these urges. They even have a "father" in common: Saresfield turns out to be Mrs. Lorimer's long-lost fiancé.

It is small wonder that Edgar reacts so powerfully, albeit unconsciously, to Clithero's strange tale, since it reveals, symbolically, his own repressed dreams and impulses. The oedipal patterns in Clithero's and Edgar's stories, only sketched here, are quite blatant to the modern reader, and one can only speculate about the degree of Brown's awareness and his intention in suggesting such patterns. What *is* clear, however, is that in the course of the novel irrational motivation and identification, whatever their source, triumph over the rational sympathy with which Edgar attempts to control his response to Clithero's story. This is the essential action of *Edgar Huntly*, and the novel is experimental precisely because it seeks for ways of imitating that action. Rational sympathy (the "charity" of sentimental fiction), having initially overcome moral judgment, is in turn undercut by unconscious, imaginative, sympathy. At the end of the novel, having fortunately missed his shot at Saresfield and having emerged from his own wilderness of guilt—having, that is, awakened from his dream of fancy—Edgar tries to work out a similar deliverance for Clithero. He rushes into the wilderness to tell him that Mrs. Lorimer is not dead, after all, but is married to Saresfield and living in New York. "I come," he announces, "to outroot a fatal but powerful illusion" (275). His information has, however, precisely the contrary effect from what he intends. He simply reanimates Clithero's compulsion to murder his benefactress, driving him to New York, where he is arrested and then commits suicide on the way to an asylum.

Edgar has maintained throughout that "the magic of sympathy, the perseverance of benevolence, though silent, might work a gradual and secret revolution, and better thoughts might insensibly displace those desperate suggestions which now governed [Clithero]" (107). At the close, he finally agrees with Saresfield that Clithero's "understanding" has been "utterly subverted" (277), rendering him immune to the workings of benevolence. But Edgar never takes the final step: he never consciously understands the implications of Clithero's insanity for his own and Clithero's narratives and for narrative appeal in general. Edgar is never willing or able to admit, even to himself, that the appeal of Clithero's tale, the "magic" of its "sympathy," derived not from "better thoughts" but from the "desperate suggestions" at its core. Edgar thus pulls back from the fullest implications of his own story. If Brown's novel records the undercutting of charity by compulsion, of "better thoughts" by "desperate suggestions," it does so only through narrative irony. Overtly, in Edgar's account, "words" do finally triumph over "sentiments."

Arthur Mervyn, the protagonist of Brown's fourth novel, even more persistently submerges "desperate suggestions" beneath the mask or veil of "better thoughts." *Arthur Mervyn* was published in two parts. The first appeared early in 1799, before *Edgar Huntly*. Part two was given to the printer early in 1800. The first part is very much in the manner of *Wieland* and *Ormond*. A sincere protagonist, this time a young man from the country, enters an alien city world, dominated by "perils and deceptions" (43).

Like Constantia Dudley, he confronts the smallpox epidemic of 1793, and he encounters an older man, Welbeck, whose character is strongly reminiscent of Carwin and Ormond.

Welbeck's villainy has mainly to do with sexual licentiousness and financial fraud, but it is also associated with literature. "My ambition," he declares, "has panted, with equal avidity, after the reputation of literature and opulence" (95). Welbeck thus assumes the familiar poses of the artist figure in Brown's fiction: as forger and as vocal impostor, counterfeiting the voices of others. In the relationship of Welbeck with Arthur Mervyn we have the familiar contest between duplicity and sincerity. As Arthur is physically wasted by fever, so his reputation is blasted by his association with Welbeck. He is saved at the end only through the charity of a Dr. Stevens, to whom he tells his story and whose own voice frames the narrative of the first part.

In part two, Arthur's adventures take a different direction. Sincerity and virtue seem to triumph. Welbeck dies repentant. Through an almost obsessive course of benevolence, Arthur rescues his reputation, rising into circles of affluence and finally marrying a rich widow. He does all this by insisting on absolute sincerity of conduct. Even his view of the city changes. Wider experience of Philadelphia convinces him "that if cities are the chosen seats of misery and vice, they are likewise the soil of all the laudable and strenuous productions of mind" (280). Part one's vision of evil is transformed, in part two, into a vision of opportunity.

Part two also transforms the earlier treatment of literary truth and deception. In part one, Welbeck's inveterate imposture is contrasted with Arthur's insistent honesty (just as, in *Wieland*, Carwin's duplicity is contrasted with Clara's sincerity). In part two, Welbeck's importance subsides, and it is Arthur himself who comes under suspicion of fraud. In fact, part two functions as a sort of commentary on the narrative that Arthur presents in part one. It begins with the efforts of Dr. Stevens's friends to convince him of the falsehood of Arthur's tale. One merchant argues, as Stevens writes,

> that Mervyn was a wily imposter; that he had been trained in the arts of fraud, under an accomplished teacher; that the tale which he had told to me, was a tissue of ingenious and plausible lies; that the mere assertions, however plausible and solemn, of one like him, whose conduct had incurred such strong suspicions, were unworthy of the least credit. [215]

The action of part two turns mainly on the question of whether or not Arthur will be able to prove his sincerity against such aspersions.

Arthur's problem recalls that of Godwin's Caleb Williams.[22] Like Caleb, Arthur has nothing to support his tale but the air of sincerity with which he tells it. But there is an important difference of emphasis in *Arthur Mervyn*. Godwin's concern with Caleb's predicament—with his inability to disprove the false accusations of Falkland—is almost entirely social and psychological; he is exploring the possibility of justice in a legal system based on corroborative evidence and with the psychological consequences of Caleb's exposure of Falkland. For Brown, what is at stake is not justice in society but truth as an abstract ideal and as a motive of narrative: "If Mervyn has deceived me," Stevens confesses to one of his suspicious friends, "there is an end to my confidence in human nature. All limits to dissimulation, and all distinctions between vice and virtue will be effaced. No man's word, no force of collateral evidence shall weigh with me an hair" (236–37).

Such confidence does have a specifically literary dimension. By shifting the narrative point of view from Arthur to Stevens, Brown calls attention to the fact that Arthur's narrative *is* a narrative—possibly a work of fiction. "Nothing but his own narrative," writes the benevolent doctor, "repeated with that simple but nervous eloquence, which we had witnessed, could rescue him from the most heinous charges. His tale could not be the fruit of invention; and yet, what are the bounds of fraud? Nature has set no limits to the combinations of fancy" (218). As Melville would do half a century later in *The Confidence-Man*, Brown in *Arthur Mervyn* links confidence in human nature with confidence in the truth of literary language, and he subjects both to powerful scrutiny. To believe in Arthur (or "author"?), one must trust the art, the "nervous eloquence," of his story.

The novel's comic conclusion seems to vindicate both Arthur and the possibility of sincerity in narrative expression. Throughout the second part Arthur insists on the efficacy of telling the truth, "without artifice or disguise" (294), and his sincerity is rewarded by the restored confidence of Stevens's skeptical friends. Yet the reader's skepticism, once aroused, is not so easily quieted. The very complexity of the novel's narrative structure raises doubts about the reliability of all narrative, and, while one hardly suspects Arthur of the deliberate sort of fraud practiced by Welbeck, one cannot avoid the suspicion that he is at least deceiving himself.[23]

For one thing, Arthur's benevolent honesty often has quite disastrous consequences for others, as he himself acknowledges. "Good intentions," he admits, "unaided by knowledge, will, perhaps, produce more injury than benefit." Yet he insists that only conscious intention matters, whatever the result. "We must not be unactive because we are ignorant. Our good purposes must hurry to performance, whether our knowledge be greater or less" (309). This obliviousness, however, is neither completely idealistic nor completely ingenuous. If Arthur ignores the hazardous consequences of his sincerity for others, he seldom forgets its possible beneficial consequences for himself. He always seems to have a *reason* for telling the truth, and his prosperity, at the novel's conclusion, suggests that virtue is perhaps to be regarded less as its own reward than as a particularly efficacious way to wealth. One recalls the friend's suspicion in the *Speculatist* essays (published four months after part two of *Arthur Mervyn* had gone to the printer) that even the benevolent man is but "performing a part in order to obtain [the world's] good opinion." Dr. Stevens, at the outset, provides Arthur's adventures with a fitting motto. "Sincerity," he observes, "is always safest" (11).

If the reader has cause to suspect the motive behind Arthur's sincerity of behavior, he has even more cause to suspect the motive behind Arthur's narrative. His story is offered as a didactic illustration of the triumph of virtue over vice, of benevolence over corruption. Each confrontation with evil simply provides another opportunity to display the corrective power of sincerity. Like Edgar Huntly, with whom he also shares a belief in the supremacy of rational will and conscious motive, Arthur believes in the power of "better thoughts" to overcome "desperate suggestions"; and this belief functions as the overt moral of his tale.

And yet, desperate suggestions emerge, in spite of Arthur's conscious narrative purpose, and they do so in a way that looks ahead to the compulsive narratives of Edgar Poe. The sense of pestilential depravity pervading Philadelphia is never quite washed away by the comic momentum of part two, and Arthur's benevolent moral is undercut by his own story: the story of a young man who idolizes his dead mother, loathes his father (for having "victimized" her), and leaves home when his father takes a second wife, a woman whose "superabundant health" (16) disturbs her stepson. The suspicions of Dr. Stevens's friends focus mainly on Arthur's account of his childhood and youth. In their view, Arthur simply rebelled against his father's just authority. They have also heard rumors, from other sources, that Arthur has had sexual relations with his stepmother.

At the end of his story, Arthur spurns the love of a beautiful young woman in order to marry his heiress, Achsa Fielding, an older widow whom he repeatedly addresses as "Mamma." Just before their marriage he confesses to feeling a "nameless sort of terror" (419) and has a dream in which Mrs. Fielding's first husband (presumably his "Papa") returns to kill him. This dream suggests that Arthur's motives, for all his overt benevolence, are not so very different from those of Clithero Edny or Edgar Huntly. The dream even induces in Arthur a brief bout of somnambulism.

What matters, however, is Arthur's utter rejection of the dream's implications, paralleling his earlier rejection of the frightening implications of Philadelphia. "I hate your dream," says Achsa; "It is a horrid thought." "Why," replies Arthur, "you surely place no confidence in dreams" (429). If Arthur feels unconscious guilt for leaving his father and marrying his

"Mamma," he refuses to admit it, either to the reader or to himself. Arthur's benevolence can be both cold and calculating. On learning of his father's death, he admits that, at first, "I was greatly shocked at this intelligence," but "better thoughts" then come to the fore; after some time, he writes, "my reason came to my aid, and shewed me that this was an event, on the whole, and on a disinterested and dispassionate view, not unfortunate" (376–77).

Many readers have noticed the irony of *Arthur Mervyn*, but they have generally been hesitant to give Brown full credit for it.[24] It would seem, however, that the book's irony is full, deliberate, and devastating. Against Arthur's profession of virtuous intention stands his unacknowledged but persistent self-interestedness. Against the novel's apparent vindication of narrative sincerity, of the rational eloquence of Arthur's "words," stands the welter of suppressed motives and "sentiments" revealed briefly in the final dream.

In 1789 Brown's Rhapsodist wrote: "It is a very whimsical situation when a person is about to enter into company, and is at a loss what character or name to assume in it" (3). Arthur is the first of Brown's protagonists to "enter into company" with complete success, without agonizing over the question of what "name or character" to "assume." But he does not resolve the Rhapsodist's doubts; he simply suppresses them. He maintains his faith in social and literary order by averting his eyes from the dangerous psychological sources of narrative expression and from the Rhapsodist's fear that all character is "assumed." Arthur turns sincerity on its head. He is a *pragmatic* idealist, willfully ignoring all those aspects of his idealism and its consequences that terrified Brown's earlier protagonists. His trick, as a good American, is to act and write artificially without knowing it. He completes the process begun by Edgar Huntly, who at least admitted that Clithero was immune to benevolent salvation. Arthur's earnestness is never daunted, but it is, as Brown's irony makes clear, the earnestness of the confidence-man.

Brown's first four novels, then, portray the complex collision of sincerity and duplicity on many levels: philosophical, psychological, political, literary. It is on this last level that they are most interesting to the student of later American fiction, for they show how the intellectual and literary climate of America, particularly the prevalence of orthodox hostility toward imagination, led an early writer toward preoccupations and formal strategies that would characterize the most stylistically interesting American fiction of the next sixty years and beyond.

Lionel Trilling and others, following the lead of such "conservative" complaints as Hawthorne's in his *Marble Faun* preface, have attributed the self-conscious symbolism of American fiction to the lack of intelligible social reality in pre–Civil War America.[25] What Brown's example suggests is that what was ultimately in question was not so much the reality to be portrayed in fiction as the authenticity of fictional portrayal. One reason why social reality is relatively unimportant in our best fiction, it would seem, is that both readers and writers, whatever their views about the intelligibility of American society, were predisposed to distrust the reality of fictional narrative. The novelist's attention was continually deflected from his world to his art, as, in Brown's novels, political and social conflict is persistently subsumed within the prior problem of artistic conflict. Hostility toward fiction and imagination, combined with the Romantic shift from a mimetic to an expressive view of artistic creation, forced the writer's attention from objective "reality" to the workings of his own mind. Thus social initiation, in Brown's novels, finally becomes a kind of metaphor for the process of literary expression. Behind the political and philosophical debates that inform their plots one finds, again and again, the Rhapsodist's question about what "character or name" an author could or should "assume" when "about to enter into company." In what "words" should he clothe his "sentiments"?

The priority of this question also explains why, in Brown's novels, the sane, controlling intelligence of the novelist-narrator, dominant in the great tradition of nineteenth-century British fiction, is replaced by the figure of the artist as impostor (the "double-tongued deceiver," as Clara describes Carwin). Brown turns from those forms in which a reliable narrator mediates between the audience and the world of the novel. He cultivates instead those forms that pretend to authenticity and immediacy: letters, memoirs, confessions; yet the paradoxical effect of this immediacy is to *subvert* authenticity by bringing narration into the action and thus making it the focus of concern and question.

All four novels reveal a basic fear, essentially similar to the fears of contemporary moralists, of the origins and effects of imaginative fiction. The romance's unreal and delusive picture of life unsettles the natural balance of the mind—both the reader's and the author's. In doing so, it releases a repressed imaginative energy that threatens not only the order of society but also the order of fiction, the narrative communication between author and audience. Deliberately writing just the sort of fiction contemporary moralists feared, and fearing it himself, Brown inevitably entangled himself in the strange relationship between narrative unreliability and irrational psychology. Whatever its overt adherence to rational moral order ("understanding," "charity," "better thoughts"), the romance ultimately probed and liberated the imagination ("passion," "unconscious necessity," "desperate suggestions").

Brown's importance does not lie, however, in his suspicion of imagination—a suspicion he shared, after all, with the great majority of his American contemporaries. What does make him important is that, by directly confronting this suspicion, he made explicit the dilemmas the earlier romancers had felt but evaded. In doing so, he discovered a new kind of narrative, or, to speak more precisely, he gave a new emphasis and focus to an old kind. Such writers as Susanna Rowson, William Hill Brown, and Hannah Foster were baffled (like Clara Wieland) by the tension between sympathy and judgment, by the need to present imaginative truth in the *form* of moral judgment. Their narratives are, as it were, unconsciously ironic or duplicitous. Brown, through a radical and deliberate development of narrative irony, brings the tension between rational judgment and unconscious sympathy, between "words" and "sentiments," to the center of the stage. In his fiction, narrative irony crosses the line into that peculiar sort of symbolism so important to later American fiction, a symbolism at once expressive and repressive, like the black veil of Hawthorne's minister: expressive largely through its ironic enactment of repression.

The aspiring romancer might idealistically declare his theoretical identification with "the man of soaring passions and intellectual energy," along with his intention to "ravish the souls of those who study and reflect." In practice, however, he was obliged to accept the need for repression, concealment, duplicity. "Sentiments," to return to Edgar Huntly's invaluable distinction, were obliged, when expressed, to assume the costume of "words."

FOUR

They all returned varying in their stories: some affected in one way, some in another; some more, some less; but all agreeing that there was a certain something about the painting that had a very odd effect upon the feelings.

I stood in a deep bow-window with the Baronet, and could not help expressing my wonder. "After all," said I, "there are certain mysteries in our nature, certain inscrutable impulses and influences, which warrant one in being superstitious. Who can account for so many persons of different characters being thus strangely affected by a mere painting?"

"And especially when not one of them has seen it!" said the Baronet, with a smile.

IRVING, *Tales of a Traveller*

FEELINGS AND EFFECTS
Washington Irving

THE PLACE OF WASHINGTON IRVING IN AN AMERICAN TRADITION OF RO-
mance is not immediately apparent. His fiction seems to avoid the intensity and the major preoccupations of other American romancers, and,
from Jonathan Oldstyle to Geoffrey Crayon, his inveterate habit of hiding
behind personae suggests, rather than sincerity, a deliberate evasion of
self-revelation. Perhaps most troubling is his cultivation of humor and
hoax. As Stanley T. Williams has written of Irving's *Tales of a Traveller:*
"we can never read these stories as we pore over the serious narratives of
Charles Brockden Brown, with possibly a smile at their absurdity but
with respect for Brown's sincere rendering of the Gothic tradition."[1]

Yet we should not too hastily dismiss Irving, either from this discussion
or from our general notion of the significant development of American
fiction. His elaborate duplicity, and especially his narrative personae,
probably reveal as much as they conceal about their author.[2] Even Brown,
after all, had his Rhapsodist and Speculatist. And Irving must be taken
seriously if only in recognition of his literary-historical importance.
Bracebridge Hall and *Tales of a Traveller* appeared while Hawthorne was an
undergraduate at Bowdoin, determining on a career as a writer of fiction;
he would later send complimentary copies of *The House of the Seven Gables*
and *The Blithedale Romance* to their author. Poe, in his 1842 review of
Hawthorne's *Twice-Told Tales*, classed Irving's *Tales* with Hawthorne's as
the only "American tales of real merit" (11:109–10).[3] Melville, in "Hawthorne and His *Mosses*," attacked the "American Goldsmith" for his
"studied avoidance of all topics but smooth ones" (413), and he burlesqued
Irving's manner in many of his own tales and sketches of the mid-1850s,
notably in "Bartleby." In 1847, however, Evert Duyckinck noted of Melville in his diary that he "models his writing evidently a great deal on

Washington Irving."[4] Poe, Hawthorne, and Melville would all go beyond Irving, but his was, at the very least, the example to be approached and surpassed.

Furthermore, and whatever his actual influence, Irving did confront in his fiction the central dilemma of American romance. James identified the romancer's art with the sacrifice of relation, the cutting of the cable anchoring the car of imagination to the solid earth. The cutting of this cable is a major preoccupation in Irving's fiction. The sacrifice of relation, the divergence of authorial sensibility from Common Sense reality, was for him a major terror. Like Brown, in spite of the many differences of tone and temperament between the two writers, he assumed a radical opposition between imagination and reality, fiction and fact. Throughout his career he sought some means of integrating the two realms, some method for anchoring James's "commodious car." His quest eventually led him away from fiction altogether, into the more reliable (or, to use James's term, "related") modes of history and biography, and it was in terms quite similar to James's that he flirted gingerly with romance.

It must be remembered that, in comparison to his long and prosperous career as a man of letters, Irving's career as a fiction writer was quite brief and far from successful. Of course he "fictionalized" his materials to a greater or lesser degree in all his works, but only in the early 1820s—in *The Sketch-Book* (1819–20), *Bracebridge Hall* (1822), and especially *Tales of a Traveller* (1824)—was he willing to identify himself or his various personae overtly as writers of fiction. Beginning with the tales interpolated into *The Sketch-Book*, he became more and more involved with fiction. He projected at least two novels, although by 1824 he had come to believe in the aesthetic superiority of short fiction.[5] *Bracebridge Hall* devoted considerably more space to tales than *The Sketch-Book*, and in *Tales of a Traveller*, for the first and only time in his career, he devoted an entire volume to works of fiction. The publication of the *Tales* marked the climax and catastrophe of this phase of Irving's career. Various circumstances, notably the book's disappointing popular and critical reception,[6] led to his rapid flight from fiction after 1824; his later volumes would include interpolated tales or "legends," but the volumes themselves would appear as works of history, biography, or personal observation.

Irving fled fiction for a variety of reasons. He consistently distrusted his powers of invention; perhaps he was afraid to make stories up. In any case, history and biography, even as they allowed a little "mingling" of "poetry," were clearly easier; for the "stories" were already there, and material was constantly being offered to him—by Everett (Spain), Astor (the West), and others. But Irving himself described his shift of mode as a deliberate and self-conscious attempt to escape the opprobrium of fictionality, of overt "romancing." The *Tales* were followed, after a silence of four years, by a work of popular history, *The Life and Voyages of Christopher Columbus*, and Irving wrote in apprehension to his friend Henry Brevoort: "if it fails it will be, most probably, what many have anticipated, who suppose, from my having dealt so much in fiction, it must be impossible for me to tell the truth with plausibility."[7] Irving had made the unreliability of historical "reality" a prime object of satire in *Knickerbocker's History of New York* (1809),[8] but it was to the role of historian that he fled, after 1824, for the security of "relation."

What fiction meant to him, by contrast, is suggested by the epigraph to Part I of the *Tales*, taken from Fletcher's *Wife for a Month:*

> *Cleanthes.*—This is a monstrous lie.
> *Tony.*—   I do confess it.
>   Do you think I'd tell you truths? [9]

And the *Tales* themselves, as the fullest development of Irving's flirtation with fiction, suggest that, among the circumstances that drove him from fiction, one must include prominently the nature of fiction itself as Irving conceived it. The book's violence, self-conscious humor, and obsession with narrative hoaxes cannot be attributed to later hostile reviews or poor sales. Irving had prepared himself beforehand for the failure of the *Tales*—so much so, in fact, that this failure becomes one of their principal themes. Again and again they turn on belief or disbelief in literary and imaginative truth and deal explicitly with frustrated artists or young men and women crazed by fiction and imagination. They reveal what it meant, for Irving, to cut the cable of relation—to "indulge," as he put it in 1857, "in *romancing*."[9]

FORBIDDEN FANCIES

In 1813 Irving sketched the plight of the imaginative writer in America with telling precision:

> Unfitted for business, in a nation where every one is busy; devoted to literature, where literary leisure is confounded with idleness; the man of letters is almost an insulated being, with few to understand, less to value, and scarcely any to encourage his pursuits. ["Robert Treat Paine," 367]

The general effect of this situation on nineteenth-century American romancers has been sketched in chapter 2. Its specific effect on Irving was crucial, both on the overall shape of his career and on the form of the fiction he produced between 1819 and 1824. Like his predecessors, contemporaries, and successors, he confronted a society that branded the writer a "deviant," an "insulated being." Moreover, such deviance surely had a good deal to do with his choice of a literary career in the first place. And yet his *"instinct . . .* to out with the Romance," to borrow Melville's phrase, was always strongly resisted by the counterforce of what Melville called "acquired wisdom."

Irving insisted repeatedly, against the objections of friends and family, on holding to his purpose of becoming a writer. Yet he atoned for his rebellion, as it were, by accepting his hostile culture's devaluation of his calling. A tone of guilty self-deprecation informs many of his personal writings. In 1821 he justified his absence from America to Henry Brevoort by declaring: "I see no way in which I could be provided for, not being a man of business, a man of Science, or in fact any thing but a mere belles lettres writer." To his family's shock at his refusing a political job in Washington in 1819, he replied to his brother Ebenezer: "I am quite unfitted for political life. My talents are merely literary."[10]

Self-belittlement of this kind clearly did not overcome the outcast's guilt and anxiety over lost wealth and status. Irving's fictions, especially such tales as "Dolph Heyliger" and "Wolfert Webber," reveal an obsession with fantasies of sudden wealth. Like Mark Twain, whose fiction reveals a similar obsession, Irving was notoriously susceptible to get-rich-quick schemes, and they absorbed much of his literary income.[11] His ultimate and paradoxical hope, however, was that literature itself, the symbol of his alienation, might secure the very status it seemed to deny him. With his 1819 letter to Ebenezer he enclosed a copy of the first number of *The Sketch-Book*, declaring: "If I ever get any solid credit with the public, it must be in the quiet and assiduous operations of my pen, under the mere guidance of fancy and feeling." Against the belittling "mere" stands the more hopeful "solid credit," implying that literature might yield just those "solid" values respected (and expected) by the orthodox. Indeed, Irving's letter of self-justification sounds less like a literary credo than a business prospectus:

> I have been for some time past nursing my mind up for literary operations, and collecting materials for the purpose. I shall be able, I trust, now to produce articles from time to time that will be sufficient for my present support, and form a stock of copyright property, that may be a little capital for me hereafter.

Accepting, at times even embracing, the loss of status a literary vocation entailed, Irving was nevertheless determined to vindicate himself in the eyes of a hostile culture by converting dispossession and alienation into repossession and control. "Do not, I beseech you," he writes to Ebenezer,

> impute my lingering in Europe to any indifference to my own country or my friends. My greatest desire is to make myself worthy of the

good-will of my country, and my greatest anticipation of happiness is the return to my friends. I am living here in a retired and solitary way, and partaking in little of the gaiety of life, but I am determined not to return home until I have sent some writings before me that shall, if they have merit, make me return to the smiles, rather than skulk back to the pity of my friends.[12]

While authorship might proclaim, symbolically, a sense of orphanhood, it might also provide the means of reclaiming a lost patrimony.

On the face of it, Irving's career as the first successful American man of letters would seem to have fulfilled this fantasy, exonerating imagination in the land of business. When he did finally return home in 1832, it *was* to the "good-will" of his country and the "smiles" of his friends. However, the fiction he published in the 1820s suggests that reconciliation on a deeper level was not so easily achieved; for to turn the life of imagination into a factory for producing and storing "solid credit" meant denying or repressing its symbolic value as a channel for escape or aggression. Irving's case is instructive. The contest between "mere" imagination and "solid" reality is an obsessive theme of American literature, and it undoubtedly owes much of its vitality to the struggle between guilt and rebellion, ambition and alienation, in young writers who wished, simultaneously, to attack and overcome the indifference of their culture.

In Irving's fiction, as in Hawthorne's and Melville's, personal uncertainty about the life of imagination enters directly as a major theme. If Ichabod Crane is defeated by imagination, by his excessive susceptibility to superstition, Brom Bones manipulates superstition to his own ends of social success. Ichabod loses Katrina, but Brom gets her. It is hardly extravagant to see in these two central figures of "The Legend of Sleepy Hollow" a reflection or projection of Irving's contradictory visions of his vocation.[13] Even more clearly to the point are three tales from *Bracebridge Hall* and *Tales of a Traveller:* "The Student of Salamanca," "Buckthorne," and "The Story of the Young Italian."[14] One deals with alchemy in Spain, one with English literary life, one with a deranged Italian painter, but all three develop a central fable of the man of imagination and his career.

This fable begins with a young man cast from his "proper" sphere, from home and status. In "Buckthorne" the rejection results from an engagement with the life of imagination, in the other two it leads to such an engagement, and in all three the hero sets out to restore his character and self-esteem through imaginative vocation. Buckthorne's literary inclinations are encouraged by his mother but scorned by his father. "Indeed," he writes of the latter, "I believe he would have pardoned anything in me more readily than poetry, which he called a cursed, sneaking, puling, housekeeping employment, the bane of all fine manhood" (232–33). This scorn is seconded by Buckthorne's beloved, Sacharissa, and by a rich uncle, who disinherits him on discovering a production of his pen. Buckthorne is left to pursue his imaginative inclinations, first as a traveling player and then as a writer in London, where he meets Geoffrey Crayon.

Antonio, the title character of "The Student of Salamanca," only partly fits the pattern of artist-hero. He has fallen from paternal favor, but he determines on reform rather than rebellion, hoping, "by further study and self-regulation," to "prepare himself to return home with credit, and atone for his transgressions against paternal authority" (151). Deflected from this worthy goal by a glimpse of the beautiful Inez de Vasques, he becomes involved in her father's alchemical experiments in order to gain access to her.[15] This old man, Felix de Vasques, conforms far more closely than Antonio to the role of artist-hero. Disinherited years before for making an improper marriage, he has turned to the "visionary schemes" (118) of alchemy—a nice symbol of the effort to make imagination pay—as a means of "raising himself from his present obscurity, and resuming the rank and dignity to which his birth entitled him" (111).

In neither of these tales, however, is the imagination capable of securing its intended rewards. Both end "happily," but in ways that simply dissipate the theme of imagination and vocation. De Vasques' experiments produce no gold; in fact, the old man is finally hauled up before the Inquisition on a charge of sorcery, against which he can only protest that he is but a "harmless visionary" (133). He is saved at the last minute by Antonio, who has returned home and convinced his father of his own reformation and of Inez's worth and rank. Alchemy and imagination abandoned, all retire to material prosperity. "It was not long," we learn at the close, "before Don Antonio succeeded to his father's titles and estates" (153).

The conclusion of "Buckthorne" is even more startling. Throughout the tale the theme of imagination is wrapped in ambiguity and uncertainty. Buckthorne's career is presented as a courageous defiance of boorish convention, but this defiance leads only to feelings of shame and failure, especially in the presence of Sacharissa. "I saw at once," Buckthorne writes of one meeting with her, "the exterminating cloud of ridicule bursting over me. My crest fell. The flame of love went suddenly out, or was extinguished by overwhelming shame" (265). The imagery here is extremely suggestive. What is more, even genuine literary success, which Buckthorne does finally achieve in London, fails to compensate for lost self-esteem and growing guilt. Thus, at the close, Buckthorne's literary ambition and defiance simply evaporate. He inherits his uncle's estate after all, renounces literature, and marries the now-admiring Sacharissa. "I find," he declares to an astonished Geoffrey Crayon, who has envied his literary eminence, "you are a little given to the sin of authorship, which I renounce" (309).

It is perhaps dangerous to take the plots of these two stories too seriously. Both exist as convenient frames on which to hang the fabric of Spanish or English local color, and both evade the serious implications of their theme in their comic conclusions. But the theme itself is clearly serious. De Vasques' trial before the Inquisition is more than a piece of gothic machinery; it is a marvelous melodramatization of Irving's own predicament. And de Vasques' defense of being a "harmless visionary" is not so far from Irving's own habitual self-denigration. Furthermore, there is a highly suggestive vocabulary of alienation and guilt, however casually presented, in both tales. Antonio returns home to "atone for his transgressions against paternal authority." Buckthorne, at the conclusion of his story, "renounces" the one "sin" his father never would have "pardoned." For all their frivolity and evasiveness, these tales skim the surface of deep and troubled waters.

This surface is finally broken in the third and best of Irving's artist fables, "The Story of the Young Italian," which was Poe's favorite among the *Tales* (see Poe's *Works*, 13:153–54). At the outset, "The Story of the Young Italian" follows the familiar pattern. Ottavio, the young Italian, is rejected by a harsh father, who prefers his older son. Ottavio develops, "when quite a child, an extreme sensibility" (100). He is early sent away to languish in a monastery run by his uncle. Here he learns to paint. His vocation will eventually promise fame and status, but what first attracts him to art is its morbid preoccupations. His first teacher, Ottavio writes, loved "to portray, either on canvas or in waxen models, the human face and human form, in the agonies of death, and in all the stages of dissolution and decay" (103–4). When Ottavio escapes to Genoa, his artistic ability secures for him the status he has previously been denied. It even brings him the love of the beautiful Bianca. His disinheritance threatens to prevent their marriage, but this last obstacle vanishes when he learns that his brother has died and that his ailing father wishes to reinherit him. At this point we seem on the verge of the same sort of easy comic conclusion that vitiates the seriousness of "Buckthorne" and "The Student of Salamanca."

The ending is, in fact, more complex. There have already been signs of quite serious conflict in Ottavio, conflict too serious for easy resolution. Art, not inheritance, has seemed to offer a route toward the repossession of rightful status. Ottavio has spoken to Bianca of the "famous masters" of painting: "their histories; the high reputation, the influence, the magnificence to which they had attained. The companions of princes, the favorites of kings, and the pride and boast of nations." "All this," he adds, "[Bianca] applied to me" (121). Yet Ottavio has never fully identified with this vision of artistic "success." It is only when he hears of his restored inheritance that he feels worthy to approach Bianca openly. "A home, a name, rank, wealth, awaited me," he writes. "I can claim you for my own," he then exclaims to Bianca. "I am no longer a nameless adventurer, a neglected, rejected outcast. Look—read—behold the tidings that restore me to my name and to myself!" (122). Ottavio can never identify his "self" with his identity as "artist." As readily as Buckthorne, he renounces his artistic vocation in the hope of returning to prosperity in the "real" world.

Ottavio's hope proves illusory. He leaves Bianca in the care of his friend, Filippo, and returns to Naples to claim his patrimony. Here he is reconciled with his father; in fact, they almost reverse roles, the old man lapsing into childishness as the son accedes to power. Ottavio, however, refuses to admit the extent to which his father's decline fulfills his own deepest impulses, his urge, as the rejected outcast, to vent his rage. "I knew that his death alone would set me free," he writes, "yet I never at any moment wished it. I felt too glad to be able to make any atonement for past disobedience" (126–27). The father takes a long time in dying, but he does die at last, and Ottavio returns to Genoa to claim his bride. Here, however, he learns that Filippo, having told Bianca that he (Ottavio) was dead, has married her himself. Ottavio succumbs to distraction, in which he slays his rival, and the violence of his vengeance—recounted in terms almost unique in Irving—reveals the repressed depths of hostility latent in the theme of the frustrated artist and skimmed over in the wish-fulfillment deaths of the older brother and father. "I sprang upon him," the Young Italian confesses, "with the blood-thirsty feeling of a tiger; redoubled my blows; mangled him in my phrenzy, grasped him by the throat, until, with reiterated wounds and strangling convulsions, he expired in my grasp" (135).

Unlike Buckthorne, Antonio, or de Vasques, Ottavio pursues to its logical conclusion the artist's vocation in a hostile culture. He holds true to the initial symbolic commitment of imaginative deviance. By acting out the deepest aggressive fantasies beneath the masks of self-denigration and "solid credit," he cuts himself off irrevocably from the easy rewards of reconciliation, just as, previously, he has rejected the promised rewards of artistic "success." He is thus trapped by the artist's defiance of society and its attendant guilt. The imagination through which he has sought success now haunts him with an image he cannot renounce, the image of the "mangled" Filippo (so like the morbid subjects of his first teacher). It is this image he paints in his remorse, producing the "Mysterious Picture" that horrifies Irving's Nervous Gentleman and leads to the host's reading of the Italian's story.

Caught between guilt and resentment, Irving himself hoped that escape might finally prove a path to reconciliation, that the deviant imagination might point the way back to "solid credit." Such wish-fulfillment is immortalized in "Rip Van Winkle," in which Rip does finally find a secure role as storyteller in the community he had fled twenty years before; and wish-fulfillment also governs the conclusions of "Buckthorne" and "The Student of Salamanca," although here it is not imaginative escape but the renunciation of art that leads to reconciliation. But "The Story of the Young Italian" indicates that Irving also understood the contradictions involved in the desire to combine deviance with success. Society, once defied, was not likely to prove so forgiving, and the "sin of authorship," once embraced, might not be so easily renounced. Ottavio's imagination is less a storehouse for imaginative "property" than a hiding-place for the Italian's repressed rage at his father, his brother, and all those who have mistreated him. Since the possibility of expressing these feelings openly is denied by guilt, Ottavio expresses them covertly in the sublimated form of art—but to no avail. At the close, the feelings escape anyway, from their psychological and aesthetic confines. "I clinched my teeth and hands," Ottavio writes of his discovery of Filippo's perfidy. "I foamed at the mouth; every passion seemed to have resolved itself into the fury that like a lava boiled within my heart" (135).

FROM RELUCTANT ROMANTIC TO NERVOUS ROMANCER

Irving's uncertainty about the nature and purpose of his career stems from a condition at once intensely personal and generally representative of the confused status the imaginative writer occupied in nineteenth-century America. One might reasonably speculate—although such things are impossible to "prove"—that in the writer's ambivalent status he found a perfect vehicle for his own conflicting impulses of aggression and ingratiation. The same conflict, in any case, appears in different forms in the fiction of Poe, Hawthorne, and especially Melville. As I suggested in chapter 2, to occupy the "neutral territory," for these men, was to execute a delicate psychological balancing act between the expression of rage and the longing for love and attention.

The same balancing act characterizes Irving's more "theoretical" comments on the nature and function of imagination in literature. Irving is no major mind as a critic, but in the conventional critical vocabulary of his day he was able to displace his psychological conflicts into the less personal, and safer, realm of "aesthetic" discourse. If this discourse often seems dry and perfunctory, that is the point: it was meant to. In calling attention to this displacement I have no intention of disparaging Irving. Let him who is without problems cast the first stone. What matters about this displacement is that it was a crucial step in the movement from individual neurosis to the disrelation of romance.

As an avowed cultivator of romantic sensibility, Irving speaks again and again for the "charms" of "romance and poetry." Yet this romantic vein in his writing is seldom consistent, and it often receives serious qualification. Beneath Irving's sentimental romanticism there lurks, moreover, a current of outright moral hostility toward imaginative indulgence. "I have a thousand times regretted with bitterness," Irving wrote to his nephew, shortly after the publication of the *Tales,* "that ever I was led away by my imagination."[16] Eleven years earlier, in an essay on the American poet Robert Treat Paine, he presented his subject's career as a virtual case study in the dangers of literary imagination. A poet of "ardent and ill-regulated imagination" (377), one who "drew his characters from books rather than from real life" (380), Paine "evinces that quick sensibility and openness to transient impressions, incident to a man more under the dominion of the fancy than the judgment" (374), whose rapid collapse into impoverished debauchery illustrates the hazards of psychological imbalance: "Surely," Irving moralizes, "if the young imagination could ever be repressed by sad example, these gloomy narratives [of Paine's career] would be sufficient to deter it from venturing into the fairy land of literature—a region so precarious in its enjoyments and fruitful in its calamaties" (366).

For all the conventional imaginative sensibility he projected onto Geoffrey Crayon, Irving himself could easily slip into the pose of rational moralist, and the orthodox line on the dangers of imagination plays no small part in his fiction. Rather than probe the hidden motives of his characters, which were perhaps too close to his own, Irving explains away their aberrations through the assumptions of Common Sense faculty psychology. Buckthorne, de Vasques, and Ottavio all fall prey to what Irving, describing the latter, calls a "strong but ill-directed imagination" (104). Crayon himself longs, as he writes at the beginning of *The Sketch-Book,* to "lose myself among the shadowy grandeurs" of Europe (17); and while he manages to maintain his own sanity, some of the stories he presents, at second hand, suggest the dangers of his enterprise. Rip Van Winkle almost literally "loses himself" in his escapist mountain reverie, and Ichabod Crane—whose last name curiously resembles Geoffrey's[17] —is vanquished by his imaginative susceptibility, his tendency to superstition.

Irving's fullest exemplum of the effects of an ill-regulated imagination is "The Adventure of the German Student," whose hero, like Robert Treat Paine or the Young Italian, is destroyed by a "visionary and enthusiastic character." "His health," we are told, "was impaired; his imagination diseased. He had been indulging in fanciful speculations on spiritual essences, until . . . he had an ideal world of his own around him" (66). He "would often lose himself [again the ominous phrase] in reveries on forms and faces which he had seen, and his fancy would deck out images of loveliness far surpassing the reality" (67–68). Again, Irving does not much probe the *nature* of Gottfried's fantasies; and this, given the nature of the tale's plot, is a bit surprising, for Gottfried meets, and goes to bed with, a beautiful woman, only to find her a corpse the next morning and discover that she had been guillotined before he met her! In Common Sense terms, however, the tale's message is as clear as the student's condition. Imaginative Gottfried Wolfgang, like Archibald in Brown's "Insanity: A Fragment," ends his life in a madhouse.

There is more to be recognized in these examples than the mere fact of Irving's concurrence in orthodox fear of imagination. Geoffrey Crayon, Gottfried Wolfgang, and their fellows are not a moralist's case studies of an external enemy, however hard Irving may try to present them as such. They are rather Irving's projections of himself, of that unconscious aggression that (in Irving's displaced aesthetic vocabulary) engaged in imaginative literature as a means of escaping "solid" responsibility. They serve the same function for Irving that Roderick Usher will serve for the narrator of his story, that Aylmer or Young Goodman Brown will serve for Hawthorne, and that Ahab will serve for Ishmael.

In the moralists' attack on fiction Irving found a vocabulary for describing his art; but this attack, hardly encouraging to an aesthetic program, also gave him an analogue, a kind of objective correlative, for his guilty defiance and a formula into which to project and rationalize that guilt. Divided personally—and well before his final commitment to literature—between responsibility and alienation, he discovered in the aesthetic conflict between reality and illusion an arena in which he could attempt to work out a "relation" of far more than aesthetic significance. His artist fables thus indicate more than his ambiguous attitude toward imaginative literature. They reveal the social context and psychological urgency of his aesthetic enterprise. As the moralists well knew, the quest for relation was ultimately a quest for sanity and normalcy, for a chance to come home to the smiles of one's friends.

This quest, as I have observed, was nevertheless acted out in aesthetic rather than psychological terms. It was in this sense that Irving exploited the platitudes of associationism. In 1814, as editor of the *Analectic Magazine*, he reprinted a review of an anonymous treatise whose argument was that "objects, in general, please by the associations which they recall to the imagination." "It appears, then," the reviewer continued, "that the association of ideas is the grand source of the pleasures of the imagination."[18]

The same terms permeate Irving's many comments on "mingling" or "connecting" history with "poetry," fact with fiction. It was through associationism that later Scottish Common Sense writers, especially Archibald Alison, accommodated their growing interest in imagination to the rigorous realism of their progenitor, Thomas Reid. Imaginary ideas, in themselves spurious, could be validated, as it were, through "association" with objects of common-sense perception. In the association of idea with object lay a potential link, a relation, between imagination and reality, fancy and judgment. Associations permitted the sentimental essayist or poet to "work up" matter-of-fact materials, but they also functioned, at the same time, to stabilize idle fancies. What must be kept constantly in mind, in reading Irving's allusions to the association between fact and fiction, is precisely this stabilizing function.

"Annette Delarbre," published in *Bracebridge Hall*, is usually dismissed as a mere exercise in tawdry sentiment, but in the present context it is a fascinating example of the substitution of conventional aesthetic discourse for psychological probing. Annette, to summarize, has offended her lover Eugene, who has fled to sea in anger and been reported lost in a storm. Why she offended him is left unclear; that his reported death gratifies her secret wishes is never, needless to say, hazarded. In any case, she sustains and defends herself—whether from sorrow at his loss or from secret guilt for having wished it—through the fancy that he has not died and will soon return. Each day she appears on the shore, searching the horizon for his ship. Her problem, as Irving presents it, is that she comes so utterly to depend on her illusion that she excludes everything else. When Eugene does in fact return, she almost dies of shock. Viewed psychoanalytically, her reaction is hardly surprising: one thinks of Roderick Usher's reaction when Madeline reappears; but Irving resorts to associationism to explain her behavior. In Annette's mind the very principle of association between idea and object has been severed. The real Eugene, instead of fulfilling her dreams, shatters them. It is only through careful efforts "to ingraft, as it were, the reality [of Eugene] upon the delusions of her fancy" (217) that her physician is able to save her from permanent insanity. Eugene is reintroduced to Annette gradually, in small doses. He thus becomes, we are told, "the real object round which her scattered ideas once more gathered, and which linked them once more with the realities of life" (218).

Now, the story suggests to modern readers more than it wants to tell us about Annette's "scattered ideas." She wants to get rid of Eugene but feels guilty about her desire. Perhaps the secret subject here—as seems the case in many of Irving's stories—is an unacknowledged and unacknowledgeable fear of sexuality. She is *happy* in her bereavement and illusion; they allow her to act out her wishes without recognizing them. She could go on walking the seacoast forever. What matters, though, is that her psychological conflicts are displaced into the rational aesthetic vocabulary of "idea" and "object," "illusion" and "reality." In "Annette Delarbre" the inner conflict of the artist is well on its way to becoming the aesthetic conflict of the artwork.

Annette's dilemma, in any case, is strikingly similar to that of the author of her tale in his lifelong effort to mingle history and romance, reality and poetry. Understood in this light, Geoffrey Crayon's journey to Europe, in quest of "storied and poetical association" (9), gains special urgency. Behind the pose of sentimental tourist is a basic need: in Europe Crayon seeks an endless succession of "real objects" around which to gather his "scattered ideas," engendered, perhaps, by secret guilt but produced in his view by idle reading and ill-regulated imagination. In Europe, with its veneer of "romance and poetry," he can "link" these ideas "once more with the realities of life" and thereby avoid the fate of Robert Treat Paine or Gottfried Wolfgang. For the lost social relation he can substitute the relation, or association, of art.

The stakes involved in Crayon's associational quest may be gauged by contrasting his suave composure with the irascibility of his alter ego, the Nervous Gentleman, narrator of "The Stout Gentleman" in *Bracebridge Hall* and of Part I, "Strange Stories by a Nervous Gentleman," in *Tales of a Traveller*. The Nervous Gentleman's morbid sensitivity functions as a kind of parody of Crayon's elegant sensibility. "I am calm, gentlemen," he declares at one point in the *Tales*, "(striking my fist upon the table,) by Heaven I am calm" (85). If Crayon is a projection of Irving, the Nervous Gentleman is a projection of Crayon. Both are sentimental tourists, and the Nervous Gentleman's plight results, not from a difference in temperament, but from his having run out of suitable objects on which to fix his scattered ideas. In the absence of such objects, it would seem, he might have to start probing the ideas themselves.

This is why the dreary innyard and inn of "The Stout Gentleman" become insupportable for him and why he seizes so eagerly upon the arrival of the portly stranger. "Here," he announces, "was a subject of speculation presented to my mind, and ample exercise for my imagination. I am prone to paint pictures to myself, and on this occasion I had some materials to work upon" (51). When one recalls what happened to the Young Italian when he painted straight from his fancy, one understands the narrator's relief. The stranger's advent offers the nearly hysterical tourist a way out of his perhaps guilty alienation.

Of course the tale is a hoax. The Nervous Gentleman never does manage to perceive the stranger, except for a brief rear view of his breeches as he enters the carriage to depart. To a critic's comment in 1848 that Irving's "most comical pieces have always a serious end in view," the author

75

replied (with perhaps a whimsical bow to the critic's figure of speech): "that man has found me out. He has detected the moral of the Stout Gentleman." [19] And the moral, for all the tale's humor, is indeed serious. The Nervous Gentleman is a Geoffrey Crayon for whom associations have failed—for whom, that is, the doctrine of associationism is ceasing to fulfill its function as a displaced vocabulary, and mask, for the more frightening truths of imagination. He can no longer convince himself that his imagination is anchored to reality. He is left, in the phrase James would apply to the condition of romance, "at large and unrelated."

The relation of the Gentleman's nervousness to the disrelation of romance begins to emerge in *Tales of a Traveller;* for when Irving at last turns to fiction in earnest, the distinction between Crayon and his alter ego breaks down. In his preface to the *Tales,* Crayon himself succumbs to apprehensive nervousness. "Waylaid in the midst of a pleasant tour," he is, like the Nervous Gentleman, "left to count the tedious minutes as they passed." Every customary "source of amusement" has grown "wearisome." [20] "I tried to read, but my mind would not fix itself." It is in this state, "at large and unrelated," that he turns to fiction. "If I cannot read a book," he announces, "I will write one" (11–12). "I am an old traveller," he continues, explaining the title of his book:

> I have read somewhat, heard and seen more, and dreamt more than all. My brain is filled, therefore, with all kinds of odds and ends. In travelling, these heterogeneous matters have become shaken up in my mind, as the articles are apt to be in an ill-packed travelling-trunk; so that when I attempt to draw forth a fact, I cannot determine whether I have read, heard, or dreamt it; and I am always at a loss to know how much to believe of my own stories. [14]

He is also at a loss to know what is wrong with him, but he is clearly going crazy.

He might have found a clue in his dreams and their connection to his bachelorhood—the perennial condition of Irving's personae, as it would be the condition of so many of Melville's. Melville's characters (one thinks especially of Redburn and of Ishmael in the opening chapters of *Moby-Dick*) and the compulsively hysterical narrators of many of Poe's tales are also foreshadowed in Crayon's repressed and unexamined nervousness, his jumpy hostility and terror.

But what matters most about Crayon's new nervousness is that, even while he cannot or will not explain it, he associates it so explicitly with fiction—with "stories" for whose truth he can no longer vouch; for it is in his nervous dislocation, whatever its source, that the origin of pure romance lies, stemming not from the "mingling" of fact and fiction but from unleashed imagination. Such fiction originates, as the skeptical Englishman later puts it, "in the heated brain of the narrator" (376).

Henry Seidel Canby, comparing the supposedly inferior *Tales of a Traveller* to the legends worked into *The Alhambra*, writes that the former "are less admirable because, paradoxically, they are more original. Here Irving trusted too much to invention, and when he left legend and history and scenes that he knew by deep experience he fell almost invariably into mawkishness or into rhetorical display."[21] We must be careful about attributing the originality of the *Tales* to actual invention. Irving seldom "made up" his fictions, preferring, as many of his contemporaries noted with displeasure, to borrow stories from other sources,[22] and he knew the "scenes" of the *Tales*—English country houses, London, Italy, New York—as well as he knew the settings (often the same ones) of his histories, biographies, and travel sketches. It is nonetheless true that in his fiction of the 1820s Irving experimented, as at no other time in his career, with something like "pure" fiction, "at large and unrelated." To say that the *Tales of a Traveller* are characterized by originality is thus not to say that they are invented but rather that they are presented as having "originated" in the imaginations of radically unreliable tale-tellers—tellers whose "scattered ideas" have come unfixed from "reality." With Crayon's nervousness the whole associationist rationale—the ability to displace compulsion into the vocabulary of associationist aesthetics—comes unglued. Between the *Tales* and *Columbus* in 1828 Irving managed to reglue the fractured joints, and they held for the rest of his life; but in the *Tales* he was compelled to explore, through both theme and form, the problem of originality, or unrelatedness, as it was linked in his mind with fiction. That such a condition led Irving invariably to "rhetorical display" is itself significant; for if psychological dislocation was the source of romance, such "display" was inevitably the condition of language cut loose from "solid" meaning and judgment. In the *Tales*, the movement from the conflicts of the artist to the conflict of the artwork has been completed.

STRANGE STORIES: IRVING'S GOTHIC

It has long been a critical truism that the tradition of gothic romance played an essential role in the development of American fiction—far more so than in England, where the tradition originated. It is curious, then, that Irving, although the bulk of his fiction falls clearly within the gothic mode, has been accorded little recognition in this connection. Scholars concerned specifically with his work acknowledge and sometimes analyze his gothicism, but they do not generally concern themselves with his place in the larger American tradition. Leslie Fiedler and Richard Chase, in their major studies of the development of American fiction, virtually ignore him.[23] Yet Irving was clearly the most important American practitioner of gothic fiction in the 1820s, when Poe and Hawthorne were beginning to write. In view of his contemporary stature, so total a lack of recognition would seem to constitute a serious oversight on the part of modern literary historians.[24]

The reasons for this oversight are not mysterious. Recent critical interest in American gothic has called attention to what Melville called "the power of blackness" in our classic writers: the terrors of unconscious motives and forbidden fantasies, the horrors of the soul and the wilderness. Such matters have more importance in Irving than is generally supposed, but, as we have seen, he is more interested in covering them up than in probing them. Furthermore, readers have had trouble in reconciling what Henry A. Pochman called Irving's "sportive Gothic" with the intensity of the major American gothicists. As Stanley T. Williams has complained: "The strength and weakness in Irving's treatment of the supernatural is that he is partly satiric; he loves to end a wild tale with a good-humored chuckle."[25] Had Irving determined the later course of American gothic, it would seem, Ligeia might simply have been a substitute lover in disguise, like the Spectre Bridegroom. Fedallah, no doubt, would have but masked a fun-loving Brom Bones figure (perhaps Bulkington), permitting Ahab to retire into cabbage patches of spermacetti prosperity, while Ishmael regaled a small-town circle in upstate New York with yarns of his twenty-year sleep on a whaling ship. Even Young Goodman Brown might have escaped to New York, following his encounter with a Satanic Pumpkin, to become a justice of the Ten Pound Court.

Yet Irving's humor is worth taking seriously. He may avoid the intensity of later writers (though they were not themselves uniformly serious, particularly Poe and Melville), but behind his humor lies a penetrating inquiry into the very mode the later writers would develop more soberly. Irving's sportive satire is directed, first of all, at gothic fiction itself, at the conventions and attitudes with which such fiction was associated.[26] Thus, for instance, the "Strange Stories by a Nervous Gentleman," which open *Tales of a Traveller*, repeatedly burlesque the central situation of Ann Radcliffe's gothic romances: the anxiety of a quivering, sensitive heroine in a haunted chamber. Only, in Irving's tales we do not have sensitive heroines; instead, there is the far from terrified and "very manly" (46) widow of "The Adventure of My Aunt," who apprehends the intruder in her chamber without a superstitious tremor, or there is the boisterous Irish soldier in "The Bold Dragoon," who grossly burlesques the Radcliffean stereotype and whose "supernatural" story is probably, in any case, an ingenious cover for alcoholic or sexual excesses.

Irving especially delights in lampooning the attention Mrs. Radcliffe's characters—like Cooper's Natty Bumppo—always manage to devote to refined aesthetic response in the midst of terrifying scenes and circumstances. Hence the Misses Popkins, in "The Adventure of the Popkins Family," who "were very romantic, and had learnt to draw in water-colors, [and] were enchanted with the scenery around; it was so like what they had read in Mrs. Radcliffe's romances" (370). Even after being robbed, we are told, "they declared the captain of the band to be a most romantic-looking man, they dared to say some unfortunate lover or exiled nobleman; and several of the band to be very handsome young men—'quite picturesque!'" (373).[27] It is small wonder that Irving's easy humor irritates those who admire the working-up of similar effects in Cooper (one thinks particularly of *The Deerslayer*, in which Natty is always registering the Claude- or Salvator-esque lighting of scenes fraught with imminent danger).

Irving's burlesque of the Radcliffean sublime does not, however, stop with the "good-humored chuckle." Mrs. Radcliffe allows her virtuous characters to thrill to the sublimity of evil without making them see the connection between their opposed aesthetic and moral responses. Irving forces this connection. In "The Painter's Adventure," the artist-narrator is captured by bandits, to whom he responds very much in the idiotic manner of the Misses Popkins. Imprisoned in a mountain hideout, with execution possible at any moment, he yet can muse: "I forgot in an instant all my perils and fatigues at this magnificent view of the sunrise in the midst of the mountains of the Abruzzi" (385). He imagines himself a Salvator among *banditti* and spends most of his time sketching his "picturesque" captors.

The tone of light comedy is dropped, however, in the interpolated "Story of the Young Robber." Here a member of the band tells the painter of his own complicity in the capture of his beloved, who was then gang-raped by his comrades and murdered by himself. This tale was universally condemned by Irving's contemporaries and is hardly more favorably regarded today, but it makes its point, and it reveals something deeper than "good humor" in *Tales of a Traveller*; for it is the purpose of the tale to affront the reader's complacency by shattering the aesthetic bounds of its genre. "I was sick at heart," the painter confesses at the close, "with the dismal story I had heard. I was harrassed and fatigued, and the sight of the banditti began to grow insupportable to me" (418).

One reason modern readers fail to appreciate the anti-Radcliffean humor of the *Tales* is that we no longer care very much about Ann Radcliffe. Even in 1824 Irving's concern with her was rather old-fashioned. In the popular mind she had been rendered obsolete by the more diabolical gothicism of Lewis, Maturin, and Byron, but Irving, unlike these writers—and unlike Hawthorne and Melville later[28]—was not often willing to break through the protective shield of sublimity to confront outright moral diabolism. Nevertheless, he was fully aware, as his Radcliffean parodies make clear, that to do so was implicit in the appeal of gothic. *True* terror had to have genuine horror as its basis. Otherwise it was a sham, a hoax.

It is this latter perception that informs Irving's most profound sportiveness. His tales—refusing the plunge into satanism, the true "power of blackness"—come to burlesque not only the gothic tradition but themselves as well. "The Adventure of My Uncle" prepares us for the explanation of a midnight apparition and then brusquely denies it when the Marquis, apparently out of family delicacy, refuses to disclose the "secret" of the portrait of his ancestress. In "The Little Antiquary" we share the title character's fear for his ring, but at the last moment the bandit declines to take it. "You think it," he explains, "an antique, but it's a counterfeit—a mere sham" (338), and so, of course, is the story, which, having built up our expectations only to deflate them, reveals to us our own complicity in the duplicitous pursuit of fictional titillation.[29] Following the incredible "Adventure of the German Student" an incredulous auditor asks: "And is this really a fact?" "A fact not to be doubted," replies the narrator. "I had it from the best authority. The student told it me himself. I saw him in a mad-house in Paris" (74). Which information also—it should be observed—incriminates the narrator.

Sir Walter Scott, in 1824, noted the gothic ambiguity of "some modern authors" who

> have exhibited phantoms, and narrated prophecies strangely accomplished, without giving a defined or absolute opinion, whether these are to be referred to supernatural agency, or whether the apparitions were produced (no uncommon case) by an overheated imagination, and the presages apparently verified by a casual, though singular, coincidence of circumstances.[30]

Such ambiguity informs the characteristic procedure of later American writers. Ishmael, for instance, never establishes the authority of Elijah's or Fedallah's prophecies. Melville was at his most mawkish in the realm of rational, Radcliffean gothic, as in the unintentionally ludicrous "explanation" of the legends surrounding Yillah's origin in *Mardi;* but he took gothic ambiguity to extraordinarily effective lengths, leaving open, for example, the question of the Confidence-Man's "supernatural" origin. Poe consistently moots the question of whether the occurrences in his tales are truly "supernal" or merely the products of the narrators' "overheated" imaginations, and Hawthorne's reliance on the formula of "multiple choice," as with the apparitions in the heavens or on Dimmesdale's chest in *The Scarlet Letter*, has received considerable discussion.[31]

Irving, too, normally establishes the supernatural in this ambiguous manner, as did his friend Scott, from whom he may have learned the trick; but unlike Scott—and well before Poe, Hawthorne, and Melville—Irving saw the crucial significance of gothic ambiguity. On the formal level it removed the narrator to the position of nonprivileged reporter, permitted only to infer motives and meanings from phenomenal appearances. It severed his relation with his material, and it severed as well what Hawthorne, in "The Custom-House," would call his "true relation" (4) with the reader. In such fiction *all* phenomena, in effect, become supernatural and ambiguous. The importance of such a stance to Hawthorne and Melville should be clear; one thinks, for example, of "The Minister's Black Veil" and of much of *Billy Budd*. Toward the end of the latter work the Surgeon defines "phenomenal," in trying to account for the strange manner of Billy's death, as "an appearance the cause of which is not immediately to be assigned" (498). Irving's experiments with gothic ambiguity might be said, in this sense, to have given currency to the "phenomenal" stance and style in American fiction.

This ambiguity is not for him, as it was for Scott, primarily a technique for compounding "betwixt ancient faith and modern incredulity." Rather, it provides a formal strategy for dealing with what Irving saw as the central problem presented by fiction itself, in any imaginative mode. Irving's parodies of Radcliffe, and his phenomenal style, force the reader from the supernatural to the psychological—to the consideration of the irrational or duplicitous motives of characters and narrators. Irving is an important transitional figure in the increasing subjectification of gothic terror.[32] But he is more than that, for in the gothic quandary over the nature and status of the supernatural he found a metaphor, and an established form, for investigating the larger question of the nature and status of fictional imagination and its appeal—a question of direct relevance to the predicament he shared with his fellow romancers. What Irving perceived in the 1820s was that the crisis of the gothic tradition—how was one plausibly to pass off the supernatural in modern times?—precisely corresponded to the crisis of romance in nineteenth-century America—how was one to pass off the literary imagination and its products in a hostile culture?

This is not to say that questions about the nature and status of imagination were not already important in the gothic tradition as it came down to Irving. In fact, Mrs. Radcliffe's great accomplishment was the conversion of the pseudo-supernatural thriller into a forum for enacting the great psychological-moral contest between fancy and judgment. In her romances the passionate terrors of the seduction novel become explicitly linked with imagination and subjectivity. The alternation between illusory terror and rational reassurance becomes the essential action of her tales. Mrs. Radcliffe may appeal to the imagination, but the virtue of her virtuous characters always consists in their ultimate adherence to "solid" reason and virtue, if only after long and interesting struggles.

Radcliffean gothic, considered in terms of its overt moral appeal, is really antigothic, since it subjects the supernatural and imaginary, in the end, to firm, rational control. Its strength and its weakness lie in Mrs. Radcliffe's ability to ignore the stark contradiction between her fiction's irrational appeal and its rational message. She refuses to see the obvious analogy between the terrors besetting her heroes and heroines and the power of romance itself as it besets the reader. There are times when she seems on the verge of such a recognition. Emily St. Aubert's adventures at Udolpho appear to her "like the dream of a distempered imagination, or like one of those frightful fictions in which the wild genius of the poets sometimes delighted"; and in *The Italian*, Ellena Rosalba reflects, after successfully surviving her various ordeals, that "contrasted with the sober truth of her present life, the past appeared like romance."[33] But Mrs. Radcliffe never becomes self-conscious about her own role as romancer. The most incredible events are reported with the earnest seriousness of the domestic novelist. Thus in her fiction the contest between imagination and judgment remains entirely a matter of theme. There is nothing in her procedure, in her handling of narrative stance and voice, to suggest that she has made the connection between her great subject and the hazards or duplicity of her own practice.

This is precisely the connection that Irving does make. Which is to say that in his best fiction—as later in Poe's, Hawthorne's, and Melville's—gothic romance becomes aesthetically self-aware. Irving's skepticism about gothic fiction is as thorough as Jane Austen's in *Northanger Abbey*, but he does not follow her when, in rejecting romantic imagination, she allies fiction instead with judgment and "novelistic" realism.[34] Rather, he continues to indulge in romance but does so in full awareness of its duplicity. What distinguishes his best gothic tales is the self-consciousness with which they simultaneously exploit and burlesque the basis of their own narrative appeal.

"The Adventure of the German Student" is a case in point. After listening to the first three of the "Strange Stories by a Nervous Gentleman," the old gentleman with the haunted head observes, so we are told, "that the stories hitherto related had rather a burlesque tendency. 'I recollect an adventure, however,' added he, 'which I heard of during a residence at Paris, for the truth of which I can undertake to vouch, and which is of a very grave and singular nature'" (65). There follows the grisly tale of Gottfried Wolfgang's copulation with an animated corpse, guillotined the day before, and of his ensuing insanity when, the black collar removed from her neck, her head rolls to the floor. The story is gruesome and compelling. Even the final revelation that it may all have been a delusion of Gottfried's "diseased" imagination hardly lessens the horror, and perhaps it increases it—like the hideous "explanation" at the end of Alfred Hitchcock's gothic masterpiece, *Psycho*. To such delusions, who would not prefer "real" specters?

But the tale is ludicrous all the same, and a "burlesque tendency," despite the narrator's disavowal, is seldom far from its verbal surface. It is indeed "grave," this tale of a reanimated corpse whom Gottfried meets in the "Place de Grève."[35] The reader, already in on the secret, is charmed to learn, of the "vicissitude" afflicting this decapitated darling, that "many a fair head, which had once been pillowed on down, now wandered house-less." She is truly one "whom the dreadful axe had rendered deso-late." By the time the narrator informs us that "she raised her head" (69)—which may also be a joking reference to "The Legend of Sleepy Hollow"—we recognize that there is a consistent employment of *double-entendre* here and, behind it, a consistent duplicity of narrative motive. We have been trapped by a tale whose verbal surface advertises it as a trap. This is not to say that we have been duped—although that is also true—but that our appreciation of the story derives from its form, its texture, rather than from the thrills it offers. Our real engagement is not with Gottfried, the Radcliffean victim, but with the narrator, with enjoying the interplay between his "heated brain" and what Canby calls his "rhetorical display." This display exists all on the surface; calling into doubt both the authority of the tale and the sanity of the teller, it provides no solid clues for a final judgment of either. The style, that is, becomes as ambiguously "phenomenal" as the world—possibly real, possibly illusory—about which it pretends to report.

Much of Irving's fiction is perfunctory, flat, even lazy, but in his best tales the Radcliffean tension between extremes of illusion and judgment is fully integrated into the act of narration. As the protective terminology of rational, associationist aesthetics breaks down, the predicament of Mrs. Radcliffe's characters becomes the predicament of Irving's narrators and auditors, including the reader. At the close of his "Strange Stories," the Nervous Gentleman is even put through the archetypal ordeal of the Radcliffean heroine. Following the evening's tale-telling, he retires to a chamber remarkably similar to "those eventful apartments described in the tales of the supper-table" (76). Here he is terrified by the "Mysterious Picture" painted by the Young Italian, which awakens in him a "horror of the mind"[36]—just as Clithero Edny's irrational tale upset the rational equipoise of Edgar Huntly. "I tried to persuade myself," he writes in true

Radcliffean fashion, "that this was chimerical, that my brain was confused by the fumes of mine host's good cheer, and in some measure by the odd stories about paintings which had been told at supper" (78). "It is my own diseased imagination," he insists, "that torments me" (80). In spite of this rational reassurance, however, he spends the night on a couch downstairs.

The next morning, the Baronet "explains" the odd effect of the Italian's painting by reading "The Story of the Young Italian"—a nice way to rationalize the effects of a work of art! Then each guest is taken to see the picture. All agree that "there was a certain something about the painting that had a very odd effect upon the feelings." The displaced, aesthetic vocabulary for rationalizing imagination is apparently vindicated in the end. The nearly hysterical fantasies of the Nervous Gentleman are "fixed" to a "real" object with "real" associations. "After all," moralizes the now less nervous Nervous Gentleman, willing to probe the unconscious once it has been rationalized and generalized, "there are certain mysteries in our nature, certain inscrutable impulses and influences, which warrant one in being superstitious. Who can account for so many persons of different characters being thus strangely affected by a mere painting?" "And especially," replies the Baronet, "when not one of them has seen it! . . . I gave the housekeeper a hint to show them all to a different chamber!" (139).

This final, wonderful hoax calls attention, once again, to the fragile complicity between artist and audience, narrator and reader, in the imaginary indulgence of romance, and it traces this imaginative complicity, finally, to those unconscious "mysteries in our nature," those "inscrutable impulses and influences," behind the serene mask of rational aesthetic discourse. One thinks of the importance of such "mysteries" and "impulses" to Brown, Poe, Hawthorne, and Melville. Yet Irving holds back—and this is, perhaps, his limitation—from any full exploration of these "mysteries" and "impulses." He does not wish, or perhaps dare, to probe the unconscious sources and implications of the imagination—to probe the "energy" (in Brown's terms) behind rational literary and psychic "order." His is a fictional world of sophisticated duplicity, of shimmering surfaces that only imply the depths their author himself refuses to enter. That he was aware of what went on in these depths is suggested by the nervousness of his Nervous Gentlemen and by the clear patterns—clear to us, anyway—of alienation, guilt, and frustrated rage that animate his artist fables and such stories as "Annette Delarbre." Perhaps he understood these patterns too well and too personally to confront them directly. His way, in any case, was not the way of sincerity.

But we can exaggerate the significance of his evasion of sincerity. Even Brown, for all his sincerity of intention, found himself trapped by the duplicitous order of rhetoric, by the tyranny of "words" over "sentiments." Poe, Hawthorne, and Melville would discover the same trap. And the Baronet's hoax, while it may undercut the authority of the Italian's painting and story, does not deny the "mysteries" and "impulses" implicit in the Nervous Gentleman's uncontrollable fantasies. In fact, it comments in a rather sinister fashion on these fantasies; for in denying them a last associational link with the "real" painting, in undercutting the last possibility of Radcliffean "explanation," it testifies that in romance the Jamesian cable of relation—psychological, social, and aesthetic—has indeed been cut. In such romance, "at large and unrelated," motive could only be ambiguous, and style "phenomenal."

FIVE

An immortal instinct, deep within the spirit of man, is thus, plainly, a sense of the Beautiful. . . . It is no mere appreciation of the Beauty before us—but a wild effort to reach the Beauty above. Inspired by an ecstatic prescience of the glories beyond the grave, we struggle, by multiform combinations among the things and thoughts of Time, to attain a portion of that Loveliness whose very elements, perhaps, appertain to eternity alone.

POE, "The Poetic Principle"

IMAGINATION, SPIRIT, AND THE LANGUAGE OF ROMANCE

Edgar Allan Poe

IN HIS CRITICAL WRITING AND IN HIS FICTION, EDGAR POE EMBRACES EX-plicitly and deliberately what is for the most part only implicit and in-advertent in the work of Irving. Irving's critical vocabulary is wholly conventional and often perfunctory; Poe's is both original and, in its way, rigorous. He was America's first fully serious theoretician of imaginative literature, and—what matters most in the present discussion—he used his role as critic to declare openly what others usually sought to obfuscate or conceal. For Poe the sacrifice of relation, in its various forms, was not an embarrassing impediment but a fundamental aesthetic principle. In his pursuit of what was still, in the 1830s and 1840s, the deviant career of romancer, he made the crucial step most of his contemporaries refused: his theory of romance was not a rationalization but a rationale. Poe did not overcome the problems that had plagued his predecessors. Rather, he brought into sharp focus, at last, the covert and irreconcilable tensions that animate their works.

"The imagination," Poe declared in 1845, "has not been unjustly ranked as supreme among the mental faculties" (*Works*, 14:187). In declaring this supremacy, Poe also uncompromisingly dismissed those strategies by which contemporary romancers sought to accommodate their art to the demands of rational and moral orthodoxy. Against the customary in-sistence on moral intention he lodged his well-known protest against "the heresy of *The Didactic*" (14:272). Moral allegory he found particularly re-pugnant in verse; but even in fiction, he argued, "it must always interfere with that unity of effect which to the artist, is worth all the allegory in the world" (13:148). Poe was equally scornful of demands for realistic "truth." "That a story is 'founded on fact,'" he declared in 1836, dismissing a

87

whole generation of apologetic subtitles, "is very seldom a recommenda-tion" (8:161). Ten years later he wrote of Charles F. Briggs: "If Mr. Briggs has a *forte*, it is a Flemish fidelity that omits nothing . . . ; but I cannot call this *forte* a virtue" (15:21).

Poe did believe in the necessity, even in works of fantasy, of giving "verisimilitude to a narration" (9:139), but that "verisimilitude" was not to be equated with fidelity to fact is clear in his meticulous hoaxes. (In an 1849 letter he described one of these, "Von Kempelen's Discovery," as an effort "to deceive by verisimilitude" [433].) Poe defined realism and fictional truth as he defined everything else: in terms of effect produced rather than of authoritative communication. "We do not paint an object to be true," he wrote in 1841, "but to appear true to the beholder. Were we to copy nature with accuracy, the object copied would seem unnatural" (10:152–53). The "appear" and "seem" are crucial here. Poe moved the criteria of artistic legitimacy from matters of extrinsic "truth," of meaning, to the work of art itself, to appearances or effects. He thus made explicit the assumptions behind what I called Irving's "phenomenal" style. To be "unnatural," in the moral universe of Common Sense orthodoxy, was to violate a social norm. For Poe the "unnatural" is a matter not of social morality but of aesthetics. Poe is a serious critic in precisely this sense: he discusses art in its own terms.

This is not to say that his aesthetic vocabulary functions any less than Irving's to mask personal or psychological conflict. Indeed, if we consider his biography and contemporary reputation, Poe conforms far more closely to the "deviant" image of the "romancer" than Irving ever did. Poe's writing, like his life, displays all the anxiety of the outcast, torn between aggression and guilt, and it would be a very great mistake to isolate Poe's commitment to imagination from its biographical and cultural contexts. Even in his defiance of orthodox norms—perhaps especially in his defiance—Poe was very much a part and product of his milieu. He may have rejected his contemporaries' denigration of the imagination, but he did not essentially differ from them in his understanding of its nature or even its consequences. His imaginative heroes almost uniformly succumb to the maladies conventionally associated with an "ill-regulated imagina-tion." William Wilson, for instance, who inherits his family's "imaginative and easily excitable temperament," attributes the disastrous events of his life, in part, to his "disordered imagination" (3:300, 315). So do Egaeus, in "Berenice," and a host of others—notably, Roderick Usher.

Poe himself was not exempt from imaginative disorder. While rebelling against the bias of his society, he ironically bore out its direst expectations and assumptions in his own career. His orthodox enemies, while they deplored his heresies, had no trouble accounting for them. In Poe's fate they found still more corroboration of their own conservative principles: he was simply another victim of overheated fancy, rather like Brown's Archibald or Irving's German Student—a genius, no doubt, but ultimately a pitiful, depraved, case-study.[1] Moral or psychological issues of this kind, often with Poe's encouragement, dominated the nineteenth-century debate over his work, and it must be admitted that the well-known misfortunes of his life—his rejection by his foster father, his effort to regain lost status through literature, the breakdowns and hallucinations of his last years—bear a striking resemblance to the cautionary artist fables of a writer like Irving.[2] Poe, we recall, particularly admired Irving's "Story of the Young Italian" (13:153–54).

The point to be stressed here is that Poe embraced his career *as* a deviant career. His insistence on the autonomy of art was, in part, an act of aggression against a "normal" society with which he could have no other relation. Yet, to focus entirely on the social-psychological context of Poe's literary vocation is to miss the real point of his example; for as consistently as Irving, and far more deliberately, he displaced psychological conflict into aesthetic terms. This displacement is at once the subject and the method of his poems and tales. He insisted that the appeal of literature, its "effect," was and should be aimed at the imagination rather than the judgment of the reader. He insisted on the primacy of imagination above all in works of literature, whatever its status elsewhere. He thus effected a strategic shift in the grounds of the debate over the nature and function of imagination, and it is this shift that marks his real departure from the thought and practice of his predecessors and contemporaries.

In Poe's fiction the relation between imagination and reality, fantasy and judgment, artist and society, is as problematic and ambiguous as in the works of Brown and Irving, but in his criticism he gives a newly explicit prominence and urgency to the relation between the work of art itself—the *product* of imagination, the deliberately "phenomenal" structure of words and images—and the judgment or reality of the reader. By the sheer pressure of his insistence on the craft of fiction he moved the debate between imagination and reality away from considerations of insanity or immorality—whatever the thematic importance of such concerns in his tales—to the central problem of experimental romance: the dissociation of artifice and meaning, "effect" and intention, rhetoric and motive. What is the relation, his works continually demand, between the romancer's words and the reader's world? Or between the romancer's words and the noumenal imaginative energy they seem simultaneously to communicate and conceal? What is the status of the language of romance?

Poe's theory of romance, of imaginative literary expression, is more rigorous than Irving's, but it is no less dualistic. In Poe's fiction the disrelation of imagination and judgment fully assumes the new form of the disrelation of inspiration and manipulation, of "supernal" vision and mechanical "effect," but the sacrifice of relation is still central. In "The Poetic Principle," for instance, literature is described in terms of imaginative mysticism, of insight into a realm beyond conventional language and consciousness. The "sense of the Beautiful" is "an immortal instinct, deep within the spirit of man. . . . It is no mere appreciation of the Beauty before us—but a wild effort to reach the Beauty above." Yet the artist is confined to "multiform combinations among the things and thoughts of Time" (14:273–74). However mystical the promptings of his imagination, the world of his art is a self-contained, self-reflexive world of words. There even seem, for Poe, to be two distinct "imaginations." One is the "immortal instinct," validated by the noumenal realm into which it provides insight; the other is the power of "combination," validated only by the mechanical unity of its phenomenal "effects." Which "imagination," then, was the "true" one? Or what was the relation between them?

IMAGINATION AND SPIRIT

Brown and Irving were deeply concerned with the imagination, but they did not much investigate its nature. Poe devoted considerable energy to precisely this investigation. He conducted it, moreover, in a new intellectual climate. If he was as steeped as Brown or Irving in the rational orthodoxy of Common Sense realism, he was also drawn to the new doctrines of Romanticism, which he encountered in the philosophy and criticism of Coleridge (and, through Coleridge, the Germans) and, in a more debased form, in the American popular and literary culture of the 1830s and 1840s. It was in the doctrines, assumptions, and contradictions of Romanticism that Poe's effort to understand the literary imagination began. This effort led, inexorably and apparently willfully, to his obsessive concern with autonomous language and effect.

The year following Poe's death in 1849 saw the onset of the great vogue of spiritualism in America—"the epoch," as Hawthorne describes it in *The Blithedale Romance*, "of rapping spirits, and all the wonders that have followed in their train—such as tables, upset by invisible agencies, bells, self-tolled at funerals, and ghostly music, performed on jewsharps" (198–99). Poe did not live to witness these phenomena, but up to his death—and, according to some mediums, long after—he was deeply interested in many of the movements that culminated in the spiritualism of the

1850s, such as phrenology, mesmerism, and Swedenborgianism.[3] Among Poe's contemporaries, moreover, concern with spiritualism was by no means confined to a deviant fringe of mesmerists and mediums or even to that group of respectable Americans who found at least some tincture of truth in their claims and doctrines. Orestes Brownson, who attacked the spiritualist movement in his 1854 novel *The Spirit-Rapper*, defined the "real aim" of Transcendentalism, in 1840, as the ascertainment of a "solid ground for faith in the reality of the spiritual world."[4] This was the aim, not just of spiritualism or Transcendentalism, but of Romanticism generally.

It was through such Romanticism, conceived in the broadest sense, that all but the most orthodox believers in the authority of Scriptural revelation set out to defend the truths of Christianity, of the immortality of the soul, against mounting skepticism. Romanticism redefined the nature and status of imagination. It was no longer a dangerous incentive to subjective introversion, a threat to reason and morality, but a major foundation of religious or quasi-religious truth. Imagination was no longer idle fantasy but that "Reason" which, as Americans generally understood him, Kant linked with intuition and distinguished from the merely rational "Understanding" of Lockean and Common Sense psychology.[5] "If the Reason be stimulated to more earnest vision," Emerson wrote in *Nature* (1836), "outlines and surfaces become transparent, and are no longer seen; causes and spirits are seen through them. The best moments of life are these delicious awakenings of the higher powers, and the reverential withdrawing of nature before its God." So conceived, the escapist imaginative revery of a writer like Irving became a form of access to divinity. "Nature," as Emerson put it, "is the symbol of spirit."[6] Here was as full a rationale for the imagination as one could possibly desire: it was not the enemy but the guarantor of true religion. Transcendentalism and spiritualism, however narrow their actual constituencies and however aberrant in some of their manifestations, were symptomatic of an extraordinarily widespread tendency in nineteenth-century America toward religious or quasi-religious "spirituality."

We should note, here, an important implication of the rise of Romantic spiritualism for the theory of American romance. It enlarged, at least in theory, both the project and the moral purpose of literary romance. For if imagination was a means of access to "spirit," would not romance be that spirit's expression? In chapter 3 I noted that romance as Brown practiced it might be defined as a kind of "subjective mimesis"—an expression in fictive language of inward, nonrational consciousness. The religiosity of popular Romanticism suggested to Poe and some of his contemporaries a further step, one never contemplated by Brown or Irving. Romance might take on a metaphysical dimension to become a form of "spiritual" mimesis. What had been conceived as the product of the author's "over-heated fancy" just might be a form of mystic utterance.

Yet there were immense problems inherent in spiritualism, and these would become problems equally for the romancer who embraced it. R. Laurence Moore writes of America's nineteenth-century spiritualists, for instance, that "in their craving for scientific respectability, they neglected philosophy. Had all their supposedly indisputable evidence been authenticated, they would have filled the world with spirits without having at all revealed a spiritual dimension in man."[7] This failure was only part of a more general failure of American Romanticism. Poe's contemporaries faced the paradoxical predicament of turning to spirituality at a time when they no longer knew with any assurance what, or where, "spirit" was. That they should have turned to it is not surprising; their very uncertainty furnished all the more motive for seizing on the "spiritual" in whatever tawdry form it was currently available. This uncertainty of theirs will help us understand the curious combination of spirituality and ghoulishness in Poe's fiction, for it was in this climate of uncertain spiritualism that Poe set out to redefine and revalidate the "supreme" faculty of imagination and to provide for its "spiritual" claims the sort of philosophical support his contemporaries by and large neglected.

Poe turned first, not to the popular Romanticism of his own literary culture, but to the writings of Coleridge, in what was to become a career-long struggle with the Coleridgean distinction between "fancy" and "imagination."[8] The distinction looked promising. What Common Sense psychology dismissed as "imagination," Coleridge labeled "fancy." From this he distinguished true "imagination"—the power that popular Romanticism would equate with intuitive spiritual insight. But at this point, for Poe, the trouble began.

Poe's most extended analysis of Coleridge's aesthetic psychology occurs in an 1840 review of Thomas Moore's *Alciphron*. Here Poe rejects the distinction between a "fancy" that "combines" and an "imagination" that "creates." "The fancy," he insists, "as nearly creates as the imagination; and neither creates in any respect. All novel conceptions are merely unusual combinations. The mind of man can *imagine* nothing which has not really existed" (10:61–62). Poe is too much the Common Sense rationalist to allow for artistic "creation" per se; but he is too much the Romantic to reject Coleridge's distinction entirely. Instead, he redefines its basis. We "*feel* and *know*" a work to be fanciful because, unlike a work of true imagination, it fails to achieve the "ideal" (62). What this last term means is suggested farther on:

The truth is that the just distinction between the fancy and the imagination (and which is still but a distinction *of degree*) is involved in the consideration of the *mystic*. . . . The term *mystic* is here employed in the sense of Augustus William Schlegel, and of most other German critics. It is applied by them to that class of composition in which there lies beneath the transparent upper current of meaning an under or *suggestive* one. [65]

This formula appears again and again in Poe's writing. Meaning in literature, to be properly "imaginative" or "mystic," must be "suggested" or "submerged." "What we vaguely term the *moral* of any sentiment," he continues in the *Alciphron* review, "is its mystic or secondary expression. It has the vast force of an accompaniment in music. This vivifies the air; that spiritualizes the *fanciful* conception, and lifts it into the *ideal*" (65). The imagination is distinct from the fancy, and superior to it, because it "spiritualizes." It exerts a *"suggestive* force which exalts and etherealizes" (67). In the most "imaginative" work of literature the relations are the most "mystic," the meanings the most "spiritual."

All this sounds like the quasi-religious spiritualism of Poe's contemporaries—the "mystic" imagination providing access to those "spiritual" truths invisible to the fancy. The trouble with Poe's mysticism, however, is that it is conceived not in terms of religious or quasi-religious experience but in terms of technique or effect. Expression, it would seem, can be made "spiritual" simply by being "submerged"—by being "suggested" rather than directly stated. Such mysticism smacks more of mystification. Poe's chief importance as a critic is that he focused on the actual techniques of producing beauty rather than on the pseudo-religious, intuitive experiences that supposedly legitimized these techniques. By doing so, he provided a necessary corrective to the visionary vagueness of so much Romantic criticism; but in supplying this corrective, he shrouded the very concept of the "mystic" or "spiritual"—so crucial to his theory of imagination—in a nearly impenetrable fog of epistemological confusion. Once the "sentiment of Poesy" had been equated with "the Faculty of Ideality"—and Poe so equated them in 1836 (8:282)—the "spiritual" was moved from supernal regions to the mind of artist or audience, where it became a product not of mystical experience but of taste.[9] If spirituality, then, was primarily a matter of effect, how could one be sure that it was anything else? Tennyson, Poe wrote in 1844, seeks or seems to seek in his poetry "a suggestive indefinitiveness of meaning, with the view of bringing about a definitiveness of vague and therefore of spiritual *effect*" (16:28). "Vague and *therefore* spiritual" tells the whole story. What defines the "spiritual" is not its relation to another world but its vagueness, its lack of apparent relation to anything in our own. In Poe's critical writings the Jamesian cable is cut with a vengeance.

Critics have long complained about the philosophical weakness of this aspect of Poe's aesthetic theory. Words like "mystic" and "spiritual" simply cannot be used with such disregard of their normal meanings. What such critics generally fail to notice, however, is that Poe himself was deeply troubled by the same problem. Indeed, by the mid-1840s his confusion had become so intense that he very nearly jettisoned spirituality altogether. When he revised the *Alciphron* review's discussion of imagination and fancy for inclusion in an 1845 essay on N. P. Willis, he dropped the final paragraph on "mystic" suggestion "spiritualizing" the fanciful into the "ideal." In its place he put a long paragraph attributing the superiority of imagination to the "harmony" of its productions, now entirely a matter of "effect." He likened the apparent creativity of its combining power, in a significantly materialistic metaphor, to a chemical reaction in which an apparently "new" substance is produced by the interaction and recombination of two others. By 1845 the mechanistic "unity of effect," celebrated in the 1842 review of Hawthorne's *Twice-Told Tales*, had replaced the earlier imagination of mystic insight.

As a result of this redefinition of "imagination," "spirit"—the object of "mystic" imagination—was also becoming untenable. By 1844 Poe could write to James Russell Lowell: "I have no belief in spirituality. I think the word a *mere* word. No one has really a conception of spirit. We cannot imagine what is not" (257).[10] Imagination is now totally confined to matter; it can only combine what already is. Literary "spirituality" is totally a matter of effect, a "*mere* word." Poe sees in matter and the effects produced by combining it the possibility of a kind of spirituality. "Spirit, we say," he writes to Lowell, "is unparticled, and *therefore* is not matter. But it is clear that if we proceed sufficiently far in our ideas of rarefaction, we shall arrive at a point where the particles coalesce. . . . The unparticled matter, permeating & impelling, all things, is God. Its activity is the thought of God—which creates" (257). This sounds a bit like Coleridge's "creative" imagination, but in fact it is all material and mechanical—a set of effects produced by the combination and manipulation of what already is. There is no "other" realm, no "spiritual" world into which to have "mystic" insight. There is only matter, and our terms for the "other" realm are "mere words." Near the beginning of *Eureka* (1848) Poe says of such words as "infinity," "God," and "spirit" (and the collocation is significant) that they are "by no means the expression of an idea—but of an effort at one," standing "for the possible attempt at an impossible conception, . . . representative but of the *thought of a thought*" (16:200). Thus inexorably did his investigation of "spirit" lead him to matter, and his investigation of "imagination" to language—"mere words." Beginning

94

with Romanticism's promise of integration and relation, Poe's philosophy drove him back to the rigid dualism of Common Sense thought.

Poe's philosophical ruminations on imagination and spirit display a seriousness almost totally lacking in Irving's casual appropriation of the terms of associationism. It does appear to be logic that drives him from spirit to language, from mysticism to extreme disrelation. His criticism thus develops the first full philosophical justification, in America, of the sacrifice of relation—the displacement of sentiments by words. Yet Poe's very insistence on logical precision smacks a good deal of personal repression; what is being justified, after all, is still displacement. Poe may be more rigorous than Irving, but one has the same sense, reading his criticism, that it is a displaced vocabulary for working out, while masking, unacknowledgable personal conflicts. "Logic" can do for Poe what he will not openly do for himself: proclaim the rejection of all relation to the "real" world.

Still—and, again, as with Irving—the personal dimension of this displacement of psychology into aesthetics is less important than its artistic consequences. What matters for the development of American romance is that Poe *did* move, and far more overtly and systematically than Irving, from the psychological to the aesthetic. Whatever personal problems this movement may have masked, it provided an aesthetic rationale for displacing "sentiments" into unrelated "words." Poe's insistence on the autonomy of language is also directly relevant to the bizarre subject matter of his "ideal" or "spiritual" fiction; for if sentiments could be known only through "mere words," might not "spirit" be knowable only through matter—and the soul through the physical corpse?

In the 1845 *Alciphron* review, Poe cites, as "the finest possible examples of the purely ideal" in literature, Shelley's "Sensitive Plant" and the now practically unknown *Undine* (1811) of Friedrich de la Motte Fouqué. The latter work, which Hawthorne and Melville also admired,[11] remained for Poe throughout his career the touchstone of excellence in imaginative prose fiction. In a review published in 1839 he praised the "loftiness of its ideality" and pronounced it "the finest romance in existence" (10:37–38). The review recounts the plot in some detail. Sir Huldebrand falls in love with the soulless water nymph, Undine. By marrying her, he enables her to acquire a soul. But his affections wander to the earthly Bertalda, whom he finally takes as his wife in Undine's place. On their wedding night, Undine, against her own will but driven by the laws of water spirits, emerges from a well (which haughty Bertalda has ordered unsealed), enters the bridal chamber, and locks the errant Sir Huldebrand in a fatal embrace. One can see why this story fascinated Poe. "Ligeia," with *its* contest between a supernal and an earthly woman, was published a year

before the *Undine* review. "The Fall of the House of Usher," whose conclusion strongly recalls that of *Undine*, appeared in the same year as the
review—in fact in the same issue of *Burton's Gentlemen's Magazine*.

By the end of the review, in any case, Poe can hardly control his
emotion. Here he declares,

> We calmly think—yet cannot help asserting with enthusiasm—that
> the whole wide range of fictitious literature embraces nothing compa-
> rable in loftiness of conception, or in felicity of execution, to those
> final passages of the volume before us which embody the uplifting of
> the stone from the fount by the order of Bertalda, the sorrowful and
> silent re-advent of Undine, and the rapturous death of Sir Hulde-
> brand in the embraces of his spiritual wife. [39]

Here is the key term again: Undine is Sir Huldebrand's "spiritual" wife.
But here, too, we see the problem with Poe's "spirituality" or "ideality."
For this "spiritual wife" is in fact a ghoul. Her embraces offer not pleasure, not life, but "rapturous death"—which event, clearly, was Poe's
great "spiritual" subject.

At times, Poe's conception of imagination is conventionally mystical. In
"The Poetic Principle" the poet's "immortal instinct" seems to give him
access to a "spiritual" realm about which he reports: "Inspired by an
ecstatic prescience of the glories beyond the grave, we struggle, by multiform combinations among the things and thoughts of Time, to attain a
portion of that Loveliness whose very elements, perhaps, appertain to
eternity alone" (14:273–74).[12] Here is Poe's rationale for an art at once
mechanical and spiritual. It is an art of "combination," of manipulated
matter and language, but it may produce the *effect* of spiritual experience.
Such an art, to quote *Eureka* again, while it is "by no means the expression
of an idea," is nevertheless "an effort at one"—a "possible attempt at an
impossible conception."

The problem with Poe's claims to spirituality, to a beauty appertaining
"to eternity alone," is that his own works so seldom move "beyond the
grave." In fact, they insist upon it and advertise it. As the poet laureate of
premature burial, Poe established the grave itself as a favorite location.
The characters who do get beyond it are usually confined to reporting on
their lives before death (as in "The Conversation of Eros and Charmion")
or to describing the physical experience of being dead, of being a corpse
(as in "The Colloquy of Monos and Una"). In a technical sense, Poe's
"spiritual" heroes and heroines are not immortal but undead—not angels
but vampires, like Undine[13]—and in spite of his alleged "wild effort to
reach the beauty above," his own beauties generally emerge, like Undine
or Madeline Usher, from the other direction. As his frequent insistence on

"submerged" meaning as a spiritual requirement suggests, the realm of Poe's spirits is subterranean. Thus he complains of merely fanciful poems, in the *Alciphron* review, that "here the upper current is often exceedingly brilliant and beautiful; but then men *feel* that this upper current *is all*. No Naiad voice addresses them *from below*" (10:66)—inviting them, presumably, to "rapturous death." What, we may well ask, is so "rapturous" about such a death? What is so "spiritual," so "ideal," about vampirism? Poe was more concerned with the epistemological vagueness of his spirituality than with its morbidness, but it is the latter quality—the ghoulishness of his "supernal" subject matter—that generally gives most trouble to modern readers.

We should be careful, however, to understand this ghoulishness in the context of its times. In 1836, Hawthorne, as editor of *The American Magazine of Useful and Entertaining Knowledge*, protested against a less pronounced but similar morbidness in his contemporaries:

> We do wrong to our departed friends, and clog our own heavenward aspirations, by connecting the idea of the grave with that of death. Our thoughts should follow the celestial soul, and not the earthly corpse. Sepulchral monuments, from the costliest marble of Mount Auburn to the humblest slate in a country graveyard, are but memorials of human infirmity—of affection grovelling among dust and ashes, instead of soaring to the sky.[14]

Poe could not disconnect the "idea of the grave" from "that of death," the "celestial soul" from the "earthly corpse": this is the essence of his "spiritual" morbidness. But the generality of Hawthorne's complaint reminds us that Poe was not alone in his confusion. Mount Auburn, harbinger of a widespread cemetery movement in nineteenth-century America, had been founded five years before Hawthorne's mention of it, and by mid-century a popular literature of dying and entombment constituted what was almost an independent literary genre, founded on precisely the confusion against which Hawthorne had complained in 1836.[15]

Such confusion extended well beyond a general obsession with the "earthly corpse." It lay at the heart of the contemporary spiritualism, which insisted on the primacy of spirit even as it failed to understand or explore what "spirit" was. The heated debate in the 1850s over the authenticity of spiritual demonstrations turned on issues and arguments remarkably similar to those Poe was debating with himself in the 1840s. As R. Laurence Moore puts it: "Spiritualists had some difficulty clarifying their views about the nature of spirit. Most agreed that 'immaterial substance' could not exist. . . . The spirit teachers seemed to concur that soul and spirit should not be considered something discontinuous from matter, but rather a higher, perfected form of matter."[16] The dilemma of the spiritualists, while few wished to analyze it with Poe's attempt at philosophical rigor, was the same as his. For if "spirit" was a *"mere* word," a mechanically induced "effect," wasn't all the rest, in the terms Coverdale applies to Westervelt's discourse in *The Blithedale Romance*, but "a delusive show of spirituality, yet really imbued throughout with a cold and dead materialism" (200)?

Most of Poe's contemporaries did not require certain knowledge of what spirit was. Exploration was touchy, possibly dangerous. And they knew at least what it was not. It was not physical, not "sensual." Whatever spirit was, might not matter itself be spiritualized simply by being softened, obscured, "etherealized"—in short, obliterated? This is one way of reading Poe's comments on "rarefaction" in his 1844 letter to Lowell. It is also a way of reading the vision of the destruction of the material universe in *Eureka*. It may also help us understand the "spiritual" charm of his corpselike and putrescent heroines, his "ideal" vampires. At times of "more earnest vision," as Emerson put it, "surfaces become transparent, and are no longer seen." Such transparency produced the *effect* of spirituality, of what one might call antimaterialist spirituality, even if nothing was revealed. Poe was hardly unique, in the nineteenth century, in equating the "vague" with the "spiritual." We now call such avoidance "Victorian," but we should recognize that it was not only a matter of prudery. It was, in its perhaps slipshod way, a metaphysical principle.

Nevertheless, prudery had much to do with this cast of mind, and its principal target was the human body, with all its disturbing "sensual" connotations. Both the connotations and the "spiritual" strategy for overcoming them are clear in a well-known passage from Irving's "Rural Funerals" (in *The Sketch-Book*):

> The grave is the ordeal of true affection. It is there that the divine passion of the soul manifests its superiority to the instinctive impulse of mere animal attachment. The latter must be continually refreshed and kept alive by the presence of its object, but the love that is seated in the soul can live on long remembrance. The mere inclinations of sense languish and decline with the charms which excited them, and turn with shuddering disgust from the dismal precincts of the tomb; but it is thence that truly spiritual affection rises purified from every sensual desire, and returns, like a holy flame, to illumine and sanctify the heart of the survivor. [115]

Whatever "spirit" was, "truly spiritual affection" could be guaranteed by a simple requirement: the death of the body. Thus matter, for Poe, is spiritualized through "rarefaction"; and God, in *Eureka*, is restored through the destruction of His created universe. No wonder, as Hawthorne put it in 1836, that Americans kept confusing the "celestial soul" with the "earthly corpse." Spirituality may have arisen, in its various forms, as a protest against the soul's annihilation in death. Yet, lacking a sense of what "spirit" was, Poe and his contemporaries could find it, finally, only in this annihilation—its ultimate "effect." Only in death, physical death, could the soul find its fullest manifestation and guarantor. Undine, this is to say, is Sir Huldebrand's "spiritual wife" *because* he finds "rapturous death" in her arms.

Is it so surprising, in this context, that Roderick Usher buries his sister? Or that Egaeus becomes fascinated with Berenice only when she begins to sicken? Or that Poe's contemporaries accepted these tales without special revulsion?[17] Yes, indeed, as Poe wrote in "The Philosophy of Composition," "the death . . . of a beautiful woman is, unquestionably, the most poetical topic in the world—and equally is it beyond doubt that the lips best suited for such topic are those of a bereaved lover" (14:201). Perverse as all this may be, it has its roots in the perversely prudish, and paradoxically materialistic, spirituality of Poe's culture. He was thoroughly of his age in distinguishing, in "The Poetic Principle," between the "Uranian" and the "Dionæan" Venus—between the "Aspiration for Supernal Beauty," whose tendency is "to elevate the Soul," and that "passion which is the intoxication of the Heart" and whose "tendency is to degrade . . . the Soul" (14:290). The same is true of his protest, in a love letter to Sarah Helen Whitman, that it is only "my diviner nature—my spiritual being—which burns and pants to commingle with your own" (388).

Poe does, in this letter, add a characteristic twist: he asserts that his love might cure his beloved's illness. But, he adds, "if *not*, Helen—if not—if you *died*—then at least would I clasp your dear hand in death, and willingly—oh, *joyfully—joyfully—joyfully*—go down *with* you into the night of the Grave" (390). Even here, however, it is hard to see how Poe is more morbid than Irving or than the host of death-sentimentalizers who followed in Irving's footsteps. Mainly, he is more graphic. What distinguishes him is not his antisensual conception of the spiritual but the sensual extremes to which he took it. He pushed the denial of flesh beyond mere prudery to actual mortification, murder, and suicide. The essential Poe fable, however elaborately the impulse may be displaced or projected onto a double or a lover, is a tale of compulsive self-murder. For Poe, in the last analysis, the soul was "elevated" in art by the vicarious experience of the body's destruction. Poe may be extreme, but behind his critical ideas and tales one always finds the compulsions of his culture.

Nevertheless, by forcing spirituality to its most extreme limits, Poe revealed its extreme consequences. Whether consciously or unconsciously, he knew that, when spirituality takes the form of sadism, its inevitable result is remorse. Suicide and homicide, even when vicarious and in pursuit of the elevation of the soul, are still murder. Poe's spiritual heroines indeed return—but not, in Irving's phrase, "like a holy flame." They return as avenging corpses. And his heroes and narrators, even as they consciously idealize or rationalize their deeds and fantasies, are always unconsciously confessing, indulging in what their creator called the "human thirst for self-torture" (14:207). Yet their acts of "spiritual" repression simply displace the sensual passion they are meant to eradicate or deny. Into their self-torture, by a final twist, is sublimated all the erotic energy supposedly annihilated with the flesh.[18]

Psychoanalytic critics have long argued that Poe's extreme conception of "spiritual" or "ideal" beauty derives from sexual obsessions, from a mixture of sexual fascination and revulsion.[19] I have no wish to quarrel with psychoanalytic criticism of Poe; no doubt his preoccupations did stem from repressed sexual obsessions. Indeed, I am arguing that his very critical vocabulary, like the "spirituality" of his protagonists, functions as a sublimation of neurotic personal conflict. But it is still important to recognize the cultural context and significance of Poe's condition, for it is precisely his obsessions that qualified him to dramatize so successfully the contradictions and consequences of the unexamined values of his age. He may never, indeed, have consummated his relationship with Virginia— but, if so, he was only acting out, literally, the rhetoric of "spiritual" love. He may have been impotent—but what, at least in a metaphorical sense, could have been more "spiritual"? To be sure, his poems and tales of homicide and self-torture are riddled with sublimated eroticism—but so is most art (or culture) that is based on a materialist spirituality, one that insists, that is, on a "spirituality" understood wholly in materialist or secular terms.

Poe's tragedy (if that is what it was) is not that he unconsciously succumbed to the repressed traumas of his childhood but that in his version of Romantic spiritualism he became inextricably enmeshed in the mortality of the body. Just as his pursuit of imagination led inevitably to "mere words," and his pursuit of "spirit" to pure materialism, so his pursuit of the "celestial soul" led back, again and again, to the "earthly corpse." Once he had accepted the terms of the spiritualist debate, rejecting Coleridge's increasingly religious sense of imaginative creativity, he was trapped, whichever side he chose to take: if spiritual belief led only to the "truly spiritual affection" of the tomb, materialist skepticism hardly offered better. The physical detritus of the soul's triumphant departure was hardly, in a phenomenal sense, to be distinguished from the physical evidence of its absence. If the mind of man could imagine nothing that had not "really"—i.e., materially—existed, then the body was all one could know. Dead flesh was dead flesh. The point to be insisted upon, though, is that

Poe's dilemma, however fueled and shaped by his own acute neuroses, was formulated by, and consonant with, the dilemmas of his culture.

"Years ago," Mr. Compson tells Quentin in Faulkner's *Absalom, Absalom!*, "we in the South made our women into ladies. Then the War came and made the ladies into ghosts."[20] Allen Tate, another Southerner, observed in 1949 that, well before the War, Poe saw and followed the extreme implications of this process: he turned the women into vampires. "If a writer ambiguously exalts the 'spirit' over the 'body,'" Tate writes, "and the spirit must live wholly upon another spirit, some version of the vampire legend is likely to issue as the symbolic situation." It should be clear by now that Poe's American contemporaries, and not only in the South, indulged freely in such ambiguous exaltation. One cannot, however, fully agree with Tate's characterization of the "archetypal condition" of Poe's characters as "the survival of the soul in a dead body."[21] The body is indeed dead or at least dying. But there is no soul; there is only, in Hawthorne's phrase, "a delusive show of spirituality, yet really imbued throughout with a cold and dead materialism." The archetypal condition of Poe's vampires is that of dead matter endeavoring, through its deadness, to simulate a spirituality—a spirituality of "effect"—that it can approach in no other manner. Berenice, Madeline, Morella, and Ligeia are animated corpses, "spiritualized" through murderous "etherealization" and then reanimated by the spiritual remorse of their lover-murderers. The latter are themselves little better than corpses, spuriously vivified by guilt into intoning their sepulchral tales. In Poe's fiction the "earthly corpse" triumphs over the "celestial soul" as surely as "words," in Brown's *Edgar Huntly*, triumph over "sentiments"—and this analogy is in no sense casual. Both Poe's theory of beauty and his theory of language derived from an aesthetic of sublimation or displacement. "Spirit," he came increasingly to insist, is unknowable; its epistemological and metaphysical status cannot be ascertained; it is therefore a "mere word." It was through "mere words" that Poe himself set out to recreate "spiritual" beauty.

ARABESQUE ROMANCE

The problem with Poe's subject matter, and especially with his ghoulish heroines, is that they seem to contradict the meaning they are intended to express or embody. Or, since Poe so frequently dismisses meaning as a legitimate goal of art, we might say that in his fiction the *achieved* "effect" contradicts that glimpsing of supernal beauty Poe claims as his *intended* "effect." The same contradiction lies at the heart of Poe's language. This language seems, in effect, at once autonomously "pure" and—sometimes even obscenely—suggestive, at once meaningless and meaningful. In Poe's self-conscious style, as in his bizarre themes, there is a profound tension between alleged "ideality" and buried implication. It is in this sense, above all, that Poe's art pursues the consequences of the sacrifice of relation.

The question of meaning—of its status in relation to verbal artifice—is of course crucial to any discussion of literary art and particularly to what I have called radical romance, with its dissociation of rational "reality" and imaginative language. But with Poe the question of meaning has a special urgency—it is in fact *the* question—because so many readers have found his tales almost totally lacking in relation, almost unintelligibly "pure." Hence Yvor Winters' famous attack on Poe's "obscurantism." Poe, according to Winters, abstracts us from reality, but to no apparent symbolic purpose: his symbolic language bears no relation to the world we know or the thoughts we think.[22] The charge of obscurantism, while leveled most frequently at Poe's poetic language, has almost equal force with respect to his fiction. Those who applaud the internal consistency of the tales, their famous "unity of effect," still have trouble relating these effects, or the structures of language that produce them, to the thoughts and things of this world. In "The Fall of the House of Usher," for instance, the dilapidated mansion may correspond with the head or mind of the demented hero. These correspondences may be worked out in the most intricate detail, but relations of this kind within the artwork suggest no obvious relations to a world of thought or experience beyond the story's moated confines. The house does not "mean" Usher's head any more than his head "means" the house; rather, both house and head, and the obsessive correspondence between them, simply establish an internally consistent set of symbols, a language, whose denotative significance seems deliberately obscure.

Poe, this is to say, took the romancer's art, the sacrifice of relation, about as far as it could go—or farther, if one agrees with Poe's detractors. Much recent criticism, bent on rescuing Poe from the charge of obscurantism, has therefore focused on ways of reestablishing a sense of relation between his work and the known world. Psychoanalysis has been used extensively in this regard. After all, we reason with relief, if your house corresponds with your head, *we* know what it means to bury your sister in the basement! For similar reasons a number of critics have lately called attention to the sociopolitical meanings hidden in Poe's abstract symbols. The black savages of Tsalal, in *The Narrative of Arthur Gordon Pym*, reveal to these readers Poe's own racial nightmares, as does the orangutang's brutality in "Murders in the Rue Morgue." Such readings find in the Ushers' decadence a hint of the isolated antebellum South and, in the fatal fissure that scars their mansion, a premonition, twenty years before Lincoln's "House Divided" speech, of national catastrophe.[23]

These approaches provide valid and valuable windows into the sealed prison of Poe's symbolic language. Psychoanalysis also helps explain his obscurantism; for his curious combination of revelation and concealment, purification and obfuscation, is clearly neurotic. Neurosis, however, seems characteristic of romance in general—given its radical dissociation of imagination and judgment, artifice and expression, phenomenal appearances and noumenal motives—and the problem of Poe's fiction lies deeper than the concealment of specific "meanings," which only mask more profound formal or linguistic questions. The Poe reader, whatever meanings he may find in the language of the tales, must first confront that language itself: a language—including the symbolic discourse of image, character, and plot—apparently drained of significant relation. Before asking what this language means, the reader must ask how it means. He must ask what sorts of relation, beneath the mask of willful obscurity, it allows and encourages.

Poe's confusion over the nature of "spirit" has a direct relevance to the problem of his obscurantism. In a very real sense his intellectual ruminations of the 1840s were linguistic in nature, precipitated by his effort to find a meaning for a "*mere*" word." Like many of his contemporaries, Poe was fond of discussing literary relation in terms of a spiritual metaphor; he complained, for instance, of artificial imitations of Gibbon's style, that in them "the body is copied, without the soul, of the phraseology" (14:93).[24] Meaning was to expression as the soul to the body, spirit to matter. His 1844 remarks on Tennyson's cultivating "a suggestive indefinitiveness of meaning, with the view of bringing about a definitiveness of vague and therefore of spiritual *effect*" (16:28), indicate the close ties between his conception of spirituality and his literary practice. Just as the body could be "etherealized" by being drained of life, so the word could be purified by draining it of meaning. Perhaps the archetypal condition of Poe's literary language—"vague and therefore spiritual"—is not so very different from the archetypal condition of his characters. It is certainly true that, just as his search for the supernal led increasingly to materialism and even necrophilia, so his scorn for "mere words" led increasingly to an obsession with the techniques for manipulating them. Thus Evert Duyckinck complained in 1850 that Poe was merely "a Swiss bell-ringer, who from little contrivances of his own, with an ingeniously devised hammer, strikes a sharp melody, which has all that is delightful and affecting, that is attainable without a soul."[25] Obscurantism, this is to say, is the stylistic equivalent of spiritual vampirism.

Poe's 1844 remarks on Tennyson have provided a major piece of evidence for those who accuse him of obscurantism. The antiobscurantists' assumption that Poe's work is intentionally meaningless is shared by those who defend him as a "pure" artist, a champion of art-for-art's-sake, creating unrelated, autonomous aesthetic structures. The latter image has its appeal and is of real importance in the history of Poe's reputation; but there are many reasons, including, as we shall see, the symbolic strategies of the tales, for suspecting that Poe's "spiritual" or "ideal" beauty is not quite the same thing as the aesthete's "purity." The key phrase, "suggestive indefinitiveness of meaning," is more complex and subtle than readers have generally supposed. Simply by giving the first two terms equal weight, one confronts the fundamental paradox at the heart of Poe's aesthetic theory and practice—namely, that his full view of literary meaning involves not merely obfuscation but a curious tension between revelation and concealment, suggestion and purification. Just as Poe's "spiritual" vampires incorporate the unacknowledgeable energy they seem overtly meant to deny, so his "pure" language suggests the very meanings it is apparently meant to mask.

The argument that Poe sought purity in fiction inevitably turns, at some point, to the title of his first story collection, *Tales of the Grotesque and Arabesque* (1840). The use of these two terms has led to one of the staples of Poe criticism: that he wrote two different kinds of fiction and meant, by his title, to distinguish between them.[26] Close attention to the 1840 preface reveals the weakness of this truism. Both terms, quite clearly, are meant to apply equally to all the stories in the volume, both meaning imaginative as opposed to realistic, "phantasy-pieces" as opposed to works of sober judgment. "The epithets 'Grotesque' and 'Arabesque,'" Poe writes in the preface, "will be found to indicate with sufficient precision the prevalent tenor of the tales here published.... During a period of some two or three years, I have written five-and-twenty short stories whose general character may be so briefly defined" (1:150). Nevertheless, the real distinction between "grotesque" and "arabesque" that Poe makes elsewhere is useful for distinguishing between the different and sometimes conflicting functions of fantasy in his fiction.

"Grotesque" implies fanciful humor, burlesque exaggeration, carica-ture, and, above all, distortion. If the reader is to appreciate it, the author must clearly communicate a sense of the reality that is being distorted. Consequently, the grotesque is inherently incompatible with "spiritual" or "ideal" beauty. In 1836 Poe cited Joseph Rodman Drake's *Culprit Fay*, in which "we are immediately overwhelmed with the grotesque" and which "it is impossible to read without laughing," as a prime example of "what *is not* Ideality or the Poetic Power" (8:299). The grotesque, whether de-liberate or (as in Drake's case) inadvertent, is humorous precisely because it is a mode of self-conscious distortion. Hence, for instance, the burlesque humor of Poe's grotesque names: "Vonderwotteimittiss," "Fum-Fudge," "Count Allamistakeo," "Mr. and Mrs. Lackobreath," and the authoritative encyclopedia, *Tellmenow Isitsoörnot*, cited in "The Thousand-and-Second

Tale of Sheherezade." Modern readers find such "humor" less than sidesplitting; it is too forced, too obvious. But this is the crucial point about grotesque imaginative language: it must insist, often crudely, on relation in order to establish its own violation of it. It is, by definition, "impure" fantasy.

In the pictorial term "arabesque," on the other hand, derived from the Moslem injunction against graphic representation of living figures, Poe found a convenient label for artistic "purity." The ornamentation of carpets and upholstery, he insists in "The Philosophy of Furniture," "should be rigidly Arabesque." "Distinct grounds, and vivid circular or cycloid figures, *of no meaning*, are here Median laws. The abomination of flowers, or representations of well-known objects of any kind, should not be endured" (14:103–4). Or, as the narrator writes of Roderick's gossamer hair, in "The Fall of the House of Usher": "I could not, even with effort, connect its Arabesque expression with any idea of simple humanity" (3:279). Poe's rationale for arabesque vagueness in "ideal" art is clear enough. Since the ineffable essence of true "beauty" is too pure for mortal comprehension, its "effect" may be reproduced only by deliberate avoidance of comprehensible meaning. Only thus, excluding an appeal to mystical power or to the truly creative imagination of Coleridgean Romanticism, could "mere words" be conceived of as groping toward nonlinguistic truth or experience.

There remains, however, the further problem that what Poe appeals to is not nonlinguistic truth but the manipulation of language. The arabesque attains to "ideality" because, quite simply, it doesn't "mean" anything. Even the names of characters and places in Poe's so-called arabesques underline the point. Compare "Vonderwotteimittiss" to "Arnheim," "Mrs. Lackobreath" to "Berenice," "Morella," "Ligeia," and all the other euphonious heroines of pure imagination. We may well question the validity of a nonlinguistic "purity" legitimized solely by the negation of language's normal function of meaning; this, surely, is deviant obscurantism at its most extreme. But if we can pass this hurdle, we must admit that in Poe's theory and practice of the prose arabesque we would seem to have something like autonomous fiction—a fictional language cut off from all normal relation.

Even so, there remain all sorts of reasons to distrust the alleged "purity" of Poe's arabesques. Verbal purity, unlike visual, is almost inconceivable; whatever the author's intention, words almost inevitably "mean" something. And the labels "grotesque" and "arabesque," while in theory they name real intentions or emphases, are hard to apply practically as a basis for classifying actual stories. Furthermore, before accepting "purity" as Poe's whole intention, we should recall that in the *Alciphron* review ideality is equated not with meaninglessness alone but with the presence of a "mystic or secondary expression," a *suggestive* force" (10:65, 67). Finally, and perhaps most significantly, there is the subjectivity of arabesque "purity"; for lack of meaning, like meaning, is an "effect," relying on assumptions about the reader (in this case, about his inability to comprehend). To maintain the appearance of arabesque "purity," the reader must conspire with the author in the suppression of meaning; he must not strike through the mask. The subjectivity of the arabesque is implicit in the derivation of the term, which grows, after all, out of a specific taboo against representation (and recognition). Such a taboo is not, first of all, a form of purity but a form of repression, more a reaction to guilt than an expression of innocence or transcendence. The "Median laws" of the "rigidly arabesque," like the masochistic tendencies of materialistic spirituality, are quite plainly not the result of a beatific state of ideality but a ritualized means of striving toward, or simulating, such a state. It is here that we see the close relationship between the "beauty" of Poe and the repressive "code" of a writer like Hemingway.

In a certain kind of modern fiction the tension between realistic and "purely" formal impulses produces a form of aesthetic distance, a movement from sordid involvement to controlled beauty, as in Joyce's "epiphanies." In Poe's terms we might call this a movement from the grotesque to the arabesque, and many of his own theoretical writings seem to call for such a program. But the movement of his stories, the reader's movement into his stories, is in fact just the opposite. Take, for instance, the narrator's detailed description in "Ligeia" of the tapestries in the sleeping apartment of his English abbey:

> The material was the richest cloth of gold. It was spotted all over, at irregular intervals, with arabesque figures. . . . But these figures partook of the true character of the arabesque only when regarded from a single point of view. By a contrivance now common, and indeed traceable to a very remote period of antiquity, they were made changeable in aspect. To one entering the room, they bore the appearance of simple monstrosities; but upon a farther advance, this appearance gradually departed; and step by step, as the visitor moved his station in the chamber, he saw himself surrounded by an endless succession of the ghastly forms which belong to the superstition of the Norman, or arise in the guilty slumbers of the monk. The phantasmagoric effect was vastly heightened by the artificial introduction of a strong continual current of wind behind the draperies—giving a hideous and uneasy animation to the whole. [2:260–61]

Is this not a fair description of the artificial but suggestive "phantasmagoric effect" of Poe's own arabesques? In them too, as in Prince Prospero's sealed chambers in "The Masque of the Red Death," purity is but the outward form of contamination. To "one entering the room" its illusion can be maintained only through repression—through denial of the relation between, say, "ghastly forms" and "guilty slumbers." The suggestion here is in fact fairly overt: the content of "the guilty slumbers of the monk" is not hard to guess. The "masque," in any case, turns out to be a "mask," the arabesque a grotesque in elaborate disguise—a disguise that the skittish reader or narrator may well labor to keep in place; but the relation it seeks to conceal is there all the same and has as much to do with the overall effect as does the artifice. This is the movement of Poe's arabesques: from "pure" forms "of no meaning" to insidious suggestiveness. What is more, it occurs, as a rule, despite the conscious wishes of the narrators. Egaeus, for example, wonders, at the beginning of "Berenice": "How is it that from beauty I have derived a type of unloveliness?" (2:16).

Egaeus's question might be asked by most of Poe's narrators as they compulsively tell or hint, in spite of their alleged ideality, the very stories their art is meant to conceal. Poe's narrators generally resort to arabesque "purity" not to call up ineffable sentiments but to control intolerable meanings, to obscure unacknowledgeable relations. They refuse the implications of their own suggestive symbols. In "Ligeia," for instance, the abbey chamber symbolically suggests a human head, topped—like Roderick Usher's house—with hairlike vines.[27] At its center, a gold flame-filled censer seems to image the narrator's disordered mind, and, although the narrator himself fails or refuses to make the connection, certain details of the censer's description suggest the content of his unacknowledged fantasies. The censer's surface, he writes, is figured with perforations, "so contrived that there writhed in and out of them, as if endued with a serpent vitality, a continual succession of parti-colored fires" (2:259–60). In this image of the censer's "writhing" flame and "serpent vitality" one can hardly escape hearing echoes of Ligeia's poem, "The Conqueror Worm":

> But see, amid the mimic rout,
>   A crawling shape intrude!
> A blood-red thing that writhes from out
>   The scenic solitude!
> It writhes!—it writhes!—with mortal pangs
>   The mimes become its food,
> And the seraphs sob at vermin fangs
>   In human gore imbued.
>
> [2:257]

We may hazard our own guesses about the repressed sexual significance of this "writhing" worm, but Poe makes very clear, through symbolic suggestion, the relation between the worm and the censer's "serpent vitality."

The narrator refuses to acknowledge the hidden relation between his own "pure" decorative art and Ligeia's poem, but to us it is clear that the motive behind the artifice is guilty repression.

Psychoanalytic critics have long been aware of the relationship between artifice and repression in Poe's fiction, but they have generally obscured the extent to which Poe himself was not only aware of it but—as the correspondence between worm and censer suggests—deliberately manipulated it in his tales. In his art as apparently in his life, Poe entertained a conception of "purity" that has much in common with the idealism of a guilt-ridden child, but, unlike the child—and unlike so many of his contemporaries who entertained the same conception in one form or another—he knew it; and this knowledge was his great formal resource. In "Tale-Writing" (1847), the expansion of his 1842 review of Hawthorne's *Twice-Told Tales*, Poe declared that allegory, the most obvious symbolic form for communicating fictional meaning, should generally be avoided. It is permissible, he continued, only "where the suggested meaning runs through the obvious one in a *very* profound under-current so as never to interfere with the upper one without our own volition, so as never to show itself unless *called* to the surface" (13:148). One has no need of Freud to see that in this formulation the line between arabesque and grotesque, between apparently "pure" form and submerged meaning, runs somewhere parallel to the line between conscious intention and contradictory unconscious impulse. Arabesque "purity," it is clear, consists primarily in the ability *not* to call submerged impulses and meanings to the surface.

It is in this sense, and in this sense only, that Roderick Usher's hair is "arabesque." The narrator cannot connect it with any meaning because he refuses to call any meaning to the surface, although there are plenty of meanings available. He enters Roderick's house like the hypothetical "visiter" to the abbey chamber in "Ligeia," except that he—like the "Ligeia" narrator contemplating the censer—refuses to probe the suggestion of the forms and figures. He characteristically represses his forebodings of meaning as "superstitions" or ridiculous "fancies," recalling, in this, so many of Anne Radcliffe's rational heroines and heroes. He ignores the obvious parallels between Roderick and his mansion—between the arabesque hair, for instance, and the fungi overspreading the building's cracked façade. His reference to the windows as "eye-like" (3:273) suggests an awareness of what is going on; but when Roderick "explains" the whole business in his peroration on "sentience," the narrator can only remark that "such opinions need no comment, and I will make none" (287). The first appearance of Roderick's sister, Madeline, fills him "with an utter astonishment not unmingled with dread." "And yet," he adds, "I found it impossible to account for such feelings" (281). No wonder he helps Roderick bury her alive. And no wonder that, when she finally comes to the surface *without* being called (at least consciously, by him), he takes to his heels. Arthur Mervyn could not have conducted himself with greater aplomb, obtusely burying "desperate suggestions" beneath "better thoughts"—even when the latter, as Poe's narrator admits, are "unsatisfactory" (274). For him the Usher domain remains arabesque to the end; but Madeline emerges, all the same, from her sepulchral grotto beneath his bedchamber.

The narrator's complicity in the "spiritual" murder of Madeline, while unacknowledged, is clear throughout his tale. *"We,"* Roderick insists, *"have put her living in the tomb!"* (296). But it is in the arabesque "purity" of his narrative intention, rather than in any specific actions within the tale, that the narrator participates most fully in the homicidal "etherealization" of Roderick's sensual sister; and, just as the vampiristic Madeline escapes from the basement, so she, and the submerged meanings she suggests, emerge continually from their formal confinement. Toward the close, the narrator's reading of the "Mad Trist" to Usher provides an object lesson in the relation between surface and submerged meaning. The narrator contrasts the romance's "uncouth and unimaginative prolixity" with the "lofty and spiritual ideality" of his friend (292). But the tale proves curiously appropriate to Roderick's situation, and he provides an interpretation of its allegory in what are almost his last words:

> And now—to-night—Ethelred—ha! ha!—the breaking of the hermit's door, and the death-cry of the dragon, and the clangour of the shield!—say, rather, the rending of her coffin, and the grating of the iron hinges of her prison, and her struggles within the coppered archway of the vault! [296]

Roderick utters what the narrator will not admit; but the crude tale suggests more than even Roderick, his defenses now collapsing, will acknowledge. For a "trist" is, among other things, a meeting of lovers; and in the prodigious deeds performed by Ethelred—forcing entrance into the hidden cavern with his uplifted mace, to kill another "vital" serpent—there lies concealed a grotesque parody of sexual penetration and sexual guilt, transmuting sexuality into murder.

In fact, such symbolic transmutation occurs throughout "The Fall of the House of Usher"—for instance, in "The Haunted Palace," the poem attributed to Roderick (although Poe had published it separately five months before the tale appeared). Despite his general scorn for overt symbolism, Poe freely admitted the "allegorical conduct" of "The Haunted Palace" (*Letters*, 161), and the allegory seems quite obvious: the onset of madness is portrayed as the unseating of the "monarch Thought" from his throne in a palace made to correspond, with Spenserian minuteness, to the human head. The problem here, as with so many of Poe's allegories, is that it refuses to explain the action it allegorically portrays. We see symptoms but not causes or motives; the poem's representation of madness is entirely phenomenal. The "evil things, in robes of sorrow," that assail "the monarch's high estate" (3:285) are not identified. Roderick Usher, it would seem, is as fond of obscurantism as his friend the narrator. Freed of their overt allegorical framework, however, the poem's symbols are more suggestive, revealing beneath the fable of unexplained insanity a deeper struggle between opposed masculine and feminine images. The stately tower is set in "the greenest of our valleys." At the close, as the castle's windows turn "red-litten," a "hideous throng" rushes into this valley, through the "pale door," "like a rapid ghastly river." Our attention is moved from palace to door, from masculine tower, sending forth "Echoes," to feminine orifice, filling the valley with its "ghastly river" (284–86).

Such hints are only hints, but they gain resonance in the context of the full story; for the House of Usher itself undergoes a similar and far more explicit transformation. At the outset it is erect and enclosed, a fit symbol for Roderick's masculine isolation; however, it rests precariously above a womblike tarn, which eventually swallows it. And in Madeline it conceals a feminine presence as well as a masculine, a presence also suggestively emblematized by its exterior. "Perhaps," writes the narrator, characteristically refusing open acknowledgment of what he sees, "the eye of a scrutinising observer might have discovered a barely perceptible fissure, which, extending from the roof of the building in front, made its way down the wall in a zigzag direction, until it became lost in the sullen waters of the tarn" (277).[28] It is this fissure, of course, that opens in the end, after Madeline's reemergence in her own blood-spattered "robe of sorrow." This final cataclysm suggests that her triumph is not only over her brother's repressive "sanity" but over his symbolic control of their shared mansion—and over the narrator's symbolic control of his story:

Suddenly there shot along the path a wild light, and I turned to see whence a gleam so unusual could have issued; for the vast house and its shadows were alone behind me. The radiance was that of the full, setting, and blood-red moon which now shone vividly through that once barely-discernible fissure of which I have before spoken. . . . While I gazed, this fissure rapidly widened—there came a fierce breath of the whirlwind—the entire orb of the satellite burst at once upon my sight—my brain reeled as I saw the mighty walls rushing asunder—there was a long tumultuous shouting sound like the voice of a thousand waters—and the deep and dank tarn at my feet closed sullenly and silently over the fragments of the "House of Usher." [297]

The narrator may find it "impossible" to account for his "feelings" toward Madeline, but in these final images—"the voice of a thousand waters," "the deep and dank tarn," the "blood-red moon" bursting through the opening fissure, whose presence he must now acknowledge—it is impossible to mistake the hidden causes of his alarm.

Of course there is nothing new in finding sexual symbolism and sexual revulsion in "The Fall of the House of Usher." What still needs to be recognized, however, is the quite calculated way in which this "arabesque" tale, through the suggestiveness of its "secondary or mystic expression," subverts its own overt narrative intention. The process can be discerned in Madeline's triumphant reemergence: the "suggestive" force can emerge only by annihilating the "purity" of the surface. Even the tale's language is sometimes self-destructive in this grotesquely "mystic" sense. Readers have long been puzzled, for instance, by the family name. Perhaps it is a genuine arabesque, a euphonious name with no meaning. Or is Roderick, as some have suggested, the guide or "usher" of the narrator? Or, again: there is an onset of "rushing" toward the end: a "rushing gust" opens the chamber door to reveal Madeline; the narrator recoils from the "rushing asunder" (or "rushing us under"?) of the mansion's walls; should we, then, render the hero's name as "R. Usher"? But there is an even more likely and significant possibility: does not this name encode the essential sexual configuration of the tale's symbolic situation, implicating all three characters in "The Fall of the House of Us/Her"?

What matters most here, however, is not what the story means in any particular reading but the status it gives to its hidden or submerged meaning in relation to its phenomenal language, its symbolic narrative form. The narrator's sexual revulsion is not the meaning toward which the tale strives; it is rather the mystic suggestion against which the narrator and his tale struggle. The story's total meaning is precisely this struggle, which is also the essence of the story's form. What must be recognized is that obscurantist displacement is both the medium and the subject of Poe's arabesques, and it is in this light that they should be read. Far more explicitly than Brown or Irving, Poe recognized and exploited the congruence between the dissociation of neurotic repression—severing conscious "purity" from unconscious fantasy—and the romance's sacrifice of relation—severing "words" from "sentiments." If "The Fall of the House of Usher" indicates the force of the taboo behind Poe's conception of "purity," it also indicates his ability simultaneously to analyze and dramatize the workings of this taboo. In his fiction, aesthetic autonomy, or the appearance of aesthetic autonomy, is presented not for its own sake but as an outgrowth of unconscious fear—fear of what the "Usher" narrator calls "the bitter lapse into every-day life—the hideous dropping off of the veil" (273). Poe knew that the veil of ideal "purity" was a form not of transcendence but of transference, displacement, symbolic concealment: the fine art of calling a spade an agricultural implement. While his own prose is frequently characterized by such protective euphemism, he was capable, when he wished, of writing with exemplary economy and clarity. The stylistic orotundity and evasiveness of his narrators, like their more general obscurantism, should be seen as deliberate dramatic characterization.

I am not implying that we should rigidly distinguish Poe from his narrators. They are all projections of his very self. He too wished, whenever and for as long as possible, to call the spade an agricultural implement, to displace the "writhing" worm into the arabesque censer. The fact that he knew what his art was up to does not mean that he endorsed what it was up against. For him as for his narrators, protective euphemism lay at the heart of the language of arabesque romance.

Unlike his narrators, however, Poe understood the limits of arabesque repression. Against the conscious narrative impulse of his tales toward the "beauty" of euphemistic "purity" there works a submerged counterimpulse toward the "hideous dropping off of the veil," toward admitting or compulsively revealing the agricultural implement to be a spade. There is always a dangerous mystic meaning in the symbols, however consciously it is obscured. Madeline does emerge from the basement; the fissure opens. Ligeia's "vitality" emerges from the aesthetic confines of the censer and the abbey chamber. The Red Death does gain entrance to Prince Prospero's chambers. At the close of "Berenice" the "thirty-two small, white and ivory-looking substances" (2:26) do spill to the floor, forcing Egaeus to confront the suppressed memory of violating his cousin's tomb—even if he will no longer utter the word, "teeth." "Indefinitiveness," in Poe's arabesque symbols, is always "suggestive" in the end.

MERE WORDS

Poe's narrators fill their tales with mystic symbols, arabesque sublimations of their deepest terrors. From first to last, theirs is a world, not of things or even of thoughts, but of obscure symbolic counters. Theirs, ultimately, is a world of words,[29] and nowhere does Poe seem more paradoxical and contradictory than in his portrayal of the powers and purposes of language. Words constitute the ultimate but far from neutral territory of Poe's arabesque romance, where the imaginary and actual meet in a pitched battle between sound and sense, "purity" and suggestion, conscious repression and unconscious revelation. Advocates of Romanticism adapted the religious idea of mystic utterance—the manipulation of language to express or suggest nonlinguistic, sacred truth—to the secular but still quasi-religious project of probing unconscious psychological mysteries. "Spirit" increasingly came to be identified with the buried self. Poe, in this sense, as in so many others, is only partially a Romantic. He sometimes speaks as if he wishes, through "pure" language, to express the inexpressible, but for his narrators such language more often functions to prohibit expression and probing, at least for as long as possible. Romanticism essayed the revelation of the buried self or of some more elusive buried "spirit," but Poe and his narrators seem as much bent on premature burial as on exhumation. Through the sacrifice of relation between sound and sense, Poe's characters seek refuge in a language liberated from all meaning, from any possible suggestion of forbidden feeling. They seek not mystic expression but aesthetic repression. Yet their "pure" aesthetic lexicon remains a displaced vocabulary of revulsion and guilt. In the end, submerged meaning not only survives; the fact of its being concealed makes its power all the more insidious.

In "Al Aaraaf" (1829), in conventional Romantic terms, Poe laments the disparity between words and the thoughts they strive to express:

> Ours is a world of words: Quiet we call
> "Silence"—which is the merest word of all.
> All Nature speaks, and ev'n ideal things
> Flap shadowy sounds from visionary wings—
> But ah! not so when, thus, in realms on high
> The eternal voice of God is passing by . . .
> [7:28]

Here again Poe is voicing his skepticism about the ability of "mere words" to express "impossible conceptions." By 1846 he could write, of his faith in "the *power of words,*" that no "thought, properly so called, is out of the reach of language" (*Marginalia;* 16:89, 88). But what was true of "thought, properly so called" was not equally true of what he called, in *Eureka,* "the *thought of a thought*" (16:200). His tales abound with what might be called, in this sense, linguistic impotence. His characters are repeatedly overcome by feelings "for which there is no name upon the earth" (2:147), by sensations "of which no words could convey to the merely human intelligence even an indistinct conception" (4:209).

One might regard this impotence, in the light of the passage from "Al Aaraaf," as but another example of the Romantic striving to express the inexpressible. Here again we encounter the rationale for Poe's obscurantism. The highest beauty being nonlinguistic, its effect can be approximated in language only by divorcing words from fixed meanings. Language must be made to transcend its rationalist bounds—the bounds of "thought, properly so called." Yet to accept this rationale is to miss the clear psychological function of linguistic "indefinitiveness" for most of Poe's characters. They are less interested in striving toward the beauty

113

above—except as a kind of rationalization for the sublimation of repressed fantasies—than in drowning out the "Naiad voice" that calls *"from below"* (10:66). Poe and his narrators are more content than they pretend with living in "a world of words," for in such a world linguistic impotence, like arabesque "purification," functions as a deliberate if unacknowledged strategy for avoiding forbidden feelings. The real terror is not that words will fail to communicate the feelings they hide but that they may succeed and in succeeding reveal the personal guilt behind the quasi-religious Romantic rationale. Poe's narrators embrace the "power of words" not as a route toward mystic expression but as a way of keeping submerged suggestions submerged.

In "Berenice," for instance, Egaeus's vague memory of his cousin's exhumation, first described as a "confused and exciting dream," soon becomes "a fearful page in the record of my existence, written all over with dim, and hideous, and unintelligible recollections." Personal guilt is metaphorically displaced into a kind of written text. Egaeus strives, he says, "in vain" to "decypher" this text (2:25); but the sincerity of his striving is cast in doubt by his earlier account of his avocations, for he loved, he says, "to repeat monotonously some common word, until the sound, by dint of frequent repetition, ceased to convey any idea whatever to the mind" (19). Brown's Edgar Huntly feared that "in proportion as I gain power over words, shall I lose dominion over sentiments" (5). The typical Poe narrator makes no genuine appeal to a realm of ineffable sentiment. Rather, he sets out to gain "dominion over sentiments" by eradicating them through structures of incomprehensible language.

In "Ligeia" the narrator is thoroughly perplexed by his own contradictory attitudes toward the suggestive and repressive powers of words. The action of his story, imaged in the transformation of Rowena's earthly body, turns on his alleged effort to express or embody the spiritual Ligeia through mere earthly language. "It is by that sweet word alone," he writes, "—by Ligeia—that I bring before mine eyes in fancy the image of her who is no more" (2:249). He even confronts the Romantic's frustration over the expressive limits of language: "Words," he confesses as Ligeia sickens, "are impotent to convey any just idea of the fierceness of resistance with which she wrestled with the Shadow" (255). Here, once again, is the Romantic rationale: the appeal to a higher, nonlinguistic realm of experience; yet the narrator rather surprisingly informs us, describing the moment when Ligeia herself began to express her suffering: "I would not wish to dwell on the wild meaning of the quietly uttered words" (255). This is not impotence but reticence.

The narrator removes to his English abbey—"which," he writes, "I shall not name" (258)—and there marries the Lady Rowena. But his thoughts are elsewhere:

My memory flew back . . . to Ligeia. . . . I would call aloud upon her name, during the silence of the night, or among the sheltered recesses of the glens by day, as if, through the wild eagerness, the solemn passion, the consuming ardor of my longing for the departed, I could restore her to the pathway she had abandoned—ah, *could* it be forever?—upon the earth. [261]

Yet, when he succeeds in evoking her, he is filled not with joy but with "a crowd of unutterable fancies connected with the air, the stature, the demeanor of the figure"—fancies that chill him "into stone" (267). "Ligeia" is a fictional enactment of the fullest power of words—the power to make real and present an "impossible conception." The narrator's horror at his success suggests, however, that his incantatory repetition of Ligeia's name has been meant as much to subdue as to summon her spirit. Just as Irving's Annette Delarbre is content to long for her lost lover and almost dies from shock at his return, so the narrator of "Ligeia" prefers her name, her verbal sign, to the reality it signifies. Her name, like the verbal structure of the story that bears the same name, seems finally meant to keep her dead and buried. When the name has the opposite, and allegedly intended, effect of raising her, the narrator's verbal control is shattered. On her return, he is overwhelmed with "*unutterable* fancies," is seized by "*inexpressible* madness" (268; my emphasis). At the close, the Romantic rationale of expressing the inexpressible collapses. Beneath the narrator's conventional laments over linguistic impotence is revealed, finally, a radical fear of the power of words.

"Morella" (1835), generally considered a kind of earlier version of "Ligeia," also turns on the ambiguous function and power of words. Here the narrator burns with spiritual love for Morella, a love whose "fires," he insists, "were not of Eros" (2:27). Nevertheless, they marry. He becomes her pupil in philosophical mysteries, listening to "the music of her voice," to "low, singular words, whose strange meaning burned themselves in upon my memory" (28). But when this love begins to threaten the bounds of language, it sours. The narrator comes to loathe Morella's voice and touch; he comes, even, to long for her death. This event soon follows, leaving him with the care of their daughter. Before Morella's death, she prophesies her husband's unhappiness as he stands by her bedside, repeating her name over and over. It is this name that fulfills her prophecy. "Morella's name," writes the narrator, "died with her at her death. Of the mother I had never spoken to the daughter;—it was impossible to speak" (33). The daughter herself, for the first ten years of her life, remains "nameless upon the earth" (32). Yet she develops into a resemblance of her mother. The father is terrified to observe "her rapid increase in bodily size," her attainment of "the adult powers and faculties of the woman," "the wisdom or passions of maturity" (31). All these he regards with "suspicions, of a nature fearful and exciting" (32). At length, the narrator writes, but with no effort at explanation: "the ceremony of baptism presented to my mind, in its unnerved and agitated condition, a present deliverance from the terrors of my destiny" (33). At this baptism, the father, activated by some "fiend" in "the recesses of [his] soul," whispers "within the ears of the holy man the syllables—Morella" (33). The budding nymphet immediately drops dead, her corpse answering, to the name, "I am here!" When the father bears her to the family tomb, he finds that his wife's body is no longer there.

"Morella" is so nearly incoherent as to verge on burlesque, yet there is a deadly serious issue at its core. The forbidden name completes the displacement of the first into the second Morella, but, even as it evokes, the word kills: its utterance annihilates its object. We might give the story a conventional Romantic reading: the narrator loses his inexpressible feelings because he insists, insanely, on naming them. But such a reading misses the deepest point of the story. The word, however much the narrator may lament the consequences of naming, is *meant* to kill. Language, naming, is the unacknowledgeable vehicle of "spiritual" murder. This is why the "ceremony of baptism" offers "deliverance from the terrors of my destiny"—relief from those "suspicions, of a nature fearful and exciting," occasioned by the daughter's precocious development. It is precisely their power to keep the allegedly "inexpressible" unexpressed that makes words so valuable to the father. Given the fact that what he is repressing is his own feelings, however, one suspects a continuing cycle of "Morellas" in his future.

Poe's heroes live in a world in which language mediates ambiguously and often fatally between conscious intentions and unconscious impulses. Hence their frequent recourse to reticence or protective incomprehensibility. As sublimations of feared and forbidden impulses, words may protect them from their surroundings and unconscious feelings. Words may protect by being "indefinitive," "vague and therefore spiritual"—the linguistic equivalent of "spiritual" vampires. But, like these vampires, they also, as sublimations, incorporate the very thoughts they are meant to eradicate. They are "spiritual," that is to say, not only in an "arabesque" but in a "mystic" sense as well. They encode, even in their arabesque obscurity, a fearful talismanic power. The word that kills inevitably bears the suggestive freight of its hidden motive. Obscurantism is, for Poe's characters, an obsessive strategy but one that almost always fails. To express a thought in language may be to kill it, but the corpse retains a hideous, if spurious, vitality. The Poe hero may wall himself in with words, but he does so only to discover that such walls, like those in

"The Pit and the Pendulum," have a terrifying life of their own—an abiding, threatening power of suggestive evocation.

EXPRESSIONS AND ORIGINS

Neither the vocation of imaginative romancer in a hostile society nor the radical dualism of romance itself "made" Poe neurotic. He was clearly neurotic to begin with, torn between ambition and alienation, eager dependence and guilty aggression. But just as the deviant label "romancer" appealed to Brown and Irving, so it undoubtedly attracted a young man whose lack of place in society, in Poe's case, began with the traumatic insecurity of life as the foster child of John Allan. The inherent neurosis of romance—its dissociation of rational discourse and irrational impulse—clearly promised a kind of objective correlative for unresolvable personal conflicts. The sacrifice of relation between conscious thought and unconscious feeling, between "better thoughts" and "desperate suggestions," offered, it would seem, just what Poe needed.

What is fascinating, however, about Poe's fiction seen in this light is the extent to which it chronicles the betrayal of its psychological promise. Again and again it dramatizes the *breakdown* of dissociation, for it is precisely suggestive relation that destroys or incapacitates so many of Poe's heroes. In a sense Poe succeeds, through symbolic indirection, in overcoming the inherent disrelation of romance; but his success is ironic, since his heroes—and, one surmises, Poe himself—turn to romance, not for the relation, but for the sacrifice.

In any case, we must not confuse the breakdown of disrelation, in Poe's work, with any genuine resolution of the conflict between fantasy and judgment, language and feeling. His symbols function not as resolutions but as unacknowledged connections between levels of experience and discourse that can be connected in no other way. Feelings enter the medium of conscious thought, in Poe's tales, only through displacement and sublimation—*as symbols*. Repression and expression do not fuse in his criticism or his fiction into a coherent, unitary aesthetic theory; instead they engage in unresolved and apparently unresolvable conflict. Verbal artifice destroys feeling only to be destroyed, in its turn, by what it has suppressed. One might thus regard Poe as a kind of case study in aesthetic pathology, since he projected his own neuroses into a literary form already implicitly neurotic.

Poe's importance is, however, far more than symptomatic. His work retains its bizarre fascination well over a century after his death, and it profoundly influenced Hawthorne and Melville, not to mention Baudelaire and the development of French Symbolism.[30] Whatever his individual neuroses, moreover, Poe managed to use them to brilliantly dramatize a complex of similar neuroses in his culture. Even his aesthetic theory goes beyond stark dualism.

One of the most important preoccupations of his criticism remains to be discussed: namely, the concept of "originality," which for Poe, as for many of his contemporaries, was a matter of crucial significance. Romanticism replaced Pope's neoclassical definition of "true wit"—"What oft was thought, but ne'er so well expressed"[31]—with a new demand for originality of conception, of genuine, organic creation. Poe grappled with this demand throughout his career. In his evolving conception of "originality" he attempted, furthermore, to find some philosophical basis for a relation between irrational impulse and the artful language that seemed at once to submerge and reveal it. He attempted to find a relation between expressions and their origins.

In *The Confidence-Man*, in 1857, Melville would make "originality" in fiction the subject of rich and resonant inquiry. "The original character, essentially such," he writes in a well-known passage,

> is like a revolving Drummond light, raying away from itself all round it—everything is lit by it, everything starts up to it (mark how it is with Hamlet), so that, in certain minds, there follows upon the adequate conception of such a character, an effect, in its way, akin to that which in Genesis attends upon the beginning of things. [205]

Compared to Melville's, Poe's idea of originality seems thin indeed. Twenty years before *The Confidence-Man*, he wrote that "original characters" are simply a matter either of "presenting qualities known in real life, but never before depicted, (a combination nearly impossible)" or of "presenting qualities (moral, or physical, or both) which although unknown, or even known to be hypothetical, are so skillfully adapted to the circumstances which surround them, that our sense of fitness is not offended" (9:261–62). Such originality does not light up its surroundings. Rather, its surroundings are of main importance, for they help to pass off its spurious novelty. "Nothing," Poe wrote in 1845, "unless it be novel—*not even novelty itself*—will be the source of very intense excitement among men" (14:153). Such "originality," one might well complain, smacks more of P. T. Barnum or Madison Avenue than of any genuinely human conception of artistic expression. It is originality wholly of "effect." Given Poe's dismissal of the genuinely creative Coleridgean imagination, this narrowness is not surprising. One recalls the stark statement of the 1840 review of Moore's *Alciphron:* "All novel conceptions are merely unusual combinations. The mind of man can *imagine* nothing which has not really existed" (10:62).

Elsewhere, however, and especially during his final years, Poe articulated a vision of originality much closer to that of *The Confidence-Man*. In 1847, for instance, he wrote in "Tale-Writing":

> The true originality—true in respect of its purposes—is that which, in bringing out the half-formed, the reluctant, or the unexpressed fancies of mankind, or in exciting the more delicate pulses of the heart's passion, or in giving birth to some universal sentiment or instinct in embryo, thus combines with the pleasurable effect of *apparent* novelty, a real egoistic delight. The reader . . . feels and intensely enjoys the seeming novelty of the thought, enjoys it as really novel, as absolutely original with the writer—*and himself*. . . . They two have, together, created this thing. Henceforward there is a bond of sympathy between them, a sympathy which irradiates every subsequent page of the book. [13:146]

Here is an originality expressive rather than spurious, involving the reader in "sympathetic" creation, "irradiating" its rhetorical context. Its "novelty" is not merely "*apparent*" or "phenomenal," a matter of superficially "pleasurable effect." It stems, rather, from precisely the sort of "suggestion" Poe's heroes so generally fear—from "bringing out the half-formed, the reluctant, or the unexpressed fancies of mankind." The reader senses not only the writer's surface art but the originating impulse—the "universal sentiment or instinct"—behind it and in his own mind.

By the time of *Eureka*, Poe's "originality" has become quite literally, in Melville's phrase, "akin to that which in Genesis attends upon the beginning of things." We appreciate in the outward form of the universe the evidence of its connection to its own beginnings, its *"originating act"* (16:220). The literary parallel to such cosmic originality is never far from the surface. Hence Poe's reference to

> an imperfect *plot* in a romance, where the *dénoûment* [sic] is awkwardly brought about by interposed incidents external and foreign to the main subject; instead of springing out of the bosom of the thesis—out of the heart of the ruling idea—instead of arising as a result of the primary proposition—as inseparable part and parcel of the fundamental conception of the book. [306]

The "bosom of the thesis," the "fundamental conception," is precisely the "originating act," the original creative impulse. Here is the ultimate "meaning" of romance, the true relation connecting its language to the writer's imagination. Language is truly original not in its novelty but in its "inseparable and inevitable" *relation* to the originating conception—the motive or sentiment—from which its arabesque, phenomenal rhetoric has sprung.

At the heart of *Eureka*, for all its analytical mechanism, operates an organicism as thoroughgoing as Emerson's. The problem with Poe, however, is that, *Eureka* notwithstanding, he seems the least organic of writers. If the "common origin," as Emerson writes in "Self-Reliance," inhabits a realm "behind which analysis cannot go," Poe and his characters remain compulsively analytical to the end. Again and again—in the detective tales, or in such adventure stories as "Descent into the Maelström" or "The Pit and the Pendulum"—intimations of terror are fought with ratiocination and logic. Emerson identifies "primary wisdom" with "Spontaneity or Instinct," with "Intuition." [32] Poe, however, frequently expressed his scorn for this Romantic trinity. "There is no greater mistake," he wrote in 1836, "than the supposition that a true originality is a mere matter of impulse or inspiration. To originate, is carefully, patiently, and understandingly to combine" (14:73). In Poe's critical writings, it would seem, one finds not an integrated theory of inspiration and expression but yet another bifurcation between two quite contradictory tendencies: organic and radically inorganic, imaginative and fanciful—one seeing in original expression the suggestion of originating impulse, the other conceiving it in terms of mere mechanical novelty of combination.

In "The Philosophy of Composition" (1846), that most analytical and least organic of critical treatises, Poe again voices his scorn of intuition, but he adds a crucial qualification: "The fact is," he writes, "that originality (unless in minds of very unusual force) is by no means a matter, as some suppose, of impulse or intuition" (14:203). The qualification is contained in the parentheses. Poe clearly regarded his own mind as one of "very unusual force," and to such a mind phenomenal surfaces yielded up their noumenal origins. Poe dramatized this force most fully in his portrait of the detective-genius, C. Auguste Dupin. Dupin's powers may be primarily analytical, but his is a very special sort of analysis, not to be confounded with "simple ingenuity." "Between ingenuity and the analytic ability," Poe explains in "Murders in the Rue Morgue," "there exists a difference far greater, indeed, than that between the fancy and the imagination, but of a character very strictly analogous. It will be found, in fact, that the ingenious are always fanciful, and the *truly* imaginative never otherwise than analytic" (4:149–50). Dupin, the *"truly"* imaginative sleuth, has indeed much in common with the Emersonian genius. "The mental features discoursed of as the analytical," Poe writes, "are, in themselves, but little susceptible of analysis. We appreciate them only in their effects." Analysis, that is to say, is, like the language of romance, phenomenal in its effect but noumenal in its origins. The analyst's "results, brought about by the very *soul* and *essence* of method [my emphasis], have, in truth, the whole air of intuition" (146). Here is the explanation for Poe's apparently contradictory statements about originality. There is simple ingenuity, the originality of common men, consisting of merely novel effects, but there is also the deeper originality of "minds of very unusual force," seeking always in phenomenal rhetoric a noumenal, generative motive.

Dupin exhibits his mental force by uncovering the originating motives behind phenomena. He seems less a romancer than a romance-reader. But he "reads" through sympathy; he identifies the buried motives of phenomena with his own. The solution of a crime, he announces in "The Purloined Letter," depends upon an "identification of the reasoner's intellect with that of his opponent"; in this way he can deduce the opponent's "thoughts or sentiments" from those that arise in the reasoner's "mind or heart" (6:41). Through such sympathetic identification Dupin solves crimes, much as Poe solves the riddle of the universe in *Eureka*, by tracing the outward form back to the "originating act" of which it is the expression. In "The Power of Words" (1845) Agathos declares that God, viewing the path of a comet, "could have no difficulty in determining, by the analytic retrogradation, to what original impulse it was due" (6:142–43). Dupin possesses this divine power, but it is shared by few of Poe's other characters, most of whom fear their own "thoughts or sentiments" too much to probe those of others. These characters remain perplexed by meaningless phenomena, by what Poe calls "the seeming absence of motive" (4:168) in the world around them. Only a Dupin, or a God, can keep expressions and origins simultaneously in view.

Even for Dupin or God, however, there are limits to this simultaneity. What distinguishes Poe's conception of originality from that of most of his contemporaries is not his rational resistance to Romantic organicism but his sense that impulse and expression, while related as different stages of the creative process, are, precisely because of this relation, separated by an impassable chasm of time. As matter, in *Eureka*, is the emanation of spirit, so is language the emanation of sentiment—as Rowena is the sublimation of Ligeia and the young Morella is the sublimation of her mother. But matter and spirit, language and sentiment, are totally irreconcilable all the same. They can have, whether in reality or in literature, no simultaneous existence.[33] Matter is not, for Poe, infused with spirit, with the abiding energy of its generation. It exists, instead, through the suppression of that energy. God, in *Eureka*, is wholly dispersed into matter; his revival necessitates matter's destruction. Similarly, to express a sentiment is to kill it. The word—like the "spiritual" vampire—is the corpse of its origin. Works of art, in Poe's system, are inevitably but the detritus of their origins, "mere words," life frozen into "spiritual" death.

That such death was, for Poe, the price of expression is indicated repeatedly in his poetry and fiction, not only in the tales and poems that deal symbolically with the fatal power of language but in those that deal literally with the creation of works of art. In the first "To Helen," for instance, the poet does not recreate his beloved's living beauty; he turns her into a frozen statue.[34] Thus too, in "The Oval Portrait" (1842), originally entitled "Life in Death," the artist kills his wife by painting her. A similar transformation is enacted in "The Assignation" (1835), an early tale whose oppressive opulence and apparent incoherence have relegated it to a position of general neglect among Poe readers. The story, however, is fascinating for a number of reasons.[35] In its opening image of the drowning child, dropped inadvertently into the Grand Canal by the Marquesa Aphrodite Mentoni, it gives us what is both Poe's most suggestive inversion of his own sense of maternal abandonment and his most personal evocation of linguistic impotence. The child struggles helplessly, "deep beneath the murky water, . . . thinking in bitterness of heart upon [its mother's] sweet caresses, and exhausting its little life in struggles to call upon her name" (2:111). But what matters most about "The Assignation" in the present context is its symbolic exploitation of literal and metaphorical works or art. The Marquesa, astonished at the loss of her child, is motionless, "statue-like," her garments hanging on her "as the heavy marble hangs around the Niobe" (111). A Byronic stranger, who turns out to be her lover, appears to rescue the child, but he too is statuesque: he emerges from a "gloomy niche," and his "classically regular" features are later compared to "the marble ones of the Emperor Commodus" (111–12, 115). The opening of the tale is eerily evocative, creating an atmosphere of almost agonizing tension between the emergency of the situation and the frozen, aesthetic composure of the participants.

The rescue of the child offers a momentary respite from this marble stasis. The stranger moves out of his niche. The child is restored, "still living and breathing" (112). The Marquesa, too, is transformed. "See!" the narrator exclaims, "the entire woman thrills throughout the soul, and the statue has started into life! The pallor of the marble countenance, the swelling of the marble bosom, the very purity of the marble feet, we behold suddenly flushed over with a tide of ungovernable crimson" (113). The narrative shift to the present tense enhances the sense of reinvigoration. But the animation is short-lived. Although the Marquesa agrees to meet with the stranger at dawn, their "assignation" turns out to be a suicide pact. When she next appears, it is not in life but in the form of a painting in the stranger's apartment, beautiful but, once again, immobile. Particularly suggestive is the passage from Chapman's *Bussy D'Ambois*, recalled to the narrator by the stranger's reaction to this painting:

> He is up
> There like a Roman statue! He will stand
> Till Death hath made him marble!
>
> [123]

And death does make the stranger, who first emerged from a "niche," marble once again. He sips his poisoned wine, faithful to his pact with the Marquesa. The narrator turns to him at the close, only to find that "his limbs were rigid" (124).

"The Assignation" is, in its way, Poe's "Bright Star" or "Ode on a Grecian Urn," but here there is no life, no hope of evoking life. In art there is only death; and life emerges briefly, at the outset, only by shattering frozen aesthetic composure. Tales like "The Assignation" or "The Oval Portrait" articulate what might be called a tragic vision of the creative process, of the disparity between the living "originating act" and the frozen language that entombs it. Many of Poe's contemporaries shared this vision, as, for that matter, do most writers and artists as they strain against the expressive limits of form; but few have gone so far as Poe, few have so completely accepted these limits as defining their own creative practice. Indeed, it is inaccurate to describe his vision as "tragic," for he simply assumed it. He may even unconsciously have desired it. Poe's pronounced sense of sexual fear and guilt hardly encouraged him to face "originating acts" directly in any form, and perhaps the "aesthetic" suicide pact of "The Assignation"—converting living impulse into marble stasis, sex into death—fulfills both Poe's desire to eradicate sexual reality and the abandoned, drowning child's "bitterness of heart."

In any case, Poe did not generally strive, in spite of his developing organic conception of originality, against the failure of expression, the burial of origins in their expressions. Instead he devoted his literary career to enacting it again and again, in poem after poem, tale after tale. In romance, as Poe developed it, the relation between expression and sentiment, language and spirit, lay in the creative process itself, but it was the nature of this process, as a process *in time*, to sever the very relation it seemed to establish. A similar vision of imaginative expression is implicit in the works of Brown and Irving; it is even more important to Hawthorne and Melville. For Poe, however, the sacrifice of relation ultimately took the form of aesthetic suicide.

Poe's vision of the deadening effect of language was characteristically extreme; his elegies over the death of sentiment always reverberate with a latent death wish. In a less extreme form, this vision was shared by many of his contemporaries. Emerson, for instance, writes in "The Poet":

Language is the archives of history, and, if we must say it, a sort of tomb of the muses. . . . The origin of most of our words is forgotten. . . . Language is fossil poetry. As the limestone of the continent consists of infinite masses of the shells of animalcules, so language is made up of images or tropes, which now, in their secondary use, have long ceased to remind us of their poetic origin.[36]

Poe would certainly have appreciated the "tomb of the muses"! And Emerson's point is very close to Poe: "poetry" has been replaced by, or displaced into, a "language" that no longer "suggests" its "origin." But Emerson is not only less extremely morbid than Poe; he adds something Poe seldom considers. His sense of the mortification of sentiments into words includes a sense of the development of history and culture. In the process of expression he finds a metaphor for the process of history, the movement from vital origins to fossilized culture and institutions.

Emerson was hardly unique in his historical extension of aesthetic theory. Eighteenth-century critics like Hugh Blair had associated poetic effusion with primitive society, just as political theory from Locke to Rousseau and beyond linked the origins of society with the original "state of nature." In *The Marble Faun* Hawthorne would explore the ambiguous relation between artworks and their originals as a means of probing the historical relation between modern civilization and its lost pagan origins. In 1857, in his *English Notebooks*, he wrote, of the English Puritans' protest against Anglican formalism, that they "showed their strength of mind and heart, by . . . lopping away all these externals, into which religious life had first gushed and flowered, and then petrified" (451). In the history of American Puritanism he saw a similar movement from "gushing" to petrifaction. For Melville, too, culture constituted, quite literally, a kind of dissociated or displaced language. *Moby-Dick* begins with an "Etymology." Queequeg and the Whale are covered with hieroglyphs—inscrutable, arabesque tokens of their primitive origins—and, toward the close, Ishmael meditates on the disparity between the archetypal, aboriginal Leviathan and its modern survivor, the petrified fossil whale. Hawthorne and Melville, that is to say, came to see the world and its history under the aspect of artistic creation and petrifaction, as a movement from "spiritual" origins to the repressive rigidity and obscurity of their own time, and in doing so they discovered a rich area of relation between romance and the "real" world—discovered it, paradoxically, in a sense of congruent disrelation in both realms. If literary language seemed out of touch with, and possibly threatened by, the energy from which it sprang, so did the institutions and culture of nineteenth-century America seem to stand in an uneasy relation with their "spiritual" or "revolutionary" origins.

Unlike Emerson, Hawthorne, or Melville, Poe had no sense of history or the past. When he extended the creative metaphor, at the end of his career, he skipped over human history entirely to embrace the saga of cosmic self-creation and self-destruction. The cosmic saga of *Eureka*, while it may strive to include all time, is in no true sense "historical." It scarcely acknowledges the existence of culture or even of human life, and for all its overt concern with astronomy and physics it remains at heart an exploration of aesthetic theory, Poe's true "Philosophy of Composition," relating language and imagination, at last, under the guise of matter and spirit. Poe was obsessed with the problematic disrelation of form and impulse, mask and motive, but he was totally uninterested in human history, in the development of myths, religions, and institutions in historical time. "I think," he wrote to Lowell in 1844, "that human exertion will have no appreciable effect upon humanity. Man is now only more active—not more happy—nor more wise, than he was 6000 years ago. The result will never vary" (256). For Poe there was no significance in historical change; it was another of the many aspects of mundane reality from which he recoiled. The area of relation exploited by Hawthorne and Melville, between the disrelations of romantic expression and those of human history, was thus unavailable to him. He was left in a world of words.

Still, Poe had much to teach Hawthorne and Melville about the aesthetic and psychological disrelation between origins and expressions, between imagination or spirit and the language of romance. He indicated, as forcefully as possible, that the program of romance, followed as strictly as he chose to follow it, led to a dead end. Imagination might be hailed as the "supreme" faculty. It might be liberated from meaning, from didactic and sensual relation. But it remained trapped in a body—alternately "pure" and "suggestive"—of language. Poe's characters create and inhabit a world even more fossilized than Melville's or Hawthorne's, a phenomenal world at once too close and too far from the noumenal energy that produced it. The difference between Poe on the one hand and Hawthorne and Melville on the other is that his phenomenal obscurity is of his or of his characters' own making, not of history's. The effort of Poe's heroes—and, one suspects, of Poe himself—to maintain the arabesque against the ever-threatening power of suggestion remains a matter of aesthetic purity or individual neurosis. It was left for Hawthorne and Melville to find in this aesthetic and psychological predicament a means for understanding the predicament of their culture.

SIX

Truth often finds its way to the mind close-muffled in robes of sleep, and then speaks with uncompromising directness of matters in regard to which we practise an unconscious self-deception, during our waking moments.

HAWTHORNE, "The Birth-mark"

Say what some poets will, Nature is not so much her own ever-sweet interpreter, as the mere supplier of that cunning alphabet, whereby selecting and combining as he pleases, each man reads his own peculiar lesson according to his own peculiar mind and mood.

MELVILLE, *Pierre*

ALLEGORY, SYMBOLISM, AND ROMANCE
Hawthorne and Melville

HAWTHORNE AND MELVILLE, THEIR BERKSHIRE FRIENDSHIP NOTWITHstanding, were clearly quite dissimilar in temperament and style, both personal and literary. And one would hardly have confused either of them with Poe. It is difficult to imagine Poe as surveyor of customs or consul at Liverpool, nor does one easily picture him sailing before the mast on a Pacific whaling cruise. The works of Hawthorne and Melville, moreover, express a sense of history and society totally lacking in Poe's fiction.

Nevertheless, there are intriguing patterns of similarity in the careers and writings of these three mid-century romancers. All three, for instance, associated the literary vocation with some degree of social alienation and perhaps turned to literature to confirm an already established sense of alienation. Hawthorne's sea-captain father died in Surinam when his son was four; Nathaniel grew up in genteel poverty. In "The Custom-House" he records his sense, as a descendant of influential Puritan ancestors, of lost family status, noting "the dreary and unprosperous condition of the race, for many a long year back" (10). After the death of his father, there was a continuous and sometimes galling dependence for support on more prosperous maternal relations. It was in such a context that Hawthorne turned, quite early and with remarkably sustained dedication, to the vocation of romancer.

He first announced his decision, albeit hesitantly and defensively, in an 1821 letter to his mother:

I have not yet concluded what profession I shall have. The being a minister is of course out of the question. I should not think that even you could desire me to choose so dull a way of life. Oh, no, mother, I was not born to vegetate forever in one place, and to live and die as calm and tranquil as—a puddle of water. As to lawyers, there are so

many of them already that one half of them (upon a moderate calculation) are in a state of actual starvation. A physician, then, seems to
be "Hobson's choice"; but yet I should not like to live by the diseases
and infirmities of my fellow-creatures. And it would weigh very
heavily on my conscience, in the course of my practice, if I should
chance to send any unlucky patient "ad inferum," which being inter-
preted is, "to the realms below." Oh that I was rich enough to live
without a profession! What do you think of my becoming an author,
and relying for support upon my pen? Indeed, I think the illegibility
of my hand-writing is very author-like. How proud you would feel to
see my works praised by the reviewers, as equal to the proudest
productions of the scribbling sons of John Bull. But authors are
always poor devils, and therefore Satan may take them.[1]

There is a good deal of adolescent bravado and mock cynicism here, but
the latent aggression against "normal" professions is quite clear, as is the
mixture of envy ("Oh that I was rich enough"), ambition ("How proud
you would feel"), and, possibly, guilt ("Satan may take them").[2]

Like Irving, Hawthorne did eventually turn his literary career into a
means of gaining "solid credit" and "real" status, but he had been a romancer for twenty-five years before The Scarlet Letter brought him anything like real success in 1850. He was a writer for twelve years—the
famous "solitary years" of 1825 to 1837—before seeing his own name
on a publication, the first volume of Twice-Told Tales. The initial
consequence—and, quite possibly, part of the motive—of his vocation was
alienation and solitude. In a well-known letter to Longfellow he described
the twelve "solitary years" of living and writing alone, in his mother's
house in Salem:

> By some witchcraft or other—for I really cannot assign any reason-
> able why and wherefore—I have been carried apart from the main
> current of life, and find it impossible to get back again. Since we last
> met . . . , I have secluded myself from society; and yet I never meant
> any such thing, nor dreamed what sort of life I was going to lead. I
> have made a captive of myself and put me into a dungeon, and now I
> cannot find the key to let myself out—and if the door were open, I
> should be almost afraid to come out. . . . For the last ten years, I have
> not lived, but only dreamed about living.[3]

For all its air of bafflement, this is the letter of a man who always associated writing with guilty isolation and who must have chosen writing,
at least in part, as a way of legitimizing such isolation.

Allan Melville died, bankrupt and delirious, when his son Herman was
twelve.[4] Herman Melville, like his future friend Hawthorne, was raised in

128

an atmosphere of frequently degrading dependence on family friends and relatives. He did not, at first, turn to writing; rather, he worked for his brother, taught school, and on two now-famous occasions went to sea before the mast. He became a writer almost by accident, but by the time of *Mardi* (1849) he had come to associate, and cultivate, the role of romancer as a form of radical protest against social "normalcy," and his writings are filled with explicit expressions of bitter alienation—most notably in the name assumed by his most famous narrator, Ishmael. The early chapters of *Typee* (1846) launch Melville's lifelong protest, as a "gentleman" unjustly deprived of his true status, against arbitrary social authority. In *Redburn* (1849) and *White-Jacket* (1850) this protest becomes a major theme, and in the first chapter of *Moby-Dick* (1851) it is developed simultaneously with the affront of Ishmael's lowly seaman's status to the "sense of honor" befitting one who comes "of an old established family in the land" (14).

Melville and Hawthorne share more with Poe, however, than a sense of alternately guilty and—at least in Melville's case—defiant isolation. In embracing the deviant role of romancer, they also embraced the neurotic dualism of romance—the tension between language and impulse, form and suggestion, repression and expression. Indeed, one might describe many of Hawthorne's tales as Poe stories translated into the third person. Were Young Goodman Brown, in his tale, or Aylmer, in "The Birthmark," to tell their own stories, they would surely sound a good deal like Poe's hysterically compulsive hero-narrators. But the differences between Hawthorne and Poe are more important than the similarities. The translation of psychological romance into the third person marks a crucial step in its development. Up to *The Blithedale Romance* (1852) the voice that addresses us in Hawthorne's fiction, and even in his criticism, is not that of the romancer but that of a "normal" man, one of "us," commenting on the psychological or aesthetic aberrations of others. Hawthorne himself quite perceptively underlines this point in his 1851 preface to *Twice-Told Tales:* "The sketches . . . have none of the abstruseness of idea, or obscurity of expression, which mark the written communications of a solitary mind with itself. They never need translation. It is, in fact, the style of a man of society" (6).[5] One could hardly better describe the essential difference between Hawthorne and Poe. Hawthorne stands at a remove from the romance's confusion of repression and expression. This confusion is neither simply nor entirely his method; it is also, often quite explicitly, his subject. In his fiction, the sacrifice of psychological, social, and aesthetic relation becomes a matter of overt authorial comment and inquiry.

Before *Pierre* (1852), Melville writes exclusively in the first person, but he uses this narrative stance, from *Typee* through *Moby-Dick*, to achieve an effect closer to Hawthorne's discursive third person than to Poe's neurotic immediacy and obscurity. Melville's narrators do not, by and large, displace their guilty alienation into repressive arabesque symbols; instead they at times discuss this alienation quite openly. There is little narrative obscurity, in Poe's neurotic sense, in Melville. In *Mardi*, when Taji's fixation on Yillah and Hautia begins to suggest Rowena and Ligeia, he more or less disappears from his own story, to be replaced by the discursive meditations of King Media, Yoomy, Mohi, and Babbalanja. At the outset of *Moby-Dick*, Ishmael, choosing whaling as a substitute or displacement for his impulse toward suicide, threatens to fall into the trap of Poe-esque compulsion, but he is saved by his own self-knowledge and by his sympathy for Queequeg. It is Ahab—Ishmael's *subject*—who acts out the neurotic logic of his compulsion, projecting his rage onto the Whale. If Ahab's furious effort to murder the Whale recalls, in its way, Roderick Usher's effort to murder his sister, the fact remains that we see this fury at one remove. Ishmael is as interested as Ahab, although in a different fashion, in the meaning of the Whale; but he is also interested, unlike Ahab, in the meaning of the quest for meaning: he is interested in probing beneath the logic of compulsion. In all of Melville's fiction the linear logic of compulsive symbolism—the inexorable displacement of sentiments by words—is balanced against a circular, ruminative curiosity, an effort to recover the noumenal energy in phenomenal order.[6] Which is to say that for Melville, as much as for Hawthorne, the sacrifice of relation becomes a matter for overt narrative comment and inquiry.

The point to be made here is relatively simple but all-important. Hawthorne and Melville are "romancers" in a special sense. While writing romance, they also write *about* romance; and it is in this light that we should read not only their fiction but their critical comments on their own aesthetic practice. It is certainly as true for them as for Irving or Poe that "aesthetic" terms functioned as a displaced, symbolic vocabulary for dealing with buried psychological conflicts at one remove. Many of these conflicts rose out of, or were exacerbated by, the ambiguous status of the romancer in a hostile culture, but Hawthorne and Melville understood and analyzed more fully than their predecessors the operation of romance's displacement of "sentiments" into "words." They combined narrative and dramatic irony not only to enact the sacrifice of relation but to probe its implications. In their work, consequently, the experimental tradition of American romance becomes self-conscious in a way it never had before.

ALLEGORY AND SYMBOLISM

It has become a commonplace of criticism that the essential distinction between Hawthorne and Melville is the distinction between allegory and symbolism.[7] This distinction raises, for the present study, a further question. What is its relevance to the theory and practice of romance in nineteenth-century America? To what extent, and in what ways, were allegorical or symbolic modes amenable to the problems and possibilities of romance expression as developed by Brown, Irving, and Poe and culminating in the works of Hawthorne and Melville?[8]

The best-known and most influential differentiation between allegory and symbolism is Coleridge's, in *The Statesman's Manual*. "An allegory," he writes,

> is but a translation of abstract notions into a picture-language, which is itself nothing but an abstraction from objects of the senses; the principal being more worthless even than its phantom proxy, both alike unsubstantial, and the former shapeless to boot. On the other hand a symbol . . . is characterized by a translucence of the special in the individual, or of the general in the special, or of the universal in the general; above all by the translucence of the eternal through and in the temporal. It always partakes of the reality which it renders intelligible.

This distinction between allegory and symbol, Coleridge adds, is analogous to the distinction between fancy and imagination. Allegories, symptomatic of a modern "hollowness of abstractions," are products "of an unenlivened generalizing understanding"; they are "but empty echoes which the fancy arbitrarily associates with apparitions of matter." Symbols, by contrast, are "living educts of the imagination."[9]

Coleridge's distinction undoubtedly describes a generally typical differentiation between Hawthorne and Melville, but in detail it raises a whole series of problems. For instance, Melville, though chiefly a symbolist, was, as *Mardi* and *The Confidence-Man* attest, hardly averse to allegorizing, and he found his central theme and torment in the ambiguity of that very "translucence of the eternal through and in the temporal" that Coleridge assumes. It is also true that Hawthorne can be described as an allegorist, but he is an allegorist of a very peculiar sort, since he denounces the "unsubstantiality" of the mode every bit as thoroughly as Coleridge. In his 1851 *Twice-Told Tales* preface, for instance, he complains of his own productions that "even in what purport to be pictures of actual life, we have allegory, not always so warmly dressed in its habiliments of flesh and blood, as to be taken into the reader's mind without a shiver" (5).[10]

There are more general problems with Coleridge's distinction as well. As many commentators have noted, his clear bias against allegory has a theoretical tendency to reduce it to something as simple, almost, as "bad" symbolism.[11] In practical epistemological or aesthetic terms, moreover, the allegory/symbolism distinction can lead to as much confusion as the fancy/imagination distinction from which it derives. One should recall the difficulty Poe had in accommodating the latter distinction to his own theory of symbolic imagination and fictional romance. Coleridge's defini- tion of symbolism relies on the very mysticism—the "translucence of the eternal"—that so troubled Poe. Lacking epistemological certainty of this "eternal," how could one finally tell symbolism from allegory, spiritual noumena from merely sensual phenomena?

Hawthorne, if he believed in the eternal, hardly believed that it could be known, that it could be glimpsed by the imagination. He was con- sistently skeptical of the spiritualism of his day. In an 1841 letter to his future wife, urging her not to be mesmerized, he asked: "What delusion can be more lamentable and mischievous, than to mistake the physical and material for the spiritual?"[12] We recall his 1836 warning against confusing the "earthly corpse" with the "celestial soul," and, in an extended 1857 discussion of spiritualism in his *English Notebooks*, he asked himself: "Do I really believe it? Of course not; for I cannot consent to let Heaven and Earth, this world and the next, be beaten up together like the white and yolk of an egg" (617). Moreover, Hawthorne associated imagination not with mystical insight but with cold intellect—with what he calls, in "The Custom-House," "the cold spirituality of the moonbeams" (36).

Melville, the symbolist, is more interested than Hawthorne in the pos- sibilities of mystic insight and imaginative power. Hawthorne's charac- teristic image of imagination is cold moonlight; Melville's is the vital sun. But, like Poe, Melville was skeptical of the creative powers attributed by Coleridge to the "esemplastic" imagination. In chapter 75 of *Mardi*, for instance, he insists that it is not imaginative conceptions that make art- works eternal; it is the materials out of which they are constructed:

> For we are not gods and creators; and the controversialists have de- bated, whether indeed the All-Plastic Power itself can do more than mold. In all the universe is but one original; and the very suns must to their source for their fire; and we Prometheuses must to them for ours. [229]

The Promethean image is distinctively Melvillean, but the first sentence recalls Poe's conviction that "the fancy as nearly creates as the imagina- tion; and neither creates in any respect"—that "all novel conceptions are merely unusual combinations" (10:61–62).

It is with such problems in mind that we must approach the function of allegory and symbolism in the works of Hawthorne and Melville. *Is* Hawthorne's customary practice "but a translation of abstract notions into a picture-language"? And, if so, what is the status of these "abstract no- tions"? What *sorts* of meaning, that is to say, do Hawthorne's allegories point to? What sorts of relation do they encourage us to seek? Do Melville's symbols, by contrast, "always partake of the reality which they render intelligible"? And what *kinds* of meaning, or "reality," do they render intelligible?

For all their differences, Hawthorne and Melville have one thing in common: they both described themselves as romancers. Whether in allegorical meaning or symbolic meaning they would appear to have sought the same thing—the elusive relation, which romance seemed to deny, between language and truth, symbol and reality. Yet in fact Melville's central preoccupation became precisely the absence or ambiguity of such a relation ("Sometimes," shrieks Ahab, "I think there's naught beyond" [144]), and Hawthorne's comments on allegory reveal that he found in the mode, even as he continued to employ it, only another form of the sacrifice of relation between art and life, imagination and actuality. Taken together, Hawthorne and Melville raise the question of whether *either* allegory or symbolism, or any combination of the two, could re-fuse the cable of relation that romance so blithely and insidiously severed.

ALLEGORICAL MODE AND ALLEGORICAL INTENTION

In 1852 E. P. Whipple wrote, in a review of *The Blithedale Romance:* "The characters are not really valuable for what they are, but for what they illustrate."[13] In this phrase he put his finger on what is most essentially allegorical about Hawthorne. Allegory is normally associated with didacticism, but it seems wise, for the moment, to defer the whole question of allegorical *intention*. What matters about allegory *as a mode* is that it is illustrative rather than realistically representational.[14] As a mode of expression it is, as Coleridge puts it, a "translation of abstract notions into a picture-language." The term "allegory," to rehearse the familiar, derives from Greek roots meaning "to speak other than openly." "In the simplest terms," as Angus Fletcher writes, "allegory says one thing and means another." What allegory "says" is not unimportant; it may have a high degree of realistic content. "The whole point of allegory," according to Fletcher, "is that it does not *need* to be read exegetically; it often has a literal level that makes good enough sense all by itself." Hawthorne, for instance, praised *Pilgrim's Progress* for "the human interest with which the author has so strongly imbued the shadowy beings of his allegory."[15] But such interest, whatever its importance in particular allegories, is not what is "allegorical" about them, for that lies in what we might call their apparent "other-meaningness"—in their seeming to point to "abstract notions" behind their "picture-language." Thus Hawthorne characteristically distinguished allegory, at least his own allegories, from the realistic fictions he always claimed to prefer.

In this light, the crucial point about allegory, as an illustrative *mode*, is that it represents reality not immediately but at one remove. In theory, at least, the elements of a realistic fiction—characters, say, or scenes—correspond directly with things in the "real" world—people, say, or places. In an allegorical fiction, by contrast, the correspondence or relation is indirect: the elements represent not things but ideas about things, "abstract notions." These elements may be fleshed out for "human interest," but the essential *relation* in allegory is nevertheless nonrepresentational, intellectual, abstract, illustrative.

For the most part, Hawthorne's practice would appear to fall within these criteria, at least with respect to the *mode* of his fiction. His tales are full of apparently allegorical characters, settings, and, especially, objects: Dr. Rappaccinni, his garden, the Maypole of Merry-Mount, Parson Hooper's black veil, Georgiana's birthmark, the scarlet letter. All of these seem insistently illustrative. In *The Scarlet Letter* we are told of the Beadle, in the opening ceremony, that he "prefigured and represented in his aspect the whole dismal severity of the Puritanic code of law" (52) and, of the scaffold, that "the very ideal of ignominy was embodied and made manifest in this contrivance of wood and iron" (55). These things, in E. P. Whipple's phrase, matter not for what they are, clearly, but for what they illustrate.

The problem, though, is that, while the *mode* of Hawthorne's tales is clearly allegorical, their *intention* is much less clearly so. The author of *The Scarlet Letter* hardly wishes to enforce upon us, as didactic imperatives, either the "dismal severity of the Puritanic code of law" or even "the very ideal of ignominy." These, to quote Coleridge, are the abstract notions for which the Beadle and the scaffold provide the "picture-language." Yet they are not Hawthorne's notions but those of the society about which he is writing. The Beadle and the scaffold, as narrative elements, are allegorical, but they are allegory observed, not allegory imagined. Moreover, what is true of them is generally true in Hawthorne, at least in Hawthorne at his best. His plots are not didactically generated by his efforts to tell us what his symbols mean, what abstract notions they picture forth; they grow instead out of his characters' efforts to find out what the symbols mean or at all events to make them mean something. It is these characters who are, in intention, the allegorists. Moreover, their allegorical tendency almost always leads to a distortion of life, a refusal to face it directly in its full complexity. Hawthorne thus apparently adopts the allegorical mode in order to turn it against allegorical intentions.

This paradoxical aspect of Hawthorne's allegory can be seen in what is probably his best-known tale. "Young Goodman Brown" can be taken as a realistic story of a young man of late seventeenth-century Salem, turned to bitterness by a real or imaginary visit to a witches' sabbath in the woods. This is the story's "human interest," and, as several readers have ably demonstrated, this interest is firmly rooted in actual seventeenth-century New England history.[16] Still, the story's *mode* of dealing with historical reality is not realistic but allegorical. The action is presented without overt attention to motive or causality. The imagery is iconographically evocative rather than verisimilar. The old man whom Brown meets in the woods is less a realized character than the illustration of and spokesman for an idea: the universality of sin. Brown's wife is scarcely characterized or even described; she exists simply as a compound of two illustrative details—her pink ribbons and her archly suggestive name, "Faith." Finally, the witches' nocturnal sabbath, for all its lurid detail, is also primarily allegorical, illustrative of the devil's statement, which comes at its climax: "Evil is the nature of mankind" (88).

If the elements of "Young Goodman Brown" thus seem to serve an illustrative function, this function can hardly be didactic; for while the characters and settings represent ideas, they are Brown's ideas, not Hawthorne's. The old man, for example, is not so much an allegorical devil—Hawthorne's symbol of abstract evil—as he is a projection either of Brown's own growing knowledge of evil or of his unacknowledged impulse toward it. Even the witches' sabbath may be, as its abrupt termination strongly suggests, Brown's own neurotic hallucination. Several critics have discussed the importance of hallucination and projection in "Young Goodman Brown," finding at the center of the tale not a moral—authority figures are "evil"—but a struggle between Brown's conscious reverence for figures of authority and his unconscious impulse to discredit them by imputing to them his own "sinful" urges.[17] We should pay special attention to what such readings suggest about the status of allegorical intention in Hawthorne's allegories. The story's elements do illustrate aspects of Brown's internal psychological conflict, and in this they are perfectly conventional (as in the temptation of Spenser's Redcross by Giant Despayre). What is not conventional is that in "Young Goodman Brown" the illustrative or allegorical *quality* of the symbols is symptomatic of Brown's psychological condition. He is torn between two rigidly "allegorical" possibilities: either humankind is "good" or it is "evil"; no other *kind* of meaning is possible for him. Abstract notions here, such as "good" and "evil," are not meanings but essential ingredients in a dramatic situation. "Evil is the nature of mankind" is the devil's meaning, a projection of Brown's self-conscious purity, a notion he finally comes to accept consciously as *his* meaning. What the story is "about" is not the meaning but the acceptance. Brown accepts abstract, allegorical meaning as a displacement for unacknowledgeable impulses—as a refuge from more personal insight.

Hawthorne is a peculiarly aloof sort of allegorist, concerned not with what reality means but with the ways his characters attribute meaning to reality or impose meaning on it. It is his characters who turn life into a picture language by making it illustrate ideas about life, as Brown must make Faith either "good" or "evil." It is in this sense that Brown is an allegorist. And so are many of Hawthorne's characters. What is the much-discussed "Unpardonable Sin," after all, but a kind of allegorical inclination to substitute illustrative meaning for true, realistic sympathy or self-knowledge? So Ethan Brand succumbs to "the Idea that possessed his life" (99), and it is thus that Young Goodman Brown, like most of Hawthorne's Puritans, ends up being trapped by an allegory of his own making.[18] Indeed, the besetting sin of Hawthorne's Puritans—and the one he most frequently scrutinizes, particularly in dealing with the second and third generations—is their insistence on allegorizing experience into rigid "iron" forms, cut off from life and suppressive of it. Through its anti-allegorical manipulation of the allegorical mode, "Young Goodman Brown" illustrates this allegorical tendency in its historical subject. "Evil" may or may not be the "nature of mankind," but there is no doubt, as the final sentence declares of Brown, that "his dying hour was gloom" (90).

ALLEGORY AND ROMANCE

Coleridge's attack on allegory in *The Statesman's Manual* is launched not so much against the literary mode as against a modern habit of thought of which the mode is symptomatic: the subordination of reality to "the hollowness of abstractions."[19] It seems to be the paradoxical intention of Hawthorne's allegories to launch a similar attack. His skepticism about allegory, about its "insubstantiality," is not confined to apologetic prefaces. It constitutes one of the major themes of his fiction. But the mode of this fiction remains allegorical in spite of its ironic self-consciousness and even, in one sense, as a result of this self-consciousness. The idea that abstract notions violate life is itself, after all, an abstract notion. An anti-allegorical allegory is still an allegory—self-reflexive but not expressive. We must ask, then, whether Hawthorne's illustrative symbols serve for him, and not just for his characters, any expressive function. What, besides discredited abstraction, lies behind his picture language? This question moves us from considerations of allegory to considerations of romance—or, rather, to a consideration of the relationship between them.

It is often difficult, however, to distinguish between allegory and romance. Both involve a departure from objective mimesis, an abstraction of actual experience. In romance, as opposed to allegory, there is, in theory, nothing necessarily symbolical in such abstraction; one can idealize without symbolizing. Nevertheless, to "idealize" implies a connection between the world of romance and some body of ideas. Much romance, as Northrop Frye observes, displays a conscious or unconscious "tendency to allegory." "The romancer," Frye writes, "does not attempt to create 'real people' so much as stylized figures which expand into psychological archetypes.... That is why the romance so often radiates a glow of subjective intensity that the novel lacks, and why a suggestion of allegory is constantly creeping in around its fringes."[20] In the hands of such self-conscious American romancers as Brown, Irving, and Poe, romance often became, as much as allegory, a way of saying one thing and meaning another, a struggle between outer language or symbol and hidden meaning or impulse.

Still, one can draw a crucial distinction, in theory, between this sort of romance and what we normally call allegory. They point to different kinds of meaning. As practiced by Brown, Irving, and Poe, romance pointed increasingly to subjective, nonrational, nonverbal levels of experience—to what Poe called "impossible conceptions." This is why the distortion inherent in language plays so important a part in nineteenth-century discussions of romance. Allegory, by contrast, appeals normally to objective ideas, *possible* conceptions, abstract notions. Instead of striving to reveal the hidden or inexpressible, it embodies ideas already verbalized. As in the case of allegorical processions of Virtues or Vices, what allegory *means* is as "verbal" as what it *says*.

Hawthorne seems, as a romancer, to appeal to both allegorical and romance kinds of meaning, to both possible and impossible conceptions. In "The Custom-House" he locates romance in the "neutral territory ... where the Actual and the Imaginary may meet, and each imbue itself with the nature of the other" (36). But what he conceives the nature of the "Imaginary" to be remains unclear. Are imaginary ideas abstract, in Coleridge's sense? Or are they subjective and nonverbal, in the tradition of Brown, Irving, and Poe? According to one prevalent view of Hawthorne, he sees imaginary ideas as abstract, conceptual, platonic, essentially verbal—as generalizations from experience.[21] His meanings, in this sense, are thus basically allegorical. But the equation of Hawthornesque romance with conceptually objective allegory stands against a good deal of contrary evidence. In his prefaces Hawthorne characteristically links romance not with objective conceptions but with subjective fantasies. In "The Custom-House," for instance, he describes romance in terms of the romancer's ability to "dream strange things, and make them look like truth" (36). In *The Blithedale Romance*, the form provides "a theatre, ... where the creatures of [the author's] brain may play their phantasmagorical antics" (1). The implications here are hardly platonic.

One finds the same sort of objective/subjective confusion in the ambiguity of Hawthorne's symbols. What is ambiguous is not just what they mean but what *sort* of meaning they convey. Brown's meanings, in "Young Goodman Brown," are clearly abstract conceptions. To the reader, however, the symbols Brown reads allegorically seem to function, additionally, as sublimations of less articulate sentiments. Parson Hooper's black veil may be, as he seems to claim, symbolic of a universal conceptual abstraction: "secret sin." But it may also—as Poe thought,[22] and as many of Hooper's parishioners surmise—express a particular subjective guilt that Hooper cannot openly acknowledge. Owen Warland's mechanical butterfly, in "The Artist of the Beautiful," may represent a platonic conception, an ideal generalization from nature. Owen seeks, we are told, "a beauty that should attain to the ideal which Nature has proposed to herself, in all her creatures, but has never taken pains to realize" (466). But the butterfly seems also to be an expression of Owen's subjective fantasies. "In the secret of that butterfly, and in its beauty," he explains to Annie Hovenden, whom he has lost in his pursuit of this beauty, "is represented the intellect, the imagination, the sensibility, the soul, of an Artist of the Beautiful!" (471). Here the butterfly is not the illustration of an abstract idea of perfection; it is rather a projection of the mind of the artist himself.

One might object to this distinction that, since Owen is an artist, the content of his imagination is precisely a sense of nature ideally generalized; but this objection misses the deepest implications of Owen's overtly deviant "sensibility," for behind the butterfly's ambiguity lie two quite different conceptions of the artistic process, even two different stories. The first story is allegorical, telling of an imaginative artist's retreat from various illustrations of the notion of physical reality: a muscular blacksmith, marriage to a "real" woman, a "real" career of useful industry. Through the sacrifice of such mundane "reality" he purifies himself in order to give form to an abstract ideal, one that transcends both the world's reality and the reality of its own physical embodiment. The first story is thus an allegory illustrating the superiority of ideal art to normal life.

The second story, however, tells of a young man who protects himself from his own impulses through idealistic rationalization but who is in fact terrified by reality and especially by sex; he manages to escape into art and there express his repressed and guilty fantasies in the sublimated, rationalized form of artistic "beauty": "If my labor be thus thwarted," Owen complains when Annie interrupts him, "there will come vague and unsatisfied dreams, which will leave me spiritless to-morrow" (452). Is it to these "dreams" or is it to his ideal of "beauty" that Owen's butterfly gives expression?[23] Are we to read the story allegorically, accepting his idealism as "true"? Or do we take the story's allegorical meaning as functioning, for Owen, as a kind of displacement of forbidden fantasy? In "The Artist of the Beautiful," it appears, conceptual and thoroughly subjective meaning, rational and irrational ideas, allegory and romance, exist simultaneously in the same literary structure.

A similar doubleness of meaning permeates "The Birth-mark," whose protagonist, Aylmer, has much in common with Owen. In his "idealism" he too sets out, as he puts it, to correct "what Nature left imperfect, in her fairest work!" (41). Instead of spurning Georgiana, as Owen spurns Annie for his "ideal," Aylmer marries and then kills her. But the motivation is the same in both cases: Owen and Aylmer commit the Unpardonable Sin of allegory, subjugating life—quite literally, in "The Birth-mark"—to abstract notions. Yet Hawthorne doesn't simply ironically undercut the allegorizing impulse; he also suggests its hidden motive and function. Aylmer, for all his idealistic perfectionism, is, like Owen, troubled by dreams, one of which is reported to us:

> He had fancied himself, with his servant Aminadab, attempting an operation for the removal of the birth-mark. But the deeper went the knife, the deeper sank the Hand, until at length its tiny grasp appeared to have caught hold of Georgiana's heart; whence, however, her husband was inexorably resolved to cut or wrench it away. [40]

The dream recalled, Aylmer sits in Georgiana's presence "with a guilty feeling" (40). Why the dream makes him guilty he refuses to investigate, but Hawthorne adds a crucial comment: "Truth," he writes, "often finds its way to the mind close-muffled in robes of sleep, and then speaks with uncompromising directness of matters in regard to which we practise an unconscious self-deception, during our waking moments" (40). What these "matters" are remains, to Aylmer, obscure, but in its grotesque sublimation of sexuality his dream recalls Lancelot Canning's *Mad Trist* in Poe's "Fall of the House of Usher"; like Canning's romance, it enacts a crucial symbolic displacement, transforming sexual penetration and guilt into grisly torture and murder.[24]

Read in this light, Aylmer's whole experiment acquires an added significance—a significance deeper than the overtly allegorical meaning of his tale. While Aylmer may fail tragically to achieve his "ideal" aspirations, he nevertheless succeeds perfectly in gratifying the repressed desires adumbrated in his dream. Aylmer is apparently two very different kinds of character: a misguided but virtuous idealist, enforcing his conscious abstract notions upon reality, and a compulsive neurotic, using allegorical "idealism" to sublimate the far from virtuous impulses he cannot consciously know or openly name. As an overt allegory, "The Birth-mark" is frequently compared to Poe's "Oval Portrait," which it does resemble; but as an allegorically veiled expression of unconscious fantasies—as a romance of "spiritual" murder—its affinities lie more with a tale like "Berenice." In motive and result, Aylmer's obsession with the birthmark corresponds precisely to Egaeus's obsession with his cousin's teeth.[25]

The symbolic duplicity of "The Birth-mark" helps clarify the relationship between allegory and romance meaning in Hawthorne's work. As allegory, the tale rests on the relation between Aylmer's emblematic experiment and his abstract notion of "purity." The meaning here is allegorical because the ideas illustrated by the emblems are abstract or conceptual. Yet these abstract meanings are themselves symbols, for behind them is another set of meanings—not abstract but vague, nonverbal rather than verbal. In short, allegorical meanings, abstract notions, serve essentially the same function for Hawthorne's characters that arabesque obscurity serves for Poe's: they are the veil by whose means the inexpressible is both masked and shadowed forth. It is true, in Coleridge's phrase, that Aylmer's allegorical experiment is but a translation of abstract notions into a picture language; but these "verbal" notions are themselves symbolic, for behind their allegorical superficiality lurks the insidious suggestion of a subjective, nonverbal depth—the realm of romance. Here, then, is what "The Birth-mark" suggests about Hawthorne's peculiar practice of allegory: that behind the allegorical *mode* of his fiction lurks something like the *intention* of the romancer. Or we might say that the form of the sacrifice of relation, in Hawthorne's fiction, is the dissociation of mode and intention.

This analysis of Hawthorne's procedure, resting on the comparably neurotic aspects of allegorical and romance disrelation, may seem over-subtle. Aylmer may be both allegorical character and compulsive neurotic, but this doubleness is quite possibly a general and inevitable characteristic of allegory. Allegorical characters are, as it were, compelled to act out apparently compulsive patterns of "irrational" behavior. They cannot acknowledge their motives because they do not properly have any; they can act only as agents of the ideas that give them being. The abstract Greed, Lust, Gluttony, and the like that drive them are experienced not as motives but as ideas of motives.[26] If allegorical characters inevitably behave as if their motives were repressed—as if their actions were sublimations of these motives—it may be argued that there is no valid basis for distinguishing between romance meaning and allegorical meaning, or at least no basis for using this distinction to differentiate the mode and the intention of Hawthorne's fiction.

This argument, however, ignores a crucial fact: namely, that Hawthorne, as his direct narrative comments make clear, was fully aware of the analogy between the form of allegory and the form of obsessive-compulsive behavior. He did not have the terminology of the Freudian, but the analogy between allegory and compulsion is one of his principal themes: allegory is the Unpardonable Sin. Thus Aylmer is not simply compelled by "the tyrannizing influence acquired by one idea over his mind"; he is also filled with a sense of "the lengths which he might find in his heart to go, for the sake of giving himself peace" (40). And, in *The Scarlet Letter*, Chillingworth goes so far as to rationalize his behavior explicitly both as a kind of fate, or compulsion, and as a kind of allegory. "It has all," he assures Hester, "been a dark necessity. Ye that have wronged me are not sinful, save in a kind of typical illusion; neither am I fiend-like. . . . It is our fate" (174). Hawthorne's emblems, we must remember, generally illustrate not his ideas but those of his characters. Thus the distinction between romance and allegory, in his fiction, is precisely the distinction between his own knowledge of motive (however darkly "veiled") and the allegorical rationalizations of his characters. In the parallels between allegory and compulsive behavior and in the distance of both from true repressed meaning or motive he found a means for turning allegory to the purposes of romance. In the overtly "verbal" relation of conventional allegory he discovered the essential disrelation of experimental romance—the disrelation between words and sentiments, verbal meaning and nonverbal suggestion, notions and dreams.

Hawthorne's characters insist on the rationality and universality of their abstract notions. Goodman Brown has his "evil," Parson Hooper his "secret sin," Owen and Aylmer their "beauty" and "perfection." These characters pay little heed to their dreams unless, like Goodman Brown, they can rationalize or allegorize them; but as Hawthorne writes, in that crucial passage in "The Birth-mark," "Truth often finds its way to the mind close-muffled in robes of sleep, and then speaks with uncompromising directness of matters in regard to which we practise an unconscious self-deception, during our waking moments" (40). It is just such "truth" that lurks suggestively behind the abstract "self-deceptions" of characters like Brown, Aylmer, and Owen and behind the "allegorical" meanings of their tales. In Hawthorne's allegory at its best, the allegorical surfaces function, like the overtly "pure" language of Poe's tales, as a simultaneously repressive and suggestive mask of "falsehood," concealing the "truths" of dream-romance.

According to Charles Feidelson, Hawthorne was limited by his concern with the opposition between imagination and actuality: "He did not see so clearly that this opposition was transected by another, more debilitating conflict—between the symbolist and the allegorist." In fact, however, this debilitating conflict is a central concern, perhaps *the* central concern, of Hawthorne's best fiction. It is true, as Feidelson writes of Hawthorne, that "symbolism at once fascinated and horrified him" and that he frequently recoiled from its imperative to explore the depths of nonverbal consciousness. Thus the future author of that remarkable passage about "truth" and "unconscious self-deception" could write to his fiancée: "It seems to me that my dreams are generally about fantasies, and very seldom about what I really think and feel." As Feidelson puts it, Hawthorne knew that "allegory was safe because it preserved the conventional distinction between thought and things."[27] But Hawthorne also knew where allegory came from, what unconscious needs it served, how it enabled the romancer "to dream strange things, and make them look like truth." If Hawthorne, as I suggested at the outset, did not so much write romance as write about it, it was this knowledge of the irrational sources of rational allegory that enabled him to do so.

SYMBOLISM AND ROMANCE

"Allegory was safe," as Feidelson puts it, "because it preserved the conventional distinction between thought and things." It preserved, that is to say, the orthodox Common Sense distinction between illusion and reality, imagination and judgment. Symbolism, by contrast, was dangerous because it refused to recognize this distinction. The symbol, as Coleridge defined it, "always partakes of the reality which it renders intelligible."[28] To the symbolist, imagined entities are as "real" as—or more "real" than—objective entities; indeed, the latter can be properly conceived only through imagination, since they are otherwise but superficial sense impressions. Reality is not in what is known, as Common Sense philosophy insisted, but in the act of knowing. What the symbolist recognizes is that all perception is symbolic, all knowledge is imaginative, and the imaginative is therefore neither necessarily nor simply fictitious. It is in this sense that Melville is described, in contrast to Hawthorne, as a symbolist.[29]

The description may accurately characterize Melville's practice, even though Hawthorne seems, at least in intention, to have been more of a symbolist than has generally been recognized. But for a study of American romance symbolism raises a central problem. For what is the relationship between symbolism and romance? It might seem that the two terms are virtually synonymous. To the extent that symbolism legitimizes imagination, it would seem to legitimize romance as well.

The problem, though, with equating symbolism and romance is that American romance grew out of and in a sense relied on the very distinction the symbolist denies—which is what James means in speaking of the romancer's sacrifice of relation. Even in the 1840s the appeal of the role of "romancer," in its more radical implications, seems to have had a good deal to do with deviance, with the rigidly dualistic separation of the "artist" from social "normalcy"; moreover, at the heart of the theory and practice of self-conscious, experimental American romance lay a virtually neurotic dualism, one that distinguished imagination from judgment, energy from order, noumenal suggestion from phenomenally obscure expression. American romance advertised not the Coleridgean "translucence" of meaning in expression but their apparent dissociation. In 1848 Melville announced his decision to "out with the Romance." We must ask if what he meant by the term was what modern critics mean by "symbolism." If so, how did he adapt this symbolism to the rigidly dualistic tradition established by his self-conscious American predecessors?

Hawthorne's letters and prefaces contain scarcely a single justification of the life of imagination or of its literary products. They consistently concur, indeed, in the low conventional estimate of imaginative literary vocation. Melville, by contrast, formulates in his critical and personal writings a full-fledged rationale for his deviant activity. He openly defies those he calls, in his 1850 review of Hawthorne's *Mosses from an Old Manse*, "the superficial skimmer[s] of pages" (418). He thus chooses, at the very beginning of the *Mosses* review, one of the few sentences Hawthorne ever wrote that might be construed as an overt rationale for artistic imagination. In the second paragraph of his essay he quotes the final sentence of "The Artist of the Beautiful": "When the Artist rises high enough to achieve the Beautiful, the symbol by which he makes it perceptible to mortal senses becomes of little value in his eyes, while his spirit possesses itself in the enjoyment of the reality" (400). The imaginary, in other words, is more real than "reality" itself. As Melville would write of works of fiction in *The Confidence-Man*, they contain "more reality, than real life itself can show" (158).

It has been argued with some justice that Melville projected his own ambitions onto Hawthorne, that "Hawthorne and His *Mosses*" is mainly Melville's advertisement for himself. This line of argument can be overdone. However atypical this sentence may be of Hawthorne, he did write it, and Melville was one of the first readers to sense Hawthorne's power of dark suggestion. Nevertheless, by quoting Hawthorne's sentence out of context, Melville does shift its emphasis. What is in Hawthorne's tale a heavily ironic conclusion becomes for Melville an unambiguous manifesto for the truth of imagination. Melville would openly declare those buried truths that Hawthorne only hints at and in regard to which his characters practice "an unconscious self-deception."

What these truths were Melville began to discover as he was writing *Mardi*—at the point when, as he wrote to John Murray, he abandoned his "narrative of *facts*" in order to write a "romance" in "downright earnest" (70).[30] His process of discovery and his new conception of literary truth are described twice in *Mardi* itself. In chapter 180 the philosopher Babbalanja describes the methods of the poet Lombardo in composing his great *Kostanza:* "When Lombardo set about his work, he knew not what it would become. He did not build himself in with plans; he wrote right on; and so doing, got deeper and deeper into himself; and like a resolute traveler, plunging through baffling woods, at last was rewarded for his toils" (595). Earlier, in chapter 169 ("Sailing On"), Melville breaks through the voice of his supposed narrator, Taji, to describe what is happening to him as he writes: "Oh, reader, list! I've chartless voyaged. With compass and the lead, we had not found these Mardian Isles. Those who boldly launch, cast off all cables" (556). The last phrase is intriguingly similar to James's image for the romancer's sacrifice of relation, but Melville does not cast off all cables merely, in James's phrase, "for the fun of it." He has a deeper purpose, the voyage of discovery that he compares to the voyage of Christopher Columbus:

> That voyager steered his bark through seas, untracked before; ploughed his own path mid jeers; though with a heart that oft was heavy with the thought, that he might only be too bold, and grope where land was none.
> So I. . . .
> But this new world here sought, is stranger far than his, who stretched his vans from Palos. It is the world of mind; wherein the wanderer may gaze round, with more of wonder than Balboa's band roving through the golden Aztec glades. [556–57]

To cast off all cables, then, was to embark on a voyage of discovery into "the world of mind"—into that realm of unfettered subjective introversion and metaphysical speculation whose exploration eventually destroyed Melville's career as a professional writer.

Increasingly, in the course of *Mardi*, the philosopher Babbalanja becomes the chief guide of this chartless voyage, and his ruminations reveal the close connection between "the world of mind" and Melville's rash decision to "out with the Romance." At the end of chapter 93 there is a crucial argument—foreshadowing those that follow the various interpolated tales in *The Confidence-Man*—over a legend just recited by Yoomy, the poet. According to the historian, Mohi, Yoomy's legend is hardly "credible." One recalls the objections of various auditors to the stories in Irving's *Tales of a Traveller*. With all the dogmatic fervor of Common Sense orthodoxy, Mohi insists that Yoomy "has not spoken the truth." To which Babbalanja replies:

> Truth is in things, and not in words: truth is voiceless. . . . And I, Babbalanja, assert, that what are vulgarly called fictions are as much realities as the gross mattock of Dididi, the digger of trenches; for things visible are but conceits of the eye: things imaginative, conceits of the fancy. If duped by one, we are equally duped by the other. [283–84]

Here already, as early as *Mardi,* is the metaphysical rationale for romance—the rationale Hawthorne never saw fit to declare openly. Fiction is at least as "real" as so-called "fact." Even as late as 1849 such a statement—complete with the condescension of "vulgarly"—was hardly calculated to ingratiate its author with critics or readers.[31] Before Melville in America, perhaps only Poe had been so willing to declare openly, against the heritage of Puritanism and Common Sense rationalism, the epistemological and metaphysical validity of imagination and romance.

Poe's rationale had rapidly run into problems, and even Babbalanja's defense of Yoomy is a bit ominous, since it does not so much assert the truth of fiction as it asserts the fictionality of what Melville's contemporaries took to be truth. Fictions are as much realities as gross matter precisely because gross matter is *not* real. It is not that romance is real; "reality," rather, is a species of romance: "If duped by one, we are equally duped by the other." The Melville of *Mardi* and of the *Mosses* review offers a welcome challenge—welcome to us, if not to his contemporary readers—to the conventional distinction between thought and thing, imaginary and actual. But even as he followed his chartless voyage into the world of imagination, Melville came more and more to recognize why his culture regarded such voyages with fear and hostility; for he discovered that the orthodox moralists, however naive their epistemology, had been right about what they didn't even know enough to call symbolism. In any case, Melville could not get far enough from their assumptions fully to reject them. Imagination did threaten psychological and social order. To admit the claims of romance was to open the doors to nihilism. If, for romance, subjective states could become valid objects of mimesis, if no subjective state was certifiably more true than any other, and if truth could only be known subjectively, then the chaos of psychological relativism was just around the corner. If "truth" was a fiction and nothing was truer than fiction, then *nothing,* quite literally, *was* the truth. It is small wonder that Evert Duyckinck attacked *Moby-Dick* for its "piratical running down of creeds and opinions."[32]

Indeed, Melville's reviewers generally reacted to his books along the predictable lines of Common Sense realism. A favorable review of *White-Jacket* in the *Knickerbocker* magazine gave thanks that "the author of 'Typee'" was, after *Mardi,* "on the right ground at last," since the story is told "without the aid of much imagination, but with a daguerreotype-like naturalness of description"; but Duyckinck denounced *Pierre*—and his review was typical of contemporary critical response—as "a mystic romance, in which are conjured up unreal nightmare-conceptions, a confused phantasmagoria of distorted fancies and conceits, ghostly abstractions and fitful shadows." Its author "is certainly but a spectre of the substantial author of 'Omoo' and 'Typee.'" As to Melville's future work,

Duyckinck continued, "let its foundation be firmly based on *terra firma*, or, if in the heavens, let us not trust our common sense to the flight of any waxen pinion."[33] What is more important than this critical hostility, however, is the fact that at least a part of Melville agreed with its premises. In 1849, for instance, he wrote to Duyckinck about the insanity of the writer Charles Fenno Hoffman: "He was just the man to go mad—imaginative, voluptuously inclined, poor, unemployed, in the race of life distanc^d by his inferiors, unmarried—without a port or haven in the universe to make" (83). This last metaphor is significant. Like the romancer of "Sailing On" or like Bulkington in "The Lee Shore" in *Moby-Dick*, Hoffman has cast off all cables. In this case, however, the result is not self-discovery but madness. Even Babbalanja, in *Mardi*, is intermittently possessed by his demon, Azzageddi, and no wonder: for the discovery that fact was fiction, that "reality" itself had cast off all cables, was hardly calculated to encourage common-sense stability. As Melville would write of imaginative truths in "Hawthorne and His *Mosses*": "it were all but madness for any good man, in his own proper character, to utter, or even hint of them" (407).

For Melville, then, the imagination clearly undermined conventional conceptions of reality, including the distinction between imagination and judgment, but it did not so clearly supply anything to take their place. In the *Mosses* review Melville speaks of "the sane madness of vital truth" (407). This association of insanity with superior insight was a staple of Romanticism, but Melville's later writings increasingly register his doubts about both the sanity and vitality of such insight. In *The Confidence-Man*, a beggar, apparently based on Poe,[34] appears, "peddling a rhapsodical tract"—apparently *Eureka;* yet "one glimmering peep of reason" suggests to him "a torment of latent doubts at times, whether his addled dream of glory were true" (167). The same doubts dominate the account of literary composition in book 25 of *Pierre*, which takes up the significant images of *Mardi* only to subvert them. From "Sailing On" we still have the chartless voyage but not the discovery: "His soul's ship foresaw the inevitable rocks, but resolved to sail on, and make a courageous wreck" (339). We still have that Columbus who "ploughed his own path mid jeers," but there is no longer an America to discover; he can only return insult for insult: "Now he gave jeer for jeer, and taunted the apes that jibed him" (339). Like Lombardo, Pierre writes "deeper and deeper into himself," but he never emerges from the "baffling woods" to be "rewarded for his toils":

For the more and the more that he wrote, and the deeper and the deeper that he dived, Pierre saw the everlasting elusiveness of Truth; the universal lurking insincerity of even the greatest and purest written thoughts. Like knavish cards, the leaves of all great books were covertly packed. He was but packing one set the more. [339]

146

The falsity of "fact," Melville came more and more to recognize, was hardly a guarantee of the truth of fiction. The only truth revealed by the diving imagination, finally, was of "the everlasting elusiveness of Truth," "the lurking insincerity of all things"—*including* products of the imagination.

The disillusionment so evident in *Pierre* no doubt reflects Melville's exhaustion and bitterness following the failure of *Moby-Dick*, particularly the failure of readers to understand or appreciate what he was doing; but we can overstress the extent to which Melville's disillusionment, either with his audience or with his form, marked a change in his basic ideas and attitudes. His hostility toward the reading public, rampant in the late works, was present from the beginning—however latent or intermittent[35]—and most of the elements of his later metaphysical and aesthetic "despair" are already implicit and even explicit in *Mardi*'s ruminations on the truth of imagination and fiction. There is no great leap from the assertion that "things visible are but conceits of the eye" to the relativistic nihilism of "The Whiteness of the Whale," where Ishmael advises that "willful travellers in Lapland" might better wear "colored and coloring glasses upon their eyes" than go blind staring into the "truth" of whiteness, its "colorless, all-color of atheism" (170, 169). The idea that things visible or imaginative are conceits and that, "if duped by one, we are equally duped by the other," might well stand as the motto of *The Confidence-Man;* and Babbalanja's notion that "truth is voiceless" reappears at the beginning of book 14 of *Pierre:* "Silence," writes the narrator, "is the only Voice of our God" (204). Although Babbalanja means to defend the truth of literature, his statement that "truth is in things, and not in words" implies the question raised explicitly in *Pierre:* "How can man get a Voice out of Silence?" (208)—a question every bit as dualistic as Edgar Huntly's fear that "in proportion as I gain power over words, shall I lose dominion over sentiments" (5).

What must be recognized is that Melville was as radically torn as Hawthorne, although in a different way, between "translucence" and "translation," between the unifying vision of symbolism and the dualistic thinking of rationalism. In Hawthorne, the overt mode of allegory is subverted or at least qualified by the suggestive, symbolistic undercurrent of romance. In Melville, an overtly symbolistic strategy is qualified by an abiding sense of dualistic division. In one of its possible meanings Babbalanja's assertion that "truth is in things, and not in words" would have met with hearty concurrence from Melville's most stringent critics. Melville may have proclaimed the superior truth of imagined reality, and he may have defined fiction, in the *Mosses* review, as "the great Art of Telling the Truth" (408), yet throughout his fiction, especially from *Pierre* on, there runs an elaborate demonstration of the dangers of fiction and imagination every bit as urgent as the warnings sounded by American moralists in the decades before Melville's birth. The crucial difference is that Melville, in his adaptation of the moralists' condemnation of fictionality, does not restrict the indictment to works of art. Even objects of normal perception, he came increasingly to believe, are artificial. "All visible objects," Ahab preaches to Starbuck, "are but as pasteboard masks" (144). When it learned to exploit the perception that "reality" itself is a fiction, American romance came at last to maturity. Hawthorne arrived at this perception by exploring the psychological and social duplicity of allegorical thinking. Melville reached the same point by attempting to act out, literally and sincerely, the imperatives of symbolism.

ROMANCE AND ROMANTICISM

The experimental tradition of self-consciously fictional romance came to maturity in America in the 1840s and 1850s, at the height of American Romanticism, but it retained the marks of its origin in the dualistic rationalism of Common Sense philosophy. Its maturation was less a matter of shifting assumptions than of broadening implications. Self-conscious American romance, which began in a radically deviant conception of fictionality and soon took to experimenting with the possibility of making imaginary or irrational subjective states the objects of literary mimesis, eventually became a forum or paradigm for the widest sort of metaphysical inquiry. Romantic spiritualism, as I noted in chapter 5, offered to romance the ultimate project and justification of spiritual mimesis. Romance might become, like Emersonian Nature, a symbol not just of irrational imagination but of spirit. Yet the central problem of American romance—its abiding testimony to its Common Sense origins—had always been the radical dissociation of expression and impulse, symbol and suggestion. This dissociation was never overcome. Rather, as romance enlarged its scope from the expression of psychological states to the embodiment of spiritual truths, its practitioners broadened the scope of romance's essential quality of disrelation by finding an analogous disrelation in their world. Experimental romance emerged, in America, in response to Common Sense rationalism. It became at last, in the works of Poe, Hawthorne, and Melville, a means for scrutinizing the disrelations or dissociations beneath the aesthetic, epistemological, and metaphysical assumptions of American Romanticism.

It should be clear by now that romance in America was less a genre than a set of attitudes or problems whose recurrence in the work of some of our best fiction writers before the Civil War constitutes something like a tradition—a tradition at once formal and intellectual. This is why the study of American romance always finds itself torn between aesthetic theory and intellectual history. For Hawthorne and Melville and their contemporaries, such things as romance, allegory, and symbolism presented not only modes to be appropriated but dilemmas to be faced; they were not so much aesthetic givens as metaphors or models for more general problems of knowledge and belief. The literary theorist may quite properly object to so loose a usage of his critical terminology, noting how it forces us to shift between theoretical questions of literary mode and intellectual-historical questions of epistemology, psychology, and even theology. To this objection one can only reply that the works of Hawthorne and Melville, and the critical terms by which we normally describe them, have their roots and their fullest meaning in the exigencies, the cultural and intellectual crises, of a particular time and place and that, moreover, the investigation of these roots—of the congruence between aesthetic and cultural dissociation—was for Hawthorne and Melville a major and explicit concern.

It is not a primary aim of this study, in any case, to contribute directly to a general theoretical vocabulary for discriminating among symbolic modes of expression. I have assumed that a "pure" vocabulary is not what we most need in order to understand the curious nature of American romance. Our romancers, notably Irving and Poe, tended to use critical discourse itself as a mode of displaced, symbolic expression, and they recognized a similar displacement in the conventional critical discourse of their culture. As I noted in chapter 1, the dominant definitions of romance at the beginning of the nineteenth century had far less to do with generic discrimination between the romance and the novel than with the more fundamental distinction between romance and "reality." It was thus inevitable that problems of literary relation should become inextricably bound up with larger questions of psychological and spiritual significance, with the meaning of "reality" itself. It is no coincidence that the romancer's sacrifice of relation became a crucial issue at a time when cultural and cosmic reality seemed equally adrift. The symbolic or allegorical strategies through which Melville and Hawthorne explored the implications of this drift were themselves deeply implicated in the mid-century crisis of belief in the spiritual significance of all outward phenomena—not just imaginative language but "all visible objects."

Indeed, it was this same crisis of belief that led Coleridge to distinguish between allegory and symbolism in the first place. His distinction does not grow out of a desire to construct a "pure" anatomy of literary modes but out of a sense of spiritual malaise. What is wrong with allegory, for Coleridge, is precisely the same thing that is wrong with Westervelt's spiritualist exhibition in *The Blithedale Romance:* it is but "a delusive show of spirituality, yet really imbued throughout with a cold and dead materialism" (200). Symbolism, by contrast and by definition, is *genuinely* spiritual. In a world whose spiritual meaning seemed "allegorically" delusive, that is to say, Coleridge turned to the notion of symbolism as a means of salvaging some vestige of threatened faith. Coleridge's distinction ultimately depends upon the different kinds of truth to which symbolism and allegory point. To return to *The Stateman's Manual*, the truths of symbolism are "eternal" or divine, those of allegory merely "temporal"— "apparitions of matter." Or, to use the quasi-psychological, neo-Kantian terms by whose means Romantics secularized the old theological distinctions, the truths of symbolism derive from imagination or reason, those of allegory from the fancy, from the "unenlivened . . . understanding." [36] More technically: the abstract notions of allegory are, in Lockean terms, complex ideas, mere abstractions of sense experience and hence nontranscendent. The truths of symbolism, however, are direct a priori insights or intuitions into the spiritual realm—simple ideas of eternal things. This is why romance, through symbolism, could be proposed as a mode of genuinely spiritual expression. All this is rehearsed to make a rather basic point. The superiority of symbolism to allegory was, strictly speaking, a matter not of aesthetics but of metaphysics or theology. What distinguished symbolism from allegory for Coleridge—however we may now understand and employ his distinction—was that symbolism, unlike allegory, provided access to a higher, transcendent truth: to a *real* "reality." But to believe in the distinction, you had first to believe in this higher truth, this "real" reality.

That was where the problem lay. As a fictional form of what Coleridge called "symbolism"—as a mode of spiritual mimesis—romance could be justified, in Melville's words, as containing "more reality, than real life itself can show." Such a defense relied, to be sure, on matters extrinsic to actual literary expression; but then, clearly, so had the Common Sense attack on fiction. What was more troubling was that the whole case for romance rested on assumptions that were, by the middle of the nineteenth century, extremely doubtful. Romantic symbolism might appear to have offered an anchor on which to reground the severed Jamesian cable, but to tie literary validity to the Romantics' quasi-religious conception of imaginative truth was like tying a leaking lifeboat to the *Titanic*—or to the *Pequod*. If the justification of romance, of its departure from Common Sense "reality," was ultimately religious, doubts about its truth, about the truth of imaginative language, could never be simply aesthetic. The fear that perhaps *all* symbolic expression might be "allegorical" in Coleridge's pejorative sense, the fear that *all* spirituality might be delusive, went far beyond the bounds of literary theory.

"Some certain significance lurks in all things," insists Ishmael in "The Doubloon," "else all things are little worth, and the round world itself but an empty cipher" (358). His statement recalls the tripartite formulation in Emerson's *Nature:*

1. Words are signs of natural facts.
2. Particular natural facts are symbols of particular
   spiritual facts.
3. Nature is the symbol of spirit.[37]

For Emerson the ideal condition of nature—its symbolic correspondence to spirit—is analogous to the ideal condition of language—its symbolic relation to meaning. Correspondence is the metaphysical equivalent of aesthetic relation. So, too, for Ishmael, correspondence between "all things" and their "certain significance" depends upon the analogy of linguistic signification. Without such correspondence, "the round world itself [is] but an empty cipher," a meaningless linguistic symbol.

For Melville, however, Emerson's assumptions were at the very least problematic. In "The Doubloon," Ishmael's "certain significance" is not serenely immanent; it "lurks." And its certainty is cast in doubt by the action of the chapter that follows—by the multiplicity of subjective meanings projected onto the doubloon by the officers and crew of the *Pequod.* Each reads his own significance into the opaque, possibly empty, symbol. "There's another rendering now," comments Stubb midway, "but still one text. All sorts of men in one kind of world, you see" (362). Even Stubb's casual "you see" is important; perhaps all meaning—as the chapter's action suggests against Ishmael's opening assurance—is only a matter of subjective vision. And what is true of the doubloon is generally true of the "text" of Nature. Ahab, in an Emersonian vein, exclaims over the "linked analogies" between "Nature" and the "soul of man" (264), but he is unable to avoid the despairing intimation that "there's naught beyond" (144). Or, as Melville's narrator puts it in *Pierre:*

> Say what some poets will, Nature is not so much her own ever-sweet interpreter, as the mere supplier of that cunning alphabet, whereby selecting and combining as he pleases, each man reads his own peculiar lesson according to his own peculiar mind and mood. [342]

Once again, metaphysical correspondence is tied to aesthetic relation: the condition of Nature, as "alphabet," is the condition of language. But both, here, are ominously ambiguous. The language of Nature has become as obscure as the language of romance.

The intensity with which Melville faced the ambiguity of Nature's "cunning alphabet," the threat of there being "naught beyond," was unusual among his literary contemporaries in America. More than any of his contemporaries, he believed, at least at the outset of his career, in the spiritual possibilities of symbolic romance. Even Emerson, after his grandiose pronouncement in *Nature* that "every natural fact is a symbol of some spiritual fact," was willing without the slightest metaphysical shudder to add the Stubb-like translation: "Every appearance in nature corresponds to some state of the mind."[38] Poe, like Melville, sought a supersensual "supernal," but he was always skeptical about its epistemological status. Moreover, it was easier for him than for Melville to relinquish the intuitive or mystic conception of imaginative truth, since for him the faculty had always revealed itself mainly in "mere" linguistic skill or taste, in the artist's "selecting and combining as he pleases."[39]

Hawthorne, finally, assumed a position close to that of Melville's Stubb: he remained content, apparently, with the most subjective, relativistic version of Emersonian correspondence: "There's another rendering now, but still one text." Hence his philosophically complacent exploitation of the formula of alternative possibilities, the device of multiple choice. The significance of his symbols is generally the significance projected onto them by his characters. In his fiction Hawthorne simply assumes as a given what so horrified Melville as a possibility—that "there's naught beyond." Thus, at their last meeting in 1856, which Hawthorne described in his *English Notebooks*, Hawthorne still puzzled over Melville's obsession with "everything that lies beyond human ken" (432). Each of these writers was forced to confront the metaphysical and epistemological ambiguity of "spiritual" significance, but each responded in his own way. Melville was impelled to "strike through the mask," to recognize even "things visible" as but "conceits of the eye." Poe was driven toward materialism and "effect." Hawthorne was driven toward psychology, "human ken," as the only viable arena of correspondence between appearances in nature and states of mind.

These metaphysical or epistemological problems provided an essential intellectual background to Hawthorne's and Melville's literary theory and practice. Through that process of displacement so typical of the theory of romance in America, these problems found their cunning duplicate in problems of literary expression and meaning. For if spiritual truth seemed ambiguous or absent in Nature, what was one to say of the *author's* truths—his meanings or feelings—in relation to the emblems, the language, in which he clothed them? Hawthorne's notebooks and letters abound with laments over the inadequacy or duplicity of language. "I have felt, a thousand times," he wrote to Sophia Peabody in 1840, employing one of his most characteristic metaphors, "that words may be a thick and darksome veil of mystery between the soul and the truth which it seeks."[40] In Melville's first novel the comic confusion between the allegedly significant terms "Typee" and "Happar" implies a similar distrust of language, and in his third work of fiction, his first avowed romance, he is far more explicit: "Words are but algebraic signs," he writes in *Mardi*, "conveying no meaning except what you please. And to be called one thing, is oftentimes to be another" (269).

For American romancers, this is to say, the crisis of correspondence manifested itself most immediately in the crisis of relation. The ambiguous duplicity of "spirit" posed its most immediate threat in the guise of those qualities of literary ambiguity or duplicity that had characterized American romance from the very beginning. "Significance," for Ishmael, "lurks" beneath appearances. As early as 1789, Charles Brockden Brown's Rhapsodist was upbraided by his skeptical correspondent in strikingly similar terms: "Your stile and manner betray you. You have not been sufficiently careful to conceal the youth and inexperience which most certainly lurk beneath your mask" (17). Ishmael contains within himself the impulses of both the wordy Rhapsodist and his skeptical correspondent. On the one hand, as the "Etymology" suggests at the outset, *Moby-Dick* is an effort to discover "by what name a whale-fish is to be called in our tongue" (1). Yet the whale's is a "nameless horror" (163). How can such inarticulate truths be expressed in language? "How," as Melville puts it in *Pierre*, "can a man get a Voice out of Silence?" (208). "The great Leviathan," Ishmael admits, "is that one creature in the world which must remain unpainted to the last" (228), yet Ishmael, for all his skepticism, sets out to paint him. He thus runs the risk, like Brown's Rhapsodist, of betraying himself through his "stile and manner." Attempting to name the nameless, he generates his own mask of words and an alphabet every bit as cunning as Nature's; yet by dealing with his problem overtly, he turns his predicament as romancer into a more general image of the predicament of his culture. This overtness is the distinguishing mark of the maturity of American romance, and it is first achieved in the works of Melville and Hawthorne.

According to Roy Harvey Pearce, *The Marble Faun* is a failure because "the form of the romance as Hawthorne knew it was no longer such as to give shape and meaning to the life which it was to comprehend." Hawthorne continued to write into what Pearce calls, in the well-known title of his essay, "the Twilight of Romance." Perry Miller, with his instinct for melodrama, preferred to call it the "lurid sunset of the Romance in America," but he too stresses the sense of decadence in the 1850s, the growing separation between form and convention on the one hand and cultural reality on the other. "Hawthorne and Melville," he insists, "do not inaugurate a 'renaissance' in American literature: they constitute a culmination, they pronounce a funeral oration on the dreams of their youth, they intone an elegy of disenchantement." "The secret of *Moby-Dick*," Miller writes, "is that it pushes the Romance to extremities which exhaust the form."[41]

Pearce and Miller tell us a great deal about the intellectual seriousness of romance, about its connection to the epistemological anxieties of the 1840s and 1850s, but their formulations overstress the idea of decadence as an actual historical process. In fact, American romance—at least experimental romance—was "decadent" from the outset; its very dawn had all the lurid marks of twilight or sunset. The divergence of the form of the romance from what Pearce calls "the life which it was to comprehend" was not a development of the 1850s; it was the central attribute of romance from the very beginning. Even Brown's *Rhapsodist* essays, in 1789, intone an "elegy of disenchantment" with "stile and manner," and all five of the writers considered in this study managed to "exhaust the form" of romance with great rapidity. Poe and Hawthorne held on longest, although there are large lacunae in Hawthorne's career, and Poe, with the possible exception of "The Cask of Amontillado" (1846), wrote no fiction after 1845 that would now be ranked with his best work. Melville moved from *Typee* to *The Confidence-Man* in ten years. Irving moved from *The Sketch-Book* to *Tales of a Traveller* in four. Brown moved from *Wieland* to *Arthur Mervyn* in three.

What Hawthorne and Melville registered in the 1850s was not the twilight of romance but the twilight of Romanticism, and this distinction is crucial. Romance was never based on Coleridgean assumptions about the reality of imagination; quite the contrary. Indeed, had imagination and reality been the same thing, or aspects of the same thing, there would have been no cable to cut, no relation to sacrifice. A fictional theory based on the Romantic justification of imagination would have looked very different from the theory implicit and explicit in the works of Brown, Irving, Poe, Hawthorne, and Melville. It would have looked, in fact, very much like the so-called "realism" enunciated by Henry James. In "The Art of Fiction" (1884) James rejects the "celebrated distinction between the novel and the romance" and insists that "the only reason for the existence of a novel is that it does attempt to represent life." "Life," however, is not in the object but in the transaction between object and "sensibility"—in the "impression"; and the highest "reality" is achieved "when the mind is imaginative." Or, as James would write to H. G. Wells, thirty years later: "It is art that *makes* life."[42] James fully believes that the imagination, however extraordinary its capacity for error, is the only route to genuine truth. His thinking about fiction is thus truly unitary. There is for him no dissociation of form from life, of imagination from "reality." The point I am making here is that, if this doctrine ties James to such Romantics as Coleridge, it separates him completely from such romancers as Hawthorne and Melville, for American romance, from Brown to Melville, remained radically dualistic, true to its deviant origins in reaction against Common Sense rational orthodoxy.

Romance came into its own in the 1840s and 1850s because, among other things, its built-in "decadence" was suddenly relevant to the decadence of Romanticism—to the Romantic spiritualism that functioned as a kind of secularized religion at mid-century. Brown and Irving were mainly baffled by the sacrifice of relation, by the duplicity and opacity they discovered in romance and in its artificial language; but by the 1840s, when God or "spirit" were barricaded, if anywhere, in inscrutably phenomenal obscurity, the world of romance was looking more and more like *the* world. Thus, for instance, Plotinus Plinlimmon's pamphlet in *Pierre*, on the dissociation of "Chronometricals" and "Horologicals," is at once a theological treatise on the disrelation of phenomenal matter and noumenal spirit and a discourse on the inevitable lurking insincerity of romance. It might be regarded, in this sense, as Melville's parodic *Eureka*.

Hawthorne and Melville both found in the sacrifice of relation far more than an aesthetic problem and far more, too, than the kind of psychological problem that beset Brown, Irving, and Poe. For Hawthorne and Melville the condition of romance, the dissociation of symbol or language from meaning, was the condition of life itself, whether in the form of Nature's "cunning alphabet" or in the form of man's "unconscious self-deceptions." For all their differences, Hawthorne used allegory, finally, as Melville used symbolism. As I put it earlier, they used allegory and symbolism as ways not only of writing romance but of writing *about* romance. and thereby writing about life. Both of them saw and exploited the connection between questions of meaning in romance and questions of meaning in the world of which romance was not only a part but perhaps the most adequate emblem. In the sacrifice of relation, in casting off all cables, romance oddly enough found the very relation it sacrificed. As Melville put it in *The Confidence-Man*, defining the sort of "reality" to be expected in romances: "It is with fiction as with religion: it should present another world, and yet one to which we feel the tie" (158). Hawthorne, unlike Melville, seldom used the disrelation of romance to explore problems of supernatural or metaphysical significance, but they both used the dissociated world of romance, its "world of words," to scrutinize the world of their contemporary American culture. It is in their work, consequently, that the tradition of romance in America becomes a tradition, at last, of American romance.

PART THREE

A WORLD OF WORDS

Every word was once a poem. . . .
For though the origin of most of our words is forgotten, each word was at first a stroke of genius, and obtained currency because for the moment it symbolized the world to the first speaker and to the hearer. The etymologist finds the deadest word to have been once a brilliant picture. Language is fossil poetry. . . .
. . . America is a poem in our eyes.

EMERSON, "The Poet"

Ours is a world of words.

POE, "Al Aaraaf"

PROLOGUE

IN THE MATURE WORK AND THOUGHT OF HAWTHORNE AND MELVILLE THE development of experimental American romance comes to its culmination and conclusion. The present study of this development might thus conceivably end with chapter 6—with the intersection of romance's disrelation and Romanticism's decadence in Hawthorne's allegorical and Melville's symbolistic fiction. The two chapters that follow are not meant to imply any further development along the lines discussed thus far. Rather, they examine the ways in which Hawthorne and Melville exploited the dilemmas of the romancer to understand what they saw as an analogous dilemma facing the national experiment.

The focus of Part Three is thus no longer solely on the romancer's social and literary strategies for exploiting or obscuring the sacrifice of relation (although I am still concerned with such strategies), for in the work of Hawthorne and Melville it is also necessary to explore the ways in which they consciously employed the psychological and aesthetic disrelation of romance as a model for comprehending what they saw as an analogous disrelation in the culture of their nation—a dissociation of nineteenth-century "America" from its allegedly "revolutionary" spiritual origins.

In parts One and Two I set forth the theory and practice of experimental American romance in the context of the romancers' experience—as "romancers"—of their culture. This context is crucial. Still, these writers were not "American" simply by virtue of being products, in a sociological sense, of their society, for they were often, in addition, social critics, social visionaries, or both. Hawthorne and Melville, particularly, undertook self-consciously to embody and examine in their fiction what they took to be the peculiar nature of their America. In Part Three, then, I am concerned with Hawthorne's and Melville's visions of America, of its culture and history.

I shall contend, moreover, that these visions depend in some significant measure on a different sort of connection between "American romance" and "America" than that discussed in the first six chapters. Instead of focusing on the sociological connection between writer and society, I shall explore a more explicitly literary connection, in works of literature, between social vision and criticism, on the one hand, and fictional theory and practice, on the other. To what extent, I ask, were Hawthorne and Melville able to make the form of romance itself, the fundamental disrelation of romance, into an instrument of social vision and social criticism?

To raise such a question is to run the risk Hawthorne might have described as entering a "fairy-land" or "cloud-land" of abstraction. The interaction between romance and cultural vision, between the theory of romance and theories of society and social history, is not the concrete "interaction" of the sociologist, for in a sociological sense it is scarcely "real" at all. The sociologist of literary vocation links fictions or theories of fiction, as examples of interactive social behavior, with the concrete conditions, the "facts," faced by authors; but to link a writer's theory of romance to his theory of society is to link an idea to an idea, a fiction to a fiction.

The all-important reason for exploring this admittedly abstract sort of interaction between the dilemmas of experimental romance and what Hawthorne and Melville saw as the dilemmas of the national experiment is the fact that such an interaction—whether "real" or not—is an explicit and important concern in the major American romances of these two writers. In other words, the self-conscious investigation of literary expression in their works is often simultaneously an investigation of the nature and meaning of "America." I have no desire to assert a "real" connection between the nature of nineteenth-century America as a culture and the nature of romance as a literary form. There are, as we shall see, intriguing similarities between problems raised by a certain kind of nationalist thought and the problems raised by experimental romance, but they are significant to the present study mainly as they engaged the attention of Hawthorne and Melville.

The call for a distinctively national American literature first arose, in the years during and following the Revolution, in the context of a general anxiety among American intellectuals to define or discover the distinctive identity of "America."[1] The nationalists' call was first answered, as we now read our literary history, by the emergence of a significant and enduring body of American literature in the years between 1820 and 1860. This was also the great age of American romance. Indeed, many of our first important national writers were also avowed romancers. This historical coincidence has led to the notion that there is a fundamental affinity between the idea of "romance" and the ideal of a distinctive "America" that was enunciated in nationalist propaganda between the Revolution and the Civil War.

The most forceful and extended assertion of such an affinity is to be found in the work of Perry Miller. At the heart of Miller's writings on American romance is the identification of romance with its subject matter and, ultimately, with the very idea of "America." Thus, in "The Romance and the Novel," Miller tells us that the romances of Cooper, Simms, and their contemporaries "were serious efforts to put the meaning of America, of life in America, into the one form that seemed providentially given, through the exemplum of Scott, for expressing the deepest passions of the continent"; similarly, in *The Raven and the Whale*, the romance is "that form in which Young America sought to prove their Americanism." The "philosophical doctrine of the romance" is thus virtually equated with the doctrine of American cultural nationalism, and the equation becomes, under the pressure of Miller's rhetoric, even deterministic. Melville turned to romance in *Mardi*, we are told, because his nationalist ambition could take only that form. National originality, Miller writes, could not be achieved "in the novel, not by Jane Austen, Bulwer, or Thackeray.... The great American book had to be big, and it had to be a romance."[2]

As historical analysis, Miller's asserted equation simply does not work. It drains the terms "America" and "romance" of any precise meaning. In what sense, for instance, can the American "continent" be said to have had "passions"? And by identifying "romance" almost completely with its American subject matter, with the rhetoric of national originality, Miller obscures the primary importance to this mode of literary expression of a central conception of the problems and possibilities of fictional *form*.[3] The truth is that American romance, except as it "mingled" American scenery and history with "poetry," was in no direct sense a response to, let alone an embodiment of, the call for a distinctively national literature or identity. As developed by Brown, Irving, Poe, Hawthorne, and Melville, its "philosophical doctrine" grew, not out of self-conscious nationalism, but out of a set of ingrained assumptions about the nature and status of romance and romancers in a society hostile to both. While these assumptions may have been especially pronounced and monotonic in America, they were hardly uniquely American. The particular forms taken by American romance may have been psychologically and socially determined by the interaction between the romancer and his culture, but it is hardly useful to describe them as "providentially given."

However much American intellectual and popular culture exacerbated the opprobrium of fictionality and hence encouraged the growth of a self-consciously "fictional" tradition in America, this self-consciousness was not in any obvious way distinctively "American." National propagandists called for the literary treatment of specifically national scenes, institutions, and history or, more vaguely, for independence from foreign models. Experimental romance, by contrast, reflects more general or universal concerns: about the relation (or disrelation) between imagination and actuality, fiction and fact, "sentiments" and "words."

There is, nevertheless, a kind of potential, metaphorical truth in Miller's asserted equation. From a certain perspective, questions of "relation" seemed as relevant to the nationalists' ideal of the nation's ambitions as to the specifically literary project of experimental romance. The Revolution and its aftermath, for those who thought about them in a certain way, posed problems intriguingly similar to the problems of the self-conscious romancer. As early as 1815 Walter Channing worried, as would so many of his contemporaries and successors, about the difficulty of finding an appropriate mode in which to express our distinctive nationality—whatever that "nationality" was. "How tame will his language sound," Channing complained, "who would describe Niagara in language fitted for the falls at London bridge, or attempt the majesty of the Mississippi in that which was made for the Thames."[4] In this view, the Revolution had, as it were, sacrificed the relation between the "language" of imported culture and those "revolutionary" canons of legitimacy that for some nationalists constituted the new "idea" of America. Ours was a new sort of truth, one for which we as yet had no words; and the invention or discovery of such words was central to the general nationalist imperative. From that point of view, the central problem of the new nation, like the central problem of romance, was one of expression, of finding valid words and forms for otherwise inarticulate sentiments.

I do not introduce this comparison of the problems facing nationalists and romancers to reinstate Miller's identification of the "romance" with "America." It is only a comparison, a metaphor—an analogy not even between fiction and actual cultural experience but between a certain kind of fiction and a certain *idea* of the nature or potential of American culture. It matters, however, because it mattered to our two greatest romancers. Hawthorne and Melville perceived, and exploited, a seeming affinity between the style of their medium and the style of their culture. Both styles presented problems that might be called "formal," and both pointed, ultimately, beyond themselves to a "truth" conceived in "revolutionary" terms.

In 1789 Charles Brockden Brown launched his literary career with a series of four periodical essays entitled *The Rhapsodist*. "I intend," he announced in the first number, "that the sincerity of my character shall be the principal characteristic of these papers. . . . I speak seriously, when I affirm that no situation whatsoever, will justify a man in uttering a falsehood" (1). In the year of Washington's first inauguration, the year of the storming of the Bastille in France, Brown spoke for the emerging Romantic cult of sincerity over calculation, of abstract justice over social custom and habit, of truth over artificial form. Such sentiments were thoroughly conventional, but Brown went on to associate this nascent Romanticism, in a way that was also becoming conventional, with the new American character and its literary expression. His essays recall various European writers of visionary sensibility, but the Rhapsodist avers that he owes his true inspiration to his home in the American wilderness, on "the solitary banks of the Ohio" (15).

Sixty-one years later, reviewing Hawthorne's *Mosses from an Old Manse*, Herman Melville still located the literary genius of America on the "banks of the Ohio" (409) and still associated that genius with the doctrine of sincerity, "the great Art of Telling the Truth" (408). Like Brown, although writing in widely different circumstances, Melville was influenced by the ideals of Rousseau and the French *philosophes*, by their desire to liberate a pure humanity smothered beneath the corrupt and deceptive forms of literature and culture. Like Brown also, he saw these ideals as being particularly appropriate to the United States. "No American writer," he declared, "should write like an Englishman, or a Frenchman; let him write like a man, for then he will be sure to write like an American" (413). The Rhapsodist, Brown's persona had insisted, "will write as he speaks, and converse with his reader not as an author, but as a man" (5). In both of these nationalistic essays the rejection of European formalism verges on a theoretical repudiation of form altogether—in the interest of American truth. The American writer defines himself simply as a "man." His literature is characterized simply by its "truth."

This claim of radical sincerity, whatever its sources in European Romanticism, was for Brown and Melville and many of their contemporaries particularly appropriate to what they saw as the "revolutionary" origins of American culture. The Puritans, themselves no friends to formal artifice in art and literature, had fled England in order to free scriptural truth from the corrupt formalism of the Church of England. A century and a half later Jefferson's *Declaration* had justified American independence on the basis of "self-evident" truths. In the years following the Revolution national propagandists insisted that the revolutionary impulse should permeate our whole culture—its social institutions, art, and literature—not just our political life. American culture, they declared, should assert its own independence by being revolutionary and sincere, expressing American truth rather than foreign influence. "Even Shakespeare," Melville wrote to Evert Duyckinck in 1849, "was not a frank man to the uttermost. And, indeed, who in this intolerant Universe is, or can be? But the Declaration of Independence makes a difference" (80).

It is hard to assess the historical significance of this ideal of America's peculiar identity and potential. Historians have long debated whether the nation born in 1776 was especially new or was rather an institution of long-established local customs and political realities. Such things as the "difference" upon which Melville insisted are difficult to quantify. Nor was the idea of America as a bastion of sincerity in the war against corrupt artifice uniformly accepted in pre–Civil War America, even among avowed nationalists. For many propagandists, America's special character was to be found not in some abstract spirit but in concrete institutions, scenery, local tradition, and history. As I noted in chapter 1, a good deal of "Americanist" cultural propaganda was fundamentally conservative and concretely "realistic." Moreover, the most important strain of nationalist thought, in historical terms, was probably not "cultural" at all but specifically political, focusing on such issues as internal economic development and the power of the federal government. The more radical conception of America's distinctive character, voiced by Brown and Melville, was only one idea among several.

Nevertheless, this idea was widespread, and it played an important part in the intellectual life of the new nation. It is the central doctrine, for instance, of William Ellery Channing's "Remarks on a National Literature," first published as a review in 1830:

> The great distinction of our country is, that we enjoy some peculiar advantages for understanding our own nature. Man is the great subject of literature, and juster and profounder views of man may be expected here than elsewhere. In Europe, political and artificial distinctions have, more or less, triumphed over and obscured our common nature.

The same idea informs Emerson's 1837 Phi Beta Kappa address, "The American Scholar," and it was generally embraced by those of Channing's Transcendental heirs who, as Benjamin Spencer puts it, "enlisted in the campaign for a national literature principally as an operation in behalf of a new freedom which they judged to be more nearly in accord with universal truth."[5]

In this view, America's nationality lay not in its history and scenery, not even in the concrete institutions established by the Revolution, but in the Revolution itself—in the originating "revolutionary" impulse. "We should have no heart to encourage native literature," wrote Channing in 1830, "did we not hope that it would become instinct with a new spirit."[6] Radical nationalism, that is to say, shifted the basis of national identity from matter to spirit, from phenomenal appearances ("artificial distinctions," for Channing) to noumenal essences. The idea of "America" was finding a new grounding in the doctrines of Romantic spiritualism. It was in such terms that Brown, in 1789, and Melville, in 1850, proclaimed their sense of America's literary and cultural mission.

Channing called for the overthrow of "artificial distinctions," for the release and revelation of "our common nature." The author of "psychological romance," writes Hawthorne in his Preface to *The Snow-Image*, burrows "into the depths of our common nature" (4). The reappearance of Channing's phrase is significant, for the supposedly revolutionary "truth" of America and the nonverbal "truth" of romance were at heart one and the same. In romance as in revolution, "our common nature" was to be liberated from imprisoning form. At the beginning of the nineteenth century, we recall, conventional opinion associated "romance and poetry" with the same "barbaric" condition, the state of nature, to which Rousseau and others appealed to justify revolution.

One may wonder whether romancers were actually moved by this sort of intellectual-historical congruence. Still, they had, perhaps, a direct and personal reason for sensing an affinity between the impulse of revolution and the obscure sources of their art. I argued in chapter 2 that a feeling of marginality or deviance, even of aggression against society and its norms, played a part in the romancer's experience and choice of his vocation. Would not the theory of justified revolution, legitimized at last by our submerged "common nature," provide the ultimate deviant rationale? Few of our experimental romancers were willing openly to proclaim such a rationale.

Brown never treated the American Revolution directly. He did begin his career as a Godwinian radical, but in his fiction the "revolutionary" characters—notably Ormond—are invariably the villains,[7] and in the years following his renunciation of fiction-writing Brown also renounced his early radicalism for the more "solid" values of Federalism. In a political pamphlet of 1809 he explicitly renounced the notion of "revolutionary" legitimacy, and did so in interesting terms. "The impulse," he wrote of the American Revolution, "was a movement of the imagination."[8]

Poe simply ignored the Revolution, just as he generally ignored the idea of Americanism and, indeed, the idea of history. There are rebellions and uprisings in his fiction, treated with a mixture of fear and fascination. One thinks of such works as *The Narrative of Arthur Gordon Pym*, "A Tale of the

Ragged Mountains," "Hop-Frog," "The System of Dr. Tarr and Professor Fether." Many of these tales draw on Poe's hostility to popular
democracy and his Southern fear of black rebellion. In many of them
rebellion is associated with the escape of imagination from rational control, and in this sense one might describe the central action of "The Fall of
the House of Usher"—Madeline's emergence from the basement—as a
kind of rebellion; but in none of these stories is revolution introduced as a
sanction for the imaginative unfettering of "our common nature."

Irving also avoided the Revolution and the revolutionary but did so in
ways that sometimes give them a kind of negative prominence. The
change through which Rip Van Winkle happily sleeps is, significantly, the
War for Independence. Brom Bones frightens off Ichabod Crane by im-
personating the ghost of a Hessian mercenary. In both of these stories,
sleepy Dutch complacency stands in opposition to alienation and violence,
and it is suggestive that the insanity of Gottfried Wolfgang, the German
Student, is tied specifically to the revolution in France. Irving's conservative contemporaries liked to distinguish our Revolution from the one
in France. Our War for Independence, they argued, was not "revolutionary" at all. Yet it is only by sleeping through America's Revolution
that Rip Van Winkle is enabled to avoid Gottfried's fate.

The truth is that, except for Melville in the 1840s, American romancers
found the affinity between romance and revolution anything but gratifying. We should not be surprised. However important a sense of deviance
may have been to these writers, they spent most of their public careers
trying to "manage" this deviance, to channel the energy of alienation or
aggression into the acceptable forms of "solid" success. For such men, one
imagines, the idea of revolution—especially if associated with their own
status or motives as artists—must have been touchy. In fact, when the
affinity between the "truths" of romance and revolution comes into focus
in the works of these romancers, it does so only briefly—and evidently as a
notion to be obscured or evaded.

Writers like Hawthorne and Melville, perhaps through the experience
of managing their own aggressive impulses, had a sense of "our common
nature" quite different from Channing's. The deepest "revolutionary" imperatives, as they understood them, were not beatific but antisocial, irrational, and violent. Jefferson might have based America's Revolution on
"truths" we hold to be "self-evident," but the author of "The Birth-mark"
knew that toward the deepest truth of our nature "we practise an unconscious self-deception during our waking moments" (40). It was against
precisely such "self-deception" that Channing and Emerson protested, but
Hawthorne understood how deeply we need it. So did Melville, who said,
in "Hawthorne and His *Mosses*," that the deepest truths are "so terifically
true that it were all but madness for any good man, in his own proper

character, to utter, or even hint of them" (407). If Hawthorne and Melville recognized such "truths" within themselves, they were scarcely pleased, consciously at any rate, to do so. Experienced in managing their own deviant impulses, they were peculiarly sensitive to the ways in which "civilized" culture generally, and the culture of "revolutionary" America in particular, subsisted through an analogous sort of management.

SEVEN

When the artist rose high enough to achieve the Beautiful, the symbol by which he made it perceptible to mortal senses became of little value in his eyes, while his spirit possessed itself in the enjoyment of the Reality.

HAWTHORNE, "The Artist of the Beautiful"

The prospect of the dissolution of that mighty nation which had embodied the best hopes of mankind was a deep pain to him; it seemed likely to be the death of that old spirit of patriotism which had come down to us from the Revolution.

JULIAN HAWTHORNE on his father's attitude toward the
Civil War, in *Nathaniel Hawthorne and His Wife*

THE DEATH OF THE SPIRIT
Nathaniel Hawthorne

HAWTHORNE'S MAIN FOCUS IN HIS AMERICAN-BASED FICTION IS THE HIS-
tory of New England, especially of the seventeenth century, but he
mined this history again and again for anticipations of the Revolution of
1776.[1] "My Kinsman, Major Molineux," set in the early eighteenth century, places its protagonist's coming-of-age in the context of a popular
uprising against British authority. "Endicott and the Red Cross" portrays a
historical event of clear revolutionary import. "We look back through the
mist of ages," Hawthorne writes at the close, "and recognize, in the rend-
ing of the Red Cross from New England's banner, the first omen of that
deliverance which our fathers consummated, after the bones of the stern
Puritan had lain more than a century in the dust" (441). And "The Gray
Champion," which combines the reappearance of one of the judges of
Charles I with the Glorious Revolution's arrival in Boston in 1689, finds in
both a "type of New-England's hereditary spirit" and a foreshadowing of
that spirit's later eruption at the Boston Massacre, the Battle of Lexington
and Concord, and the Battle of Bunker Hill (18).

As we shall see in the next chapter, Melville found in such "revolutionary" events a direct analogue and sanction both for his own rebellious
impulses and for his writings. Hawthorne's attitude toward the "revolutionary," by contrast, is far from the easy patriotism of nationalist propaganda. He may invoke America's "deliverance," but he does not proclaim his own. He keeps his distance. The popular uprising in "My
Kinsman, Major Molineux" is more unruly than noble, and the humilia-
tion of the title character is handled with evident distaste. While Endicott
asserts New England's freedom, he does so primarily through violence—
and by denying the freedom of many of its residents. Even the apparently
patriotic message of "The Gray Champion" is not exactly "revolutionary."

At the beginning of *Nature* Emerson complains that "our age is retrospective. It builds the sepulchres of the fathers." "Why," he urges, "should not we also enjoy an original relation to the universe? . . . Let us demand our own works and laws and worship."[2] If such demands are "revolutionary," they are surely to be distinguished from the "hereditary spirit" of "The Gray Champion," from the title character's "pledge, that New-England's sons will vindicate their ancestry" (18).

Hawthorne, seldom willing to identify the voice of his prefaces and fiction with the irrational sources of his art, was also consistently skeptical of the "revolutionary" spirit proclaimed by Emerson, Channing, and others. "Begin all anew!" Hester exhorts Dimmesdale in the forest. "Hast thou exhausted possibility in the failure of this one trial? Not so! The future is yet full of trial and success. . . . Exchange this false life of thine for a true one" (198). In this spirit of revolutionary sincerity, Hester casts off her scarlet letter and the "false life"—what Channing called the "artificial distinctions"—of which it is the symbol. But she is soon compelled to reassume the letter and the identity imposed upon her by Puritan Boston. "An evil deed," Hawthorne writes at the close of the forest scene, "invests itself with the character of doom" (211). The false vestments of habit and social distinction, in Hawthorne's view, were not so easily to be renounced.

In terms of conscious inclination, Hawthorne was as hostile as Brown or Irving to the radical ideal of revolution. In an 1840 letter to Sophia Peabody he recounted a curious dream. "I was engaged," he writes, "in assisting the escape of Louis XVI and Marie Antoinette from Paris, during the French revolution. And sometimes, by an unaccountable metamorphosis, it seemed as if my mother and sister were in the place of the King and Queen."[3] This looks, surely, like the fantasy of a counterrevolutionary. A notebook entry of 1842 indicates a similar bias, proposing for consideration "the emerging from their lurking-places of evil-characters, on some occasion suited to their action—they having been quite unknown to the world hitherto. For instance, the French Revolution brought out such wretches" (240).

Yet Hawthorne's position is more complex and ambiguous than his conscious assertions and easy labels—"evil-characters," "wretches"— might first suggest. Behind the "unaccountable metamorphosis" of his Revolution dream one surely senses, at the very least, a certain frustration with social and family piety. It is Hawthorne himself, after all, who dreams his mother and sister into the place of the threatened royal couple. And for all his overt distaste, Hawthorne turned again and again to the "emerging" of buried dark forces from their "lurking-places"—to the eruption of repressed "truth," as he puts it in "The Birth-mark," into the waking world of "unconscious self-deception." "The mind is in a sad note," he writes in "The Birth-mark," "when Sleep, the all-involving, cannot confine her spectres within the dim region of her sway, but suffers them to break forth, affrighting this actual life with secrets that perchance belong to a deeper one" (40). Such breaking-forth was Hawthorne's great subject and great model for his own art from first to last—from the half-repressed fantasies of Young Goodman Brown to the emergence of Miriam's dark model from the catacombs in *The Marble Faun*. Hawthorne may have recoiled, in his own proper character, from rebellion as he recoiled from any personal avowal of the artist's willful animus against society; but he saw the essential connection between the unleashing of fantasy and the unleashing of revolutionary violence.

Hawthorne sensed, moreover, the connections between his own uneasy fear of buried fantasy and his society's fearful management of its allegedly "revolutionary" origins. Personally adept at the arts of repression, he nevertheless understood what he was repressing and why. It was less clear to him that his society possessed such understanding. Elevating "revolutionary" or "spiritual" truths into canons of legitimacy, slogans of social control, it denied the deepest implications of these truths as Hawthorne understood them. Like Aylmer, therefore, it lost sight of the distinction between "sentiments" and "words," between "revolutionary" origins and waking "self-deceptions." Hawthorne's three American-based romances—*The Scarlet Letter, The House of the Seven Gables*, and *The Blithedale Romance*—chart the historical process that produced this situation.

"When the aritist rose high enough to achieve the Beautiful," Hawthorne writes at the close of "The Artist of the Beautiful," "the symbol by which he made it perceptible to mortal senses became of little value in his eyes, while his spirit possessed itself in the enjoyment of the Reality" (475). The same sense of tension between invisible "Reality" and inadequate "symbol" governs Hawthorne's vision of social history. But in American society, as Hawthorne read its history, it was neither easy nor wise to dismiss the "perceptible"—to insist, instead, on the abiding "reality" of originating "spirit." If one's artwork had not an ideal butterfly but an ideal society, one had to recognize that the visible forms of social life, however inadequate to their original inspiration, had a "reality" of their own.

"The founders of a new colony," begins the second paragraph of *The Scarlet Letter*, "whatever Utopia of human virtue and happiness they might originally project, have invariably recognized it among their earliest practical necessities to allot a portion of the virgin soil as a cemetery, and another portion as the site of a prison" (47). What was the relation, then, between "practical necessities" and the original project—between the actual, "perceptible" culture of cemetery and prison and the ideal of Utopia? Was the "word," in any sense, still a "poem"? Or was "America" simply another in a long, invariable line of fallible human societies—another demonstration, this time in the realm of social history, that "spirit," when expressed, becomes a "mere word"?

Hawthorne usually, if sometimes sadly, opted for the latter conclusion. Hester Prynne, at the end of her story, finds more "real life" in Boston than in the revolutionary assertion of her "individuality." At the end of his career, in his preface to *Our Old Home*, Hawthorne confessed a similar resignation in terms suggesting how closely, for him, the spirit of romance was bound up with the ideal spirit of America. The Civil War, he writes, upset his project for a romance based on the materials of his essays: "The Present, the Immediate, the Actual, has proved too potent for me. It takes away not only my scanty faculty, but even my desire for imaginative composition." So far, this sounds like the many complaints of conservative romancers, including Hawthorne himself, about America's excessive and barren "reality." But the sentence goes on. The war, Hawthorne continues, "leaves me sadly content to scatter a thousand peaceful fantasies upon the hurricane that is sweeping us all along with it, possibly, into a Limbo where our nation and its polity may be as literally the fragments of a shattered dream as my unwritten Romance" (4). The parallel could scarcely be clearer.

The Civil War, in Hawthorne's view, did more than interfere with the writing of romance. It shattered America's original dream, its originating impulse, as surely as Robert Danforth's baby shattered Owen Warland's butterfly; and Hawthorne, whatever his attitude toward Owen's butterfly, saw little hope that America's spirit could survive the collapse of the nation that had made it perceptible to mortal senses. Julian Hawthorne, in his biography of his parents, records his father's troubled meditations on the war. For the most part, Julian writes, Hawthorne tried to see the conflict in terms of "practical necessities." He saw no point in a Union won through military victory: "compulsion could effect nothing worth having." "At the same time," Julian continues, "the prospect of the dissolution of that mighty nation which had embodied the best hopes of mankind was a deep pain to him; it seemed likely to be the death of that old spirit of patriotism which had come down to us from the Revolution."[4]

For Hawthorne, "the death of that old spirit" was the invariable and irreversible course of history in general and of American history in particular, and realization was as great a threat as the destruction that seemed imminent after 1860. As the sentiments of the romancer became the words of the romance, so the Utopian vision, in expressing itself, assumed the mask of empty forms and "practical necessities."

"Ours is a world of words," Poe wrote in "Al Aaraaf." Perhaps "national spirit" was as merely a word as "spirit" itself. Still, Emerson insisted in "The Poet," "every word was once a poem"; and "though the origin of most of our words is forgotten, each word was at first a stroke of genius, and obtained currency because for the moment it symbolized the world to the first speaker and to the hearer. The etymologist finds the deadest word to have been once a brilliant picture." For Hawthorne, as also for Melville, it was in these terms the ultimate task of the national romancer to trace the expressions of his culture back to their origins, like the God of Poe's *Eureka* deducing live Spirit from dead Matter, "impossible conceptions" from "mere words." The American romancer was to function as etymologist for that most mysterious of words, "America." "Genius," Emerson declared, "is the activity which repairs the decay of things."[5] Neither Hawthorne nor Melville was so sanguine about the possibility of repairing such decay, but they both set out to understand it—to understand what they saw as the historical transformation of America's originating "spirit" into the verbal mask, the rhetoric, of nineteenth-century culture.

Every word might once have been a poem, but for Hawthorne, as for Melville, the deepest historical implication of this Emersonian doctrine was the conviction that every poem became, inevitably, a word and that efforts at "revolutionary" or "poetic" revival were ultimately fruitless or worse. In Hawthorne's view, America had moved from warm inspiration to cold artificiality over the course of the seventeenth century and again in the years since the Revolution. The word, Poe discovered, was the corpse of its origin. So, added Hawthorne, was the nation. Genius, Emerson insisted, might repair "the decay of things." But such decay, as Hawthorne read our history, had stemmed in the first place from the eruption of revolutionary genius.

THE DECAY OF THINGS

Society, when it appears in Hawthorne's fiction, is usually presented as a mass spectacle. One thinks of the witches' sabbath in "Young Goodman Brown," the hostile or puzzled Puritan congregations of "The Gentle Boy" or "The Minister's Black Veil," the crowds of "Endicott and the Red Cross" or "Wakefield," the processions of "My Kinsman, Major Molineux," *The Scarlet Letter*, and *The House of the Seven Gables*. Social differentiation or conflict is rendered, at best, through rival masses: the royalist procession and Puritan crowd in "The Gray Champion," the gay revelers and somber Puritans in "The May-Pole of Merry Mount." In Hawthorne's short stories and, for the most part, in his four romances, society is mainly an abstraction. Crowds, or individual representatives of social tendencies, act as counters for some conception of society as it functions in the story or affects the protagonist. Thus we have evil in "Young Goodman Brown," intolerance in "The Gentle Boy," utilitarian "reality" in "The Artist of the Beautiful." In terms of density or complexity of rendering, with the possible exception of *The Scarlet Letter*, there is rather little "society" in Hawthorne's fiction. It focuses, rather, on individual conflict.

Nevertheless, this individual conflict, especially in Hawthorne's historical tales, is profoundly social in its import. Endicott, Brown, Robin, and the rest function, for their times, as what Emerson called "representative men." Their tales consequently demand to be read, among other ways, as what we might call fictional psychohistories. So read, they tell a clear story of the initial inspiration and subsequent decline of the Puritan experiment in New England, a story I have described elsewhere in detail.[6] Briefly put: the first generation courageously asserted its independence of British tyranny, but the discipline demanded by this assertion led to intolerance and to a rigid, "iron" formalism of enforced social conformity. The ultimate legacy of this fierce independence was the repression of passion, "gayety," and freedom of imagination in New England, especially for the children and grandchildren of the founders.

This vision of New England's social history had direct relevance to Hawthorne's practice and problems as a romancer. Was not the great danger of romance, as of Puritanism, the inevitable sublimation of imaginative freedom into empty formalism, of "sentiments" into "words"? Moreover, Puritan formalism had, for Hawthorne, a specifically allegorical dimension. Hawthorne's Puritans—notably Young Goodman Brown but many others as well—formalize and repress life by allegorizing it, by subordinating it to abstract conceptions such as "good," "evil," or "Adulteress." In 1854 Philip Schaff, the German theologian and student of American culture, noted the "nationalistic nakedness and . . . barrenness for the imagination and the heart" of America's Puritanic forms (or antiforms) of worship. In their war against "symbolical forms," he writes, "the Puritans displayed . . . the same pedantry and fanaticism, nay, we may even say the same formalism—only reversed, negative—as the Papists and Episcopalians in their zeal for them; and gave proof, that an extreme spiritualism, which overlooks the true import of the divinely created body, very easily passes unawares into its own opposite."[7] In this sense even the overtly antisymbolical gestures of Hawthorne's Puritans—such as Endicott's cutting down the May-Pole or his tearing the Red Cross from the British flag—exhibit a kind of "reversed" allegorical fanaticism.

All of these implications are clear in the sketch "Main Street" (1849), Hawthorne's fullest examination of Puritan history before *The Scarlet Letter*. Hawthorne is more sympathetic than Schaff to the original revolutionary impulse of Puritanism:

How could they dispense with the carved altar-work?—how, with the pictured windows, where the light of common day was hallowed by being transmitted through the glorified figures of saints? ... They needed nothing of all this. Their house of worship, like their ceremonial, was naked, simple, and severe. But the zeal of a recovered faith burned like a lamp within their hearts, ... being, in itself, that spiritual mystery and experience, of which sacred architecture, pictured windows, and the organ's grand solemnity, are remote and imperfect symbols. [58]

The original Puritans did not need the material culture of art. They were directly in touch with the "spiritual mystery" that stood as the originating source of both art and culture.

In Hawthorne's account, however, this direct experience of "spiritual mystery" did not last:

All was well, so long as their lamps were freshly kindled at the heavenly flame. After a while, however, whether in their time or their children's, these lamps began to burn more dimly, or with a less genuine lustre; and then it might be seen, how hard, cold, and confined, was their system,—how like an iron cage was that which they called Liberty! [58]

The original impulse was confined by the detritus of its expression. "In truth," Hawthorne continues,

when the first novelty and stir of spirit had subsided,—when the new settlement, between the forest-border and the sea, had become actually a little town,—its daily life must have trudged onward with hardly any thing to diversify and enliven it, while also its rigidity could not fail to cause miserable distortions of the moral nature. Such a life was sinister to the intellect, and sinister to the heart; especially when one generation had bequeathed its religious gloom, and the counterfeit of its religious ardor, to the next; for these characteristics, as was inevitable, assumed the form both of hypocrisy and exaggeration, by being inherited from the example and precept of other human beings, and not from an original and spiritual source. The sons and grandchildren of the first settlers were a race of lower and narrower souls than their progenitors had been. [67–68]

It was with the historical course of Puritanism as with the expressive course of romance: the "original and spiritual source" expressed itself in increasingly rigid forms of belief, behavior, and social expectation—in a kind of increasingly "arabesque" social language. When the first "stir of spirit" subsided, only the language remained.

By the time of the second or third generation in New England, Puritan culture had become literally allegorical. It had come to be dominated by what Coleridge, speaking of his own culture, called a "hollowness of abstraction."[8] It had also, as Hawthorne saw it, produced his own nineteenth-century America. As he writes in "Main Street," at the close of his gloomy summary of the decline of Puritanism: "Nor, it may be, have we even yet thrown off all the unfavorable influences which, among many good ones, were bequeathed to us by our Puritan forefathers" (68). The legacy of Puritanism was a world of hollow abstractions, shells of spirit—a world of words.

The Scarlet Letter opens only twelve years after the initial migration to Boston, but the first "stir of spirit" has, clearly, already subsided. In spite of its historical youth, this community, as Hawthorne describes it, is principally characterized by age and rigidity. "The wooden jail," we are told, "was already marked with weather-stains and other indications of age.... The rust on the ponderous iron-work of its oaken door looked more antique than any thing else in the new world.... It seemed never to have known a youthful era" (47–48). In 1857, commenting in his *English Notebooks* on the elaborateness of the Anglican service, Hawthorne wrote of his own ancestors that they "showed their strength of mind and heart, by ... lopping away all these externals, into which religious life had first gushed and flowered, and then petrified" (451). By the opening of *The Scarlet Letter* the Puritans have themselves repeated the process against which they originally rebelled. Looking at the crowd around the prison door, Hawthorne notes "the grim rigidity that petrified the bearded physiognomies of these good people" (49). The Puritan impulse to repair the decay of things has only instituted another cycle of decay.

Set against this formal petrification is the vitality of Hester Prynne.[9] She is early associated with the Catholic "image of Divine Maternity" (56), as Pearl will later remind Bellingham of court masques and Wilson of "the sun ... shining through a richly painted window, ... of those naughty elfs or fairies, whom we thought to have left behind us, with other relics of Papistry, in merry old England" (109–10). Like the rosebush outside the prison, Hester stands for the qualities of passion and imagination repressed by the Puritans and, in her case, literally imprisoned. The opening ceremony has a clear and deliberate import: Hester is being made to play the role of Adulteress in the allegorical social drama through which the Puritans maintain their community against, among other things, any further eruptions of the "spiritual mystery" that first established it.

Hester rebels, at first implicitly, then openly. This is the central "story"

176

of *The Scarlet Letter*. As an artist, she transforms by her needlework what are meant to be badges of her shameful status—the letter and Pearl—into images of her passionate "individuality." She accordingly comes to incarnate the Utopian spirit lost to Boston as a whole:

> It was an age in which the human intellect, newly emancipated, had taken a more active and a wider range than for many centuries before. Men of the sword had overthrown nobles and kings.[10] Men bolder than these had overthrown and rearranged—not actually, but within the sphere of theory, which was their most real abode—the whole system of ancient prejudice, wherewith was linked much of ancient principle. Hester Prynne imbibed this spirit. [164]

Like Brockden Brown's Ormond, Hester turns from circumstance to the impulse of sincerity. Like Melville's Ahab, she long masks what would appear to her community as madness or blasphemy.[11] And in the forest, in her insistence to Dimmesdale that "the past is gone!" (202), she attempts to put this "spirit" into practice. Like the Emersonian genius, she sets out, at least for herself, for Pearl, and for Dimmesdale, to repair the decay of things.

Hester's revolutionary sincerity is complicated, however, by a number of factors. Despite her status as victim of allegory, she often sublimates her own impulses into allegory, or projects them onto others, as rigidly as any Puritan. She stays in Boston, she tells herself, to work out her repentance. Is the hope of possible reunion with Dimmesdale among her motives? "She barely looked the idea in the face, and hastened to bar it in its dungeon" (80). What the Puritans do to Hester, as a figure of impulse, Hester does to her own impulses in a way that recalls the comment about secret "truth" and waking "self-deception" in "The Birth-mark." "What she compelled herself to believe," we are told, "—what, finally, she reasoned upon, as her motive for continuing a resident of New England,— was half a truth, and half a self-delusion" (80). Characters in *The Scarlet Letter* have a habit of projecting their secret motives onto others, and, if these others respond by uttering the secrets too openly, of demanding that they "hush." "Mother!—Mother!" Pearl implores, "Why does the minister keep his hand over his heart?" "Hold thy tongue, naughty child!" answers Hester. "Do not tease me; else I shall shut thee into the dark closet!" (172). In such a spirit of mixed sincerity she sets out to meet Dimmesdale in the woods.

In the forest, to be sure, Hester utters openly what she has heretofore kept secret in the prison of her heart, but even here the light of revolutionary sincerity is clouded with irony. Chillingworth, argues Dimmesdale, "violated, in cold blood, the sanctity of a human heart." His sin was deliberate, Hester's and Dimmesdale's spontaneous. "What we did," pleads Hester, "had a consecration of its own. We felt it so! We said so to each other! Hast thou forgotten it?" "Hush, Hester!" Dimmesdale replies before admitting: "No; I have not forgotten" (195). There is a deeper problem here than Dimmesdale's projective hypocrisy, his guilty "Hush!"; for Hester's call to spontaneous action fails to meet her own criteria. Maybe what she and Dimmesdale did, seven years before, was spontaneous, but to do it again, deliberately, could scarcely be equally so. This is the tragic inference behind the Utopianism both of Hester and of the now-formalistic community from which she seeks to escape. To act on the Utopian impulse—to express it or socialize it—is inevitably to allegorize and hence to falsify it. Hawthorne sees clearly the distinction between Dimmesdale's past capitulation to impulse and his present plan of escape with Hester. "This [past deed] had been a sin of passion, not of principle, nor even purpose" (200). To convert "passion" into "principle" or "purpose," in the world of *The Scarlet Letter*, is to trap life in an idea about life. The neutral territory between ideal and actual is a chasm after all.

At the close, Hester still hopes for some reconciliation, if not on earth then in Heaven. "Shall we not meet again?" she whispers. "Shall we not spend our immortal life together?" "Hush, Hester," Dimmesdale replies, "Hush!" And the rest of his response is hardly more comforting: "The law we broke!—the sin here so awfully revealed!—let these alone be in thy thoughts!" (256). Hawthorne's irony here is so devastating as to move from criticism into a kind of awe. As Dimmesdale foresakes overt hypocrisy for overt sincerity, he too falls into the trap of allegory, and in an especially hideous way. Even confronting the spiritual realm, the ultimate Utopia, he smothers what Edgar Huntly called "desperate suggestions" beneath "better thoughts" by projecting the former onto Hester, once again, with his admonitory "Hush." One suspects that, if Dimmesdale were the narrator of *The Scarlet Letter*, the book might sound a bit like a tale by Poe. Even God, in Dimmesdale's final vision, becomes a kind of allegorical double, manipulating on the stage of the world the symbols of the minister's guilty self-justification:

> "He hath proved his mercy, most of all, in my afflictions. By giving me this burning torture to bear upon my breast! By sending yonder dark and terrible old man, to keep the torture always at red-heat! By bringing me hither, to die this death of triumphant ignominy before the people! Had either of these agonies been wanting, I had been lost for ever! Praised be his name! His will be done! Farewell!" [256–57]

Those readers who find Dimmesdale admirable in his confession should pay attention to his image of a God willing to damn Chillingworth in order to bring on the allegorical spectacle of Dimmesdale's "salvation." If the minister's self-serving sense of Providence is plausibly accurate to Puritan rhetoric, as it is, this is only to say that he shows how far the allegorical sublimation of forbidden impulse could go in seventeenth-century New England.[12]

The historical action of *The Scarlet Letter* thus bears out the general analysis of "Main Street": the gradual discovery by Puritan society of "how like an iron cage was that which they called Liberty!" (58). Hester looks from an "estranged point of view at human institutions . . . ; criticizing all with hardly more reverence than the Indian would feel for the clerical band, the judicial robe, the pillory, the gallows, the fireside, or the church. The tendency of her fate and fortunes had been to set her free" (199). The irony of the last sentence should not go unnoticed. And Hester's repudiation of the outward language of culture—"the clerical band, the judicial robe," and the like—is finally as futile as the Puritans' original rejection of Anglican forms of worship. To repudiate the past, in *The Scarlet Letter*, is only to repeat it; for the past as it exists in the rigid formalism of Puritan Boston is but the petrified detritus of an earlier repudiation. Extreme gestures of sincerity, as Dimmesdale's case indicates, lead only to even more extreme formalism and repression.

Petrifaction and Renewal

In the nineteenth-century Salem of "The Custom-House," Hawthorne himself confronts a world of spiritual shells and petrified forms. The town presents a vista of physical ruin; the Custom-House, with its collection of superannuated hangers-on, offers a gallery of human decay. Faced with this community of ruins and near-corpses, Hawthorne is drawn to the vision of freedom he embodies in Hester in the story that follows. "Henceforth," he writes of Salem, "it ceases to be a reality of my life. I am a citizen of somewhere else" (44). The somber irony of Hester's fate, however, hardly supports this exuberant repudiation of the past's "reality." As Hawthorne writes of his heroine, at the close of her story: "There was more real life for Hester Prynne, here, in New England, than in that unknown region where Pearl had found a home" (262–63).

As a romancer, however, Hawthorne finds a freedom denied by the actuality of Puritan Boston or nineteenth-century Salem. In his imagination, in the creative energy behind the romance, he successfully, if only momentarily, repairs the decay of things. "The past was not dead" (27), he writes as he introduces us to the second story of the Custom-House, where he finds Surveyor Pue's manuscript and the frayed scarlet letter. First, however, he finds a pile of commercial documents, recording "the names of vessels that had long ago foundered at sea or rotted at the wharves, and those of merchants, never heard of now on 'Change, nor

179

very readily decipherable on their mossy tombstones." He glances at these documents "with the saddened, weary, half-reluctant interest which we bestow on the corpse of dead activity,—and exerting my fancy, sluggish with little use, to raise up from these dry bones an image of the old town's brighter aspect" (29). If Hawthorne's allusions and imagery here look ahead to Eliot's *Waste Land,* so does his ambition: to make the "dry bones" of the past live in imagination.

Imagery of death and renewal permeates "The Custom-House." We even learn of Surveyor Pue, the original source of Hester's story, that "his remains in the little grave-yard of St. Peter's Church" were dug up eighty years before, "during the renewal of that edifice." Nothing was found, Hawthorne notes, save a wig, some rags of clothing, and "an imperfect skeleton" (30). But Hawthorne's real engagement, adumbrated by this imagery of death and renewal, is with himself. He must revive his own imagination, deadened by the empty formalism of life at the Custom-House. "A gift, a faculty, if it had not departed, was suspended and inanimate within me. There would have been something sad, unutterably dreary, in all this, had I not been conscious that it lay at my own option to recall whatever was valuable in the past" (26). Yet the project of recovering this "gift"—which constitutes the main action of "The Custom-House," as Hester's rebellion constitutes that of *The Scarlet Letter*—is not easily accomplished. "My imagination," Hawthorne reports,

> was a tarnished mirror. It would not reflect, or only with miserable dimness, the figures with which I did my best to people it. The characters of the narrative would not be warmed and rendered malleable, by any heat that I could kindle at my intellectual forge. They would take neither the glow of passion nor the tenderness of sentiment, but retained all the rigidity of dead corpses. [34]

There is more than a touch of Poe in all this metaphorical talk of reviving or reanimating "corpses," and the relevance of these concerns to the story that follows need hardly be mentioned. *The Scarlet Letter* begins and ends with a graveyard. There is something of Hawthorne's impulse toward imaginative renewal in Hester's needlework—in her projection of inner vitality into a dead, allegorical social form. Moreover, the project of Hawthorne's imaginative art, like that of Hester's more overt rebellion, is conceived as running counter to the inevitable course of history. If the Puritans turned life into petrified forms, "hollow abstractions," Hawthorne sets out to return petrified forms to imaginative life.

In this he succeeds, but he does not, in "The Custom-House," confuse what the imagination can momentarily achieve in romance with what individual or social rebellion can accomplish in history, and this point is crucial. Just as Ishmael drifts out of the action of *Moby-Dick*, so the imaginative action of "The Custom-House" is never incorporated into the historical action of *The Scarlet Letter*. If the narrator dramatically revives the past in chapter 1, he just as dramatically allows it to wither again in the "Conclusion." The letter first appears in "The Custom-House," "much worn and faded," its embroidery "greatly frayed and defaced" (31). Hester, filtered through Surveyor Pue and those older citizens from whom he gathered his information, first appears "as a very old, but not decrepit woman" (32). Both are revived, in the book, as in their first bloom, but, by the end, the letter is again on its way to decay and Hester is a corpse.

These points may seem too obvious to mention, but I belabor the distinction for a simple and important reason. In Hawthorne's next two romances, his last published fictions with American settings, the distinction is not so strictly observed. Much of the power of *The Scarlet Letter* stems from Hawthorne's perception and exploitation of the parallels between the course of romance and the course of history—of the shared tension between inspiration and expression, sentiments and words. But the book owes its power, equally, to its careful separation of these two congruent realms.

Richard Poirier, in *A World Elsewhere*, says of "the greatest American authors" that they try, "against the perpetually greater power of reality, to create an environment that might allow some longer existence to the hero's momentary expansions of consciousness." Yet, he recognizes, such permanence can be achieved only in art, not in "reality" itself. The feelings so stabilized "have, as it were, no place in the world, no place at all except where a writer's style can give them one." *The Scarlet Letter* resists the pressure of reality, it achieves the fictive renewal of dead history, because that renewal remains fictive. In *The House of the Seven Gables* Hawthorne attempts to break down this distinction between fictive and "real" (or ideal and actual) renewal, and in *The Blithedale Romance* he portrays a society that no longer understands this distinction. "Style," as Poirier puts it, might "temporarily . . . free the hero (and the reader) from systems"—from imprisoning "pressures of time, biology, economics," and the like;[13] but the "style" of such freedom might also, as Hawthorne increasingly understood, create the most imprisoning and enervating system of all.

In *The House of the Seven Gables* and *The Blithedale Romance*, imaginative renewal, of the sort that occupies Hawthorne in "The Custom-House," is brought into the historical action to become a principle, not just of the artwork, but of society. In both books, what Poirier calls "a world elsewhere" is established here. In *The House of the Seven Gables* this movement from art to society leads to crippling confusion. The contradictions of the book's

ending have been much discussed and need not long detain us here.[14] All
along, Holgrave, the daguerreotypist, has represented the idea of revolutionary progress; he has incarnated the impulse to which Hester gives
utterance in the forest. He is thus opposed to the cyclical sense of tragedy
symbolized by the history of the Pyncheons and by their ancestral mansion. At the close, Judge Pyncheon is dead, Clifford is free, Holgrave
marries Phoebe, and they all move out of the house and presumably out of
the past. It is never clear, however, just how they will avoid recapitulating
the historical cycle that produced the house in the first place. Holgrave
and Phoebe declare their mutual love in a chapter called "The Flower of
Eden," but how they will avoid the fate of the first family is not indicated.
The surviving characters leave the House of the Seven Gables at the close
but do so only to move into another of the Judge's residences. Hawthorne
may intend irony here; if so, it is an irony he refuses to explore.

In *The Scarlet Letter*, Hawthorne portrayed the descent from momentary
inspiration to repressive formalism as an inevitable psychological and historical process. In *The House of the Seven Gables*, he sets out to deny this
inevitability. One of the more striking historical tableaux in *The Scarlet
Letter* is the picture of Governor Bellingham's garden, in which the original attempt to cultivate foreign flowers has been overrun by domestic
vegetables. In 1844 Hawthorne wrote to his friend George Hillard: "I do
not agree with you that poetry ought not to be brought into common life.
If flowers of Eden can be made to grow among my cabbages and squashes,
it will please me so much the better; those excellent vegetables will be just
as good to eat, and the flower no less delightful to see and smell."[15] Here
The Scarlet Letter's stark vision of the irreconcilability of imaginative impulse and material articulation is replaced by the conservative romancer's
program of "mingling" the imaginary and the actual. In culture as in
romance, such "mingling" might overcome the sacrifice of relation. It is in
this spirit that Hawthorne sets out, at the close of *The House of the Seven
Gables*, to mingle tragedy and renewal, darkness and sunshine—to bring
"poetry" back into a world of words. The Judge's death and the return of
the sunlight force into bloom, amid the gables of the corpselike house, the
posies Alice Pyncheon had brought, long ago, from Italy. The implications of Bellingham's garden are reversed. "They . . . seemed, as it
were," we are told, "a mystic expression that something within the house
was consummated" (286). And the next chapter, in which Holgrave's and
Phoebe's love is at least metaphorically consummated, is "The Flower of
Eden."

It seems clear that Hawthorne meant this chapter, and the love it cele-
brates, as both the climax and the moral center of his romance. In love and
light he set out to establish, as an alternative to the empty forms of the
past, a new and direct source of spiritual inspiration. His effort was deeply

rooted in personal experience. "Phoebe" was one of his favorite nicknames for his wife, and in "The Flower of Eden" he is appealing directly to what his marriage, at the age of thirty-eight, had meant to him. In an 1843 letter to Horatio Bridge, responding to Bridge's feeling "that there is nothing worth living for," Hawthorne wrote that he and Sophia recommended falling in love. "It would renew your youth—you would be a boy again, with the deeper feeling and purposes of a man."[16] Such sentiments are characteristic of Hawthorne's comments on his own marriage, and they appear again in "The Flower of Eden." Holgrave declares to Phoebe:

> "The presence of yonder dead man threw a great black shadow over everything; he made the universe, so far as my perception could reach, a scene of guilt, and of retribution more dreadful than the guilt. The sense of it took away my youth. I never hoped to feel young again! . . . But, Phoebe, you crossed the threshold; and hope, warmth, and joy, came in with you! The black moment became at once a blissful one. It must not pass without the spoken word. I love you!" [306]

Love both renews Holgrave and rescues him from the dead formalism of the past. One almost expects the orchestra to strike up, in the background, the accompaniment for a duet about "hope, warmth, and joy."

There is no reason to doubt the happiness and passion of Hawthorne's marriage. It was clearly, for him, a personal renewal. But such happiness raises problems when it is used as a symbol of *social* or *historical* renewal, and this seems to be the case in "The Flower of Eden." As a spontaneous testimony to the moment's power, Holgrave's "I love you!" is one thing, but as an effort to make the moment permanent—to make it, even, the basis of a new social system—his need to express his feeling in "the spoken word" has possibly ominous implications. Holgrave, we are told, "gathered a wild enjoyment—as it were, a flower of strange beauty, growing in a desolate spot, and blossoming in the wind—such a flower of momentary happiness he gathered from his present position" (305). In their moment of blissful love, Holgrave and Phoebe "were conscious of nothing sad nor old. They transfigured the earth, and made it Eden again, and themselves the two first dwellers in it" (307). Yet Holgrave's prophecy of the social expression of his happiness is totally at odds with the source of his inspiration:

> "The world owes all its onward impulse to men ill at ease. The happy man inevitably confines himself within ancient limits. I have a presentiment, that, hereafter, it will be my lot to set out trees, to make fences—perhaps, even, in due time, to build a house for another generation—in a word, to conform myself to laws, and the peaceful practice of society." [306–7]

That Holgrave's new conservatism simply and suddenly overthrows his former radicalism is an important index of the confusion of *The House of the Seven Gables*, but it is even more important to recognize how fully this capitulation to social forms contradicts that momentary experience, that "first stir of spirit," upon which it is apparently based. Love does not renew society; it does not change the social order. It simply provides a new, and highly contradictory, legitimacy for society as it already exists.

Hawthorne is at least partly aware of the contradiction between momentary and systematic happiness in "The Flower of Eden." When "the world" intrudes, on the return of Clifford and Hepzibah, the spell is broken, the moment past. It is only in the ritual comic conclusion of the final chapter that love is apparently made the basis of a new symbolic social order. We can perhaps understand, if not quite forgive, Hawthorne's succumbing to comic convention and the wishes of his readers; for when he could avert his eyes from his darker knowledge, these wishes were his own. In *The Blithedale Romance*, however, he would subject to stricter scrutiny the effort to make the fleeting personal experience of love into a systematic social ideal.

The deadness of the language of social forms is, in *The House of the Seven Gables*, less directly relevant to Hawthorne's aesthetic concerns than it is in either *The Scarlet Letter* or *The Blithedale Romance*. What lies behind the Pyncheon legacy is not a "first stir of spirit" but a brazen act of capitalist appropriation. Neither the nineteenth-century Judge nor his seventeenth-century progenitor, "the original perpetrator and father of this mischief" (185), was ever involved in the heroic assertion of spiritual truth against the tyranny of corrupt forms; but in the relationship of Holgrave to Phoebe there is a fascinating hint that Hawthorne is investigating his art as well as his society, for "Phoebe," symbol of sunlight, is more than a representative of moral regeneration—she symbolizes, as well, the source of Holgrave's art. As Holgrave explains the role of sunlight in daguerreotypy: "There is a wonderful insight in heaven's broad and simple sunshine. While we give it credit only for depicting the merest surface, it actually brings out the secret character with a truth that no painter would ever venture upon, even could he detect it" (91). One thinks of Hawthorne's description of his own art in his preface to *The Snow-Image:* as "burrowing, to [my] utmost ability, into the depths of our common nature, for the purposes of psychological romance" (4). In loving Phoebe, perhaps, Holgrave is turning from the outward forms of his art to its source, from words to sentiments.

The problem here is that the source of art, as Hawthorne understood it, was scarcely so moral or respectable as Phoebe is. It was more like Hester's love, a repressed, imaginative passion, or like those "spectres," those "affrighting . . . secrets," that, according to "The Birth-mark," escape the heart's dungeon in dreams. Phoebe, by contrast, serves mainly to legitimize as "truth" what the Hawthorne of "The Birth-mark" understood to be waking "self-deception." Hawthorne would be closer to his full sense of artistic imagination, of the mysterious source of art, in the obscure relationship of Miriam to her demonic model in *The Marble Faun*. When Hawthorne wrote *The House of the Seven Gables*, Melville was also exploring the principle of sunlight as original and originating source in *Moby-Dick;* but the "colorless, all-color of atheism from which we shrink" (169), which Ishmael discovers in "The Whiteness of the Whale," is a far cry from Phoebe's slightly idealized but nevertheless solidly respectable "reality."

FROM SENTIMENTS TO SENTIMENTALITY

Hawthorne discovered, in the gap between original spirit and formal expression, a common ground between the duplicity of his art and the history of his society. The process of imaginative expression thus provided, for him, a kind of paradigm for America's tragic movement from beginnings to results, from living mystery to "the death of that old spirit." "In proportion as I gain power over words," Brown's Edgar Huntly complained, "shall I lose dominion over sentiments." In proportion as Puritan New England gained institutional or cultural articulation, as Hawthorne read its history, it lost dominion over its originating spirit.

In *The Scarlet Letter* this sense of common ground between artistic expression and historical process creates a subtle relationship but one that Hawthorne never literalizes. In *The House of the Seven Gables* he does try to literalize it, with unfortunate results. In *The Blithedale Romance* the relationship is again literal, but the confusion of aesthetic or psychological and social or political is no longer Hawthorne's strategy, it is his subject. One might well say of *The Blithedale Romance* what Allan Seager said of Nathanael West's *The Day of the Locust*: it is "not fantasy imagined, but fantasy seen."[17] Like West's Los Angeles, Hawthorne's Blithedale has not just lost sight of the distinction between social actualities and social ideals; it has lost sight of the more fundamental distinction between the rhetoric of society and the rhetoric of art.

The main theme of *The Blithedale Romance* is once again renewal—the revival of empty forms into spiritual youth and warmth. This theme operates on many levels: not only social or cultural but also personal, aesthetic, and perhaps even religious. The Utopian experiment, like the love of Holgrave and Phoebe in *The House of the Seven Gables*, is a "scheme for beginning the life of Paradise anew" (9). It is a return to lost origins—to a fresh air, as Coverdale puts it, that has "not been spoken into words of falsehood, formality, and error" (11). Coverdale himself moves to

Blithedale in search of a renewal at once personal—the discovery of a new purpose in life—and aesthetic—the connection of his poetry with something "real" or "substantial." Priscilla, too, like Coverdale's insubstantial fancies, is revived by being "mingled" with substantial reality. Even the drinking of the old topers, in the saloon where Coverdale seeks out Old Moodie, is tied to the general theme of renewal—in terms that again recall Holgrave's appeal to Phoebe. "The true purpose of their drinking," Coverdale explains, "—and one that will induce men to drink, or do something equivalent, as long as this weary world shall endure—was the renewed youth and vigor, the brisk, cheerful sense of things present and to come, with which, for about a quarter-of-an-hour, the dram permeated their systems" (178).[18]

Coverdale's "for about a quarter-of-an-hour" is ominous. All the efforts at renewal in *The Blithedale Romance*, including the Utopian experiment itself, are equally, if not always so rapidly, evanescent, and Coverdale implies a historical development more enervating, even, than the displacement of original spirit into empty formalism. For the saloon images a Utopian impulse that has moved from "spirit" to "spirits"—from genuine inspiration to artificial stimulants. The account of Westervelt's spiritualism reveals how fully, in the nineteenth-century America of *The Blithedale Romance*, even the antiformal impulse of spiritual regeneration has become a species of formal, mechanical artifice. It is in this sense that America, as a culture, has literalized the direst implications of the romance. Westervelt promises spiritual rebirth, but it is to be sought, apparently, through chemical means.[19]

Coverdale is careful to distance himself from Westervelt's bogus spiritualism, yet he has earlier admitted (102) to a sense of kinship with the professor. The night before setting out for Blithedale, we learn in the book's first sentence, Coverdale had attended "the wonderful exhibition of the Veiled Lady" (15), and he returns to it toward the close; he is, in fact, well on his way to becoming a regular customer. There are more than a few suggestive similarities between Westervelt's spurious art and the art of Miles Coverdale, as romancer,[20] and the account of Westervelt's plans for the regeneration of the world sounds a good deal like the project of the Blithedale Utopians. "He spoke," writes Coverdale, "of a new era that was dawning upon the world; an era that would link soul to soul, and the present life to what we call futurity, with a closeness that should finally convert both worlds into one great, mutually conscious brotherhood" (200).

Of course, the community's failure—its betrayal of its ideals—is to some extent a result of practical policital or social problems. The bond of the community is, as Coverdale puts it, "not affirmative, but negative"

(63). Theirs is a rebellion without a positive program. The one bond or ideal they do espouse in common, "familiar love" (19), is difficult to implement. They eschew competition only to find themselves in commercial competition with the outside world, and, internally, the ideal of "familiar love" soon gives way to the nasty reality of sexual competition among Zenobia, Priscilla, Hollingsworth, and Coverdale. As with the "Utopia of human virtue and happiness," described at the outset of *The Scarlet Letter*, so, at Blithedale, "practical necessities" soon overwhelm the ideals of the "original project."

Coverdale's artistic ideals also succumb, in his view, to a tyranny of inevitable circumstance. He sets out, through immersion in the "reality" of farming, to produce verse at once "poetic" and "real." His is the ideal of the conservative romancer: he will "mingle" the Imaginary and the Actual. But actuality overwhelms his poetry as surely as it overwhelms the idealism of the Utopians. "Our labor," Coverdale laments, "symbolized nothing, and left us mentally sluggish in the dusk of the evening. Intellectual activity is incompatible with any large amount of bodily exercise" (66).

There is something disingenuous, however, in this explanation. The real failure, of the Blithedale experiment and of Coverdale's art, is not a triumph of actual over ideal. It is, rather, a prior failure of idealism—a failure of the artist and his society to confront the true nature of the originating spirit of literary and social order. What Coverdale and his cohorts call an appeal to imagination or spirit is in fact an evasion of both. Several cultural historians have recently described what they see as a failure of Romanticism in nineteenth-century America, namely, the refusal of accepted cultural spokesmen and spokeswomen to acknowledge the reality of social and psychological disrelation, the dark night of the soul, confronted by their great European and British contemporaries.[21] I suggested at the end of chapter 6 that American romance came to maturity, in the works of Hawthorne and Melville, when it learned to examine and exploit precisely this cultural crisis.

In this sense, and nowhere more clearly than in Coverdale's musings on his purpose as an artist, the failure of American Romanticism is the great subject of *The Blithedale Romance*; for in Coverdale's theory and practice of literary art we see the ultimate extension of his society's corruption of regenerative "spirit." Zenobia, he writes,

> should have made it a point of duty . . . to sit endlessly to painters and sculptors, and preferably to the latter; because the cold decorum of the marble would consist with the utmost scantiness of drapery, so that the eye might chastely be gladdened with her material perfection, in its entireness. [44]

The duplicity of this appeal to artistic etherealization—the tension between "chastely" and "gladdened"—is suggested even more forcefully in
Coverdale's account of the realistic paintings of roast beef, sirloins and the
like, that he encounters later in the saloon. In these paintings, he insists
"you seemed to have the genuine article before you, and yet with an
indescribable, ideal charm." Earlier, however, he has speculated: "Some
very hungry painter, I suppose, had wrought these subjects of still life,
heightening his imagination with his appetite, and earning, it is to be
hoped, the privilege of a daily dinner off whichever of his pictorial viands
he liked best" (176). It is interesting to read this idea back to the passage
about being "chastely . . . gladdened," through art, by Zenobia's "material
perfection." Coverdale's "aesthetic" prurience, his sublimation of "appetite" into "ideal charm," suggests at the very least that Hawthorne understood a good deal about what went on beneath the "chaste" surface of his
culture's bogus "idealism." Like Washington Irving, Coverdale displaces
his guilty fantasies into the safer realms of "spiritual" or "aesthetic"
platitude, and Hawthorne is fully aware of the operation of this displacement.

Coverdale's unacknowledged prurience, moreover, provides a kind of
paradigm for the general failure of Blithedale. Of the Utopians we meet,
only Zenobia comes anywhere near to trusting the community's alleged
"spirit." She is the only one whose love is open and passionate, untinged
by opportunism, and the community suppresses her sincerity and sexuality, her frank awareness that "familiar love" may have something to do
with sex, as thoroughly as does the romancer, Miles Coverdale. Like
Coverdale's art, the community's treatment of Zenobia forces upon her
precisely the fate that Aylmer, in his refusal to face and acknowledge the
"truth" obscured by his scientific "self-deception," forces upon Georgiana.
As a result of Aylmer's experiment, Georgiana's cheek assumes a "marble
paleness" (54); in death she becomes literally a statue. Coverdale wishes
"chastely" to indulge his repressed sexual fantasies about Zenobia by
displacing her into "the cold decorum of . . . marble." Zenobia, at the close
of *The Blithedale Romance*, becomes "the marble image of a death-agony"
(235). Zenobia, to be sure, has her faults and excesses, but it is in the
community's refusal to acknowledge in her the truths masked by its
"idealism" that we see the strong parallel between Blithedale and Coverdale's romance about it—in the repressiveness and shallowness of that
"ideal" toward which both strive.

The ideal's fullest incarnation, if one may use so strong a term, is
Priscilla. She is *already* "ideal." She is already, in Coverdale's terms, "ar-
tistically" safe. Indeed, she is a literalization of a fictional stereotype, the

sexless, "girlish" woman, and the community, at Hollingsworth's suggestion, happily accepts its treatment of her as the test of its adherence to its
ideals. But the ideal represented by Priscilla is highly suspect.[22] Her
initial appearance of ethereality is just that, an appearance. It has more in
common with the emaciation of Poe's "spiritual" vampires than with any
true spiritual quality. And Priscilla, we must not forget, *is* the Veiled
Lady, the star of Westervelt's spurious show. Finally, Priscilla's actions
and apparent motives, whatever her appearance, are hardly admirable.
She comes to Blithedale to test Zenobia's sisterly love, but she conceals
from Zenobia the fact that they are sisters. As a result, Old Moodie takes
his money from Zenobia and transfers it to Priscilla, who then, apparently
as a consequence, gets Zenobia's man.

If this is "ideality," it is ideality of a peculiarly acquisitive and ultimately prosperous sort. It reminds one of Arthur Mervyn's equally successful pursuit of sincerity; and Priscilla's success, like Arthur's, involves
the deliberate sublimation of "desperate suggestions" into "better
thoughts." With Priscilla an "artistic" ideal enters directly into the action
of *The Blithedale Romance*, but hers is an "art," not of expression, but of
repression. She is "ideal" largely in appearing sexless. She exists and
prospers entirely as an evasive sublimation of all those fantasies Coverdale
can indulge only "chastely." Coverdale's evasion of Zenobia, his turning
instead to the "ideality" of art or of Priscilla, is ultimately an evasion of
himself, of the impulses he cannot face openly without guilt. It is an
evasion of true Romanticism, of truly imaginative self-discovery. His
confession of "love" for Priscilla, on the other hand, is a capitulation to
bogus Romanticism, to sentimentality. Passion is made safe by being
surrounded with all the trappings of spiritual religion. But this rhetoric,
Hawthorne's irony makes clear, still has as its basis the very guilty fantasy
it is meant to repress; and sentimentality, as Priscilla's prosperity reveals,
is the rhetoric not only of Coverdale's repressed imagination but of his
culture.

What has been sentimentalized most fully, in *The Blithedale Romance*, is
the very impulse toward regeneration that lay at the heart of the Puritan
migration and that supposedly lies at the heart of Blithedale. The faith of
the founders, Hawthorne writes in "Main Street," was in itself a genuine
"spiritual mystery" (58). At Blithedale, a community that has retreated in
guilty fear from *true* "spirit" and "mystery," such terms are used in a
curious fashion. The "freedom" of Zenobia's "deportment" leads a nervous Coverdale to surmise that she is "a woman to whom wedlock had
thrown wide the gates of mystery." "What are you seeking to discover in
me?" asks Zenobia. "The mystery of your life," answers Coverdale (47).

Earlier, he meditates on the peculiarities of the little purses Priscilla manufactures, which Old Moodie, we learn later, is in the habit of "quietly insinuating under the notice" of young gentlemen in the saloon (178):

> Their peculiar excellence, besides the great delicacy and beauty of the manufacture, lay in the almost impossibility that any uninitiated person should discover the aperture; although, to a practised touch, they would open as wide as charity or prodigality might wish. I wondered if it were not a symbol of Priscilla's own mystery. [35]

Worst of all is Coverdale's grisly account of the search for Zenobia's body:

> Hollingsworth at first sat motionless, with the hooked-pole elevated in the air. But, by-and-by, with a nervous and jerky movement, he began to plunge it into the blackness that upbore us, setting his teeth, and making precisely such thrusts, methought, as if he were stabbing at a deadly enemy. I bent over the side of the boat. So obscure, however, so awfully mysterious, was that dark stream, that—and the thought made me shiver like a leaf—I might as well have tried to look into the enigma of the eternal world, to discover what had become of Zenobia's soul, as into the river's depths, to find her body. [233]

For all its sentimental rhetoric, this passage, like Aylmer's gruesome dream or the *Mad Trist* of Poe's Lancelot Canning, transforms sexual fantasy into guilty aggression. Such is the course of the "love" that Blithedale has set out to embody as a social ideal. It fails not so much because of the counterforce of individual selfishness as because it is itself no "ideal" but a hollow abstraction, a denial or evasion of its own most central reality.

The obscene *double-entendres* in these passages are clearly not deliberate on Coverdale's part, but they are just as surely deliberate on Hawthorne's and may thus suggest what "dale" it is the narrator wishes to "cover." The point is that a culture that has sublimated sexuality into a quasi-religious vocabulary of "spirit" and "mystery," a sentimentalized displacement of the truths of imagination or fantasy, is inevitably going to slip into unintended *double-entendre* in its "spiritual" discourse. For this discourse and the culture that sustains it no longer *have* any genuine basis in "spiritual" experience; they have sacrificed that relation. What drives them is the unacknowledgable force of their evasion, of their sacrifice. Characters in *The Scarlet Letter*, I noted earlier, have a habit of silencing those who hint at their own deepest impulses with an admonitory "Hush." In the spiritual "ideality" of Blithedale, this "Hush" has become an aesthetic and social principle.

We must be very clear about what happens in *The Blithedale Romance*. In a sense we might say that the suppression or repression of Zenobia is

190

simply a nineteenth-century version of what happens to Hester in *The Scarlet Letter*. The Puritan fathers, however, are quite open about what they are doing: they suppress Hester's rebellious passion because it threatens their civil system. While they may imprison and punish her, they do not sentimentalize either her motives or their own. Her ideals, whatever their connection to the community's "first stir of spirit," are not their ideals. The Utopians at Blithedale, on the other hand, claim to espouse the very individualism for which Zenobia stands. Hester at least had the support of coherent opposition. Zenobia confronts a world, by contrast, in which a sentimentalized language of social and spiritual "idealism" has become a medium of psychological repression and social control. In the allegorical social drama of *The Scarlet Letter*, the Beadle and the scaffold may also be forces of social control, but this control is overt. The Beadle and the scaffold, in this sense, mean what they say. In the "ideal" social drama of Blithedale, things mean precisely what they do not say.

Blithedale's sentimental language of social control finds its objective correlative in Priscilla and does so with a straight face. The irony of this language, as it functions to conceal the guilty fears and fantasies at its heart, is never openly acknowledged. The whole culture has taken on the quality of one of Poe's "arabesques." If Zenobia behaves at times melodramatically or theatrically, as in the mode of her suicide, we can hardly blame her. Hester was forced to play a part in a drama that, for all its allegorical coerciveness, was rooted in "practical necessities," but Zenobia acts in a world in which such necessities, and the regenerative impulse that stands against them, have taken on the character of fiction.

"A veil may be needful," Hawthorne wrote in his *American Notebooks* in the mid-1830s, "but never a mask" (23). Coverdale accuses Zenobia of using her name as "a sort of mask" (8); he prefers the spurious spirituality of Priscilla, the Veiled Lady. But it is Coverdale and his community who, in their refusal to confront the full implications of the imaginative regeneration they claim to espouse, turn the veil of symbolic expression into a mask of evasion. They thus turn their social life—quite literally, when Coverdale returns to Blithedale—into a masquerade. It is in this sense that Coverdale's guilty obfuscation becomes symptomatic of a more general social obfuscation. Seventeenth-century New England, in Hawthorne's view, displaced sentiments into words. Their nineteenth-century descendants at Blithedale have lost sight of the distinction. For sentiments they have substituted sentimentality.

It was against precisely such sentimental evasion that Melville spent the bulk of his career protesting. Zenobia strikes the Melvillean note in her final speech to Coverdale, before his first departure from Blithedale: "It needs a wild steersman when we voyage through Chaos! The anchor is up!

Farewell!" (142). But no one at Blithedale is willing to cast off all cables. At their next meeting Coverdale accuses Zenobia, in his mind, of turning herself into "a work of art" (164), but she has no choice in a society whose only surviving values are, in the worst sense, "artistic." Even in asserting that he "malevolently beheld the true character of the woman" beneath her outward style, Coverdale can describe this character only in "aesthetic" terms: "passionate, luxurious, lacking simplicity, not deeply refined, incapable of pure and perfect taste."[23] It is small wonder that in Zenobia's gestures Coverdale sees "something like the illusion which a great actress flings around her" (165), for the world in which she acts is less a community than an audience. In such a world, as the one-legged cynic puts it in Melville's *Confidence-Man*, "to do, is to act; so all doers are actors" (27).

"A man tries to be happy in love," Hawthorne wrote in his Notebook in 1837; "he cannot sincerely give his heart, and the affair seems all a dream. In domestic life, the same; in politics, a seeming patriot; but still he is sincere, and all seems like a theatre" (153). In the vision of New England's history articulated in Hawthorne's three American-based romances, the plight of this hypothetical man is finally the plight of the actual nation. What had begun in the sincere energy of spiritual sentiment had ended in the cold order of theatrical artifice, of sentimentality. Under the sway of the first, revolutionary, "stir of spirit," America had sacrificed its relation to England, to the language of established social tradition. Over the next two centuries American culture had sacrificed or repressed, as well, its relation to this originating impulse. American actuality had lost touch with America's supposed ideals.

To describe Hawthorne's picture of America in terms of the disparity between the actual and the ideal is to make his work sound like political criticism—comparable, say, to the political and social fiction of James Fenimore Cooper.[24] But the "ideals" with which Hawthorne concerns himself are not political values like "justice" and "equality." They are, rather, "spiritual," experiential. What separates American actuality from American ideals, in Hawthorne's fiction, is not political imperfection but an inevitable historical process—an invariable movement from gushing to petrifaction. Hawthorne's vision of America thus has less in common with political criticism than with such theories of psycho- or sociohistorical process as Max Weber's routinization of charisma or Norman O. Brown's cultural sublimation.[25]

Hawthorne, of course, never read Weber or Brown, but similar theories of history, seeing in the rise of civilized order the repression of originating energy, were as current in his day as in ours. Orthodox eighteenth- and nineteenth-century moralists, even as they dissociated civilization from "primitivism," saw the former as growing out of the latter. Rousseau appealed to the state of nature to legitimize revolution against artificial tyranny. Emerson spoke repeatedly of history as a process of petrifaction. Hawthorne hardly shared the faith of Rousseau or Emerson in the possibilities of revolutionary renewal, for he understood too well the compulsion, both for the individual and for the culture, to displace the "truth" of originating experience into the order of "unconscious self-deception." Still, his sense of historical process itself is not so far from that of Rousseau or Emerson.

Nevertheless, Hawthorne also found a paradigm for the disrelation of historic development in the disrelation of romance, of imaginative literary expression. Both processes, for him, led inexorably to "the death of that old spirit." In *The Blithedale Romance* the importance of this paradigm is clear in the many similarities between Coverdale's repressive art and the repressive community in which he practices it, and in *The Marble Faun*, moving from the history of America to the whole history of the West, Hawthorne would analyze simultaneously the dissociation of Christian civilization from its pagan origins and of artistic expression from imaginative inspiration. "Your stile and manner," wrote the skeptical Correspondent to Brown's sincere Rhapsodist in 1789, "betray you" (17). So had the "spirit" of America, in Hawthorne's vision of its history, been "betrayed" by its "stile and manner."

America, so the radical nationalist argument went, was to be a land in which the ideal became actual, the visionary a fact of life—a land in which "our common nature" could live free of "artificial distinctions," to use Channing's terms. But there was always the fear articulated in Brown's *Speculatist* essays in 1800:

> No man is willing to acknowledge, even to himself, the sinister views which sometimes prompt him to action; nor to examine, with a rigid scrutiny, the little artifices with which he sometimes degrades himself, much less to acknowledge to the world, that he is but performing a part in order to gain its good opinion.... Hence it is that life appears like one great masquerade, at which every object is decked in false colours, and the attention of observers diverted from an useful analysis of the genuine character, by the vagaries of the one which is assumed. [26]

The Blithedale Romance portrays an America in which these fears have been fully realized.

EIGHT

We Americans are the peculiar, chosen people—the Israel of our time; we bear the ark of the liberties of the world. . . . Long enough have we been skeptics with regard to ourselves, and doubted whether, indeed, the political Messiah had come. But he has come in us, *if we would but give utterance to his promptings.*

MELVILLE, White-Jacket

He chanced to come to a placard nigh the captain's office, offering a reward for the capture of a mysterious impostor, supposed to have recently arrived from the East; quite an original genius in his vocation, as would appear, though wherein his originality consisted was not clearly given; but what purported to be a careful description of his person followed.

MELVILLE, The Confidence-Man

MASKS OF SINCERITY
Herman Melville

MELVILLE'S WRITINGS STAND AS THE CULMINATION OF THE TRADITION OF experimental American romance. Chronologically, of course, his public career as a fiction writer, beginning with the appearance of *Typee* in 1846, naturally follows the careers of Brown, Irving, Poe, and Hawthorne. More significantly, Melville concludes this study because his career and writings comprehensively recapitulate the concerns, problems, and practices of his predecessors. Like these predecessors he followed the imperative of subjective mimesis, the impulse of sincerity, into the imprisoning arabesque trap of language. Like Hawthorne, moreover, he found in the duplicity of his medium a kind of metaphor or model for portraying the duplicity of his society.

However, what particularly distinguishes Melville, in addition to his evident genius, is that he engaged in the fully "deviant" or "revolutionary" project of romance more openly than any of his predecessors. Like Hawthorne, he sensed the underlying connection between the originating "spirits" of romance and of "revolutionary" America. Unlike Hawthorne, however, and unlike most of his literary contemporaries, he openly celebrated this connection. Again and again, at least up to *Moby-Dick*, his writings explicitly and hopefully identify the spirit of romance with the revolutionary impulse to strip away what William Ellery Channing called "artificial distinctions." Genuine literature, as Melville defines it in "Hawthorne and His *Mosses*," holds to "spiritual truth" in a "world of lies" (408). And "the Declaration of Independence," he wrote to Evert Duyckinck, "makes a difference" (80). Thus it is that in the chapter "Sailing On," in *Mardi*, the romancer's "chartless voyage" is explicitly linked to the voyage of Christopher Columbus:

That voyager steered his bark through seas, untracked before;
ploughed his own path mid jeers; though with a heart that oft was
heavy with the thought, that he might only be too bold, and grope
where land was none.

So I.   [556–57]

And thus it is that in "Knights and Squires," in *Moby-Dick*, Ishmael's
invocation of the "Spirit of Equality," the "great democratic God" (105), is
at once a celebration of American political liberty and an appeal for literary inspiration and legitimacy.

Melville's literary career begins, in *Typee*, with Tommo jumping ship at
Nukuheva to escape "the unmitigated tyranny of the captain" (21). It ends
with a British captain justifying the execution of an innocent Billy Budd
on the grounds that he can thereby suppress mutiny, that is to say, revolution. From first to last the legitimacy not just of social authority but of
the impulse to rebel against it constituted for Melville a theme of overwhelming importance.[1] *Mardi*, like *Typee*, begins with the hero-narrator
jumping ship. Parts of the book take up, in allegorical form, the European
revolutions of 1848; at the close, King Media departs to deal with a similar
uprising in his own kingdom. It is possible that a mutiny against Ahab's
arbitrary power was to have been a central event of the first version of
Moby-Dick, the way a similar mutiny dominates the interpolated "Town-
Ho's Story."[2]

In a more general sense, *Omoo*, *Redburn*, *White-Jacket*, and much of
Melville's short fiction of the 1850s deal with the nature and the effects of
social oppression, either ashore or in the microcosmic society of the sailing
ship. The characteristic tone of Melville's heroes or early hero-narrators is
one of rage—repressed, frustrated, or openly defiant—against the con-
strictions of the social system. In *Moby-Dick*, for instance, Ishmael's
opening discussion of his shabby treatment by "those stage managers, the
Fates" (16), grows directly out of his prior ruminations on the tyrannical
behavior of sea captains, and *Pierre*, finally, sets out to defy all the for-
malities and falsehoods of an arbitrary social system.

That authority and rebellion should have been important to Melville is
hardly surprising. His own father was notoriously strict. Allan Melville,
so his great-granddaughter writes, "kept close watch on his sons: when
they were not in school they were confined to the house except for visits to
his office."[3] Herman, generally regarded as lazy or slow, was never accorded the kind of serious attention granted his older brother, Gansevoort,
and Allan Melville's bankruptcy, illness, and death seem to have left him
with both an abiding sense of guilt and a feeling of unjust loss of status—a
feeling shared by many of his fictional heroes, notably Redburn and
Ishmael. Melville's sense of unjust neglect, even of persecution, was

further exacerbated by the pressure of publishers, critics, readers, and family members to conform his writings to their standards. "Try to get a living by the Truth," he wrote to Hawthorne in 1851, "and go to the Soup Societies. . . . Though I wrote the Gospels in this century, I should die in the gutter" (*Letters*, 127, 129).

The point of this biographical information is not to shore up a psychoanalytic reading of Melville or to reduce his themes to expressions of personal neurosis. The point, rather, is to stress that, for Melville, the tension between arbitrary authority and revolutionary impulse was more than just a theme. The contest between tyranny and truth was, for him, at once generally political and specifically personal.

It was in terms of this contest that he most profoundly understood the purposes and the problems of literary expression. Indeed, if my hypothesis in chapter 2 is correct—that "being a romancer" functioned for Brown, Irving, Poe, and Hawthorne as a covertly or marginally "deviant" career—then Melville's open and celebratory identification of romance with revolution is only a final extension or literalization of the sacrifice of relation. In identifying romance with social protest, Melville was returning it at last, explicitly and hopefully, to its primary social and psychological meaning. Yet such identification, even in the first flush of enthusiasm, proved difficult. The full story of Melville's career as a romancer is the story of his increasingly wary engagement with "revolutionary" romance and of his ultimate disillusionment.

In the light of this full story—the story of Melville's disenchantment with both "revolutionary" romance and "revolutionary" ideology—we should be cautious about stressing the distinction between his radicalism and the conservatism of such predecessors or contemporaries as Hawthorne. Both Hawthorne and Melville responded to a sensed connection between the sources of romance and the sources of revolution, as, less directly, did Brown, Irving, and even (if more abstractly) Poe. What distinguishes Melville from Hawthorne is not his understanding of these linked forces but his attitude toward them. Later, especially in *Pierre* and the other works of the middle 1850s, his attitude came more and more to resemble Hawthorne's. In *Moby-Dick* the political implications of "chartless" voyaging are already becoming ominous. Ishmael may identify with Bulkington's defiance of "artificial distinctions." "As in landlessness alone resides the highest truth," he writes, "shoreless, indefinite as God—so, better is it to perish in that howling infinite, than be ingloriously dashed upon the lees, even if that were safety!" (97). But when Ahab smashes the quadrant in a similar spirit, his allegorical ship of state is pushed inexorably toward its fated destruction—a symbolic foreshadowing of national cataclysm.

In his notebook, in 1842, Hawthorne described the French Revolution as the "emerging from their lurking-places of evil-characters," of "wretches" (240). Ishmael's metaphysical ruminations about things "beyond human ken" far surpass these easy moral labels, but Hawthorne's "evil-characters" and "wretches" have nevertheless a good deal in common with that elusive "significance" which, according to Ishmael, "lurks in all things" (358). Melville proclaimed clearly and fully what most of his predecessors only intermittently hinted at: that the unleashing of these lurking energies was the essence at once of romance and of revolution. Still, in the wake of his revolutionary optimism swam growing doubts about the beneficence of what Channing called the "common nature" to be released from imprisoning "distinctions."

The growth of these doubts, and of their relevance to Melville's understanding of literary expression, are the central story of Melville's career as experimental romancer. From *Typee* to *White-Jacket* he warily explored the violent underside of those revolutionary promptings with which he at first identified his own literary vocation. These explorations bore rich fruit in *Moby-Dick*—and bitter fruit in *Pierre*. In *The Confidence-Man*, finally, Melville surveyed a culture whose surface had come to seem to him as duplicitous and arabesque as the rhetorical surface of romance. In *The Confidence-Man* as in *The Blithedale Romance*, the ambiguous ontological status of fictional narrative, as the lying mask of its allegedly sincere motive, becomes at last an explicit paradigm of the ambiguous ontological status of the style of America's allegedly "revolutionary" culture.

More than thirty years after publishing *The Confidence-Man*, in *Billy Budd*, Melville returned again to what he saw as the linked "formal" qualities of literary expression and social organization. "With mankind," muses Captain Vere, "forms, measured forms, are everything; and that is the import couched in the story of Orpheus with his lyre spellbinding the wild denizens of the wood." "And this," adds Melville's narrator, "he once applied to the disruption of forms going on across the Channel and the consequences thereof" (501).

My immediate concern, however, is with the works published between 1846 and 1857, coming at the twilit culmination of the major "flowering" of American romance.

REVOLUTIONARY PROMPTINGS

Whatever personal psychological importance the revolutionary theme may have had for Melville, he was also, in turning to it again and again, responding to the political and social realities not only of a world still coming to terms with the French Revolution and its aftermath but of a "revolutionary" America, supposedly conceived in liberty but fast approaching a crisis over capitalist exploitation and chattel slavery. Melville's fiction, in any case, is filled with images of the abuse and corruption of political authority. Here is Wellingborough Redburn describing the statue of Lord Nelson in Liverpool:

> At uniform intervals round the base of the pedestal, four naked figures in chains, somewhat larger than life, are seated in various attitudes of humiliation and despair. . . . These woe-begone figures of captives are emblematic of Nelson's principal victories; but I never could look at their swarthy limbs and manacles, without being involuntarily reminded of four African slaves in the market-place. [155]

Throughout Melville's fiction, heroic figures of traditional political authority are transmuted into emblems of raw power and social injustice.

Against such injustice Melville set—and set out to incarnate in his writings—the ideals of revolution in general and of revolutionary America in particular. "We Americans," proclaims White-Jacket, "are driven to a rejection of the maxims of the Past. . . . We are the pioneers of the world; the advance-guard, sent on through the wilderness of untried things, to break a new path in the New World that is ours" (150–51). This revolutionary Americanism, recalling Emerson or Hester Prynne in the forest, had for Melville specific literary implications. "Long enough have we been skeptics with regard to ourselves," White-Jacket continues, "and doubted whether, indeed, the political Messiah had come. But he has come in *us*, if we would but give utterance to his promptings" (151).

For Melville, then, as for such radical nationalists as Emerson or William Ellery Channing,[4] both new justice and new "utterance" were to be discovered in the liberation of the new American self. It is in this spirit that Tommo and his successors jump ship or cast off all cables and that Ishmael goes whaling and determines to describe the Whale to landsmen; but the pursuit of this spirit, like the pursuit of the elusive spirits of romance and Romanticism, soon led into territory as baffling as the maze that trapped Pierre. In part the problem was political. How could our revolutionary character be institutionalized without being betrayed? The sailor Jackson, in *Redburn*, and Captain Ahab, in *Moby-Dick*, embody the fear, represented to many of Melville's contemporaries by the apotheoses of Napoleon and Andrew Jackson, that the toppling of tyrants in the name of democratic revolution might lead only the the elevation of new "democratic" despots in their place.[5]

Ultimately, Melville's exploration of the revolutionary spirit moved beyond politics to questions of epistemology and irrational psychology. What *was* this "true" character, to be liberated by revolution against corrupt authority and formalism? How was it to be known? And what, psychologically, were the consequences of responding to its "Messianic" promptings?

Melville's sense of the "true" self or character, oppressed by tyranny and to be liberated by revolution, springs most immediately from a kind of Rousseauian or Jeffersonian primitivism. "The grand principles of virtue and honor," writes Tommo in *Typee*, "are the same all the world over"— except as "they may be distorted by arbitrary codes." "It is to this in-dwelling, this universally diffused perception of what is *just* and *noble*, that the integrity of the Marquesans in their intercourse with each other is to be attributed" (201). The primitives of *Typee* enforce the same point as the Indians of Jefferson's *Notes on the State of Virginia*. "If truth and justice," Tommo asks rhetorically, "and the better principles of our nature, cannot exist unless enforced by the statute-book, how are we to account for the social condition of the Typees?" (203).

In *Typee*, this primitive virtue is set against the "arbitrary codes" en-forced by Western adventurers and missionaries. By the time of *White-Jacket*, Melville has shifted his anatomy of the contest between truth and tyranny to the class system of the West itself, as emblematized by the codes of the man-of-war. Jack Chase, White-Jacket writes of his shipboard friend, "was a gentleman. What though his hand was hard, so was not his heart, too often the case with soft palms" (14). In the hearts of the op-pressed, and not in outward social distinction, lies your "true" gentility. "Though bowing to naval discipline afloat," we are told of Jack, "ashore, he was a stickler for the Rights of Man, and the liberties of the world" (17). Or, as Jack himself explains to his young friend:

> "There are many great men in the world besides Commodores and Captains. I've that here, White-Jacket"—touching his forehead— "which, under happier skies . . . might have made a Homer of me. But Fate is Fate, White-Jacket; and we Homers who happen to be cap-tains of tops must write our odes in our hearts, and publish them in our heads." [271]

As Ishmael will later, Jack blames Fate for the neglect of his greatness. But there is a more immediate threat to his liberty. "But look!" he adds, apparently casually, "the Captain's on the poop" (271).

At the heart of Jack's ideology—as apparently, too, at the heart of Melville's—is the belief that true character is inward or noumenal and that social systems and identities are merely arbitrary, constricting appear-ances. The truth of personality, like the truth of romance, is spiritually obscure. Jack's declaration is important in other ways as well, for he, like Melville, links this noumenal or spiritual personality with the sources of literary expression, with "odes in our hearts." To give "utterance" to its "promptings" is at once an act of literary self-expression and a revolu-tionary assertion of the Rights of Man.

But there are problems beneath Jack's confident bravado. For one thing, there is Melville's growing doubt, from *White-Jacket* to *The Confidence-Man*, as to whether a personality so well hidden or oppressed can be said to exist at all. In a world of usages and codes, usages and codes are all that we can know. In such a world, "liberty," like Poe's "spirit," may be but a "mere word." In the rather ominous words of the title to chapter 12, "The Good or Bad Temper of Men-of-war's men, in a great Degree, [are] attributable to their Particular Stations and Duties aboard Ship" (44). How explain the gaiety of the top-men on the *Neversink?* "The reason of their liberal-heartedness," White-Jacket explains, "was, that they were daily called upon to expatiate themselves all over the rigging. The reason of their lofty-mindedness was, that they were high lifted above the petty tumults, carping cares, and paltrinesses of the decks below" (47). White-Jacket is persuaded of the truth of his deterministic theory of character, so he claims, "in my inmost soul" (47). In the light of the theory, however, one can only wonder what this "inmost soul" amounts to.

A still more immediate problem was raised by founding the hope of revolutionary renewal on the liberation of a secret self. Supposing that this self *did* exist and that "utterance" *could* be given to its "promptings," how could one be so sure that these "promptings" bore any relation to what Tommo calls "this universally diffused perception of what is *just* and *noble*" (201)? What if the savage turned out not to be noble but quite the reverse? This is the standard argument turned against the Rousseauian rationale for revolution by its critics, including Melville's own Captain Vere. Melville, however, takes it far beyond questions of psychology or social order. His investigation of the ambiguous spirit of revolution leads him deep, as well, into the originating sources both of romance and of culture.

To the extent that the neglect of Jack Chase's greatness stems not from Fate but from the captain on the poop, his most obvious recourse would seem to be, not to solitary composition ("odes in our hearts"), but to escape or even to the violent overthrow of the captain's arbitrary authority. Jack has in fact, prior to White-Jacket's shipping on the *Neversink*, deserted and been recaptured. "He abandoned the frigate," we are assured, "from . . . glorious motives": to embrace "the Rights of Man, and the liberties of the world" by joining the partisans in Peru (17). On the *Neversink* itself, however, revolutionary motives are apparently neither so "glorious" nor so easy to espouse in one's own cause; Jack, we recall, consistently bows to naval discipline when afloat.

"Depravity in the oppressed," writes White-Jacket, "is no apology for the oppressor; but rather an additional stigma to him, as being, in a large degree, the effect, and not the cause and justification of oppression" (142). This is the classic revolutionary ideology: that all evil, finally, is social evil—that the evil unleashed by revolution is ultimately the product of the tyranny against which revolution is launched. Melville accepted the argument only intermittently and with steadily decreasing confidence.

This ideology appears in *Redburn*, in the title character's reaction to the apparent depravity of the sailor Jackson. In his malevolent power over the crew, Jackson anticipates what Melville, describing Claggart in *Billy Budd*, would call "depravity according to nature" (457). Redburn, however, is more sympathetic: "There seemed," he writes, "even more woe than wickedness about the man; and his wickedness seemed to spring from his woe" (105). Depravity, that is to say, is the *result* of authoritarian oppression. It is not "according to nature"; it is the product of tyranny. Thus revolution, in disposing of tyranny, should also dispose of evil.

But the situation in *Redburn* is more complex than the statement about "wickedness" and "woe" at first suggests. If Jackson and the common sailors represent the oppressed class in a totalitarian society, they also embody the revolutionary "promptings" that stand in opposition to totalitarianism. And the implications of these "promptings" are ominous. Here is Redburn, speculating on Jackson's mysterious power:

> It is not for me to say, what it was that made a whole ship's company submit so to the whims of one poor miserable man like Jackson. I only know that so it was; but I have no doubt, that if he had had a blue eye in his head, or had had a different face from what he did have, they would not have stood in such awe of him. [59]

Whatever the abstract virtue of its *cause*, the *power* of democracy here is clearly the power of innate evil. For all the "woe" to which Redburn so compassionately responds, it is to Jackson's "wickedness" that the sailors "democratically" subordinate themselves.

In Redburn's fearful fascination with Jackson there is more than a little of that unacknowledgeable, unconscious sympathy that bound Brown's Edgar Huntly to Clithero Edny; and just as Clithero symbolically shadows forth what Edgar cannot confront in himself, so Jackson adumbrates those unconscious impulses that Redburn, in his own proper character, feels compelled to repress. Early on, increasingly isolated, Redburn glimpses this obscure self. "At last," he writes, "I found myself a sort of Ishmael in the ship, without a single friend or companion; and I began to feel a hatred growing up in me against the whole crew—so much so, that I prayed against it, that it might not master my heart completely, and so make a fiend of me, something like Jackson" (62).

Jack Chase's motives in espousing the Rights of Man may appear "glorious" to White-Jacket, but in Jackson—and especially in Redburn's nervously sympathetic response to him—Melville hints that the source of revolutionary "promptings" has less to do with glorious disinterestedness than with guiltily aggressive rage or "hatred"; and Melville, prophet of the "political Messiah," was capable, with Redburn, of praying against such "promptings." In the theme of revolution he ultimately discovered an objective correlative for his own unconscious anger against society, but he found it increasingly difficult to embrace the secret, hardly Rousseauian self that this discovery revealed. As determinedly as Roderick Usher, he set out to bury his secret in the basement, but, unlike Roderick, and with far more sympathy and awareness, he also set out to explore the subterranean chambers. Even as he enacts the crucial symbolic displacement of romance, Melville subjects it to wonderful scrutiny. "What the White Whale was" to the crew, writes Ishmael in "Moby Dick," "or how to their unconscious understandings, also, in some dim, unsuspected way, he might have seemed the gliding great demon of the seas of life,—all this to explain, would be to dive deeper than Ishmael can go" (162). Yet dive he does. Which is why, paradoxically, he alone remains floating at the end.

"At dinner," wrote Melville in his journal, of an 1849 visit to the ubiquitous John Murray, "the stiffness, formality, & coldness of the party was wonderful. I felt like knocking all their heads together" (44–45). The first sentence's frustration with empty formalism is typically Melvillean, but the violence of the second sentence is perhaps even more important. Such violence is seldom very far from the surface in Melville. However masked by patriotic rhetoric, it lies at the heart of those revolutionary "promptings" to which White-Jacket hopes to give "utterance." But it is precisely this violence that Melville's characters usually seek to evade, repress, displace, or rationalize. They seek, that is to say, to give utterance to revolutionary feelings while avoiding the deepest implications of those feelings.

In *Typee*, Tommo is "revolutionary" in only a rather limited sense, and these limitations, one suspects, are quite deliberate. However outraged he may be by the captain's "unmitigated tyranny," he turns not to violent mutiny but to escape. This escape leads to a confrontation with the primitive—not with the primitive self of Tommo but with a valley-full of Rousseauian "savages." Tommo keeps his distance, largely by maintaining a comic perspective on his material. It is nevertheless hinted repeatedly that these savages are somewhat less than noble; hence Tommo's almost pornographic fascination with the titillating suggestions of cannibalism. But Tommo never makes overt the connection between the possible violence of the Marquesans and his own rage at the captain or his more general rage—as one who has moved "in a different sphere of life" (32)—at the "state-room sailors" (3) of the opening paragraph.

At the very close, however, these violent feelings *do* erupt, though they are directed against one of the "savages." Mow-Mow approaches the boat

in which Tommo is finally making good his escape. "In another instant,"
Tommo writes, "he would have seized one of the oars."

> Even at the moment I felt horror at the act I was about to commit,
> but it was no time for pity or compunction, and with a true aim, and
> exerting all my strength, I dashed the boat-hook at him. It struck him
> just below the throat, and forced him downwards. I had no time to
> repeat my blow, but I saw him rise to the surface in the wake of the
> boat, and never shall I forget the ferocious expression of his counte-
> nance. [252]

Here the protective idealization of the "savage" and the protective distance
Tommo has until now maintained between himself and the "savages,"
displacing his own impulses into their strangeness, seem to be breaking
down. Tommo seems on the verge of full identification of his own violence
with the "savagery" of the Typees. There is even something of Poe's
"William Wilson" here, or of Irving's "Young Italian." In striking out at
Mow-Mow's "ferocious countenance," Tommo in a sense both attacks and
confirms his own deepest impulses. But the incident comes at the very end
of *Typee*, perhaps by conscious or unconscious design, and its implications
remain undeveloped.

In *Mardi* a strikingly similar incident occurs much earlier: Taji's killing
of the priest, Aleema, in order to rescue Yillah. Taji, like Tommo, initially jumps ship. What he wishes to escape is the boredom of a calm,
rather than the fury of a tyrannical captain, but the theme of rebellion
and guilt is much in evidence. On shipboard, writes Taji, the sailor has
abandoned "his glorious liberty of volition. . . . He has taken the ship to
wife, for better or for worse, for calm or for gale; and she is not to be
shuffled off" (10).[6] To jump ship, then, may be to reassert one's "liberty,"
but Taji's last phrase, curiously, is drawn from Hamlet's meditation on
suicide: "For in that sleep of death what dreams may come / When we
have shuffled off this mortal coil, / Must give us pause" (III.i. 66–68).
This hint is important. Taji's voyage of escape becomes increasingly, if
obscurely, entangled in patterns of guilty rebellion and apparently mo-
tiveless self-destruction. In the course of his story, Taji, a common sailor
at the outset, comes to control a series of allegorical ship-kingdoms. At the
close, he makes the goal of his quest specific: "Now, I am my own soul's
emperor; and my first act is abdication! Hail! realm of shades!" (654).

At the beginning, Taji insists that he and his companion, Jarl, are
blameless in quitting the *Arcturion*. His time of service was up, and even
the captain said he might quit the ship if he could. Still, Taji grieves "to

tell how I deserted [the] Maternal craft, that rocked me so often in [her] heart of oak" (24); for after Taji's desertion nothing was heard of the *Arcturion,* and he feels inexplicably guilty for having "unconsciously eluded a sailor's grave" (25). "It is impossible for me so much as to imagine," Taji rationalizes, "that our deserting her could have been in any way instrumental in her loss" (25); yet, he admits, "I can not repress a shudder when I think of that old ship's end" (25). What Taji cannot admit is that he perhaps feels guilty because, however blameless in action, he unconsciously longed for the ship's destruction.

Edgar Huntly, faced with Clithero Edny's tale of "blameless" murder, hopes that "the magic of sympathy, the perseverance of benevolence, though silent, might work a gradual and secret revolution, and better thoughts might insensibly displace those desperate suggestions which now governed [Clithero]" (107). In the opening chapters of *Mardi,* Taji, too, is torn between "better thoughts" and "desperate suggestions"—and in a way directly relevant to Melville's response to the revolutionary theme. For Taji, like Edgar, wants his "revolution" to be "secret"; he wants to displace the desperate "promptings" of rebellion into the "better thoughts" of rational self-exoneration. But the guilt endures. He may pray that "the spirit of that lost vessel"—the *Arcturion*—"roaming abroad through the troubled mists of midnight gales . . . may never haunt my future path upon the waves" (24), but within two chapters he has simply internalized the guilt against which he prays. Adrift at sea and presumed dead by those he has deserted, he writes: "one feels like his own ghost unlawfully tenanting a defunct carcass" (29).

Taji, in overt act, seems blameless—his rebellion is legitimized by his "rights"; yet even his justified escape leads to unconscious guilt. He has, moreover, illegally seized the ship's boat, the *Chamois,* in which he and Jarl sail West, and before reaching Mardi he overcomes two more boats. The first, the *Parki,* has a complex revolutionary history, foreshadowing the *San Dominick* in "Benito Cereno." First seized violently from its white officers by a coalition of Cholo half-breeds and natives, it was then as violently seized from these rebels by Samoa and his termagent wife, Anatoo. Taji next takes command, not violently, he insists, but "tacitly" (97). He nevertheless assumes with pleasure the illegitimate rank of captain. Anatoo interferes with this pleasure, and, with Jarl, Taji contemplates her murder; but he is again spared the guilt of overt action: a convenient storm, stirring up drops of brine "heavy as drops of gore" (117), kills Anatoo for him, although it also sinks the *Parki.* Taji, Jarl, and Samoa return to the *Chamois,* in which they encounter the altar-like canoe of the priest, Aleema, and his sacrificial captive, Yillah.

It is in overcoming this last vessel that Taji's unconscious violence becomes, at last, overt. Threatened by Aleema, he responds:

> A thrust and a threat! Ere I knew it, my cutlass made a quick lunge. A curse from the priest's mouth; red blood from his side; he tottered, stared about him, and fell over like a brown hemlock into the sea. [133]

But Taji still has excuses: he acted unconsciously, "Ere I knew it." As he tells the story, it was not he but his cutlass that "lunged" at the priest. Moreover, Aleema *was* planning to sacrifice Yillah. In this light, Taji simply, like any good revolutionary, struck out in the name of liberty. But his doubts remain:

> By this hand, the dead man had died. Remorse smote me hard; and like lightning I asked myself, whether the death-deed I had done was sprung of a virtuous motive, the rescuing a captive from thrall; or whether beneath that pretense, I had engaged in this fatal affray for some other, and selfish purpose. [135]

With the killing of Aleema, Taji's obscure guilt finally acquires a correlative in action. He represses this guilt, however, in an additional (if now metaphorical) act of violence. Perhaps, he speculates, his motives were selfish. "But throttling the thought, I swore to be gay" (135). Tommo maims Mow-Mow at the very end of *Typee*. One hundred fifty-four chapters of Taji's narrative follow the killing of Aleema. But the rest of *Mardi* mainly dissipates the theme of violent rebellion and guilt, first by substituting for it the allegorical quest for Yillah ("truth"), then by elaborating the allegorical satire of the Mardian archipelago, and finally, and above all, by dissipating Taji almost completely as a character—until the very end.

Still, Taji's doubts suggest the depth of Melville's ambivalence toward the nature and consequences of revolutionary "promptings." Was the revolutionary impulse a "virtuous motive"? Or was revolutionary ideology a "pretense," a mask for that unconscious, violent aggression against authority that both Tommo and Taji try hard to repress, displace, or rationalize? Was the whole revolutionary rationale only what Hawthorne, in "The Birth-mark," called an "unconscious self-deception"?

The allegorical burgeoning and ultimate intellectual and artistic chaos of *Mardi* have generally been attributed to Melville's rapid intellectual development at the time he was writing it, a development that produced in him a compulsion to incorporate all his new readings and ideas into his fiction as fast as they came to him.[7] It seems equally reasonable to surmise, however, that the difficulty of the revolutionary theme played an important part in the process of that theme's dissipation. What could not be *dis*placed could, just possibly, be *re*placed. Only at the very end, in Taji's suicidal refusal of the complacencies of Serenia, does the theme directly reappear. Its difficulties would, however, surface again, albeit more furtively, in the two books that rapidly followed *Mardi: Redburn* and *White-Jacket*.

Redburn's disillusionment with authority, as he presents it to us, stems from his discoveries of corruption and social oppression, both aboard the *Highlander* and ashore in Liverpool; but it also stems, by means of a process about which Redburn is less candid, from impulses within the victimized hero himself. The fundamental rhythm of the earlier portions of Redburn's experience—as it will be the fundamental rhythm of Ishmael's—is an alternation between a sense of desperation and a sense of contented acceptance. Early on, Redburn travels to New York on a Hudson River packet. Excluded from the genteel society of the cabin, young Wellingborough is possessed by "demoniac feelings" (13). These are "ejected" when he is taken in and fed by his brother's New York friend, Mr. Jones. Similarly, on board the *Highlander*, Redburn alternates between the "hatred growing up in me against the whole crew" (62) and the "delight" and "wild delirium" (115) of being part of that same crew in action.

This emotional vacillation is important, because it is Redburn's "demoniac" feeling of exclusion that first threatens his reverence for authority. The opening of his story is dominated by a strange symbolic glass ship, whose figurehead foreshadows Redburn's disillusionment:

> Her figure-head, a gallant warrior in a cocked-hat, lies pitching head-foremost down into the trough of a calamitous sea under the bows—but I will not have him put on his legs again, till I get on my own; for between him and me there is a secret sympathy; and my sisters tell me, even yet, that he fell from his perch the very day I left home to go to sea on this *my first voyage*. [9]

The glass figure is fallen, a victim of time; his plight is hardly Redburn's responsibility. Yet Redburn participates in his fall, at least in this: "I will not have him put on his legs again."

Redburn has stated, somewhat earlier in the book, that as a child he had actively threatened the glass ship and its captain:

> When I was very little, I made no doubt, that if I could but once pry open the hull, and break the glass all to pieces, I would infallibly light upon something wonderful, perhaps some gold guineas, of which I have always been in want, ever since I could remember. And often I used to feel a sort of insane desire to be the death of the glass ship, case, and all, in order to come at the plunder; and one day, throwing

out some hint of the kind to my sisters, they ran to my mother in a great clamor; and after that, the ship was placed on the mantle-piece for a time, beyond my reach, and until I should recover my reason.

I do not know how to account for this temporary madness of mine. [8]

Redburn's conscious reverence for authority, this memory makes clear, is in conflict with his unconscious desire to have some of the "plunder" for himself or at least to smash the ship to pieces. Redburn longs for wealth, power, or violent release, but because of his reverence for father figures he can acknowledge his longing only as a "sort of insane desire," a "temporary madness." This "madness" is one with the desperation he feels on the Hudson River packet or on the *Highlander*. Redburn never comes consciously to hate the father whose death consigned him to poverty, but his loathing of the *Highlander*'s at first fatherly Captain Riga clearly owes as much to a personal sense of exclusion as to an objective sense of the captain's corruption. "No gentleman," Redburn complains, "would have treated another gentleman as he did me" (71).

The "plunder" has been placed out of Redburn's reach. He must worship the fathers (whether Lord Nelson, Captain Riga, or his own father) without any expectation that he himself will ever reap the rewards of fatherhood: access to power and authority. It is out of this frustration that he turns, albeit unconsciously, on the fathers themselves: "I will not have him put on his legs again, till I get on my own." Redburn's unconscious aggression against figures of paternal authority is crucial. Even more important, however, is his inability, or refusal, to acknowledge these feelings. "I do not know," he writes, "how to account for this temporary madness of mine."

White-Jacket, too, falls victim on occasion to such "temporary madness," most notably when he is on the point of being flogged by Captain Claret. The protest against flogging, in *White-Jacket*, is couched mainly in terms of abstract justice, but in chapter 67 the issue becomes intensely personal. It is only with difficulty that White-Jacket recounts his desperation when threatened with the scourge:

> There are times when wild thoughts enter a man's heart, when he seems almost irresponsible for his act and his deed. The Captain stood on the weather-side of the deck. . . . I stood a little to windward of him, and, though he was a large, powerful man, it was certain that a sudden rush against him, along the slanting deck, would infallibly pitch him headforemost into the ocean, though he who so rushed must needs go over with him. My blood seemed clotting in my veins; I felt icy cold at the tips of my fingers, and a dimness was before my eyes. [280]

Even more interesting than the deed White-Jacket contemplates—symbolic parricide and suicide—is his nervous handling of his feelings. At such a time, he insists, a man "seems almost irresponsible for his act and his deed." "I can not analyze my heart," he writes, "though it then stood still within me" (280).

In the event, the crisis is averted. Captain Claret is dissuaded from pursuing his petty tyranny by a corporal of marines. White-Jacket's violent "promptings" are never put to the test of "act and deed." "I," he writes in conclusion, "who, in the desperation of my soul, had but just escaped being a murderer and a suicide, almost burst into tears of thanksgiving where I stood" (281).

In both *Redburn* and *White-Jacket* the "temporary madness" of rebellious rage almost erupts, but in both books it is successfully displaced or deflected. In *Redburn* it is deflected by the narrator's growing defeatism and passivity and by his projection of his own capacity for "insane hatred" onto Jackson. In *White-Jacket* it is deflected, paradoxically, by the very "revolutionary" rhetoric in which White-Jacket espouses the Rights of Man and that he idealizes in the figure of Jack Chase. We must recognize that Jack and the rhetoric that surrounds him *are* displacements. Through them, revolutionary impulse is projected into a realm that, by its abstraction, is rendered as safe as, say, the aesthetic vocabulary into which Washington Irving displaces his fear of what the Nervous Gentleman, in *Tales of a Traveller*, describes as "certain mysteries in our nature, certain inscrutable impulses and influences" (139).

Beneath the abstract "revolutionary" rhetoric of *White-Jacket*—energizing that rhetoric even as it is masked by it—lurks a sense of "our nature" that is neither abstract nor, in the political sense, ideal. The evil of Master-at-Arms Bland—like that of his successor, Claggart, in *Billy Budd*—cannot be fully explained away by his association with tyranny. "What he was," White-Jacket writes, in partial exoneration of Captain Claret, "the usages of the Navy had made him." None of his tyrannical acts "proceeded from any personal, organic hard-heartedness" (367). But Bland, White-Jacket writes earlier, "was an organic and irreclaimable scoundrel" (188). Especially chilling is an apparently casual comment White-Jacket makes to explain the special tyranny of midshipmen, given power at so early an age over other human beings:

> But since what human nature is, and what it must forever continue to be, is well enough understood for most practical purposes, it needs no special example to prove that, where the merest boys, indiscriminately snatched from the human family, are given such authority over mature men, the results must be proportionable in monstrousness to the custom that authorizes this worse than cruel absurdity. [218]

Was "human nature," then, not the ideal alternative to tyrannical oppression but rather its raw source? The "arbitrary codes" of tyranny were perhaps only a system of institutionalized violence; but in an objective view, antiinstitutional violence, as the essence of "what human nature is, and what it must ever continue to be," was hardly preferable. Moreover, the "arbitrary codes" of tyranny had been so fully internalized by those subject to their dominion that rage could no longer operate with primordial purity. As the institutional system took over the application of violence, the individual was left with "promptings" that led mainly to guilt and finally to self-destruction.[8]

In "Hawthorne and His *Mosses*" Melville defines literature as "the great Art of Telling the Truth" (408). His insistence on radical sincerity, on the rejection of all corrupt forms, is more than revolutionary. When he speaks of those Americans "who look forward to the coming of a great literary genius among us" (409–10), his tone is positively millenarian. The creation of a new national literature will be the "coming" of a redeemer, the advent of a divine being, an incarnation of "truth" in "this world of lies" (408). Hence White-Jacket's declaration that "the political Messiah . . . has come in *us*, if we would but give utterance to his promptings" (151). Hence, too, Melville's response to discovering Shakespeare, "the divine William," as he described it in an 1849 letter to Duyckinck: "Ah, he's full of sermons-on-the mount, and gentle, aye, almost as Jesus. . . . And if another Messiah ever comes twill be in Shakesper's person" (77).

All of this is fascinating to the reader of *The Confidence-Man*, which begins with the "advent" of a Christ-like "stranger" (1), or to the reader of *Pierre*, in which the narrator writes, of his hero's conversion to revolutionary sincerity, "Thus, in the Enthusiast to Duty, the heaven-begotten Christ is born" (106). This pervasive collocation of revolutionary sincerity, nationalism, and messianism underscores the more general point that for Melville the implications of revolution were simultaneously political, psychological, and literary. Yet it became increasingly difficult for him to reconcile this messianic expectation with what Pierre, for instance, discovers to be "the everlasting elusiveness of Truth" (339).

For one thing, how could one know that the noumenal "truths" of America's literature and messianic character were "true"? White-Jacket's partial exoneration of Captain Claret has already been mentioned: his contention that none of Claret's evil acts "proceeded from any personal, organic hard-heartedness. What he was, the usages of the Navy had made him" (367). In a similar vein, White-Jacket writes in excuse of those British officers who rejoiced at Napoleon's return, as offering new hope of carnage: "I urge it not against them as *men*—their feelings belonged to their profession. Had they not been naval officers, they had not been rejoicers in the midst of despair" (209). These exculpations are ominous. The British officers are innocent, not "as *men*," but because in the noumenal, Rousseauian sense they are scarcely "men" at all: even "their feelings belonged to their profession." Similarly, Captain Claret's very being has apparently been subsumed by the "artificial codes" of the political system. If he is innocent on the "personal, organic" level, it is only because he has no such level.

At first appearance, *White-Jacket* seems meant as a protest novel, an attack on the perversion of "true" value and character by "artificial codes" and systems. Beneath the surface, however, there lurks a growing recognition that perhaps the "artificial" is all the "truth" there is. How can the "personal" and "organic" be asserted as revolutionary values when they can scarcely be said to exist? White-Jacket may protest that the Articles of War are antithetical to the Declaration of Independence (297), yet he has trouble maintaining his faith that the ideal spirit of the Declaration is truer than the practical spirit of the Articles—or even as true. "Ah!" he laments, "the best righteousness of our man-of-war world seems but an unrealized ideal, after all; and those maxims which, in the hope of bringing about a Millennium, we busily teach to the heathen, we Christians ourselves disregard" (324). We do not simply fall short of our messianic professions; perhaps our doing so is inevitable. As White-Jacket writes:

> In view of the whole present social frame-work of our world, so ill adapted to the practical adoption of the meekness of Christianity, there seems almost some ground for the thought, that although our blessed Savior was full of the wisdom of heaven, yet his gospel seems lacking in the practical wisdom of earth—in a due appreciation of the necessities of nations at times demanding bloody massacres and wars; in a proper estimation of the value of rank, title, and money. [324]

Here already, as early as *White-Jacket*, Melville is drifting from messianic sincerity to the somberly ironic dualism of *Pierre*.

In the mysterious pamphlet Pierre finds on his journey to New York, Plotinus Plinlimmon distinguishes between two kinds of "truth": "chronometrical" (heavenly, noumenal) and "horological" (earthly, phenomenal). Their practical incompatibility is the sardonic point of the pamphlet. "But why then," Plinlimmon archly asks, "does God now and then send a heavenly chronometer (as a meteoric stone) into the world, uselessly as it would seem, to give the lie to all the world's time-keepers?" (212). This question—especially the wonderful ambiguity of "give the lie"—foreshadows the central situation of *The Confidence-Man*. And White-Jacket is hardly less sardonic than Plinlimmon. Does "the wisdom of heaven" seem irrelevant to "the practical wisdom of earth"? "All this," he reasons, "only the more crowns the divine consistency of Jesus; since

211

Burnet and the best theologians demonstrate, that his nature was not merely human—was not that of a mere man of the world" (324). Which was the "truth," then? That the Messiah had "come in *us*, if we would but give utterance to his promptings"? Or that the only "truth" of human character, after all, was the "merely human"? If the latter, then the "literary Shiloh of America," whose "coming" Melville had prophesied in "Hawthorne and His *Mosses*" (419), would be only a spurious priest, a deceiver, a confidence-man.

There was a yet more horrifying possibility. It is suggested by what Tommo, Taji, Redburn, and White-Jacket hint· about their deepest "promptings" and is revealed more clearly by Melville's remarks on "truth" in the "*Mosses*" essay. Suppose the hidden chronometrical "truths" *were* "true." And suppose them to be the sort of "truths" Shakespeare found "at the very axis of reality" (407). What sort of "political Messiah" might they indicate? Melville writes of Shakespeare:

> Through the mouths of the dark characters of Hamlet, Timon, Lear, and Iago, he craftily says, or sometimes insinuates, the things which we feel to be so terrifically true that it were all but madness for any good man, in his own proper character, to utter, or even hint of them. Tormented into desperation, Lear the frantic king tears off the mask, and speaks the sane madness of vital truth. [407]

The great "truth" in Hawthorne's fiction, Melville insists, is its "great power of blackness . . . [which] derives its force from its appeals to that Calvinistic sense of Innate Depravity and Original Sin, from whose visitations, in some shape or other, no deeply thinking mind is always and wholly free" (406). Melville's Lear, "tormented into desperation," sounds a good deal like many of Melville's early hero-narrators. They, to be sure, labor hard to keep the mask in place, and one can well understand why, since messianic salvation, on the basis of such "truths," sounds more like damnation.

Thus it is that beneath the overtly messianic revolutionary rhetoric of Melville and his characters lurks the compulsion to deny the promptings of desperate but buried aggression. Even their fear that "the wisdom of heaven" cannot be known or practically applied may function as a defensive means of denying its less than "heavenly" suggestions and of obscuring the relation between these suggestions and the primal desperation of the buried self. So Tommo displaces his own violence into the "ferocious countenance" of wounded Mow-Mow. So Taji, at the last, turns his guilty, unacknowledgeable hatred of others against himself.

In this light, Charles Olson's wonderful account of Melville's mythology is instructive:

Melville was agonized over paternity. He suffered as a son. He had lost the source. He demanded to know the father.

Kronos, in order to become god, armed himself with a sickle and castrated his father Uranus. Saturn used a pruning knife. Kronos and Saturn in turn were overthrown by their sons banded together in a brother horde. The new gods of Jupiter were, in their turn, attacked by other sons. These sons—they were the "Giants"—lost. They are described as more akin to men.

Enceladus was among them. He is a constant image in Melville. Melville saw his likeness in defeated and exiled heroes, not in successful sons who, by their triumph, become the fathers.[9]

Again and again, in Melville's writings, rebellious defiance is turned into repressive evasion, guilty self-destruction, or—increasingly—a curious sort of passive enervation. The Messiah—from "Hawthorne and His *Mosses*" to *Billy Budd*—is known less by his "heavenly wisdom" than by the crucifixion, ordained by his father and enforced by a hostile social system, that he passively, almost willfully, suffers.

Tommo and White-Jacket, for the most part, manage to deflect or abstract their aggressive impulses. Taji, convinced that he is the unlawful tenant even of his own body, turns to Byronic suicide, as Pierre and Ahab will do after him. Redburn—like Bartleby, later, or like Billy Budd—simply withers away. On the level of rhetoric he may confront the fathers' failure to pass on their "plunder" by dispensing with fathers altogether. "We are not a nation," he declares,

> so much as a world; for unless we may claim all the world for our sire, like Melchisedec, we are without father or mother.
>
> For who was our father and our mother? . . . Our ancestry is lost in the universal paternity. . . . We are the heirs of all time, and with all nations we divide our inheritance. [169]

But Redburn cannot exercise the will to claim this "inheritance"; such willfulness becomes, for him, insane "hatred" or "temporary madness." He would prefer not to. Those who find "growth" or "initiation" in *Redburn*[10] miss the chilling effect of the protagonist's admission, near the beginning, that "I had learned to think much and bitterly before my time; all my young mounting dreams of glory had left me; and at that early age, I was as unambitious as a man of sixty" (10).

Ishmael, contemplating the "Titanism of power" suggested by the whale's tail, is lead to meditate on the first two persons of the Trinity:

> When Angelo paints even God the Father in human form, mark what robustness is there. And whatever they may reveal of the divine love

in the Son, the soft, curled, hermaphroditical Italian pictures, in which his idea has been most successfully embodied; these pictures, so destitute as they are of all brawniness, hint nothing of any power, but the mere negative, feminine one of submission and endurance, which on all hands it is conceded, form the peculiar practical virtues of his teachings. [315]

Hence, perhaps, the "phenomenal" absence of "muscular spasm" in the execution of Billy Budd. The surgeon may be correct in refusing to attribute it to "will power" (498), for it seems to stem from the will's own self-annihilation. When Billy is hanged, there is no spontaneous orgasm.

Redburn, even in his youth, is "as unambitious as a man of sixty." Melville's typical persona in the short fiction of the 1850s is an unambitious middle-aged bachelor. The narrator of "Bartleby" is "one of those unambitious lawyers who never address a jury." He has been praised for prudence by John Jacob Astor, "a personage little given to poetic enthusiasm." He is "an eminently *safe* man" (40).

Such a man, too, is Amasa Delano, the bachelor sea captain of "Benito Cereno." In his case, indeed, cautious self-effacement leads to an almost willful blindness. He never guesses, until told directly by Cereno, that a brutal slave revolt has taken place on board the *San Dominick*. Babo's masquerade remains, to use Poe's term, as "arabesque" to him as Roderick's hair remains to the narrator of "The Fall of the House of Usher." Roderick's companion, like so many of Poe's narrators, works hard to keep the mask of arabesque "purity" in place. And so, one suspects, does Delano. Like Edgar Huntly, Delano is repeatedly "relieved by . . . better thoughts" (259), by whose means he combats the "return of involuntary suspicion" (260).

Delano has named his ship's boat *Rover*, in token of its likeness to "a Newfoundland dog" (271). That he also likens Babo, leader of the slave uprising, to a Newfoundland dog seems to slip his mind. As his boat approaches, the white water at its bow suggests a strange fancy: "Ha! glancing towards the boat; there's *Rover*; good dog; a white bone in her mouth. A pretty big bone though, seems to me" (272). Here Delano glimpses, symbolically, the "truth" of the situation on board the *San Dominick*, where the bleached bones of slaughtered Aranda are tied and covered beneath the bowsprit; but by keeping this glimpse symbolic he keeps it arabesque, repressed. He never makes the connection between the horror of Babo's revolt and whatever violent impulses, lurking in his own heart, come to be emblematized by his own boat. Having denied his own nature, he is blind to the nature of others. But Plinlimmon was right: Delano's "horological" blindness to "chronometrical" truth saves his life.

Delano's avoidance of revolutionary promptings—in his world and in himself—is usually contrasted with the patriotic optimism or Byronic defiance of Melville's earlier protagonists, but the extent and importance of this contrast can be exaggerated. To be sure, Delano lacks, say, Ishmael's probing curiosity, and the ironic prose of his story lacks the resonant richness of Ishmael's as it lacks the thrusting energy of Ahab's. Nevertheless, Delano's avoidance is implicit in Melville's heroes from Tommo onwards. However extreme his obtuseness, such avoidance is what Melville's more "revolutionary" figures were striving toward from the very beginning.

So also, in Melville's view, was their "revolutionary" culture. *Israel Potter* is Melville's one direct treatment of the American Revolution. In it, John Paul Jones conceals a tattooed arm beneath a civilized sleeve. This "jaunty barbarian in broadcloth," writes Melville, is

> a sort of prophetical ghost, glimmering in anticipation upon the advent of those tragic scenes of the French Revolution which levelled the exquisite refinement of Paris with the bloodthirsty ferocity of Borneo; showing that broaches and finger-rings, not less than nose-rings and tattooing, are tokens of the primeval savageness which ever slumbers in human kind, civilized or uncivilized. [88]

This prophecy is later applied to the country for whose revolution Jones is fighting. "Intrepid, unprincipled, reckless, predatory," Melville writes, "with boundless ambition, civilized in externals but a savage at heart, America is, or may yet be, the Paul Jones of nations" (170).

Yet Jones's daring is fully under the manipulative control of Benjamin Franklin's calculated prudence. At the center of *Israel Potter* is Franklin's horological reduction of the messianic impulse, which Jones finds in *Poor Richard's Almanac:* "God helps them that help themselves" (185). Franklin is a kind of apotheosis of the Melvillean figure of unassailable paternal authority, the "liberal" tyrant. "Every time he comes in," Israel reflects, "he robs me, . . . with an air all the time, too, as if he were making me presents. If he thinks me such a very sensible young man, why not let me take care of myself?" (74). Forbidding nocturnal wanderings in Paris, Franklin instead gives Israel a guidebook—and a copy of *Poor Richard.*

Israel never strikes out at Franklin. He does, however, have his moment of violence—a moment whose details recall Olson's comment on Melville's mythology. Impressed onto a British revenue cutter, Israel, when his ship is attacked by Jones, turns on its British officers. What White-Jacket only contemplates, Israel achieves, smiting the captain over the taffrail into the sea. He next engages an officer who "as he fell . . . caught Israel by the most terrible part in which mortality can be grappled. Insane with pain, Israel dashed his adversary's skull against the sharp iron. The officer's hold relaxed, but himself stiffened" (125). The remaining officer Israel catches "round the loins, bedding his fingers like grisly claws into his flesh, and hugging him to his heart. The man's ghost, caught like a broken cork in a gurgling bottle's neck, gasped with the embrace" (125–26). Israel throws him against the bulwarks. Unlike Tommo or Taji, Redburn or White-Jacket, Israel feels no apparent guilt about his violence. But then, he is fighting for a worthy cause, the liberty of America.

After forty years of exile in London, however, Israel ends up as enervated as any "unambitious . . . man of sixty," and his revolutionary energy is little remembered in the country it helped to establish. This veteran of Bunker Hill, returning to Boston on the Fourth of July, narrowly escapes "being run over by a patriotic triumphal car in the procession, flying a broidered banner inscribed with gilt letters: 'BUNKER-HILL /1775/ GLORY TO THE HEROES THAT FOUGHT!'" (238). Returning to his native Berkshires and unable to secure a veteran's pension, "he died the same day that the oldest oak on his native hills was blown down" (241). John Paul Jones may suggest "the primeval savageness which ever slumbers in human kind, civilized or uncivilized." The narrator may claim that America, "the Paul Jones of nations," is "a savage at heart." But by the end of *Israel Potter* America's "primeval savageness" has died of neglect and been buried.

America had betrayed its revolutionary origins and possibilities. From the allegorical America of *Mardi*'s Vivenza chapters through *Pierre, Israel Potter*, and *The Confidence-Man*, Melville denounced both the hypocrisy and the tragedy of this betrayal. He also knew that it was inevitable. It was indeed the function of "arbitrary codes," both conscious and unconscious, to repress revolutionary energy. "Savages" were such precisely because they did not *know* they were "savage." With such knowledge, inevitably, came guilt. Civilized culture had its relation to "savage" energy, but it maintained itself as those in its thrall maintained themselves: by sacrificing this relation—or at least by repressing conscious awareness of it. The willful traveller in Lapland, writes Ishmael at the close of "The Whiteness of the Whale," refuses to wear "colored and coloring classes" upon his eyes. He thus "gazes himself blind at the monumental white shroud that wraps all the prospect around him" (170). Culture endured by keeping the glasses in place.

To speak of culture's sacrificing its relation to revolutionary energy is to raise, for Melville, a crucial question. Issues of politics and psychology notwithstanding, this is, after all, a study of the development of American romance. Melville, in his overt comments on his art, sees the impulse to give "utterance" to revolutionary "promptings"—"the great Art of Telling the Truth"—as the essence of literary expression. Yet in his fiction this impulse, as it is engaged by his protagonists, is cast into question and is finally, perhaps, subverted. Expression looks more and more like repression; sincerity gives way to guilt. What, then, *was* the nature or purpose of literary expression? In a world where self-assertion was repeatedly transmuted into suicide or self-enervation, and revolutionary "truth" into unconscious repression and irony, what did or could it mean "to out with the Romance"? In *Moby-Dick* and *Pierre*, at last, Melville faced these questions—if not necessarily the answers to them—openly and directly.

FIERY HUNTS

Ishmael, at the outset of *Moby-Dick*, emerges as a familiar character. His casual good humor in the face of constricting circumstance perhaps sets him apart. "Not ignoring what is good," he writes, "I am quick to perceive a horror, and could still be social with it—would they let me—since it is but well to be on friendly terms with all the inmates of the place one lodges in" (16). But his "would they let me" is ominous, and beneath Ishmael's easy tolerance lurks the frustrated anger of Melville's earlier hero-narrators. The status of common sailor touches the "sense of honor" of one who comes "of an old established family in the land" (14).[11] As for his motives, he goes to sea "whenever I find myself involuntarily pausing before coffin wharehouses" or following funerals—whenever, that is, "it requires a strong moral principle to prevent me from deliberately stepping into the street, and methodically knocking people's hats off." Going to sea, he writes, "is my substitute for pistol and ball. With a philosophical flourish Cato throws himself upon his sword; I quietly take to the ship" (12).

Like Redburn, Ishmael is possessed by irrational "demoniac feelings" against total strangers. Like Taji, he takes to the sea as a substitute for acting out suicidal compulsions. Not even, perhaps, as a substitute; for the attraction he feels for the "nameless perils of the whale" (16) and the somber testimony of the memorial tablets in the Whaleman's Chapel hint that he may embrace whaling as *a form of* suicide.

But, as is the case with so many of Melville's earlier heroes, Ishmael is largely able to deflect the promptings of his buried rage. For defiance he substitutes good humor. The affront of tyranny he transforms into the compensatory rhetoric of democratic dignity, or he resorts to abstract rationalization: "Who aint a slave?" (15). He may feel resentful, similarly, that the Fates "put me down for this shabby part of a whaling voyage, when others were set down for magnificent parts in high tragedies, and short and easy parts in genteel comedies, and jolly parts in farces" (16). But here, too, his recourse is clear: through his art he can transform his "shabby part" *into* high tragedy, genteel comedy, and jolly farce. And just as Tommo, Taji and White-Jacket turn from personal frustration to apparently impersonal observation, so does Ishmael, for large portions of his narrative, turn from the unspeakable personal implications of "the overwhelming idea of the great whale himself" (16) to the relatively safe and arbitrary cataloguing of the cetology chapters.

Ishmael's principal recourse, however, is to projection. His unacknowledgeable impulses—about which, as about his personal history, we learn very little—are displaced into the world around him or projected onto other characters, whose actions, after the opening chapters, constitute the only plot of *Moby-Dick*.[12] Especially important as alter egos in Ishmael's drama of sublimation are Queequeg, Ahab, and Starbuck.

Queequeg permits Ishmael, like Tommo before him, to turn from desperate outcast into "objective" anthropologist. Having transferred his own desperate fantasies to this "savage," he can then assure himself that Queequeg's "savagery" is only skin deep. A good deal has been made, quite properly, of the idea that Ishmael's "democratic" love for Queequeg saves him from the obsessive diabolism that overwhelms Ahab.[13] But this is a "love" based on maintaining mostly comic distance. Ishmael may dismiss Queequeg's skin color and "heathenish" tattooing as superficial and hence inessential, but he steadfastly recoils at any hint of what slumbers beneath this surface or beneath the surface of his own complacency. He prefers the charitably abstract consolation that "through all his unearthly tattooings, I thought I saw the traces of a simple honest heart" (52).

The mode of Ishmael's rapport with Queequeg also has an unsettling tendency to shift from anthropological comic to Radcliffean gothic, substituting for the ironic interplay of "civilized" and "savage" the quick-cut alternation of inexplicable terror and rational reassurance, "desperate suggestions" and "better thoughts." Queequeg's Ramadan, for instance, transforms Ishmael's tolerant amusement at quaint custom into something like the jumpy irascibility of Irving's Nervous Gentleman. "I cherish the greatest respect towards everybody's religious obligations," Ishmael assures us, "never mind how comical" (78). But Queequeg's continued failure to open the locked door elicits a far different response: "'Queequeg!—Queequeg!'—all still. Something must have happened. Apoplexy! I tried to burst open the door; but it stubbornly resisted" (78). When Ishmael finally does break the door open, Queequeg's composure is too much. "I almost felt like pushing him over," Ishmael confesses, "so as to change his position, for it was almost intolerable" (80). Ishmael may turn from violent fantasies to the companionship of his "bosom friend," but even in this friendship the fantasies, from time to time, threaten new eruption. Ishmael returns to reason, trying to convince Queequeg that "frantic" religion should be dismissed as being "uncomfortable" (81), but a casual mention of "dyspepsia" draws from Queequeg the memory of a banquet upon human flesh. "No more, Queequeg," says Ishmael, shuddering, "that will do" (82). Ishmael turns to Queequeg to escape his own secret self, not to find it.

In Ahab, Ishmael finds this self. He joins Ahab's fiery hunt, he writes, "because of the dread in my soul"—the dread which, with Queequeg, he strives to obscure. "A wild, mystical, sympathetical feeling was in me; Ahab's quenchless feud seemed mine" (155). Ahab acts out the full implications of Ishmael's "desperate suggestions," and by doing so he allows Ishmael to maintain his precarious hold on "better thoughts." By projecting his secret rage into Ahab's suicidal quest, Ishmael is spared having to embark on such a quest in his own interest. He is enabled to remain, as he puts it in the "Epilogue," "floating on the margin of the ensuing scene, and in full sight of it." This distance saves him from the full power of the *Pequod*'s "closing vortex" (470). And Queequeg's arabesque and empty coffin bears him up.

Ahab is more than Ishmael's alter ego. In his defiance of the entire universe, from the ship's owners to the gods, he gives utterance to the promptings latent in all of Melville's heroes from Tommo on. He does so, however, only to dramatize a set of interlocking paradoxes implicit from the first in the messianic ideal of revolutionary self-assertion.

Tommo, Taji, Redburn, and White-Jacket are paralyzed by guilt. Ahab ignores this guilt, as it would seem, and strikes back. But it is hard to see how Ahab's projection of "all his intellectual and spiritual exasperations" onto the Whale is any less evasive of sincerity than is Ishmael's calculated good humor. By piling "upon the whale's white hump the sum of all the general rage and hate felt by his whole race from Adam down," by making it "the monomaniac incarnation of all those malicious agencies which some deep men feel eating in them" (160), Ahab is mainly striving to deny his own agency. He is blaming the Whale for his own violent impulses. In the event, his assertion of liberty ends in death. Ahab's allegorical exploitation of the Whale is analogous to Aylmer's allegorical exploitation of Georgiana in Hawthorne's "Birth-mark." Aylmer at least had the sense to pick on somebody his own size. Moreover, to the extent that Ahab, in pursuing the Whale, is pursuing a guilty sublimation of his secret self, the hidden meaning of his quest is, from the first, suicide.

In seeming to assert his buried self, Ahab loses it. This may have been his hidden purpose all along, but his overt revolutionary rhetoric of self-assertion, which perhaps masks this purpose, leads on its own terms to inexorable confusion. Ahab's sense of tyranny, like Ishmael's, expands rapidly to cosmic proportions. It is against Fate itself that he asserts his freedom. "I own thy speechless, placeless power," he shouts at the corposant fire, "but to the last gasp of my earthquake life will dispute its unconditional, unintegral mastery in me. In the midst of the personified impersonal, a personality stands here" (417). In his quest, Ahab sets out to realize this "personality"; yet, when compassion for Pip touches his "inmost centre" (428), the "self-realizing" quest is, paradoxically, threatened, and so is Ahab's rhetoric of personal assertion. "There is that in thee, poor lad," says Ahab to Pip, "which I feel too curing to my malady. Like cures like; and for this hunt, my malady becomes my most desired health" (436). Self-assertion becomes a "malady." By the close, in "The Symphony," Ahab argues that only Fate drives him on, "against all natural lovings and longings." What began in assertion of "personality" ends in bafflement: "Is Ahab, Ahab?" (445). Pursuing the promptings of personal freedom, Ahab only recreates the impersonal Fate against which he rebelled in the first place.

The same paradoxical transmutation lies at the heart of the political meaning of *Moby-Dick*. "Who's over me," shouts Ahab in "The Quarter-Deck." "Truth hath no confines" (144). "Who's over him, he cries," reflects Starbuck; "aye, he would be a democrat to all above; look, how he lords it over all below!" (148). As had Napoleon and Andrew Jackson, in the eyes of many of Melville's contemporaries, so Ahab asserts democratic freedom only to institute an even more oppressive tyranny. "Ye are not other men," he declaims to his boat's crew on the last day of the chase, "but my arms and legs; and so obey me" (465).

It is in this light that Starbuck is most important, for he alone, as far as we know, contemplates mutiny. The reasons for his failure are instructive. Many readers of *Moby-Dick* see at its center a conflict between the active, linear, despotic energy of Ahab and the passive, circular, democratic vision of Ishmael. Yet this conflict is never resolved. Like so many American classics, *Moby-Dick* rides on unresolved conflict, a kind of contest between characters for domination of the book itself.[14] In *Moby-Dick* this conflict is not only unresolved; it is never really engaged. What happens to Starbuck suggests why it is not—why neither Ishmael nor Bulkington (as may have been Melville's original intention)[15] rises up to save the ship from Ahab's despotic monomania.

Starbuck's problem is not that he doesn't understand Ahab but that he understands him too well. He knows what dark "truths" Ahab has seen; he has glimpsed them himself. He has felt in himself the outraged promptings that fuel Ahab's fiery hunt. But he will consciously acknowledge neither the truths nor the promptings. Gazing at the doubloon, he tries to make the hills the Trinity, "in some faint earthly symbol," and the sun an abiding "beacon and a hope." "Yet, oh," he involuntarily reflects, "the great sun is no fixture; and if, at midnight, we would fain snatch some sweet solace from him, we gaze for him in vain!" Then Starbuck slams on the brakes: "This coin speaks wisely, mildly, truly, but still sadly to me. I will quit it, lest Truth shake me falsely" (360). An interesting phrase, that last. We could as easily be in the House of Usher with Roderick's companion. In "The Gilder," Starbuck's avoidance, as he stares into the sea, is even more overt: "Let faith oust fact; let fancy oust memory; I look deep down and do believe" (406).

Starbuck seems something of a fool, but his foolishness has its function—a function of which he is fully aware. "Oh! I plainly see my miserable office," he soliloquizes; "to obey, rebelling; and worse yet, to hate with touch of pity! For in [Ahab's] eyes," he adds, "I read some lurid woe would shrivel me up, had I it" (148). Like Redburn contemplating Jackson, Starbuck sees "more woe than wickedness" in Ahab; and like Redburn praying against the hatred that might turn him into Jackson, Starbuck recognizes that to contest Ahab would be to become Ahab, by acknowledging in himself the capacity for violence that has overwhelmed his captain. The dawning idea of mutiny, suggested by the rack of muskets outside Ahab's cabin, horrifies him: "Starbuck was an honest, upright man; but out of Starbuck's heart, at that instant . . ., there strangely evolved an evil thought" (421). He strives to rationalize the impulse. Perhaps he could imprison Ahab? But in chains, Starbuck recognizes, Ahab "would be more hideous than a caged tiger. . . . I could not endure the sight; could not possibly fly his howlings; all comfort, sleep itself, inestimable reason would leave me on the long intolerable voyage" (422). Starbuck, should he act, would become like Tommo, haunted by Mow-Mow's "ferocious countenance," or like Irving's Young Italian, haunted by the image of mangled Filippo.

As a good liberal, a man whose very religion is belief in the beneficence of "arbitrary codes," Starbuck knows that even the killing of Ahab would be just. But he also knows that it would awaken in him promptings he cannot, as a good liberal, liberate. The gate of justice is blocked by guilt. "Starbuck," writes Ishmael in "Knights and Squires," "was no crusader after perils; in him courage was not a sentiment; but a thing simply useful to him" (103). For Starbuck, as for the Franklin of *Israel Potter*, violence is acceptable only if it is socially instrumental; to the extent that it is primary, to the extent that it expresses personal rage, it is forbidden. His is "that sort of bravery, chiefly visible in some intrepid men, which . . . cannot withstand those more terrific, because more spiritual terrors, which sometimes menace you from the concentrating brow of an enraged and mighty man" (104).

Yet Starbuck is no simple coward. Ahab possesses precisely the sort of courage Starbuck lacks; and the course and outcome of Ahab's sincere defiance could hardly encourage proponents of mutiny. It never occurs to

Ishmael, as far as we know, to resist his captain, and this is not the only similarity between Starbuck and Ishmael; for the First Mate's habit of avoidance, his determination to quit dark thoughts, "lest Truth shake me falsely," bears an intriguing resemblance to Ishmael's characteristic narrative manner.

"There are times," says White-Jacket, "when wild thoughts enter a man's heart, when he seems almost irresponsible for his act and his deed" (280). Ahab perishes in acting out his thoughts, and he takes the others with him. Ishmael survives, it would seem, because he is able to displace his own "wild thoughts" into the "acts and deeds" of others. Yet Ishmael is not just an avoider, a displacer. He is also a writer, an artist. Or perhaps we should say that it is in the very process of displacement, rather than in revolutionary promptings themselves, that he finds the key to his utterance. He survives because he accepts, and even implicitly advertises, the sacrifice of the relation between his promptings and his utterance.

Starbuck, after the first day's chase, stares in horror at Ahab's wrecked whaleboat. "'Tis a solemn sight," he declares; "an omen, and an ill one." "Omen? omen?" snaps Ahab, "—the dictionary! If the gods think to speak outright to man, they will honorably speak outright; not shake their heads, and give an old wives' darkling hint" (452). Ahab, for all his rage against cosmic insincerity, pays heed to Fedallah's omens, which are finally confirmed. And Ishmael's mode is not noumenally "outright" but rigorously phenomenal. His insights into mysterious depths are always, like those of the narrator of *Billy Budd*, deductions from obscure or contradictory appearances, not communications of direct, mystical insight. He communicates to us through "darkling hints." His is the language of irony, not that of sincerity.

He relies, for instance, on what might be called ironic montage. Like the Shakespeare of "Hawthorne and His *Mosses*," he may insinuate "things which we feel to be so terrifically true that it were all but madness for any good man, in his own proper character, to utter, or even hint of them," but, unlike the Lear of the "*Mosses*" essay, he never "tears off the mask" (407). Thus his darkest "truths" are often shadowed forth not by the chapters themselves but by the empty spaces between the chapters, marked by abrupt transitions upon which Ishmael himself, "in his own proper character," bestows no comment.

Chapter 6, for instance, ends with a revery on the "bloom" of "the women of New Bedford," "perennial as sunlight," and on Salem, "where they tell me the young girls breathe such musk, their sailor sweethearts smell them miles off shore, as though they were drawing nigh the odorous Moluccas instead of the Puritanic sands" (39). Immediately thereafter, chapter 7, introducing the Whaleman's Chapel, presents the sardonically contrasting image of storm-blasted widows, left destitute by sailor sweethearts who never returned. Similarly, Father Mapple's sermon is followed immediately—and with no narrative comment on the transition—by Ishmael's participation with Queequeg in the pagan worship of Yojo. There are also numerous undiscussed transitions within chapters. Ishmael, in "The Ramadan," never comments on his own rapid shifts from good-humored tolerance to gothic terror, and in "The Doubloon," as I noted in chapter 6, the opening assurance that "some certain significance lurks in all things" (549) is ironically contradicted, and again without narrative recognition, by what happens in the chapter that follows.

Even Ishmael's apparently "outright" communication is riddled with self-conscious irony. What it indirectly insinuates is precisely what it claims, overtly, to deny. In "The Honor and Glory of Whaling" we are assured that the "Grecian story of Hercules and the whale is considered to be derived from the still more ancient Hebrew story of Jonah and the whale; and vice versa." The implications of this "vice versa," respecting the authority of the Old Testament, are passed over. In the face of the attack of comparative mythologists on the truth of Scripture—of their argument that Old Testament "history" was largely a corruption of older, pagan "stories"—Ishmael simply says of his two myths: "certainly they are very similar" (306).[16] In "Jonah Historically Regarded," Ishmael's overt attack on skeptical debunking of Scripture ironically supports such skepticism. Do Nantucketers, bothered by their knowledge of cetological anatomy, doubt the story of Jonah and the whale? There were also "some skeptical Greeks and Romans," observes "orthodox" Ishmael, "who, standing out from the orthodox pagans of their times, equally doubted the story of Hercules and the whale, and Arion and the dolphin; and yet their doubting those traditions did not make those traditions one whit the less facts, for all that" (306–7).

"I think it may safely be asserted," wrote Charles Brockden Brown in the early 1790s, "that of all the virtues mankind is most universally deficient in sincerity. . . . How many motives are there for concealing our real sentiment . . . ? And how many occasions are there, on which, if its immediate and temporary effects only be considered, sincerity is criminal?"[17] Ahab's fiery hunt certainly illustrates the notion that sincerity, pursued to the exclusion of all else, may be "criminal" and possibly insincere as well. Ishmael's rhetoric, on the other hand, illustrates, even as it ironically obscures, the "many motives" we may have "for concealing our real sentiment." Ishmael willfully displaces "sentiments" into "words." But even as Ahab dramatizes the lurking insincerity of sincerity, so

Ishmael paradoxically demonstrates that insincerity—for Starbuck only a form of evasion—may hold the key to "the great Art of Telling the Truth."

Emerson, in a well-known passage in "The Poet," differentiates between the "poet" and the "mystic." The "mystic," he writes,

> nails a symbol to one sense, which was a true sense for a moment, but soon becomes old and false. For all symbols are fluxional; all language is vehicular and transitive. . . . Mysticism consists in the mistake of an accidental and individual symbol for an universal one.[18]

If Ahab is a "mystic," Ishmael is a "poet."

Melville almost literally echoes Emerson in an 1851 letter to Hawthorne: "What plays the mischief with the truth is that men will insist upon the universal application of a temporary feeling or opinion" (131). Thus "The Whiteness of the Whale" describes what the white whale was to Ishmael "at times": the "vague, nameless horror concerning him, which at times by its intensity completely overpowered all the rest" (163). Ishmael, in "The Try-Works," is wrapped in darkness "for that interval" (354). The "truth" of Ishmael's rhetoric is the phenomenal truth of experience in human time, not the atemporal, noumenal revelation of the mystic. Or, to speak more precisely, Ishmael's rhetoric embodies the recognition that even mystic promptings are only "temporary feelings or opinions." Nothing, in every sense of the word, is *wholly* "true"—which is the point of "The Whiteness of the Whale."

There is, to be sure, something defensive in all of this. Ishmael has a great deal in common with the Redburn who prays that "hatred . . . might not master my heart completely, and so make a fiend of me" (57). He has, too, some of the evasive obscurantism of Starbuck or of Amasa Delano. The difference is that his vision includes what his rhetoric ultimately overcomes. "Look not *too long* in the face of the fire, O man!" he writes in "The Try-Works." "Give not thyself up, then, to fire, lest it invert thee, deaden thee; as *for the time* it did me" (354–55; my emphasis). "There seemed even more woe than wickedness about the man," writes Redburn of Jackson. "There is a wisdom that is woe," writes Ishmael; "but there is a woe that is madness" (355).

It is in this spirit that Ishmael displaces the "mystic" promptings of enraged "woe" into the "fluxional" artifice of language. Ahab's is the suicidal sincerity of Hamlet: "Seems, madam! Nay it is; I know not 'seems'" (I. ii. 75). "The rushing Pequod," Ishmael writes in "The Try-Works," "freighted with savages, and laden with fire, and burning a corpse, and plunging into that blackness of darkness, seemed the material counterpart of her monomaniac commander's soul." "So," he adds, "seemed it to me, as I stood at her helm" (354). The Whale's is a "nameless horror" (163). Its whiteness is the "mystic sign" of "nameless things" (169). Poe located the "effect" of romance—its power at once to evoke and to conceal its "mystic" energy—in its "suggestive indefinitiveness of meaning" (16:28). Whiteness, writes Ishmael, "by its indefiniteness . . . shadows forth the heartless voids and immensities of the universe" (169). Nay, replies Ishmael to Hamlet/Ahab, it seems; I know not "is." Nothing "is."

Ishmael's absolute nihilism is of a piece with his tolerant optimism. The white whale's "dumb blankness, full of meaning," his "colorless, all-color of atheism from which we shrink" (169), is implicit from the outset in Ishmael's liberal insistence that Queequeg's skin is "only his outside" (29), that in spite of superficial differences we all belong to "the same ancient Catholic Church" (83). What distinguishes Ishmael is that, even as he dismisses surfaces as inessential, it is to surfaces that he holds. It is through the artificial acceptance or manipulation of surfaces that he hopes to compensate for the empty horror that lies, as it seems, beneath them. Ahab, suspecting that "there's naught beyond," strikes out in suicidal defiance. He cannot stand indefiniteness. Ishmael, by contrast, embraces the phenomenal indefiniteness of appearances and of language. "How can I hope to explain myself here," he writes in "The Whiteness of the Whale"; "and yet, in some dim, random way, explain myself I must, else all these chapters might be naught" (163).

Ishmael's cosmopolitan nihilism is first hinted at, and first linked to the "dim, random way" of language, in the opening "Etymology." The handkerchief of the consumptive "pale Usher" is "mockingly embellished with all the gay flags of all the known nations of the world" (1). Each colorful flag mocks the truth of the white cloth's (and the "pale" Usher's) "colorless, all-color," as each of the names that follow mocks the "nameless horror" of the whale. Words both partially hint at and partially suppress the truth. Even as they testify to their origins, they falsify the truth of those origins; as names, they sacrifice their relation to primal namelessness. But theirs is a saving sacrifice. Queequeg's hieroglyphic tattooings are "the work of a departed prophet and seer of his island." Their "mysteries," Ishmael writes, "not even himself could read, though his own live heart beat against them." To Ahab their arabesque obscurity is a "devilish tantalization of the gods" (399). But it is Queequeg's coffin—similarly engraved, and buoyant because it contains "naught" within—that saves Ishmael.

Appalled by the silence of the whale, Ahab extends his outrage to a more comprehensive muteness: "O Nature, and O soul of man! how far beyond all utterance are your linked analogies! not the smallest atom stirs or lives in matter, but has its cunning duplicate in mind" (264). Queequeg's coffin, at the close, is "liberated by reason of its cunning spring" (470), and Ishmael is not outraged by such "cunning"; torn between deep promptings and empty utterance, he turns to the hollow buoyancy of artifice. Language may be only another "cunning duplicate," a parody, of unutterable truth. Thus the coffin's emergence parodies the breaching of the whale: "rising with great force, the coffin life-buoy shot lengthwise from the sea, fell over, and floated by my side" (470). Even this empty box challenges the truth of language, being at once "life-buoy" and "coffin," preserver of life and receptacle of death. But while Ahab's craft goes down, Ishmael's craft keeps him afloat.

"I am horror-struck," writes Ishmael, "at this antemosaic, unsourced existence of the unspeakable terrors of the whale, which, having been before all time, must needs exist after all humane ages are over" (380). In this horror Ishmael finds the correlative of his own initial desperation. It is at once the timeless source of history and the primal source of Ishmael's voyage and of his story. It is the terrible "truth" of *Moby-Dick; or The Whale*. The book exists, however, not by speaking "outright" but by "hints." However "antemosaic" his meanings, Ishmael weaves his fable on a "loom of time." [19] Even as it testifies to the power of that *"instinct"* whose primacy Melville proclaimed to John Murray in 1848, the phenomenal verbal structure of Ishmael's romance—with its "seemings," its "for a times," its parodic play—displaces the terrible relation at its heart. Ahab pursues the Whale and perishes. Ishmael pursues *The Whale*, in the "dim, random way" of language, and escapes alone to tell his tale. Redburn prayed against succumbing to the "wickedness" of Jackson and of his own smoldering hatred. "I have written a wicked book," wrote Melville to Hawthorne of *Moby-Dick*, "and feel spotless as the lamb" (142).

Pierre, in most respects, seems as different from *Moby-Dick* as one could imagine. There are the shifts of scene from sea to land and of narration from first person to third person. There is the new prominence given to plot—to the formulas of genteel sexual melodrama that Melville apparently set out to exploit or imitate and ended up parodying. [20] More fundamentally, there is a radical shift in implicit attitude toward language. Literary expression, which redeemed Ishmael from Ahab's suicidal compulsion, becomes Pierre's equivalent to Ahab's fiery hunt.

At the beginning, moreover, Pierre is not an outcast. He still occupies that "proper" position in society from which Tommo, Redburn, and Ishmael—for reasons never very fully explained—have fallen. In *Pierre*, consequently, the story of the hero's rebellion is one with the story of his fall, and this collocation is important; for in *Pierre*, at last, the deepest implications of Melville's revolutionary theme are revealed: the hero's rebellion is the *cause* of his fall. Beneath Pierre's idealistic rhetoric of revolutionary sincerity swims the dark hint that self-destruction was his motive all along.

It is hard to find any other sense in which Pierre's motives and actions are "revolutionary." To be sure, his early faith in the rational, respect-able, phenomenal truth of Saddle Meadows—the "Joy" linked to Lucy—is soon undermined by unconscious intimations of a deeper, darker, noumenal truth—the "Woe" of Isabel and New York. At first "the streams of these reveries" leave no "conscious sediment in his mind." But soon "irresistible intuitions" (85)—first suggested by the chair portrait of his father and confirmed by the appearance of Isabel—triumph. It is not just that Pierre must accept Isabel as his illegitimate half-sister. More impor-tant, his whole conception of "truth" is irrevocably altered:

> Oh, not long will Joy abide, when Truth doth come; nor Grief her laggard be. . . . Oh, men are jailers all; jailers of themselves; and in Opinion's world ignorantly hold their noblest part a captive to their vilest. . . . The heart! the heart! 'tis God's anointed; let me pursue the heart! [91]

In this spirit of radical sincerity Pierre renounces Lucy, his mother, and his inheritance to head for New York with Isabel and, in his writing, to "cast off all cables." This is his fiery hunt.

In substituting belief in "Grief" for belief in "Joy," Pierre succumbs to the same monomaniac fixation that overwhelmed Ahab. By the end, even this fixated belief has been shattered. Isabel's evidence that she is Pierre's half-sister, and hence that Pierre's father deviated from rectitude, is called into question. Lucy will not stay spurned: she joins Pierre and Isabel in New York. Neither "Joy" nor "Grief" can be fully believed in—or escaped. Thus does Pierre's story illustrate "the everlasting elusiveness of Truth" (339).

But there are problems in Pierre's rebellion deeper than the "elusiveness of Truth." For one thing, however sincere Pierre may be in intention, his sincerity is repeatedly compromised by his behavior. "In the Enthusiast to Duty," proclaims the narrator of Pierre's renunciation of "all common conventional regardings," "the heaven-begotten Christ is born" (106). Yet Pierre does not openly own Isabel as his sister; he pretends, rather, to marry her. In his pursuit of truth, he embraces not defiance but "a most singular act of pious imposture, which he thought all heaven would justify in him, since he himself was to be the grand self-renouncing victim" (173).

The conscious motives behind this duplicitous sincerity are important. Pierre turns to "pious imposture," he assures himself, because he is "de-termined at all hazards to hold his father's fair fame inviolate from any thing he should do in reference to protecting Isabel . . . ; and equally de-termined not to shake his mother's lasting peace by any useless exposure of unwelcome facts" (172–73). This is a curious sort of sincerity and a curious sort of rebellion. Pierre does not turn against his father, nor does he mean to shock his mother. Rather, the motive for his "revolution" is to *defend* his

227

father. He may renounce the past and "all common conventional regardings"; yet he appeals to the authority of heaven to "justify" him, and,
in his far from chartless voyage, he repeatedly appeals to the past, especially to the literary past, for guidance.[21] Prohibited, apparently, from
venting his promptings on his real or symbolic parents, he turns them on
himself. It is significant that what will "justify" him in the eyes of heaven,
and presumably in his own, is the fact that "he himself was to be the grand
self-renouncing victim." Only thus can he deal with the guilt that lurks,
from the very beginning, at the heart of his story.

"A noble boy," thinks Mary Glendinning of her son, "and docile" (19).
Yet as she gazes at the baton of her father, the Revolutionary War general,
she recognizes the problem couched in her praise:

> "This is his inheritance—this symbol of command! and I swell out to
> think it. Yet but just now I fondled the conceit that Pierre was so
> sweetly docile! Here sure is a most strange inconsistency! For is
> sweet docility a general's badge? . . . Now I almost wish [Pierre]
> otherwise than sweet and docile to me, seeing that it must be hard for
> man to be an uncompromising hero and commander among his race,
> and yet never ruffle any domestic brow." [20][22]

Pierre confronts the same problem. It is indeed hard for him to be a hero
without ruffling any domestic brow. How can he give utterance to his own
promptings, the violence of his buried self, without turning them on his
mother and on the memory of his father? How can he escape the civilized
rebel's guilt and thereby lay claim to the heritage of his heroic "revolutionary descent" (20)? It is because he cannot answer these questions, or
even openly face them, that Pierre is compelled to turn to "pious imposture." The impulse of open aggression repressed by guilt, Pierre can
indulge it only covertly, in the sublimated form of an abstract messianic
rhetoric, which, he unconsciously hopes, will absolve him of conscious
responsibility for his actions.

The effect of the actions nevertheless reveals their hidden motive. Outraged at Pierre's defiance of her will, his mother, whose "peace" Pierre
vowed never to "shake," dies. Pursued by Lucy and Isabel, Pierre shoots
down Glen Stanly, thereby extinguishing "his house in slaughtering the
only unoutlawed human being by the name of Glendinning" (360). At the
close, drinking Isabel's poison, he kills himself—Isabel and Lucy dying
with him.

Beneath the surface of benevolent purpose works the forbidden energy
of primordial violence. For all his rhetoric, Pierre has unconsciously
known this all along. Even vowing to protect his mother's peace, we are
told, "he in embryo, foreknew, that the extraordinary thing he had resolved, would, in another way, indirectly though inevitably, dart a most

228

keen pang into his mother's heart" (173). But this violence can only appear in the mask of "sweet docility." In the end, it can only be turned against itself. "The sins of the father," insists the Reverend Falsgrave, "shall be visited upon the children to the third generation" (100). Pierre, having fully internalized the taboos of his culture and being thus incapable of rebelling consciously against ancestral authority, turns from the assertion of his buried self to benevolent rhetoric and, ultimately, by his guilty self-destruction, to fulfillment of the biblical prophecy.

Together with Ahab's suicidal fiery hunt, Pierre's guilty pursuit of aggression in the names of "Duty" and "Truth" culminates Melville's effort to give utterance to revolutionary promptings. The problem with *Pierre* is that in it the promptings are apparently deflected into neither ironic observation nor the actions of others but into lurid melodrama. In the character of Pierre, it would seem, Ishmael has turned into Ahab. But this is true only in a sense, for it is not Pierre but the nameless narrator who functions as the Ishmael of the book. It is as if Melville, once he had detached his own voice from the character of his persona, could allow that persona, in his own proper character, to act out the full implications of his guilty rage.

But if *Pierre*'s anonymous narrator is the book's Ishmael, he is an Ishmael much reduced. Pierre, like Ahab, illustrates Ishmael's moral, in "The Try-Works," that if "there is a wisdom that is woe" there is also "a woe that is madness," but the narrator never completes Ishmael's affirmative circle. There is, in *Pierre*, no "Catskill eagle in some souls that can alike dive down into the blackest gorges, and soar out of them again and become invisible in the sunny spaces" (355); nor is there in *Pierre*, for either the hero or the narrator, anything like Ishmael's "insular Tahiti, full of peace and joy, but encompassed by all the horrors of the half known life" (236). Unlike Ishmael, the narrator of *Pierre* cannot, "amid the tornadoed Atlantic of my being, . . . still for ever centrally disport in mute calm; and while ponderous planets of unwaning woe revolve round me, deep down and deep inland . . . still bathe me in eternal mildness of joy" (326).

Nevertheless *Pierre*'s narrator, like Ishmael, uses language to maintain his distance from the story he tells. Pierre founders on "the everlasting elusiveness of Truth; the universal lurking insincerity of even the greatest and purest written thoughts" (339). The narrator delights in these things: "lurking insincerity" is his favorite mode. He delights in subversively ironic rhetorical display. Introducing Lucy, for instance, he digresses into a grotesquely parodic encomium on female beauty:

> A lovely woman is not entirely of this earth. Her own sex regard her
> not as such. A crowd of women eye a transcendent beauty entering a

room, much as though a bird from Arabia had lighted on the window sill. Say what you will, their jealousy—if any—is but an after-birth to their open admiration.

Many narrators, having managed to derive jealousy and afterbirth from female beauty, might stop. But not the narrator of *Pierre:*

> A beautiful woman is born Queen of men and women both, as Mary Stuart was born Queen of Scots, whether men or women. All mankind are her Scots; her leal clans are numbered by the nations. A true gentleman in Kentucky would cheerfully die for a beautiful woman in Hindostan, though he never saw her. Yea, count down his heart in death-drops for her; and go to Pluto, that she might go to Paradise. He would turn Turk before he would disown an allegiance hereditary to all gentlemen, from the hour their Grand Master, Adam, first knelt to Eve. [24]

Mary Queen of Scots, beheaded by her sister, is hardly an example to quell rumblings about female jealousy, and by the end of the passage we have managed to get from female beauty to Original Sin! This narrator is a master of the deliberately and subversively unfortunate phrase or metaphor. In lovers' eyes, he writes, "swim the strange eye-fish with wings, that sometimes leap out, instinct with joy; moist fish-wings wet the lover's cheek" (33). Or, of amorous Pierre: "the striped tigers of his chestnut eyes leaped in their lashed cages with a fierce delight" (35).

It has been said that the language of *Pierre* is out of control.[23] This is surely true of many of Pierre's own speeches and soliloquies, but it is not generally true of the narrator's voice. There the problem, if any, is that its irony is too dense. His is not, however, the open, buoyant irony of Ishmael.[24] The ironic interplay of the narrative voice of *Pierre* is not between utterance and promptings, "words" and "sentiments," but between words and other words. The metaphorical meaning of "after-birth" fights with its literal meaning. The rhetoric of courtly fealty fights with the biblical context of Adam's fall. "Eye-fish" fight with actual wet fish, soiling lovers' cheeks. Lucy's name is subverted, along with its Wordsworthian associations, by its closeness to "Lucifer." Even "Joy" and "Grief," for the narrator, are finally "mere words."

The narrator displaces the simultaneously expressive and repressive dynamic of sublimation into Pierre's melodramatic mania. Then, like the distant cynic Plinlimmon, he cuts the cable. His language floats—to quote James's phrase again—"at large and unrelated." It no longer suggests any deeper, repressed meaning; all that "lurks" in it is its insincerity. It subverts only itself.

Some of Hawthorne's stories, writes Melville in the *"Mosses"* essay, "are directly calculated to deceive—egregiously deceive—the superficial skimmer of pages" (418). Ishmael deceives to open the reader to, and at the same time protect himself from, immensities beyond the superficial surface of conscious knowledge and verbal artifice. The narrator of *Pierre* deceives, it would seem, for the sake of deception. He sets out, with deliberate insincerity, to burlesque the role of a "good man, in his own proper character." He turns his performance from the promptings of the secret self to the tenuous clichés, the conventional utterance, of his culture. Perhaps this shift, for Melville, was inevitable. Pierre lives in a world that has thoroughly confused rebellion and "duty," self-assertion and "sweet docility." We may be tempted to trace this confusion to a personal neurosis in Melville, and not without reason. But in Hawthorne's *Blithedale Romance*, published in the same year as *Pierre*, we confront a culture dominated by a similar confusion of sentiment and sentimentality. Like the Hawthorne of *The Blithedale Romance*, the Melville of *Pierre*, in the voice of his narrator, turns from the impulse of renewal to the petrifaction of his unrenewed culture and, especially, to the petrifaction of its language. When Melville no longer resisted this petrifaction, as it would seem he did not, what begins to emerge in the narrative voice of *Pierre* is the almost terminally phenomenal rhetoric that wholly dominates *The Confidence-Man*.

The shift from messianic expression to phenomenal observation was implicit in Melville's fiction from the beginning. Tommo flees his rage at the captain's tyranny to observe the strange customs of Marquesan "savages." In *The Confidence-Man* Melville turns his anthropologist's eye—and ear—on the culture of his own America. In his view, this culture was the product of an evasion similar to Tommo's: it existed through the repression of its origins; it endured by denying its relation to these origins. The Melville of *The Confidence-Man* seems no longer concerned, as he was in his earlier works, with giving utterance to his own "revolutionary" promptings. Instead, he sets out to explore the buried relation between his culture and its origins, between its ordered world of words and the energy these words seemed meant to conceal.

INSTINCT AND IMPOSTURE

"There is no quality in this world," writes Ishmael, "that is not what it is merely by contrast. Nothing exists in itself" (55). Experience is a pattern of contrasting phenomenal "truths." The difficulty of integrating them into a more comprehensive vision is suggested to Ishmael by the sperm whale's head, which is described in a chapter nicely subtitled "Contrasted

View." The whale's eyes, which face sideways and are separated by the vast bulk of his head, simultaneously register two totally different images. "Is his brain," Ishmael wonders, "so much more comprehensive, combining, and subtle than man's, that he can at the same moment of time attentively examine two distinct prospects, one on one side of him, and the other in an exactly opposite direction?" Rather, Ishmael suspects, whales must be beset by a "helpless perplexity of volition, in which their divided and diametrically opposite powers of vision must involve them" (280). The same perplexity besets many of Melville's characters, torn as they are between the "truths" of primitive and civilized, faith and doubt, "Joy" and "Woe." Every "truth," Melville wrote to Hawthorne, is but "the universal application of a temporary feeling or opinion" (131). Beset by the perplexity of double vision, his characters nevertheless set out to find some larger truth behind or beyond the apparently random succession of contradictory feelings or opinions, of contrasted views. They seek some basis for confidence in the meaning of appearances.

They do so, however, only to discover that in culture, as in personal experience, "nothing exists in itself." In *Omoo*, for instance, viewing a wrecked American whaler at Tahiti, Tommo indulges in a curious fantasy:

> What were my emotions, when I saw upon her stern the name of a small town on the river Hudson! She was from the noble stream on whose banks I was born; in whose waters I had a hundred times bathed. In an instant, palm-trees and elms—canoes and skiffs—church spires and bamboos—all mingled in one vision of the present and the past. [102]

Here we have an almost pure example of what we might call Melville's cultural double vision. Such vision often leads to a search for some meaningful distinction between "civilized" and "savage," one that suggests the relation of both to a universal or original conception of human nature; sometimes, again, it leads to the "helpless perplexity" of relativism and nihilism. Melville, like Poe's Dupin, in general sets out to discover the originating truth (in this case, of culture) by inferring noumenal motives from phenomenal expressions. What universal truth lies, say, behind the contrasting surfaces of "church spires and bamboos"? Or might this contrast have no meaning?

Tommo's "church spires" are neither "truer" nor less "true" than his "bamboos." So, too, with the "Joy" and "Woe" of *Moby-Dick* and *Pierre*. And in *The Confidence-Man*, in the *Fidèle*'s April Fools' Day voyage down the Mississippi, the debate between confidence and distrust leads, again, only to "helpless perplexity." Whatever noumenal origins might unify and explain the contrasted views of the *Fidèle*'s American masquerade have wholly given way to a game of shifting, contradictory appearances.[25] As Frank Goodman—the final, "Cosmopolitan" avatar of the elusive title figure—says to the barber toward the close: "You can conclude nothing absolute from the human form" (193). It is with the "human form"—with contrasted views of the forms of human character, culture, and literature—that *The Confidence-Man* concerns itself.

Moby-Dick raises perplexing ontological questions about the "truth" of Nature. Similar questions are raised in *The Confidence-Man* about culture and, initially, about the self, about *human* nature. Of course the cosmic nihilism of *Moby-Dick* seems to rise out of anxieties about the self—out of simultaneous fears of its violence and of its possible nonexistence; and in *The Confidence-Man* Melville is still concerned, at least indirectly, with the "spiritual" meaning of natural phenomena. But it is clear that in *The Confidence-Man* the chief emphasis falls on the psychological and social. As Paul Brodtkorb puts it, in one of the best discussions of this complex romance: "The universal void of *Moby-Dick* has here become focussed into the potential void at the center of personality."[26]

The central problem of *The Confidence-Man* is summarized in chapter 14, in the narrator's digression on the suddenly "altered mien" (57) of the Merchant, diddled by wine "into making disclosures—to himself as to another—of the queer, unaccountable caprices of his natural heart" (58). The arch ambiguity of "to himself as to another" is crucial: how many "selves" can one character have? In chapter 14, in apparent defense of this incident, the narrator argues that in "fiction based on fact" a consistent character is impossible because, "in real life, a consistent character is a *rara avis*" (58). "No writer has produced such inconsistent characters as nature herself has." The essentials of human nature, "in view of its contrasts," are, like those of the divine nature, "past finding out" (59).

Melville's narrator employs, nevertheless, the standard Romantic vocabulary for locating the true self beneath the phenomenal "inconsistencies" and "contrasts" of outward character. "More earnest psychologists," we are told toward the end of chapter 14, "still cherish expectations with regard to some mode of infallibly discovering the heart of man" (60). Such discovery may seem the motive of the Confidence-Man, in his various guises: to force "good men" like the Merchant into unwonted self-revelation. But if chapter 13 discloses the Merchant's "natural heart," chapter 14 finds only meaningless inconsistency even at the heart of nature. Moreover, there is no reason to believe that the Merchant's involuntary distrust is any "truer" than his customary geniality. In this masquerade even the revelation of the "heart" is only another mask. "The grand points of human nature," argues the narrator in chapter 14, "are the same to-day they were a thousand years ago. The only variability in them is in expression, not in feature" (60). This sounds very like Ishmael's tolerant dismissal of Queequeg's "heathenish" tattooing in favor of his "simple, honest heart" until we note that "features" are every bit as superficial as "expressions."

The notion that "inner" personality is in fact as external as "outward" character is insinuated more fully by the introduction of the Gentleman with Gold Sleeve-Buttons:

> The inner-side of his coat-skirts was of white satin, which might have looked especially inappropriate, had it not seemed less a bit of mere tailoring than something of an emblem, as it were; an involuntary emblem, let us say, that what seemed so good about him was not all outside; no, the fine covering had a still finer lining. [30]

The impulse of renewal, at Hawthorne's Blithedale, has become as formal and petrified as the culture against which it supposedly struggles. Nonverbal "sentiment" has given way to verbal "sentimentality." So, on the *Fidèle*, inner personality has itself become a mode of outward character. Even sincerity has become only another social role.

The external inwardness of the Gentleman with Gold Sleeve-Buttons is matched by the language in which he is described. The allegedly noumenal meaning of which his coat-lining is the "emblem" can be judged only "as it were," as we might "say." How it "might have looked" can be validated only in terms of how it "seemed." The language may ironically subvert the message of the lining, but it does not probe beneath it. Ishmael, also devoted to the phenomenal stance and style of "seems," turns to such language for salvation. He uses language, nevertheless, to hint at "nameless" terrors, "unspeakable" horrors—at truths beyond language. "Goodness," writes the narrator of *The Confidence-Man*, "is no such rare thing among men—the world familiarly know the noun" (30). Inner qualities exist here only as they appear, whether in outward gesture or linguistic sign. The noumenal has been fully replaced by the nominal. Even the figure whose "advent" opens the book is identified as a "stranger" only in "the extremist sense of the word" (1).

"No man, for any considerable period," writes Hawthorne of Dimmesdale, "can wear one face to himself, and another to the multitude, without getting bewildered as to which may be the true" (216). The same "helpless perplexity" lies at the heart, or rather all on the surface, of *The Confidence-Man*. In its labyrinth of contrasted views it undermines all sorts of confidence, especially self-confidence. And Melville goes one step beyond Hawthorne. Egbert, assuming the role of Charlie Noble, tells the Story of China Aster to the Cosmopolitan, who listens in the role of a friend seeking charity. At the close, the Cosmopolitan, apparently enraged, seems "disdainfully to throw off the character he had assumed." Egbert, however, is left "at a loss to determine where exactly the fictitious character had been dropped, and the real one, if any, resumed" (192). That casual "if any" pushes us beyond perplexity into psychological nihilism. All "character," it seems, may be "fictitious." This is wholly, so far as we know, a world of roles and poses—including the pose of sincerity. The world of the *Fidèle* is a world of words, floating "at large and unrelated." What is more, it floats, not because the cable has been cut, but because, apparently, there is literally nothing to attach it to.

The buried motive or meaning of both character and culture, Melville's Romantic contemporaries liked to assume with confidence, was the human heart. In it lay the fountain of liberty and the imaginative source of "true" literary expression. All this was threatened by the possibility of psychological nihilism—a possibility that emerges in Melville's fiction at least as early as *White-Jacket*. What Captain Claret "was," we recall, "the usages of the Navy had made him" (367); even the "feelings" of the bloodthirsty British officers "belonged to their profession" (209). Such doubts, only hinted at in *White-Jacket*, dominate *The Confidence-Man*.

The book also takes up, but transforms, Melville's sense that if the "heart" does exist, its "truths" are "terrible"—that our "Messianic" promptings are at heart satanic. Except for the eruption of the Titan against the Herb-Doctor in chapter 17, there is little actual violence in *The Confidence-Man*. Like everything else on the *Fidèle*, violence has been sublimated into artificial gesture and language. Aggression now takes the duplicitous form of the Confidence-Man's charming verbal advance. Still, this obscurely supernatural figure, like the "truth" of the *"Mosses"* essay, seems alternately Christlike or satanic or somehow both at once.[27] But the issue between Christ and Satan takes here a new turn. The title character's diabolism does not lurk beneath his benevolence; his aggression does not lurk beneath his genial exterior. Rather, these distinct and opposite qualities alternate; or, like the prospects presented to the whale's double vision, they appear simultaneously. The reader and the passengers are not subjected to "darkling hints" but are reduced, like the baffled whale, to "helpless perplexity." The cosmic ambiguity of the Confidence-Man is not multileveled, insinuating chronometrical "truth" beneath the mask of horological artifice. The ambiguity is all horological, a contrasting pattern on a flat surface.[28]

This perplexing flatness overtakes Melville's earlier sense of the tension, in "civilized" culture, between arbitrary external order and repressed inner violence, as in *Israel Potter*'s image of an America "civilized in externals but a savage at heart" (170). Almost in the middle of the book Charlie Noble, allegedly in the words of Judge James Hall, tells the Cosmopolitan the Story of Colonel John Moredock, the Indian-Hater. That this story is central to the meaning of *The Confidence-Man* has long been recognized, although there has been much disagreement about how it should be understood. In one view, Moredock is Melville's ideal, a man whose distrust is the only sure defense against confidence-men and wily Indians. In another view, Moredock, like Ahab, illustrates the self-destructive consequence of hatred, of what Ishmael calls staring "*too long into the face of the fire*" (354).[29]

Given the nature of *The Confidence-Man*, such debates can again lead only to perplexity; for the critic as for the whale, certainty can be achieved only by closing one eye. But the story is fascinating, for it takes up, once more, the idea that primal violence lurks at the heart of society. Here the idea is associated with the views "of one evidently not so prepossessed as Rousseau in favor of savages" (124). Moredock, turning in vengeance against the violence of "savages," unleashes the savage violence in himself. He remains genial, nevertheless, in the settlements. The Cosmopolitan objects to this inconsistency: "If the man of hate, how could John Moredock be also the man of love?" (136). But, as Hershel Parker observes, "there is ample biblical authority for being both a man of hate and a man of love. In Amos 5:15 the duality is stated baldly: 'Hate the evil, and love the good.'"[30] And Moredock's inconsistency in fact reflects the value system of his culture. It too maintains the "good" order of "civilization" by carefully distinguishing it from the "evil" of "savagery."

Yet the story told by Judge Hall and/or Charlie Noble tends to call all such distinctions into question.[31] The prophet Amos may be reassuring if we have confidence in the truth of Scripture; but how are we to distinguish the "evil" from the "good"? The backwoodsman, says Charlie, "learns that a brother is to be loved, and an Indian to be hated" (127). Yet a propensity to villainy can scarcely serve to distinguish between Indian and white, for "histories of Indian lying, Indian theft, Indian double-dealing, Indian fraud and perfidy, Indian want of conscience, Indian blood-thirstiness, Indian diabolism," we are told, "are *almost* as full of things unangelic as the Newgate Calendar or the Annals of Europe" (126–27; my emphasis). Wily Chief Mocmohoc, we learn, is "deemed a savage *almost* perfidious as Caesar Borgia" (128; my emphasis). "Yet," comments the Cosmopolitan to Charlie Noble, "the annals of neither Rome nor Greece can produce the equal in man-hatred of Colonel Moredock, as the judge and you have painted him" (136).

The overt purpose of chapter 26, "The Metaphysics of Indian-hating," is to make the contrast between two views—"love"/"hate" and "civilized"/"savage"—into a moral distinction. The effect of the ambiguously narrated essay, however, is to subvert both the distinction and its supposed moral meaning. "Savagery" no longer "slumbers" beneath the surface of "civilization," as the narrator claimed in *Israel Potter*. They are simply contrasting, perhaps even identical, aspects of meaningless human nature.

If there is any difference, it is that, of the two, the "civilized" may be the more "savage."

As if this were not enough, there is an even more fundamental problem raised by the Story of Colonel John Moredock. To believe in "Indian lying, Indian theft," and so on, you must first have grounds for confidence in the "histories" of them. The Cosmopolitan carefully limits his objection to the inconsistency of Moredock "as the judge and you have painted him," and there is good reason to distrust this verbal "painting"; for, on close inspection, the disquisition on Indian-hating and the Story of Moredock look a good deal like one of Washington Irving's hoaxes. We should look at least twice, for instance, at the name of the perfidious Indian chief, "Mocmohoc." Is he, like the pale Usher's handkerchief, only "mockingly embellished"? Charlie, unwilling to vouch for the truth of his own story, refers to the authority of Judge Hall, whose narrative he nevertheless considerably distorts and embellishes.[32] In his boyhood, Charlie claims, he almost had a sight of Moredock in the flesh, when he stopped at a cabin where the Indian-hater was said to be "sleeping on wolf-skins in the corn-loft above." But when he climbed part way into the loft, Charlie saw only "a bundle of something, like a drift of leaves; and at one end, what seemed a moss-ball." Charlie supposes this "moss-ball" may have been the Colonel's "curly head" (123). But we may well wonder whether Moredock exists at all. We should reflect, in any case, on the sort of "colonel" one might expect to find in a "corn-loft" and on whether there is any "kernel" of truth in this narrative. Which is to say that, whatever its meaning, the authority of this moral tale is highly questionable. Like everything else in *The Confidence-Man*, including *The Confidence-Man* itself, the Story of Colonel John Moredock is only a story.

The principal activity on board the *Fidèle* is in fact the telling of stories and the discussion of their ambiguous meaning and authority. The problem presented by these fictions is identical with the problem presented by the phenomenal duplicity, the flat ambiguity, of "fictitious character." Egbert, for instance, provides a strange preface to his rendition of the Story of China Aster. "I wish," he explains to the Cosmopolitan, "I could [tell it to you] in my own words, but unhappily the original story-teller here has so tyrannized over me, that it is quite impossible for me to repeat his incidents without sliding into his style." He claims, however, to approve "the main moral, to which all tends" (177). The Cosmopolitan couches the idea of meaning, as distinguished from style, in significantly different terms. "With what heart," he asks at the close, "have you told me this story?" (190). These terms are ominous. Is the "style" of fiction, like the masquerade of character, all there is? Can we understand fictional narrative by seeking out its motive? Or is fiction, too, void at its "heart"?

In its use of a group of travelers to frame the telling of stories, *The*

Confidence-Man recalls *The Canterbury Tales.* Chaucer, whose pilgrimage also takes place in April, is in fact mentioned in chapter 2 (6). But in its use of tale-telling to explore and burlesque the authority and motive of fictional narrative, Melville's romance is closer to the framing narratives of Irving's *Tales of a Traveller.* Irving's skeptical Englishman denounces the "Adventure of the Popkins Family" as "a mere piece of romance, originating in the heated brain of the narrator" (376). Melville, too, sets out to investigate the relation between romance and its origins, between its "style" and its "heart," but in *The Confidence-Man* we seldom even know with confidence in whose words a story is being told. We never meet, it seems, "the original story-teller."

In raising questions of literary theory, *The Confidence-Man* is still exploring the nature and meaning of character and culture. "Taken altogether," writes Michael Kammen in *People of Paradox,* "an accumulation of 'stylistic modes' just might lead toward an ontological approach to American history—a quest for its very being, its historic drive and destiny."[33] Melville lacks Kammen's confidence. In *The Confidence-Man* he explores and burlesques fictional theory, the theory of the romance, to suggest that perhaps "America" itself is a fiction—that its "very being," like "the original story-teller," has decamped.

Melville's narrator twice stands back, in chapters 14 and 33, to comment theoretically about fiction. But here, too, as everywhere else in *The Confidence-Man,* we get not a comprehensive "truth" but two contrasted views, leading again to "helpless perplexity." Chapter 14 argues that "while to all fiction is allowed some play of invention, yet, fiction based on fact should never be contradictory to it" (58). Chapter 33 responds to the reader's possible objection to the "antics" of the preceding chapter: "How unreal all this is!" "Strange," replies the narrator,

> that in a work of amusement, this severe fidelity to real life should be exacted by any one, . . . strange that any one should clamor for the thing he is weary of; that any one, who, for any cause, finds real life dull, should yet demand of him who is to divert his attention from it, that he should be true to that dullness. [157]

Or, as the Cosmopolitan says of his Story of Charlemont:

> It is a story which I told with the purpose of every story-teller—to amuse. Hence, if it seem strange to you, that strangeness is the romance; it is what contrasts it with real life; it is the invention, in brief, the fiction as opposed to the fact. [160]

In chapter 33 we get what looks like a reconciliation of these contrasting motives of truth to nature and imaginative diversion. Though readers want "novelty," the narrator writes, "they want nature, too; but nature unfettered, exhilarated, in effect transformed. . . . It is with fiction as with religion: it should present another world, and yet one to which we feel the tie" (158). This sounds like Melville's earlier theory of expression: literature, like religion, is the incarnation or utterance of messianic promptings. Yet the passage—taken on its own, and especially taken in context—is loaded with self-subversive irony. If the essential quality of "real life" is its "dullness," to present nature "exhilarated" is inevitably to falsify it. Romance, here, rests apparently on relation, presenting a world "to which we feel the tie." Yet it presents nature "unfettered." Romance, like religion, symbolically testifies to a noumenal world beyond our own, but romance confines itself rigorously to our own phenomenal "reality": it gives us nature "*in effect*" transformed.

Taken in context, the passage is even more subversive. What seems meant as a quasi-religious defense of the romancer's "invention" ("It is with fiction as religion") too easily reverses itself to become an ironic attack on the "truth" of religion, as being only an analogous "invention." Moreover, the taint of fictionality extends beyond religion to infect *all* "reality." "*The Confidence-Man*," as Edgar Dryden puts it, "presents a world where the real and fictitious are indistinguishable and interchangeable."[34] Hence Egbert's puzzlement, following the Cosmopolitan's sudden metamorphosis, to know "where exactly the fictitious character had been dropped, and the real one, if any, resumed" (192). The phenomenal duplicity of the Cosmopolitan the Gentleman with Gold Sleeve-Buttons is not simply an effect of the voice that speaks to us about them. It is also, it would seem, a quality of the world about which the voice speaks. In this work of "fiction based on fact," the "fact" is itself "fiction," "reality" is itself "invention."

In this sense, *The Confidence-Man* does manage to reconcile the contrasting views of chapters 14 and 33, but it can do so only because the apparent distinction between them—like the distinctions between character and personality, good and evil, civilized and savage, confidence and distrust—are finally rendered meaningless. What is true of the narrator's ironic language in *Pierre* is true of the whole world of *The Confidence-Man:* words and gestures are related not to hidden "sentiments" but only to other words and gestures. It is with culture as with fiction: "There is no quality in the world," as Ishmael puts it, "that is not what it is merely by contrast" (55). This is why Melville's most ironic anatomy of literary expression, of the art of romance, is simultaneously his most ironic examination of the duplicitous surface of his culture. In a world where even "facts" are "fictions," there is no longer any distinction between fictional theory and cultural anthropology. Both deal with ambiguous "texts" that, like Hawthorne's Blithedale, have sacrificed all relation to their origins.

The evasive displacement that characterizes Melville's earlier protagonists, that energizes Ishmael's rhetoric, has in *The Confidence-Man* been literally and fully realized by the culture of Melville's America.

Frank Goodman, the Cosmopolitan, dominates the second half of *The Confidence-Man*. His name seems to combine two crucial and antithetical Melvillean conceptions of character, culture, and literary expression. On the one hand there is sincerity. "Even Shakespeare," Melville wrote to Duyckinck in 1849, "was not a frank man to the uttermost. And, indeed, who in this intolerant Universe is, or can be? But the Declaration of Independence makes a difference" (80). On the other hand there is prudent circumspection, role-playing. The deepest truths, Melville writes in the "*Mosses*" essay, are "so terrifically true that it were all but madness for any good man, in his own proper character, to utter, or even hint of them" (407). Frank Goodman can resolve this apparent contradiction because on board the *Fidèle* even sincerity, it seems, is only another "fictitious character."

The terms in which Goodman describes himself to Pitch are also familiar:

> "A cosmopolitan, a catholic man; who, being such, ties himself to no narrow tailor or teacher, but federates, in heart as in costume, something of the various gallantries of men under various suns. Oh, one roams not over the gallant globe in vain. Bred by it, is a fraternal and fusing feeling. No man is a stranger." [115]

Here is the tolerant cosmopolitanism of Ishmael and his "everlasting First Congregation of this whole worshipping world" (83). Yet fraternity has become only a pose, and sincerity itself a mask. Frank is indeed as he appears; he is "in heart as in costume."

Here, too, is realized the nihilism implicit in Ishmael's tolerance. The Cosmopolitan's costume, like the handkerchief of *Moby-Dick*'s pale Usher, is "mockingly embellished with all the gay flags of all the known nations of the world" (1). What it mocks most of all is the truth it denies, Ishmael's "colorless, all-color of atheism, from which we shrink." But even this utterly nihilistic truth can hardly be said to exist on the *Fidèle*. The Cosmopolitan glimpses in Shakespeare a certain "hidden sun, . . . at once enlightening and mystifying." To Charlie Noble's question—"Do you think it was the true light?"—he declines to give an answer (149), and to Pitch he insists that, just as there are various men, so there are "various suns." Ishmael's "true" sunlight—the "antemosaic" source of character, culture, and literature—is in itself white, meaningless. But it exists. The colorful Cosmopolitan appears only at sunset, and at the close of the book, at midnight, he extinguishes even the ship's artificial solar lamp.[35] What, then, is the relation of the Confidence-Man, and of the *Fidèle*'s passengers, to the original source?

The barber, duped at last, judges the Cosmopolitan "QUITE AN ORIGINAL" (204). Melville's narrator digresses on this phrase in chapter 44:

> The original character, essentially such, is like a revolving Drummond light, raying away from itself all round it—everything is lit by it, everything starts up to it..., so that, in certain minds, there follows upon the adequate conception of such a character, an effect, in its way, akin to that which in Genesis attends upon the beginning of things. [205]

Here we would seem to have the "true light." In the Cosmopolitan, consequently, we would seem to have an incarnation of that originating energy otherwise absent on the *Fidèle*. The "original character" is the "true" personality, "essentially such"—the source of artificial roles as white light is the source of artificial color. And behind the various roles assumed by the Confidence-Man would seem to lurk the "secret sun" of Shakespeare, "the original story-teller," using fiction to rebuke an America for which the Declaration of Independence has made no difference at all.

We should be cautious, however, about placing our own confidence in such a reading. The character's "originality," like the romance's "transformation" of "nature," can be known only by its "effect," and the case for identifying Frank Goodman with the figure described in chapter 44 is at best tenuous. "There can be but one such original character to one work of invention," we are told in chapter 44, "for much the same reason that there is but one planet to one orbit" (205). Before accepting the Cosmopolitan as the "original story-teller"—as an incarnation of the repressed, unitary "heart" behind character, culture, and fiction—we should recall his remark to Pitch about "various suns."

We would do well to return to Egbert's strange introduction to the Story of China Aster: "the original story-teller here has so tyrannized over me, that it is quite impossible for me to repeat his incidents without sliding into his style" (177). The ambiguous placement of Egbert's "here" might bolster one's sense that the Cosmopolitan, the only other figure then present, must be "the original story-teller," but a closer look at Egbert's apology indicates that it is the style, not the teller, that tyrannizes. Egbert has fully cut himself off from originating energy, from promptings, from the creative process. He can therefore tell only the stories of others; he can have no utterance of his own. If this is tyranny, it is a tyranny he willingly accepts, just as he happily, for the sake of argument, assumes the roles of Mark Winsome and Charlie Noble. He may console himself (whatever that might mean) by distinguishing between the "style" of another and "the main moral, to which all tends," which "I fully approve" (177); but this distinction is no more meaningful than any of the others on which the *Fidèle*'s passengers depend. In the America of *The Confidence-Man* the "secret sun" hasn't just been repressed. It has gone out.

At the beginning of chapter 8, in the guise of the Man in Gray, the Confidence-Man is momentarily "left to himself, with none to charm forth his latent lymphatic." In this solitude, "he insensibly resumes his original air, a quiescent one, blended of sad humility and demureness." The nature of this "original air" has already been hinted at in the image of a "sea-breeze, blowing off from a thousand leagues of blankness" (37). Ishmael's "dumb blankness" has become, in *The Confidence-Man*, a blankness in the empty heart of the now wholly arabesque phenomenal language of character, culture, and literary fiction. Ishmael's blankness was "full of meaning" (169). The only essential quality of this new blankness is its emptiness.

The sacrifice of relation led, for the romancer and for the romance, to a complex set of interlocking tensions: between alienation and ingratiation, "deviance" and "normalcy," "fiction" and "fact," fantasy and rationalization, energetic impulse and ordered symbol, nonverbal suggestion and overt language, origin and expression. Such tensions are characteristic, to a greater or lesser degree, of most literary expression. What distinguishes the experimental traditon of American romance is the extremity of these tensions, the irreconcilability of these dualistic oppositions. From Brown to Melville, the impulse of extreme sincerity struggles with the mask of equally extreme artifice.

Melville confronted and enacted the sacrifice of relation in many forms. His writing, from 1846 to 1857, alternates between "acquired wisdom" and "instinct," between the desire to please and the desire to outrage his audience. His characters, like Brown's or Poe's, alternate between "desperate suggestions" and "better thoughts." His early narrators, especially Ishmael, embrace the artifice of language and symbol at once to express and to repress the "darkling hints" of unfettered imagination. In its full and rich incorporation of the tension produced by the sacrifice of relation, testifying simultaneously to the presence and absence of the Jamesian cable, the language of *Moby-Dick* is the culmination of the experimental tradition of American romance.

It is precisely this sense of tension between expression and repression that is missing from *The Confidence-Man*, as it is also missing from Hawthorne's *Blithedale Romance*. The vital dualism of romance, central to *The Scarlet Letter* and *Moby-Dick*, becomes confused in *The House of the Seven Gables* and *Pierre*. The status of nonverbal impulse, in these books, is both more literal and more ambiguous than in their predecessors. Such im-

pulse, as distinguished from the superficial *language* of impulse, has van-
ished utterly in *The Blithedale Romance* and *The Confidence-Man*. These
works often seem parodies of their more resonant predecessors. Hester
and Ishmael, to be sure, employ strategies of evasion, but always in some
awareness of what it is they are evading. At Blithedale and on the *Fidèle*
there is only evasion.

Perhaps Hawthorne and Melville were exhausted. Perhaps, as Roy
Harvey Pearce and Perry Miller put it, the form of the romance was
exhausted. But the romance, as I argued at the end of chapter 6, was at
least implicitly exhausted from the very beginning. In any case, there is an
additional factor to be recognized: the books in which Hawthorne and
Melville first seem to "exhaust" the romance are also the first full-length
fictions in which they turned from the past or the ocean to examine
directly the culture of their own contemporary America.[36] This gave rise
to the problem Hawthorne mentions in the *Seven Gables* preface: that a
contemporary setting exposed the romance "to an inflexible and exceedingly dangerous species of criticism, by bringing ... fancy-pictures almost
into positive contact with the realities of the moment" (3). The greater
problem, however, may have been not the force but the failure of the
contrast; for the "realities of the moment," in *The Blithedale Romance* and
The Confidence-Man, seem finally indistinguishable from the "fancy-
pictures" of the romancer. Indeed, they were possibly even more
"fictional." The romancer at least knew that his pictures were pictures.
His culture, even as it denied or evaded the full truth of imagination,
insisted that its "fictions" were "facts."

In the face of that culture, it is understandable that a romancer might
lose his hold on the distinctions and tensions that animated his art. In the
Puritan revolution or the War for Independence, as Hawthorne and Melville read our history, America had cut the cable tying the car of imagination to the reality of earth. But it had then forgotten which was which.
One could no longer tell at which end America had been standing when
the cable was severed. One could no longer distinguish fiction from fact or
sincerity from its masks.

In his 1879 book on Hawthorne, James pauses to speculate on the
difficulty an American confronts when, divorced from the social
categories and conventional identities of Europe, he tries to understand
the national character. "The individual," he writes, "counts for more, as it
were, and, thanks to the absence of a variety of social types and settled
heads under which he may be easily and conveniently pigeonholed, he is
to a certain extent a wonder and a mystery."[37] The exploration and obfuscation of this "mystery"—the "mystery" of the unrelated self, the unleashed imagination—was from the first the project of experimental
American romance. What makes Irving's Nervous Gentleman nervous is

his sense of "certain mysteries in our nature, certain inscrutable impulses and influences, which warrant one in being superstitious" (139). So Hester, cast out of normal social relations, must come to terms with her "individuality." And Ishmael, the ultimate Melvillean *isolato*, must confront the mysterious "imaginative impressions" (167) suggested by the Whale.

This exploration comes to a dead end, for Hawthorne and Melville, because, in the contemporary America of *The Blithedale Romance* and *The Confidence-Man*, the imaginative impulse has disappeared, leaving only its petrified verbal detritus. "Mystery," like "spirit," has become a "mere word"; mysterious promptings have been replaced by the effect of mystification. The word "mystery," for instance, stands at the center of Coverdale's inadvertently obscene language of sentiment, and in *The Confidence-Man* we get not "mystery" but the "mysterious impostor" advertised on the wanted poster "nigh the captain's office": "quite an original genius in his vocation, as would appear, though wherein his originality consisted was not clearly given; but what purported to be a careful description of his person followed" (1).

In 1842 Hawthorne jotted in his Notebook the idea for a story based on the search for the American Genius:

> Great expectation to be entertained in the allegorical Grub-street of the appearance of the great American writer. Or a search warrant to be sent thither to catch a poet. On the former supposition, he shall be discovered under some most unlikely form; or shall be supposed to have lived and died unrecognized. [243–44][38]

Melville's "wanted" poster, like Hawthorne's search warrant, is in a sense an advertisement not just for the American Genius but for the mysterious American character—what Michael Kammen calls the "very being" of America. It was thus that experimental romance engaged in the effort to understand the national experiment.

The failure of American romance, enacted in *The Blithedale Romance* and *The Confidence-Man*, points finally to what Hawthorne and Melville saw as a prior failure of the American experiment. Hawthorne's Genius has "lived and died unrecognized," and the "originality" of Melville's "mysterious impostor" can be communicated only "as would appear." Wherein it consists is "not clearly given." However mysteriously spiritual or noumenal this character's originality may be alleged to be, the account we get of him, both in the "wanted" poster and in *The Confidence-Man* as a whole, is comically phenomenal. We get no inner view of this character, not even a "careful description of his person," but only "what *purported* to be a careful description of his person." All these "seemings," "appearings," and "purportings" hearken back to the phenomenal style of Irving's

244

sportive gothic, but they are not defensive responses to subjective terror, nor do they simply indicate that the American character can be known only through its shifting style. This shifting style, in *The Confidence-Man*, seems literally all there is. "Something further," we are told at the close, "may follow of this Masquerade" (217), but there is little felt threat of revolutionary eruption. There is apparently nothing left to erupt. In *The Confidence-Man* the mysterious American spirit, the prompting to which White-Jacket longed to give utterance, is still the source and subject of the romance, but it has fully invested itself in the mask of sincerity; it has *become* the mask of sincerity. The sacrifice of relation has been fully and fatally realized.

NOTES

INTRODUCTION

1. Lionel Trilling, "Manners, Morals, and the Novel," in *The Liberal Imagination: Essays on Literature and Society* (New York: Scribner's, 1976), p. 212

2. Richard Chase, *The American Novel and Its Tradition* (Garden City, N.Y.: Doubleday, 1957); Perry Miller, "The Romance and the Novel" (originally delivered as lectures in 1956), in *Nature's Nation* (Cambridge, Mass.: Harvard University Press, 1967), pp. 241–78. Terence Martin studied the intellectual and historical backgrounds of the rise of romance in *The Instructed Vision: Scottish Common Sense Philosophy and the Origins of American Fiction* (Bloomington: Indiana University Press, 1961). For more recent elaborations of the "romance" argument, see, for instance, Joel Porte, *The Romance in America: Studies in Cooper, Poe, Hawthorne, Melville, and James* (Middletown, Conn.: Wesleyan University Press, 1969), and John Caldwell Stubbs, *The Pursuit of Form: A Study of Hawthorne and the Romance* (Urbana: University of Illinois Press, 1970).

3. See, for instance, Nicolaus Mills, *American and English Fiction in the Nineteenth Century* (Bloomington: Indiana University Press, 1973), and Robert Merrill, "Another Look at the American Romance," *Modern Philology* (forthcoming).

4. See, for instance, David H. Hirsch, *Reality and Idea in the Early American Novel* (The Hague: Mouton, 1971), pp. 32–36 (and, for a similar objection to Chase's assumptions, pp. 36–48).

5. As Richard Poirier puts it: "it is regrettable that Hawthorne chose to elevate distinctions about environment, which is after all only one aspect of fiction, into distinctions between genres. . . . Genres have no instrumentality for expression, especially those of 'novel' and 'romance.' These so-called genres have none of the ascertainable conventions of style that can legitimately be associated with such genres as the pastoral or the epic" (*A World Elsewhere: The Place of Style in American Literature* [New York: Oxford University Press, 1966], pp. 8, 11).

6. For a guide to parenthetical page references, see the Bibliographical Appendix.

7. Leo Marx, "Comment" on C. Vann Woodward's "The Aging of America," *American Historical Review* 82 (1977): 597.

8. The fullest exposition of the similarities between nineteenth-century American literature and modern experimentalism is in Charles Feidelson, Jr.'s *Symbolism and American Literature* (Chicago: University of Chicago Press, 1953).

PROLOGUE TO PART ONE

1. For a useful listing of American novels and romances published up to 1820, see the Bibliography in Henri Petter, *The Early American Novel* (Columbus: Ohio State University Press, 1971), pp. 466–75. Among other general studies that deal wholly or substantially with early American fiction, I have consulted Herbert Ross Brown, *The Sentimental Novel in America, 1789–1860* (Durham: N.C.: Duke University Press, 1940); Alexander Cowie, *The Rise of the American Novel* (New York: American Book Company, 1948); Lillie Deming Loshe, *The Early American Novel* (New York: Columbia University Press, 1930); and Arthur Hobson Quinn, *American Fiction* (New York: Appleton-Century, 1936).

2. See William Charvat, *The Profession of Authorship in America, 1800–1870*, edited by Matthew J. Bruccoli (Columbus: Ohio State University Press, 1968), p. 68.

CHAPTER ONE

1. Henry James, *The Art of the Novel: Critical Prefaces by Henry James*, edited by Richard P. Blackmur (New York: Scribner's, 1934), p. 33.

2. Ibid.

3. Ibid., pp. 33–34.

4. See Congreve's preface to *Incognita* (1692); see also Reeve's *The Progress of Romance* (1785) (reprint, New York: Facsimile Text Society, 1930), esp. pp. 110–11.

5. J. M. S. Tompkins, *The Popular Novel in England, 1770–1800* (London: Constable, 1932), p. 210; Sir Walter Scott, "On the Supernatural in Fictitious Composition," in Ioan Williams, ed., *Sir Walter Scott on Novelists and Fiction* (London: Routledge & Kegan Paul, 1968), p. 314.

6. General William Sullivan, "Address of the Bunker Hill Monument Association to the Selectmen of the Several Towns in Massachusetts," in George Washington Warren, *The History of the Bunker Hill Monument Association . . .* (Boston: James R. Osgood, 1877), p. 85; Pratt, *Autobiography of Parley Parker Pratt* (Salt Lake City: Deseret Book Co., 1938), p. 227; Charles Brockden Brown, "The Difference between History and Romance," *The Monthly Magazine and American Review* 2 (1800): 251–53.

7. Washington Irving, in Pierre M. Irving, *The Life and Letters of Washington Irving* (New York: Putnam, 1864), vol. 4, p. 236; Hawthorne, quoted in Randall Stewart, *Nathaniel Hawthorne: A Biography* (New Haven: Yale University Press, 1948), p. 133.

8. Thomas Jefferson to Nathaniel Burwell, March 14, 1818, in Paul Leicester

Ford, ed., *The Works of Thomas Jefferson* (New York: Putnam, 1899), vol. 10, pp. 104–5; Samuel Miller, *A Brief Retrospect of the Eighteenth Century* (New York: T. J. Swords, 1803), vol. 2, pp. 179, 176. For further discussions of hostility toward fiction and imagination in early America, see William Charvat, *The Origins of American Critical Thought, 1810–1835* (Philadelphia: University of Pennsylvania, 1936); G. Harrison Orians, "Censure of Fiction in American Romances and Magazines, 1789–1810," *PMLA* 52 (1937): 195–214; and, especially, Terence Martin, *The Instructed Vision: Scottish Common Sense Philosophy and the Origins of American Fiction* (Bloomington: University of Indiana Press, 1961).

9. See, for instance, Tompkins, "The Stirring of Romance, and the Historical Novel," in *The Popular Novel in England*, esp. pp. 210–17. Clara Reeve's *Progress of Romance* was mainly intended to combat hostility toward imaginative fiction in England, giving respectability to romance by associating it with the ancient epic; and Scott's various critical writings testify to his sense of the abiding suspicion of fiction in England in the early nineteenth century.

10. See, for instance, Perry Miller, *The New England Mind: The Seventeenth Century* (Cambridge, Mass.: Harvard University Press, 1939), esp. pp. 257–60. Miller contends, among other things, that "Anne Hutchinson and Roger Williams were banished from Massachusetts Bay because they were altogether too gifted with imagination" (p. 259).

11. On the pervasiveness of Common Sense thought in America see, for instance, Merle Curti, *The Growth of American Thought* (New York: Harper & Bros., 1951), p. 236; Herbert W. Schneider, *A History of American Philosophy* (New York: Columbia University Press, 1946), pp. 246–50; and Sydney E. Ahlstrom, *A Religious History of the American People* (New Haven: Yale University Press, 1972), pp. 355–56. The Scottish School was founded by Thomas Reid. Far more influential in America, and considerably more interested in the function of imagination (which Reid largely dismisses), were Hugh Blair's *Lectures on Rhetoric and Belles Lettres* (1783), Archibald Alison's *Essays on the Nature and Principles of Taste* (1790), and Dugald Stewart's *Elements of the Philosophy of the Human Mind* (1792).

12. Martin, *The Instructed Vision;* Dugald Stewart, *Elements of the Philosophy of the Human Mind* (Boston: Wells & Lilly, 1821), vol. 1, pp. 276–78.

13. Hugh Blair, *Lectures on Rhetoric and Belles Lettres* (Philadelphia: James Kay, 1844), pp. 72, 66, 421; Miller, *A Brief Retrospect of the Eighteenth Century*, vol. 2, p. 175.

14. William Dunlap, *The Life of Charles Brockden Brown* (Philadelphia: James P. Parke, 1815), vol. 1, p. 27; Edd Winfield Parks, *Edgar Allan Poe as Literary Critic* (Athens, Ga.: University of Georgia Press, 1964), p. 10; Randall Stewart, *Nathaniel Hawthorne: A Biography*, pp. 16–17.

15. Irving had undoubtedly been exposed to Scottish aesthetics and psychology by the time he wrote *The Sketch-Book*. In 1817 he was introduced into the literary circles of Edinburgh, and as early as 1810, in an essay on Thomas Campbell, he took note of Dugald Stewart's favorable opinion of the poet (148). Melville entered the Albany Academy in 1830, where the English textbook was Murray's *English Reader*, three-fourths of which consisted of writings by Blair; in 1835 he was admitted to the Albany Young Men's Association, whose library would have made

the standard Scottish writers available to him (see William H. Gilman, *Melville's Early Life and "Redburn"* [New York: New York University Press, 1951], pp. 55, 73–74).

16. Irving, *Letters, Volume II, 1823–1838*, edited by Ralph M. Aderman, Herbert L. Kleinfield, and Jenifer S. Brooks (Boston: Twayne, 1979), p. 84.

17. James Gray, quoted in Martin, *The Instructed Vision*, p. 67.

18. *Life and Letters of Washington Irving*, vol. 4, p. 157.

19. The most complete study of American literary nationalism, although it does not attempt to measure the effect of literary propaganda on the nature of American literary achievement, is Benjamin T. Spencer's *The Quest for Nationality: An American Literary Campaign* (Syracuse: Syracuse University Press, 1957). See also Robert E. Spiller's excellent collection of primary materials, *The American Literary Revolution* (Garden City, N.Y.: Doubleday, 1967); Spiller, *The Third Dimension: Studies in Literary History* (New York: Macmillan, 1965); Harry Hayden Clark, "Nationalism in American Literature," *University of Toronto Quarterly* 2 (1933): 429–519; E. K. Brown, "The National Idea in American Criticism," *Dalhousie Review* 14 (1934): 133–47; William Ellery Sedgwick, "The Materials for an American Literature: A Critical Problem of the Early Nineteenth Century," *Harvard Studies and Notes in Philology and Literature* 17 (1935): 141–62; John J. McCloskey, "The Campaign of Periodicals after the War of 1812 for National American Literature," *PMLA* 50 (1935): 262–73; Robert W. Bolwell, "Concerning the Study of Nationalism in American Literature," *American Literature* 10 (1939): 405–16; and Earl L. Bradsher, "The Rise of Nationalism in American Literature," in Nathaniel M. Caffee and Thomas A. Kirby, eds., *Studies for William A. Read* (University, La.: Louisiana State University Press, 1940), pp. 269–87.

20. William Gilmore Simms, *The Yemassee: A Romance of Carolina* (1835), C. Hugh Holman, ed. (Boston: Houghton Mifflin, 1961), p. 6.

21. Tudor, *North American Review* 1 (1815): 120; see Robert E. Streeter, "Association Psychology and Literary Nationalism in the *North American Review*, 1815–1825," *American Literature* 17 (1945): 243–54; Longfellow, "Our Native Writers," in Spiller, ed., *The American Literary Revolution*, p. 387.

22. William Hedges, *Washington Irving: An American Study, 1802–1832* (Baltimore: Johns Hopkins University Press, 1965), pp. 114–15.

23. Longfellow, in Spiller, ed., *The American Literary Revolution*, p. 387; James Kirke Paulding, quoted in *Life and Letters of Washington Irving*, vol. 2, p. 239; Edward Everett, in *North American Review* 41 (1835): 14. On the importance of associationist aesthetics to Hawthorne's handling of historical materials, see Michael Davitt Bell, *Hawthorne and the Historical Romance of New England* (Princeton: Princeton University Press, 1971), pp. 197–200.

24. Paulding, "National Literature," in Spiller, ed., *The American Literary Revolution*, pp. 381–82.

25. *American Quarterly Review* 2 (1827): 42, 43.

26. Richard Chase, for instance, concludes from the *Marble Faun* preface that "Hawthorne was... convinced... that romance, rather than the novel, was the predestined form of American narrative" (*The American Novel and Its Tradition* [Garden City, N.Y.: Doubleday, 1957], p. 18). Yet Hawthorne's overt point in that preface, as Nicolaus Mills rightly observes, is "his assertion of how difficult it

is to write a romance in America" (*American and English Fiction in the Nineteenth Century* [Bloomington: Indiana University Press, 1973], p. 25).

27. *American Quarterly Review* 2 (1827): 46.

28. Irving, *Letters, Volume II*, p. 415.

Chapter Two

1. On this matter see, especially, G. Harrison Orians, "Censure of Fiction in American Romances and Magazines, 1789–1810," *PMLA* 52 (1937): 195–214.

2. William Hill Brown, *The Power of Sympathy*, William S. Kable, ed. (Columbus: Ohio State University Press, 1969), pp. 32n–33n.

3. Ibid., p. 33.

4. Susanna Rowson, *Charlotte Temple: A Tale of Truth*, Clara M. Kirk and Rudolf Kirk, eds. (New Haven: College and University Press, 1964), pp. 102, 71, 117, 103, 146, 150. Precisely speaking, of course, *Charlotte Temple* is not an "American" novel, since Mrs. Rowson had not yet settled in America when the book appeared in London in 1791. She did settle in America, however, and from the book's first American publication in 1794 its American setting and American popularity, along with Mrs. Rowson's move to the United States, placed it for better or worse within the American tradition.

5. *The Power of Sympathy*, p. 179.

6. Hanna Foster, *The Coquette; or, the History of Eliza Wharton* (1797) (New York: Columbia University Press, 1939), pp. 13–14, 39.

7. Ibid., pp. 244, 236, 229.

8. John Caldwell Stubbs has argued, largely on the basis of writers' increasing willingness to use the term "romance" in titles or subtitles, that American hostility toward imaginative romance had subsided somewhat by the middle of the century; "during the 1840s," he writes, "the term came under serious scrutiny, and the genre was recognized as valid" (*The Pursuit of Form: A Study of Hawthorne and the Romance* [Urbana: University of Illinois Press, 1970], p. 4). One suspects, however, that what was recognized as "valid" was for the most part not fiction as opposed to fact but the "mingling" recommended by the conservative theory of romance.

9. Martin, *The Instructed Vision*, p. 145 (see chap. 1, n. 8).

10. Kai Erikson, *Wayward Puritans: A Study in the Sociology of Deviance* (New York: John Wiley, 1966), pp. 19–20.

11. For an objection to the failure of recent critics of the "novel"-versus-"romance" persuasion to understand the status of "reality," in the nineteenth century, as social norm rather than philosophical concept, see David H. Hirsch, *Reality and Idea in the Early American Novel* (The Hague: Mouton, 1971), pp. 32–36.

12. Erikson, *Wayward Puritans*, pp. 20–21.

13. Howard Becker, *Outsiders: Studies in the Sociology of Deviance*, rev. ed. (New York: Free Press, 1973), pp. 9, 14. Other sociological works consulted include Albert K. Cohen, *Deviance and Control* (Englewood Cliffs, N.J.: Prentice-Hall, 1966); Edwin M. Lemert, *Human Deviance, Social Problems, and Social Control*, 2nd ed. (Englewood Cliffs, N.J.: Prentice-Hall, 1972); David Matza, *Becoming Deviant* (Englewood Cliffs, J.J.: Prentice-Hall, 1969); and Edwin M. Schur, *Labeling Deviant*

Behavior: Its Sociological Implications (New York: Harper & Row, 1971). I am grateful to Donald Light, Jr., of the Center for Biomedical Education, City College of New York, for guiding me to this material.

14. For Becker's discussion of his "sequential model" see *Outsiders*, pp. 22–39.

15. For an excellent discussion of the conditions facing the professional writer in America at the beginning of the nineteenth century, see William Charvat, *The Profession of Authorship in America, 1800–1870*, edited by Matthew J. Bruccoli (Columbus: Ohio State University Press, 1968), esp. pp. 5–48.

16. For my understanding of Melville's career I am especially indebted to William Charvat's discussion of it, ibid., pp. 203–61.

17. Richard Mather, quoted in Perry Miller and Thomas H. Johnson, eds., *The Puritans* (New York: Harper & Bros., 1938), p. 672.

18. The consequence of this state of mind for Boston's literary culture is the subject of Martin Green's *The Problem of Boston: Some Readings in Cultural History* (New York: Norton, 1966). Green begins by pointing out that in Boston, as opposed to the rest of nineteenth-century America, literary activity was a "normal," even an elite, activity. Yet the effect of this approval, he seems almost reluctantly to conclude, was the failure of the writers nurtured by it to achieve literary greatness. The moral of Green's story, although he does not express it in quite these terms, is that Boston's establishment writers were not "deviant" enough.

19. Becker, *Outsiders*, p. 39.

20. See Charvat, *The Profession of Authorship*, p. 71.

21. Hawthorne to Fields, February 11, 1860, reprinted in George Perkins, ed., *The Theory of the American Novel* (New York: Rinehart, 1970), p. 68.

22. Compare Edwin Lemert's speculation on the "various situations or conditions where negative identities, i.e., those generally stigmatized, may offer temporary or relatively stable solutions to life problems"—on the ways, that is, in which a "deviant status or role gives access to rewards and satisfactions" (*Human Deviance, Social Problems, and Social Control*, pp. 74, 262). See also Lemert's discussion of the social dynamics of paranoia: "It is arguable that occupying the role of the mistrusted person becomes a way of life for these paranoids, providing them with an identity not otherwise possible" (ibid., p. 254). Lemert's whole discussion of the "spurious interaction" between "paranoids" and "normals" suggests a number of intriguing comparisons with the perhaps equally spurious interaction between writers and their audiences.

CHAPTER THREE

1. These periodicals were *The Monthly Magazine and American Review* (1799–1800) and *The Literary Magazine and American Register* (1803–7) and its successor, *The American Register, or General Repository of History, Politics, and Science* (1807–9).

2. The Advertisement for *Sky Walk* appeared in the Philadelphia *Weekly Magazine*, March 17, 1798. A brief extract from the novel followed on March 24. Publication of the novel itself, which had been set in type, was delayed by the death of the publisher and by complications raised by his heirs. Rather than

renegotiate his contract, Brown simply abandoned the novel, using portions of it in other works, especially *Edgar Huntly*.

3. The three main sources of biographical information on Brown, all of which contain otherwise unavailable primary material, are William Dunlap, *The Life of Charles Brockden Brown*, 2 vols. (Philadelphia: James P. Parke, 1815); Harry R. Warfel, *Charles Brockden Brown: American Gothic Novelist* (Gainesville: University of Florida Press, 1949); and David Lee Clark, *Charles Brockden Brown: Pioneer Voice of America* (Durham, N.C.: Duke University Press, 1952).

4. Kai Erikson, *Wayward Puritans: Studies in the Sociology of Deviance* (New York: John Wiley, 1966), p. 20.

5. Brown, *Literary Magazine and American Register* 1 (1803): 4.

6. Brown, "Journal Letters to Henrietta G.," in Clark, *Charles Brockden Brown*, p. 102. Clark dates these letters, which may in fact be a fragmentary draft of an epistolary novel, to the period 1790–93.

7. Timothy Dwight, *The Duty of Americans, at the Present Crisis* (New Haven: Thomas and Samuel Green, 1798), p. 12. Brown met Dwight at meetings of the Friendly Club in New York. On Brown's own exploitation of popular alarm about the Illuminati, see Lillie Deming Loshe, *The Early American Novel* (New York: Columbia University Press, 1907), pp. 41–43, and Clark, *Charles Brockden Brown*, pp. 188–92. On general American hysteria about the Illuminati, see Vernon Stauffer, *New England and the Bavarian Illuminati* (New York: Columbia University Press, 1918), and, for a brief account, Howard Mumford Jones, *America and French Culture* (Chapel Hill: University of North Carolina Press, 1927), pp. 397–400.

8. See, for instance, Larzer Ziff, "A Reading of *Wieland*," *PMLA* 77 (1962): 51–57. An earlier and fuller reading of *Wieland* along these lines is contained in "*Wieland*: Reason and Justice," chapter 5 of Warner Berthoff's unpublished Harvard Ph.D. dissertation, "The Literary Career of Charles Brockden Brown" (1954). The fullest study of the breakdown of Lockean assumptions in all of Brown's fiction is Arthur Kimball's *Rational Fictions: A Study of Charles Brockden Brown* (McMinnville, Ore.: Linnfield Research Institute, 1968). Kimball develops his argument more briefly in his article "Savages and Savagism: Brockden Brown's Dramatic Irony," *Studies in Romanticism* 6 (1967): 214–15.

9. Brown, "A Lesson on Sensibility," *Weekly Magazine* (Philadelphia) 2 (1798): 71.

10. Ibid., p. 72.

11. *Port Folio* 3d ser. 1 (1809): 168. On the relationship between these two stories, and for evidence that they were written by Brown, see Robert Hemenway, "Brockden Brown's Twice-Told Insanity Tale," *American Literature* 40 (1968): 211–15.

12. *The Monthly Magazine and American Review* 3 (1800): 161–62. David Clark concludes that although "Brown's authorship of the *Speculatist* is uncertain . . . it is reasonably safe to assign these essays to his pen" (*Charles Brockden Brown*, p. 142n). Given the internal evidence of style and theme, even this statement seems conservative.

13. *Literary Magazine and American Register* 1 (1803): 150.

14. On this point see Terence Martin, *The Instructed Vision: Scottish Common Sense*

Philosophy and the Origins of American Fiction (Bloomington: University of Indiana Press, 1961), pp. 61–63.

15. In view of its principal theme, it is interesting to read *Wieland* in the light of Charles Chauncy's statement, made in 1742, that it is no "just ground of exception against the Spirit's *operations*, that they may be counterfeited; that men may make an appearance, as if they were acted by the Spirit, when, all the while, they have no other view in their pretences, but to serve themselves" (*Enthusiasm Described and Caution'd Against*, in Darrett B. Rutman, ed., *The Great Awakening: Event and Exegesis* [New York: John Wiley, 1970], p. 59). The aftermath of the Awakening, particularly the conservative effort to preserve doctrine while repudiating enthusiasm, is clearly of considerable importance to Brown's novel.

16. M. H. Abrams, *The Mirror and the Lamp: Romantic Theory and the Critical Tradition* (New York: Norton, 1958), p. 22.

17. For helping me to clarify my thinking on this point I am greatly indebted to Don Gifford, of Williams College.

18. Brown, "The Difference between History and Romance," *Monthly Magazine* 2 (1800): 251–53.

19. Brown, "Journal Letters to Henrietta G.," in Clark, *Charles Brockden Brown*, p. 102.

20. Archibald Alison, *Essays on the Nature and Principles of Taste* (Boston: Cummings & Hilliard, 1812), pp. 18–19.

21. On Brown's use of landscape for psychological symbolism in *Edgar Huntly*, see Kenneth Bernard, "Charles Brockden Brown and the Sublime," *The Personalist* 45 (1964): 235–49, and Paul Witherington, "Image and Idea in *Weiland* and *Edgar Huntly*," *The Serif* 3 (December, 1966): 19–26. For a more general discussion of the psychological dimensions of *Edgar Huntly* and of Brown's fiction as a whole see chapter 5 of Leslie Fiedler's *Love and Death in the American Novel* (Cleveland: Meridian, 1960).

22. The influence of *Caleb Williams* (1794) on Brown's fiction, and particularly on *Arthur Mervyn*, is quite evident and has received much comment. Dunlap assures us that in the 1790s Brown "was an avowed admirer of Godwin's style, and the effects of that admiration, may be discerned in many of his early compositions" (*Life*, vol. 2, p. 15). Describing a work in progress—"something in the form of a romance"—in his journal in 1797, Brown referred to *Caleb Williams* as the standard by which such a work should be judged.

23. On the question of the truthfulness of Arthur's narrative, see, especially, Patrick Brancaccio, "Studied Ambiguities: *Arthur Mervyn* and the Problem of the Unreliable Narrator," *American Literature* 42 (1970): 18–27. The novel's elaborate narrative structure is described in detail in Kenneth Bernard, "*Arthur Mervyn:* The Ordeal of Innocence," *Texas Studies in Literature and Language* 6 (1965): 441–44.

24. Warner Berthoff, for instance, writes that "the moral irony in the contrasts between the hero's priggish reflections on events and the melodrama of his actual career is remarkably consistent," but feels compelled to insist that "one does not wish to claim too much for Brown as a comic artist manqué, nor as an ironist" (Introduction to Berthoff's edition of *Arthur Mervyn*, p. xviii). James H. Justus gives Brown more credit in his excellent article, "Arthur Mervyn, American," *American Literature* 42 (1970): 304–24.

25. See Trilling, "Manners, Morals, and the Novel," in *The Liberal Imagination* (New York: Scribner's, 1950), pp. 205–22, and Richard Chase, *The American Novel and Its Tradition* (Garden City, N.Y.: Doubleday, 1957).

CHAPTER FOUR

1. Stanley T. Williams, *The Life of Washington Irving* (New York: Oxford University Press, 1935), vol. 1, p. 274.

2. On the significance of Irving's various personae, see William L. Hedges, *Washington Irving: An American Study, 1802–1832* (Baltimore: Johns Hopkins University Press, 1965). I am doubly indebted to Hedges. His book is the best study of Irving to date; specifically, Hedges is the first modern critic—perhaps the first critic since Poe—to take the fictional experiments of *Tales of a Traveller* seriously. I have also profited immensely from Hedges' detailed and invaluable comments on an earlier version of the present chapter.

3. Five years later, in "Tale-Writing" (his expansion of the 1842 Hawthorne review), Poe qualified his praise, objecting to the *Tales* that "in many of them the interest is subdivided and frittered away, and their conclusions are insufficiently *climacic* [sic]." Yet he acknowledged them to be nonetheless "graceful and impressive narratives," especially "The Young Italian" (Poe, *Works*, 13:153–54). These qualifications, it might be noted, accompanied a corresponding devaluation of his 1842 estimate of Hawthorne. In an 1838 letter to Nathan C. Brooks, in which he declined a request to write a general review of Irving for the Baltimore *American Museum*, Poe wrote that "Irving is much overrated" (*Letters*, 112). This harsh estimate, however, had more to do with Irving's more recent works of popular history and biography than with the fiction of the early 1820s. Poe remained consistently an admirer of *Tales of a Traveller*.

4. Evert Duyckinck, quoted in Jay Leyda, *The Melville Log: A Documentary Life of Herman Melville, 1819–1891* (New York: Harcourt, Brace, 1951), p. 253.

5. "In these shorter writings," Irving wrote to Henry Breevoort on December 11, 1824, "every page must have its merit—The author must be continually piquant—woe to him if he makes an awkward sentence or writes a stupid page" (Irving, *Letters, Volume II, 1823–1838*, edited by Ralph M. Aderman, Herbert L. Kleinfield, and Jenifer S. Banks [Boston: Twayne, 1979], p. 91). On Irving's two projected novels, see Williams, *Life*, vol. 1, p. 162, and vol. 2, pp. 289–90, 324. The first of these, "Rosalie," was the work of 1817–18; a portion appeared as "Mountjoy" in *Wolfert's Roost* (1855). The second finally led to the section "Buckthorne and His Friends" in *Tales of a Traveller*.

6. For an account of the critical reception of the *Tales*, see Williams, *Life*, vol. 2, pp. 294–96 Both typical and prophetic was the pronouncement of the *Metropolitan Literary Chronicle:* "Above all let [Irving] shun tale-writing: it is not his forte" (quoted ibid., p. 296).

7. Irving, *Letters, Volume II*, p. 274. According to William Hedges: "For Irving, history remained fiction, even though his tone shifted from the comic to the romantic. *Columbus* is—as much as any American novel—a romance" (*Washington Irving*, p. 250). Such a statement may accurately describe the *effect* of Irving's later historical writing, but it remains true that, after 1824, he took pains to cultivate the

stance of "historian." Romance might be indulged in covertly, "mingled" with history, but it was not to be indulged in openly.

8. On this matter see especially chapter 3, "The Fiction of History," in Hedges, *Washington Irving*, pp. 65–85.

9. Irving to S. Austin Allibone, in Pierre M. Irving, *The Life and Letters of Washington Irving* (New York: Putnam, 1864), vol. 4, p. 236.

10. Irving, *Letters, Volume I, 1802–1823*, edited by Alderman, Kleinfeld, and Banks (1978), pp. 614, 540.

11. The principal financial nightmare of Irving's early years was the bankruptcy of his brothers' business, "P. and E. Irving"—a proceeding in which Irving himself became personally involved. Nonetheless, in 1820, with his brother Peter and against the advice of his other brothers, he began to invest in French navigation companies. The losses incurred in this venture did not prevent his similarly fruitless speculation in the Bolivar Copper Mines in 1825.

12. Irving, *Letters, Volume I*, pp. 540, 541.

13. On the importance of the contest between imagination and "substantial" achievement to "The Legend of Sleepy Hollow" and "Rip Van Winkle," see, especially, Robert A. Bone, "Irving's Headless Hessian: Prosperity and the Inner Life," *American Quarterly* 15 (1963): 167–75; Daniel G. Hoffman, *Form and Fable in American Fiction* (New York: Oxford University Press, 1965), pp. 83–98; Terence Martin, "Rip, Ichabod, and the American Imagination," *American Literature* 31 (1959): 137–59; and Donald A. Ringe, "New York and New England: Irving's Criticism of American Society," *American Literature* 38 (1967): 455–67.

14. "The Student of Salamanca" appeared in *Bracebridge Hall*, "The Story of the Young Italian" in *Tales of a Traveller*. "Buckthorne," originally projected as a novel, concludes the section "Buckthorne and His Friends" in *Tales of a Traveller*. Irving had planned, for a time, to include some version of this section in *Bracebridge Hall*.

15. The basic situation of "The Student of Salamanca"—a young man, through his attraction to an old scientist's daughter, becomes implicated in the scientist's experiments—bears an intriguing similarity to the situation of Hawthorne's "Rappacini's Daughter." Similarity of this sort is hardly proof of influence, but it is nevertheless suggestive. Even more suggestive is the description of de Vasques' alchemy: "In all his visionary schemes there breathed a spirit of lofty, though chimerical, philanthropy, that won the admiration of the scholar. Nothing sordid, nor sensual; nothing petty nor selfish seemed to enter into his views, in respect to the grand discoveries he was anticipating. On the contrary his imagination kindled with conceptions of widely dispensed happiness" (118). One thinks, here, of a whole series of idealistically deluded scientists and reformers in Hawthorne, especially of Aylmer in "The Birth-mark."

16. Irving, *Letters, Volume II*, p. 85.

17. This similarity is noted in Hedges, *Washington Irving*, p. 141.

18. *Analectic Magazine*, vol. 3, 356–57. The review, reprinted in volumes 3 (pp. 353–70) and 4 (pp. 105–17), was taken from the *Ecclectic Review*.

19. Irving, in *Life and Letters*, vol. 2, p. 57.

20. This conversion of Crayon into Nervous Gentleman has a relation to the biographical background of the *Tales*. Irving had set out to write not a collection of stories but a "German Sketch-Book," very much in the Crayon manner. It was

only his inability to produce such a book that led to the form of the *Tales* as they finally appeared. In this sense, Crayon's predicament in the midst of his "pleasant tour"—even though it somewhat recalls Sterne's *Sentimental Journey*—might well be regarded as a fictionalization of Irving's predicament with respect to his "German Sketch-Book."

21. Henry Seidel Canby, *Classic Americans* (New York: Harcourt, Brace, 1931), p. 90.

22. For a guide to the sources on which Irving drew in composing the *Tales*, see Williams, *Life*, vol. 2, pp. 286–94. For a contemporary complaint about their lack of originality, see *American Writers: A Series of Papers Contribured to Blackwood's Magazine (1824–25) by John Neal*, Fred Lewis Pattee, ed. (Durham, N.C.: Duke University Press, 1937), p. 139.

23. Richard Chase, *The American Novel and Its Tradition* (Garden City, N.Y.: Doubleday, 1957); Leslie Fiedler, *Love and Death in the American Novel* (Cleveland: Meridian, 1960). Chase's omission of Irving is understandable; dealing only with long fictions, he also excludes Poe. Fiedler, however, who devotes forty-four pages to Poe (and the "Development of the Gothic") and forty-two pages to Brown (and the "Invention of American Gothic"), mentions Irving only once—in a reference to "such popular histories as Irving's *Astoria* or *Adventures of Captain Bonneville*" (*Love and Death*, p. 371). Similarly, Joel Porte, who discusses Poe at length in *The Romance in America* (Middletown, Conn.: Wesleyan University Press, 1969), virtually ignores Irving.

24. Chase, Fiedler, and Porte all stress the importance of Cooper, and quite rightly. He had his own debts and contributions to the gothic tradition; moreover, his writings were certainly as influential as Irving's, and (together with the influence of Scott) they spawned a host of imitations. Yet to exclude Irving seems perversely myopic. Poe and Hawthorne, for instance, in turning to the short gothic tale rather than the long historical romance, began their careers by following Irving's example, not Cooper's.

25. Henry A. Pochman, "Irving's German Sources and *The Sketch-Book*," *Studies in Philology* 27 (1930): 506; Williams, *Life*, vol. 1, p. 274.

26. Lady Lillycraft, in *Bracebridge Hall*, "places the Castle of Otranto at the head of all romances" (22). But Irving was not quite so old-fashioned. The principal target of the *Tales* is the rational English gothic of Ann Radcliffe, whom Irving placed "at the head of her line" (Williams, *Life*, vol. 2, p. 288). He also undoubtedly read Lewis and Maturin and, as well, a good deal of the German literature that influenced them. The effect of such reading can be detected in such tales as "The Story of the Young Italian" and "The Story of the Young Robber." Also, the opening pages of Maturin's *Melmoth the Wanderer* seem very much in force in the description of Buckthorne's miserly uncle. On these matters, see Henry A. Pochman, "Irving's German Tour and Its Influence on His Tales," *PMLA* 45 (1930): 1150–87, and Williams, *Life*, vol. 2, pp. 286–96 (esp. pp. 288–89).

27. This "exiled nobleman" suggests that Schiller's *Die Räuber*, or at least its immense and abiding popularity, lies behind the Misses Popkins' sensationalism. Schiller's play, which gave birth to the literary vogue of *banditti*, clearly influences the "Italian Banditti" section generally and "The Story of the Young Robber" in particular. For an argument that it also lies behind "The Story of the Young

Italian," see Pochman, "Irving's German Tour," pp. 1172–73; for a rejoinder, see Williams, *Life*, vol. 2, pp. 288–89.

28. Poe is often included in lists of American gothic diabolists. In fact, however, he consistently expressed his scorn for diabolism. In 1831 he dismissed "the devil in Melmoth" as one who "labors indefatigably through three octavo volumes, to accomplish the destruction of one or two souls, while any common devil would have demolished one or two thousand" (*Works*, 7:xxviii; cf. 11:13). "Pure Diabolism," he wrote in 1849, "is but Absolute Insanity. Lucifer was merely unfortunate in having been created without brains" (16:160). "Absolute Insanity" was not, of course, without interest for Poe, and there may be some defensive special pleading in his dismissal of "Pure Diabolism." But his interest was more in self-torture or passive victimization than in external, proselytizing evil. In "The Pit and the Pendulum," for instance, the Inquisition, that great subject of gothic fiction, is simply a convenience. As an active presence it is not "treated" at all. What matters are its effects, not its motives.

29. It must be admitted that some of the deflations in Irving's tales seem to result more from indolence than from calculation. For instance, following the spectral shenanigans in "Wolfert Webber," we are simply told: "In fact, the secret of all this story has never to this day been discovered" (*Tales*, 540). Irony may be intended here, but one's impression is that Irving, having written himself into a corner, wishes to extricate himself as rapidly as possible.

30. Sir Walter Scott, "Ann Radcliffe," in Ioan Williams, ed., *Sir Walter Scott on Novelists and Fiction* (London: Routledge & Kegan Paul, 1968), p. 116.

31. On this aspect of Hawthorne, see, for instance, Yvor Winters, *In Defense of Reason* (Denver: Alan Swallow, 1947), p. 170, and F. O. Matthiessen, *American Renaissance* (New York: Oxford University Press, 1941), pp. 276–77.

32. This aspect of Irving's achievement is discussed in John Clendinning, "Irving and the Gothic Tradition," *Bucknell Review* 12 (1964): 90–98.

33. Ann Radcliffe, *The Mysteries of Udolpho* (1794) (New York: Dutton, 1931), vol. 1, p. 301, and *The Italian: or, the Confessional of the Black Penitents* (1797) (New York: Oxford University Press, 1968), p. 302.

34. Jane Austen's attack on gothicism also includes her most sustained defense of her own chosen mode (which she carefully distinguishes from romance): the "realistic" novel of manners, "in which the most thorough knowledge of human nature, the happiest delineation of its varieties, the liveliest effusions of wit and humour, are conveyed to the world in the best-chosen language" (*Northanger Abbey* [1818] [New York: New American Library, 1965], p. 30). What distinguishes Irving is his refusal to make this kind of distinction. In these contrasting responses to Mrs. Radcliffe—burlesque rejection as opposed to burlesque indulgence—one comes perhaps as close as one can to the point of divergence between the "realistic" "Great Tradition" of nineteenth-century British fiction and the tradition of American romance.

35. Gottfried's first encounter with the female victim of the Terror is strikingly similar to Tobias Pearson's first encounter with Ilbrahim, victim of the Puritan persecution of the Quakers, in Hawthorne's "The Gentle Boy" (first published in 1832, in *The Token*). Gottfried, wandering alone at night, sees the spectral woman at the foot of the guillotine. Pearson, wandering alone at evening, sees Ilbrahim at

the foot of the gallows. "What is your name," Pearson asks the strange boy, "and where is your home?" "They call me Ilbrahim," replies the boy, "and my home is here" (*Twice-Told Tales*, 72). "But you have a home," Gottfried suggests to the stranger, to which she replies: "Yes—in the grave!" (70). Gottfried, in compassion, takes her to his home; Pearson, in compassion, takes Ilbrahim to his. One scarcely wishes to argue, here, deliberate allusion by Hawthorne to Irving's story or even conscious imitation. One feels, nevertheless, that Hawthorne read his Irving carefully.

36. The terrifying, mysterious portrait was a standard, even hackneyed, device in gothic fiction; but given Poe's special admiration for "The Young Italian," it is interesting to note how close Irving's uses of the device, here, is to Poe's use of it in the narrative frame of "The Oval Portrait."

CHAPTER FIVE

1. Typical of this contemporaneous image of Poe is the infamous "Ludwig" obituary, in which Rufus Griswold began his long-successful campaign to destroy Poe's reputation: "He was at times a dreamer—dwelling in ideal realms—in heaven or hell, peopled with creations and the accidents of his brain.... His poems... illustrate a morbid sensitiveness of feeling, a shadowy and gloomy imagination" (quoted in Eric Carlson, ed., *The Recognition of Edgar Allan Poe* [Ann Arbor: University of Michigan Press, 1966], pp. 32, 35).

2. The most comprehensive biography of Poe is Arthur Hobson Quinn's *Edgar Allan Poe: A Critical Biography* (New York: Appleton-Century-Crofts, 1941).

3. On spiritualism and its precursors, see Slater Brown, *The Heyday of Spiritualism* (New York: Hawthorn, 1970), pp. 1–97; Howard Kerr, *Mediums, and Spirit-Rappers, and Roaring Radicals: Spiritualism in American Literature, 1850–1900* (Urbana: University of Illinois Press, 1972), pp. 3–21; R. Laurence Moore, *In Search of White Crows: Spiritualism, Parapsychology, and American Culture* (New York: Oxford University Press, 1977); and Frank Podmore, *Modern Spiritualism: A History and a Criticism* (London: Methuen, 1902), vol. 1, pp. 154–76. For Poe's views on phrenology, see Edward Hungerford, "Poe and Phrenology," *American Literature* 2 (1930): 209–31. Poe attended some of the sessions, between 1845 and 1847, in which Andrew Jackson Davis, mesmerized into supposed communion with the other side, dictated *The Principles of Nature, Her Divine Revelations and a Voice to Mankind*—a major text of the later spiritualist movement, which one Poe biographer claims to have been the inspiration for *Eureka* (see Hervey Allen, *Israfel: The Life and Times of Edgar Allan Poe* [New York: Doran, 1926], p. 206). Such Poe pieces as "Mesmeric Revelation" and "The Facts in the Case of M. Valdemar," drawing on the supernal side of contemporary mesmerical exhibitions, aroused interest and sometimes credence among protospiritualists.

4. Orestes Brownson, in "Two Articles from *The Princeton Review*," in Perry Miller, ed., *The Transcendentalists: An Anthology* (Cambridge, Mass.: Harvard University Press, 1960), p. 243.

5. On the adaptation and misreading of German philosophy and aesthetics in England and America, see, for instance, René Wellek, *Confrontations: Studies in the Intellectual and Literary Relations between Germany, England, and the United States*

NOTES TO PAGES 91–100

during the Nineteenth Century (Princeton: Princeton University Press, 1965), especially pp. 153–212 (for discussions of German philosophy and American Transcendentalism).

6. *Selected Writings of Ralph Waldo Emerson*, Brooks Atkinson, ed. (New York: Modern Library, 1940), pp. 27–28, 14.

7. Moore, *In Search of White Crows*, pp. 36–37.

8. The fullest discussion of Poe's treatment of this issue is in Floyd Stovall's "Poe's Debt to Coleridge," *University of Texas Studies in English* 10 (1930): 70–127. Also relevant are chapter 2, "Aspects of a Philosophy of Poetry," in Edward H. Davidson, *Poe: A Critical Study* (Cambridge, Mass.: Harvard University Press, 1966), and Margaret Alterton, *Origins of Poe's Critical Theory* (*University of Iowa Humanistic Studies* 2, no. 3 [1925]).

9. On Poe's shift from mysticism to the psychology of taste, see George Kelly, "Poe's Theory of Beauty," *American Literature* 27 (1956): 521–36.

10. Eight days after writing this letter to Lowell, Poe developed the same ideas more briefly in a letter to Thomas Holley Chivers (*Letters*, 260). These ideas also lie behind a tale written in the same year (1844), "Mesmeric Revelation."

11. Hawthorne mentions *Undine* twice, in a tone of great familiarity, in his letters to his future wife, Sophia Peabody (*Love Letters of Nathaniel Hawthorne, 1839–1863* [Washington: National Cash Register, 1973; reprint of 1907 Dofobs edition], vol. 1, pp. 97, 219). Melville, as Leon Howard argues, seems to have drawn on *Undine* in his portrayal of Yillah in *Mardi* (*Herman Melville: A Biography* [Berkeley: University of California Press, 1951], pp. 113–14).

12. "The Poetic Principle," published only after Poe's death, was prepared as a lecture in 1848. Many of its most important sections, however, were lifted from an 1842 review of Longfellow's *Ballads and Other Poems*. The passage here quoted, except for very minor verbal changes, is entirely the work of 1842 (cf. *Works*, 11:72).

13. On the importance of vampirism to Poe see D. H. Lawrence, *Studies in Classic American Literature* (Garden City, N.Y.: Doubleday, 1951), pp. 78–79; Allen Tate, "Our Cousin, Mr. Poe," *Collected Essays* (Denver: Alan Swallow, 1959), pp. 455–71; Lyle H. Kendall, "The Vampire Motif in 'The Fall of the House of Usher,'" *College English* 24 (1963): 450–53; and J. O. Bailey, "What Happens in 'The Fall of the House of Usher'?" *American Literature* 35 (1964): 445–66.

14. Hawthorne, in *The American Magazine . . .* 2 (1836): 319.

15. See chapter 6, "The Domestication of Death: The Posthumous Congregation," in Ann Douglas, *The Feminization of American Culture* (New York: Knopf, 1977), pp. 200–226. The specific relevance to Poe of nineteenth-century burial customs and related matters is also discussed in Davidson's *Poe: A Critical Study*, pp. 105–21.

16. Moore, *In Search of White Crows*, pp. 23–24.

17. Thomas W. White, editor of the *Southern Literary Messenger*, did apparently find "Berenice" a bit too much. "Your opinion of it," Poe wrote to him in 1835, "is very just. The subject is by far too horrible. . . . I allow that it approaches the very verge of bad taste" (*Letters*, 57–58). But White *did* publish "Berenice," and he subsequently hired its author to edit the *Messenger*.

18. Compare Daniel Hoffman's point that Poe's "delicacy, or squeamishness,

fooled several generations of readers into thinking that [he] was a spiritual writer—if they didn't take him for a fiend. Of course we can now . . . recognize that it is this suppressed erotic intensity which throbs and shudders throughout" such tales as "Ligeia" (*Poe Poe Poe Poe Poe Poe Poe* [Garden City, N.Y.: Doubleday, 1972], p. 256). Or, as Joel Porte writes of Egaeus in "Berenice": "He grasps the paradox that an act supposedly carried out to obliterate a sexual temptation also represents his giving in to his darkest desires" (*The Romance in America* [Middletown, Conn.: Wesleyan University Press, 1969], p. 84).

19. The most comprehensive and single-minded psychoanalytic study of Poe is Marie Bonaparte's *The Life and Works of Edgar Allan Poe: A Psycho-Analytic Interpretation*, John Rodker, trans. (London: Imago, 1949), originally published in French in 1933. Many of Bonaparte's ideas were anticipated in Joseph Wood Krutch, *Edgar Allan Poe: A Study in Genius* (New York: Alfred A. Knopf, 1926). Since the publication of these two studies, psychoanalysis, in various forms and with varying degrees of rigorousness, has played an important role in many of the most important discussions of Poe.

20. William Faulkner, *Absalom, Absalom!* (New York: Random House, 1936), p. 12.

21. Allen Tate, "Our Cousin, Mr. Poe," *Collected Essays*, pp. 464, 461.

22. "The underlying defect in all of Poe's work," Winters argues, is "the absence of theme." "We have, in brief, all of the paraphernalia of allegory except the significance" ("Edgar Allan Poe: A Crisis in the History of American Obscurantism," in Carlson, ed., *The Recognition of Edgar Allan Poe*, pp. 197, 192). Even those critics who pull back from Winters' outright rejection of Poe find the status of meaning in his work problematic. Edward H. Davidson writes, of the similes and metaphors of his poetry, that they exist in "some private, very special discourse, the vocabulary of which [has], as it were, long ago been established but the key to which [has] long been lost" (*Poe: A Critical Study*, p. 101). And Daniel Hoffman wonders, in reaction to the famous line in Mallarmé's commemorative sonnet: "did Edgarpoe *really* 'donner un sens plus pur aux mots de la tribu'? . . . Or did he obfuscate—not purify—the language of the human tribe, in order to disembody language from its gross husks of meaning?" (*Poe Poe Poe Poe Poe Poe Poe*, p. 73).

23. See especially, in this respect, Harry Levin's *The Power of Blackness* (New York: Alfred A. Knopf, 1958); Leslie Fiedler's *Love and Death in the American Novel* (Cleveland: Meridian, 1960); and Ishmael Reed's surreal historical novel *Flight to Canada* (New York: Avon, 1977). For a different sort of "social" reading, one that finds a relation between Poe's fiction and America's fascination with the unexplored West, see Edwin Fussel's *Frontier: American Literature and the American West* (Princeton: Princeton University Press, 1965), pp. 132–74.

24. Compare the description of the "motley drama" in "The Conqueror Worm," containing "much of Madness, and more of Sin, / And Horror the soul of the plot" (7:87). Poe refers elsewhere to "that purity and perfection of *beauty* which are the soul of the poem proper" (15:15), and in "The Philosophy of Furniture," to cite only one more example, he writes: "The soul of the apartment is the carpet. From it are deduced not only the hues but the forms of all objects incumbent" (14:103).

25. "Poe's Works" (a review of Griswold's 1850 edition, first published in *The Literary World*), in Carlson, ed., *The Recognition of Edgar Allan Poe*, p. 43.

26. As Arthur Hobson Quinn puts it: "Generally speaking, the Arabesques are the product of powerful imagination and the Grotesques have a burlesque or satirical quality" (*Edgar Allan Poe: A Critical Biography*, p. 289).

27. On Poe's use of physical/psychological allegory, using architecture, for example, to represent conflicting psychological states, see, especially, Richard Wilbur, "The House of Poe" (1959), in Carlson, ed., *The Recognition of Edgar Allan Poe*, pp. 255–77.

28. The feminine connotations of this fissure are noted in Bonaparte, *The Life and Works of Edgar Allan Poe*, pp. 239–40.

29. The tendency of Poe's hero-narrators to convert their world into something like a literary text is one of the concerns of David Halliburton's *Edgar Allan Poe: A Phenomenological View* (Princeton: Princeton University Press, 1973).

30. On Poe's reputation and influence in France, see, especially, Patrick F. Quinn, *The French Face of Edgar Poe* (Carbondale: Southern Illinois University Press, 1957).

31. Pope, "Essay on Criticism," lines 297–98.

32. *Selected Writings of Ralph Waldo Emerson*, p. 155.

33. Compare Georges Poulet's statement that "the dreams of Poe are never magical. Though once they were, they are so no longer. Thence their unreal, vaporous character, like a thought which in losing its actuality has also lost its consistency" (*Studies in Human Time*, Elliott Coleman, trans. [Baltimore: Johns Hopkins University Press, 1956], p. 331).

34. As Daniel Hoffman notes: "The price of pure idealism is the extinction of reality, as Poe acknowledged in 'To Helen,' transforming his beloved into a statue" (*Form and Fable in American Fiction* [New York: Oxford University Press, 1961], p. 212). One might compare Edward Davidson's comment that "Poe more and more sought physical embodiments for his abstract ideas; and once he found such a representation, the object became a thing-in-itself and its attendant idea almost nothing" (*Poe: A Critical Study*, p. 77).

35. The interest and importance of "The Assignation" were first urged upon me by Professor Ann Douglas, of Columbia University. I am indebted throughout this chapter both to her criticism and comments on earlier versions of the chapter itself and to her many valuable suggestions about Poe.

36. *Selected Writings of Ralph Waldo Emerson*, p. 329.

CHAPTER SIX

1. Nathaniel Hawthorne, quoted in Julian Hawthorne, *Nathaniel Hawthorne and His Wife* (Boston: Houghton Mifflin, 1884), vol. 1, pp. 107–8. I have also, for biographical information, relied on Randall Stewart, *Nathaniel Hawthorne: A Biography* (New Haven: Yale University Press, 1948).

2. For a different view of Hawthorne's initial commitment to literature— arguing that he became a writer with confidence and only later associated his vocation with alienation—see Nina Baym, *The Shape of Hawthorne's Career* (Ithaca: Cornell University Press, 1976).

3. Hawthorne's letter to Longfellow is reprinted in George Perkins, ed., *The Theory of the American Novel* (New York: Rinehart, 1970), pp. 65–66. In 1854

Hawthorne recorded in his *English Notebooks* a recurring dream, with similar implications: "that I am still at college—or, sometimes, even at School—and there is a sense that I have been there unconscionably long, and have quite failed to make such progress in life as my contemporaries have; and I seem to meet some of them with a feeling of shame and depression that broods over me, when I think of it, even at this moment. This dream, recurring all through these twenty or thirty years, must be one of the effects of that heavy seclusion in which I shut myself up, for twelve years, after leaving college, when everybody moved onward and left me behind" (98). Randall Stewart and Nina Baym, among others, minimize the significance of the "solitary years," arguing that the importance of Hawthorne's early alienation has been exaggerated—that he in fact "enjoyed," as Baym puts it, "a range of deep human ties during his life" (*The Shape of Hawthorne's Career*, p. 29). No doubt he did, especially in the years following his marriage; but only by ignoring letters and notebook entries of the kind I have just quoted can one close one's eyes to the fact that Hawthorne, from the beginning, associated imaginative literary vocation with alienation.

4. The most comprehensive sources of biographical information are Leon Howard, *Herman Melville: A Biography* (Berkeley: University of California Press, 1951) and the complementary volume by Jay Leyda, *The Melville Log: A Documentary Life of Herman Melville, 1819–1891* (New York: Harcourt, Brace, 1951).

5. For a fascinating discussion of Hawthorne's narrative rhetoric, his effort "to open an intercourse with the world," see Kenneth Dauber, *Rediscovering Hawthorne* (Princeton: Princeton University Press, 1977).

6. For my sense of the importance of the opposition, in Melville, between the linear and the circular, I am especially indebted to John Seelye, *Melville: The Ironic Diagram* (Evanston: Northwestern University Press, 1970).

7. See chapter 7, "Allegory and Symbolism," in F. O. Matthiessen, *American Renaissance: Art and Expression in the Age of Emerson and Whitman* (New York: Oxford University Press, 1941), pp. 242–315. Matthiessen is careful to qualify the distinction. "Both allegory and symbolism," he notes, "can arise from the same thinking." Moreover, neither Hawthorne nor Melville observed the distinction between "allegory" and "symbolism" in critical discourse. Nevertheless, Matthiessen argues, "the differentiation . . . between Melville and Hawthorne at their most typical" is "the differentiation between symbolism and allegory" (ibid., pp. 248–50). Also see Charles Feidelson, Jr., *Symbolism and American Literature* (Chicago: University of Chicago Press, 1953), esp. pp. 14–15, 32. Unlike Matthiessen, Feidelson tends to use the distinction to praise Melville at Hawthorne's expense.

8. Although the third part of Matthiessen's chapter on "Allegory and Symbolism" is entitled "The Crucial Definition of Romance" and deals with Hawthorne's remarks on romance (especially in the preface to *The House of the Seven Gables*), it never directly addresses the question of how Hawthorne's meditations on romance are related to Coleridge's conceptions of either allegory or symbolism.

9. *The Complete Works of Samuel Taylor Coleridge* (New York: Harper & Bros., 1871), vol. 1, pp. 436–38. One might compare Coleridge's definition of "symbol" in *Aids to Reflection* (Coleridge's best-known prose work in America in the first half of the nineteenth century) as "a sign included in the idea which it represents;—that is, an actual part chosen to represent the whole. . . . And this definition of the

word is of great practical importance, inasmuch as the symbolical is hereby distinguished *toto genere* from the allegoric and metaphorical" (ibid., p. 270).

10. A similarly "Coleridgean" bias, although not specifically concerned with allegory, is evident in Hawthorne's remarks in an 1846 review of William Gilmore Simms's *Views and Reviews:* "Mr. Simms . . . possesses nothing of the magic touch that should cause new intellectual and moral shapes to spring up in the reader's mind, peopling with varied life what had hitherto been a barren waste. . . . His style . . . is composed of very good words, exceedingly well put together; but, instead of being imbued and identified with his subject, it spreads itself over it like an incrustation" (reprinted in Randall Stewart, "Hawthorne's Contributions to *The Salem Advertiser,*" *American Literature* 5 [1934]: 332).

11. On the theoretical problems raised by Coleridge's distinction, see, especially, Angus Fletcher, *Allegory: The Theory of a Symbolic Mode* (Ithaca: Cornell University Press, 1964), pp. 13–18, and Edwin Honig, *Dark Conceit: The Making of Allegory* (New York: Oxford University Press, 1966), esp. pp. 45–50.

12. *Love Letters of Nathaniel Hawthorne, 1839–1863* (Washington, D.C.: National Cash Register; reprint of 1907 Dofobs edition), vol. 2, p. 64.

13. E. P. Whipple, *Graham's Magazine*, September, 1852; reprinted in J. Donald Crowley, ed., *Hawthorne: The Critical Heritage* (London: Routledge & Kegan Paul, 1970), p. 255.

14. Compare Robert Scholes' and Robert Kellogg's definition of "allegory" as "the kind of didactic narrative which emphasizes the illustrative meaning of its character, setting, and action" (*The Nature of Narrative* [New York: Oxford University Press, 1966], p. 107).

15. Fletcher, *Allegory*, pp. 2, 7; Hawthorne, *American Magazine of Useful and Entertaining Knowledge* 2 (1836): 419.

16. See David Levin, *In Defense of Historical Literature* (New York: Hill & Wang, 1967), pp. 78–87, and Michael Colacurcio, "Visible Sanctity and Specter Evidence: The Moral World of Hawthorne's 'Young Goodman Brown.'" *Essex Institute Historical Collections* 110 (1975): 259–99.

17. See, especially, Frederick C. Crews, *The Sins of the Fathers: Hawthorne's Psychological Themes* (New York: Oxford University Press, 1966), pp. 98–106.

18. Michael Colacurcio suggests such a view of the relationship between Hawthorne's allegorical practice and his treatment of Puritanism in his reference to the "perfectly historical but almost antiallegorical process" of "Young Goodman Brown" ("Visible Sanctity and Specter Evidence," p. 275).

19. Coleridge, *Complete Works*, vol. 1, p. 436.

20. Northrop Frye, *Anatomy of Criticism* (Princeton: Princeton University Press, 1957), pp. 306, 304. See also, in this connection, Fletcher, *Allegory*, pp. 3–10.

21. John Caldwell Stubbs, for instance, glosses the "neutral territory" passage by explaining that for Hawthorne romance "involved the interplay of real life with conceptual abstraction." In this view, romance sounds very much like Coleridgean "allegory." When Hawthorne speaks of "truth," according to Stubbs, he "is not talking of subjective truth; he is talking of discovering and picturing scenes of universal truth. His notion is platonic" (*The Pursuit of Form: A Study of Hawthorne and the Romance* [Urbana: University of Illinois Press, 1970], pp. 8–9, 12–13).

22. For most readers, Poe wrote, "the *obvious* meaning of this article will be

found to smother its insinuated one. The *moral* put into the mouth of the dying minister will be supposed to convey the *true* import of the narrative; and that a crime of dark dye, (having reference to the 'young lady') has been committed, is a point which only minds congenial with that of the author will perceive" (*Works*, 11:111).

23. Compare Frederick Crews's reading of "The Artist of the Beautiful" (*The Sins of the Fathers*, pp. 167–70).

24. Compare Crews, ibid., p. 126.

25. One might note, in connection with Poe, the significant description of Aylmer's "scientific" method: "He handled physical details, as if there were nothing beyond them; yet spiritualized them all, and redeemed himself from materialism, by his strong and eager aspiration towards the infinite. In his grasp, the veriest clod of earth assumed a soul" (49). This apparently approving passage represents not the narrator's point of view but Georgiana's as she reads Aylmer's journal; and her "reverence" for him, which seems to increase with her discovery that his experiments generally end in failure, raises questions about her own suppressed motives, questions ignored by those who see her simply as a projection or helpless victim of Aylmer's repressed urges. For if Aylmer is a "spiritual" sadist, what are we to think of his wife, who chooses him out of a phalanx of more healthy-minded suitors and who keeps reinforcing his "ideal" view of his homicidal enterprise? Unlike Poe, Hawthorne became increasingly interested in the woman's stake in "spirituality" and, by the time of *The Scarlet Letter*, in her rebellion against it.

26. See Fletcher's chapter 6, "Psychoanalytic Analogues: Obsession and Compulsion" (*Allegory*, pp. 279–303), where he points out that "We are not talking about the compulsive behavior of authors as men; we are talking about literary products which have this form, a form we can discern regardless of its causes, a form which for our purposes exists as a thing in itself." Fletcher discusses many "compulsive" aspects of allegory, but what he has to say about allegorical characters (or "agents") is, for our purposes, especially pertinent: "The well-known stubbornness, conscientiousness, and idealism of the compulsive neurotic come through in fictional works as the undeviating, totally committed, absolutist ethics of characters like the creative thinkers in Hawthorne" (ibid., pp. 286, 288).

27. Feidelson, *Symbolism and American Literature*, p. 14; Hawthorne, *Love Letters*, vol. 1, p. 70; Feidelson, *Symbolism and American Literature*, p. 15.

28. Coleridge, *Complete Works*, p. 437.

29. "*Moby-Dick*," writes Matthiessen, "is, in its main sweep, an example of the reconcilement of the general with the concrete, of the fusion of idea and image" (*American Renaissance*, p. 250). "Unlike Hawthorne," writes Feidelson, "the Melville of *Moby-Dick* does not verge toward allegory, because he locates his symbols in a unitary act of perception" (*Symbolism and American Literature*, p. 32).

30. For a full account of the stages of composition of *Mardi* and of Melville's changing conceptions of what he was doing as he wrote, see Merrel R. Davis, *Melville's "Mardi": A Chartless Voyage* (New Haven: Yale University Press, 1952), pp. 45–99.

31. See William Charvat, *The Profession of Authorship in America, 1800–1870*, Matthew J. Bruccoli, ed. (Columbus: Ohio State University Press, 1968), p. 216.

32. Evert Duyckinck, New York *Literary World* (November 22, 1851); reprinted in Hershel Parker, ed., *The Recognition of Herman Melville* (Ann Arbor: University of Michigan Press, 1967), p. 41.

33. Duyckinck, *The Knickerbocker* (May, 1850) and New York *Literary World* (August 21, 1852); reprinted in Parker, ed., *The Recognition of Herman Melville*, pp. 30, 55. Melville's conflict with the orthodox taste of critics and public is discussed at length in Perry Miller, *The Raven and the Whale: The War of Words and Wits in the Era of Poe and Melville* (New York: Harcourt, Brace & World, 1956), esp. pp. 223–34. Melville's family, who generally agreed with the preferences of the critics, also discussed his career on the basis of Common Sense "realist" assumptions. Thus his mother wrote to her brother in 1853, urging that he find Herman a position that would free him of the need to write: "This constant working of the brain, & excitement of the imagination, is wearing Herman out." This same brother insisted, four years later, that Melville mistook his "sphere" in turning from "Narrative" to "Criticism" in a recent series of lectures. He ought, so the uncle reasoned, to work up a *Typee*-like narrative of his recent Mediterranean tour, for "such work would not make a requisition on his imagination" (Eleanor Melville Metcalf, *Herman Melville: Cycle and Epicycle* [Cambridge, Mass.: Harvard University Press, 1953], pp. 147, 169).

34. See Harrison Hayford, "Poe in *The Confidence-Man*," *Nineteenth-Century Fiction* 14 (1959): 207–18.

35. See Charvat, *The Profession of Authorship in America*, esp. pp. 204–5.

36. Coleridge, *Complete Works*, pp. 436–37.

37. *The Selected Writings of Ralph Waldo Emerson*, Brooks Atkinson, ed. (New York: Modern Library, 1940), p. 14.

38. Ibid., p. 15.

39. Compare, for example, the language of Poe's 1845 essay on N. P. Willis: "From novel arrangements of old forms which present themselves to it, [the imagination] selects only such as are harmonious;—the result, of course, is *beauty* itself.... The pure Imagination chooses, *from either beauty or deformity*, only the most combinable things hitherto uncombined" (12:38).

40. Hawthorne, *Love Letters*, vol. 1, p. 193.

41. Roy Harvey Pearce, "Hawthorne and the Twilight of Romance," *Yale Review* 37 (1948): 487; Perry Miller, "The Romance and the Novel," *Nature's Nation* (Cambridge, Mass.: Harvard University Press, 1967), pp. 257, 255, 246.

42. James, in Morton Dauwen Zabel, ed., *The Portable Henry James* (New York: Viking, 1951), pp. 405, 393, 401, 489.

Prologue to Part Three

1. For a listing of discussions of American nationalist thought, see chapter 1, note 19.

2. Perry Miller, "The Romance and the Novel," *Nature's Nation* (Cambridge, Mass.: Harvard University Press, 1967), p. 245, and *The Raven and the Whale: The War of Words and Wits in the Era of Poe and Melville* (New York: Harcourt, Brace & World, 1965), pp. 339, 257.

3. One might compare John Caldwell Stubbs' objection, to a similar emphasis in

Joel Porte's *The Romance in America*, that while he "treats the theme of exploration of the wilderness, either geographical or psychological, . . . Porte does not occupy himself much with the *form* of the romance" (*The Pursuit of Form: A Study of Hawthorne and the Romance* [Urbana: University of Illinois Press, 1970], p. 4n).

4. Walter Channing, "Essay on American Language and Literature," *North American Review* 1 (1815): 309.

5. William Ellery Channing, "Remarks on a National Literature," in Robert E. Spiller, ed., *The American Literary Revolution, 1783–1837* (Garden City, N.Y.: Doubleday, 1967), p. 362; Benjamin Spencer, *The Quest for Nationality: An American Literary Campaign* (Syracuse: Syracuse University Press, 1957), p. 175. It might be objected that to stress America's revolutionary origins is to exaggerate the extent to which the War for Independence was in fact "revolutionary." This question has vexed historians for two centuries, and I have no wish, here, to join their fray. But whatever its causes, the Revolution—the deliberate and successful defiance of British authority—clearly *fostered* a "revolutionary" temper or at least a generalized crisis of legitimacy. As Bernard Bailyn has summarized the matter: "In no obvious sense was the American revolution undertaken as a social revolution. No one, that is, deliberately worked for the destruction or even the substantial alteration of the order of society as it had been known. Yet it was transformed as a result of the Revolution. . . . What did now affect the essentials of social organization—what in time would help permanently to transform them—were changes in the realm of belief and attitude" (*The Ideological Origins of the American Revolution* [Cambridge, Mass.: Harvard University Press, 1972], p. 302. It is in this realm of "belief and attitude," particularly respecting attitudes toward traditional canons of legitimacy, that the Revolution would seem most profoundly to have affected the thinking of American writers and intellectuals about the nature of "America," and it matters little whether such changes in attitude were caused, or simply made manifest, by the successful War for Independence. What does matter is that such attitudes of skepticism or distrust were associated by our writers, whether favorably or unfavorably, with the origins of the new nation and its culture. The Revolution, as Bailyn puts it, encouraged the faith "that a better world than any that had ever been known could be built where authority was distrusted and held in constant scrutiny" (ibid., p. 319). Even in the absence of such faith, the distrust endured.

6. William Ellery Channing, "Remarks on a National Literature," in Spiller, ed., *The American Literary Revolution*, p. 364.

7. Ormond's sister, Martinette de Beauvais, has participated in the American Revolution dressed in male clothing. These patriotic associations do not, however, make her any less a match for her brother in disinterested bloodthirstiness. Constantia asks her: "Does not your heart shrink from the view of a scene of massacre and tumult, such as Paris has lately exhibited and will probably continue to exhibit?" "Have I not been three years in a camp?" Martinette answers, alluding to her American experience. "What are bleeding wounds and mangled corpses, when accustomed to the daily sight of them for years? Am I not a lover of liberty? and must I not exult in the fall of tyrants, and regret only that my hand had no share in their destruction?" (170–71).

8. Charles Brockden Brown, *An Address to the Congress of the United States, on the*

Utility and Justice of Restrictions upon Foreign Commerce... (Philadelphia: C. & A. Conrad, 1809), p. iv. The importance of this pamphlet as an index of Brown's intellectual transformation is discussed in chapter 5, "Anarchia, A Species of Insanity," of Arthur Kimball's *Rational Fictions: A Study of Charles Brockden Brown* (McMinnville, Ore.: Linnfield Research Institute, 1968).

CHAPTER SEVEN

1. On Hawthorne's reading of the Revolution back into seventeenth- and eighteenth-century New England history, see Michael Davitt Bell, *Hawthorne and the Historical Romance of New England* (Princeton: Princeton University Press, 1971), esp. pp. 17–81. Also see John P. McWilliams, Jr., "'Thorough-going Democrat' and 'Modern Tory': Hawthorne and the Puritan Revolution of 1776," *Studies in Romanticism* 15 (1976): 549–71.

2. *Selected Writings of Ralph Waldo Emerson*, Brooks Atkinson, ed. (New York: Modern Library, 1940), p. 3.

3. *Love Letters of Nathaniel Hawthorne, 1839–1863* (Washington, D.C.: National Cash Register; reprint of 1907 Dofobs edition), vol. 1, p. 153.

4. Julian Hawthorne, *Nathaniel Hawthorne and His Wife: A Biography* (Boston: Houghton Mifflin, 1884), vol. 2, p. 270. Julian had his own motives for stressing his father's sorrow at the prospect of dissolution, namely, to counter the lingering charge of want of patriotism arising from Hawthorne's friendship with Franklin Pierce (to whom he dedicated *Our Old Home* in the midst of the Civil War) and from his failure to take a strong stand in favor of the Union or in opposition to slavery. Still, the son's account seems fair in the light of his father's comments at the time, recorded in his letters and in his essay "Chiefly about War Matters."

5. Emerson, *Selected Writings*, pp. 327, 329–30.

6. See *Hawthorne and the Historical Romance of New England*.

7. Philip Schaff, *America: A Sketch of Its Political, Social, and Religious Character*, Perry Miller, ed. (Cambridge, Mass.: Harvard University Press, 1961), pp. 114–15.

8. *The Complete Works of Samuel Taylor Coleridge* (New York: Harper & Bros., 1871), vol. 1, p. 436.

9. For an intriguing discussion of the historical implications of Hester's rebellion, see Michael Colacurcio, "Footsteps of Ann Hutchinson: The Context of *The Scarlet Letter*," *ELH* 39 (1972): 459–94.

10. Here Hawthorne links Hester's symbolic "revolution" with the actual Puritan Revolution in England, culminating in the execution of Charles I in 1649. It may thus be significant that the dates of the historical action of *The Scarlet Letter*, 1642 to 1649, are identical with the duration of the English Civil War, which also began in 1642 (cf. H. Bruce Franklin, "Introduction," *"The Scarlet Letter" and Related Writings* [Philadelphia: Lippincott, 1967]). If so, the significance of historical timing is ironic, hinting at the growing irrelevance of the New England experiment in the face of the outbreak of fighting in England. Hawthorne's sense of the transformation of New England Puritanism—his sense that, having lost their central role in the Work of Redemption, they were forced to insist all the harder on what had initially been only means—is in this respect quite close to that of Perry

Miller, in "Errand into the Wilderness" (*Errand into the Wilderness* [New York: Harper, 1956], pp. 1–15). On the dates of the historical action of *The Scarlet Letter*, see Charles Ryskamp, "The New England Sources of *The Scarlet Letter*," *American Literature* 31 (1959): 257–72.

11. "It is remarkable," Hawthorne writes in "Another View of Hester," "that persons who speculate the most boldly often conform with the most perfect quietude to the external regulations of society" (164). "The subtle insanity of Ahab respecting Moby Dick," writes Ishmael, "was noways more significantly manifested than in his superlative sense and shrewdness in foreseeing that, for the present, the hunt should in some way be stripped of that strange imaginative impiousness which naturally invested it.... Ahab plainly saw that he must still in a good degree continue true to the natural, nominal purpose of the Pequod's voyage; observe all customary usages" (183–84).

12. Not that Hawthorne saw *all* such Providential rhetoric as egocentric; rather he saw it as potentially so, especially as Puritanism was handed down from the founders to their sons and grandsons. Hence the significant distinction, in "The Minister's Vigil," between Dimmesdale and the community of the fathers. "It was, indeed, a majestic idea," Hawthorne writes, "that the destiny of nations should be revealed, in these awful hieroglyphics, on the cope of heaven. A scroll so wide might not be deemed too expansive for Providence to write a people's doom upon.... But what shall we say, when an individual discovers a revelation, addressed to himself alone, on the same vast sheet of record! In such a case, it could only be the symptom of a highly disordered mental state, when a man, rendered morbidly self-contemplative by long, intense, and secret pain, had extended his egotism over the whole expanse of nature, until the firmament itself should appear no more than a fitting page for his soul's history and fate" (155).

13. Richard Poirier, *A World Elsewhere: The Place of Style in American Literature* (New York: Oxford University Press, 1966), pp. 15, ix, 5.

14. "Hawthorne," as F. O. Matthiessen put it in 1941, "assumed with confidence the continuance of democratic opportunity. Yet in the poetic justice of bestowing opulence on all those who had previously been deprived of it by the Judge, [he] overlooked the fact that he was sowing all over again the same seeds of evil" (*American Renaissance: Art and Expression in the Age of Emerson and Whitman* [New York: Oxford University Press, 1941], p. 332).

15. Quoted in Moncure D. Conway, *The Life of Nathaniel Hawthorne* (London: Walter Scott, 1890), p. 101.

16. Hawthorne to Horatio Bridge, May 3, 1843; MS. copy in unknown hand, Henry W. and Albert A. Berg Collection, The New York Public Library, Astor, Lenox, and Tilden Foundations, quoted by permission.

17. Allan Seager, quoted in Jay Martin, *Nathanael West: The Art of His Life* (New York: Farrar, Straus, & Giroux, 1970), p. 305.

18. One might compare an 1838 entry in *The American Notebooks*, concerning the behavior of one "Uncle John" in a barroom: "Mr. Smith, unbidden, gave him a glass of gin, which the old man imbibed by the warm fireside and grew the younger for it" (140). I am indebted, here, to Joel Porte's acute discussion of the saloon chapter, especially his observation that "for Coverdale, art, like alcohol, should contain and engender pleasure, not pain; and an illuminating set of

analogies between these two illusion-producers obviously underlies all of Hawthorne's aesthetic theorizing in this chapter" (*The Romance in America: Studies in Cooper, Poe, Hawthorne, Melville, and James* [Middletown, Conn.: Wesleyan University Press, 1969], p. 132).

19. In the same vein, Hawthorne wrote to Sophia Peabody in 1841, urging her not to resort to mesmerism for relief from headaches: "Without distrusting that the phenomena which thou tellest me of, and others as remarkable, have really occurred, I think that they are to be accounted for as the result of a physical and material, not of a spiritual, influence" (*Love Letters*, vol. 2, p. 63).

20. I am indebted here to Porte's discussion of *The Blithedale Romance* (*The Romance in America*, pp. 125–37) and to two discussions of the book by Frederick Crews—"A New Reading of *The Blithedale Romance*," *American Literature* 29 (1957): 147–70, and *The Sins of the Fathers: Hawthorne's Psychological Themes* (New York: Oxford University Press, 1966), pp. 194–212. Crews's later reading is apparently meant as a repudiation of the earlier one; I have nevertheless profited greatly from both.

21. See, for instance, Ann Douglas, *The Feminization of American Culture* (New York: Knopf, 1977), especially chapters 8 and 9, and Martin Green, *The Problem of Boston: Some Readings in Cultural History* (New York: Norton, 1966).

22. Not all critics accept this reading of Priscilla's moral status in *The Blithedale Romance*. For a quite different reading, which sees Priscilla as truly virtuous and Zenobia as "a woman deeply guilty of violating the sanctity of essential human relationships," see Marius Bewley, *The Eccentric Design: Form in the Classic American Novel* (New York: Columbia University Press, 1963), pp. 147–60.

23. Dimmesdale displays a similar "aestheticism" in his response to Hester's confession, in the forest scene, that Chillingworth is her husband. "The shame!" he murmurs, "the indelicacy!—the horrible ugliness of this exposure of a sick and guilty heart to the very eye that would gloat over it!" (194).

24. For readings of Hawthorne's fiction in such terms, see, for instance, Lawrence Sargent Hall, *Hawthorne: Critic of Society* (New Haven: Yale University Press, 1944), and A. N. Kaul, *The American Vision: Actual and Ideal Society in Nineteenth-Century Fiction* (New Haven: Yale University Press, 1963), pp. 139–213.

25. See Max Weber, *Economy and Society: An Outline of Interpretive Sociology*, Guenther Roth and Claus Wittich, eds. (New York: Bedminster Press, 1968), pp. 246–54, 1121–23, and Norman O. Brown, *Life against Death: The Psychoanalytic Meaning of History* (New York: Vintage, 1959).

26. Charles Brockden Brown, *Monthly Magazine, and American Review* 3 (1800): 161–62.

CHAPTER EIGHT

1. On the contest between authority and revolution in Melville, see, for instance, John Bernstein, *Pacificism and Rebellion in the Writings of Herman Melville* (The Hague: Mouton, 1964); Nicholas Cannaday, Jr., *Melville and Authority* (Gainesville: University of Florida Press, 1968); Robert Zaller, "Melville and the Myth of Revolution," *Studies in Romanticism* 15 (1976): 607–22; and, especially, the discussion of *Billy Budd* in Hannah Arendt, *On Revolution* (New York: Viking,

1965), pp. 74–83. In fact, however, this contest is so central to Melville, and consequently to Melville criticism, as to make citation of relevant critical works meaningless. I have tried, in notes to the discussion that follows, to indicate particular debts and/or disagreements. In general, I have profited especially from: D. H. Lawrence, *Studies in Classic American Literature* (Garden City, N.Y.: Doubleday, 1923), pp. 142–74; Lewis Mumford, *Herman Melville: A Study of His Life and Vision*, rev. ed. (New York: Harcourt, Brace & World, 1962); F. O. Matthiessen, *American Renaissance: Art and Expression in the Age of Emerson and Whitman* (New York: Oxford University Press, 1941), pp. 371–514; William Ellery Sedgwick, *Herman Melville: The Tragedy of Mind* (Cambridge, Mass.: Harvard University Press, 1944); Richard Chase, *Herman Melville: A Critical Study* (New York: MacMillan, 1949); Newton Arvin, *Herman Melville: A Critical Biography* (New York: Viking, 1957); Lawrance Thompson, *Melville's Quarrel with God* (Princeton: Princeton University Press, 1952); Warner Berthoff, *The Example of Melville* (Princeton: Princeton University Press, 1962); H. Bruce Franklin, *The Wake of the Gods: Melville's Mythology* (Stanford: Stanford University Press, 1963); Paul Brodtkorb, *Ishmael's White World: A Phenomenological Reading of "Moby-Dick"* (New Haven: Yale University Press, 1965); William Charvat, *The Profession of Authorship in America, 1800–1870*, Matthew J. Bruccoli, ed. (Columbus: Ohio State University Press, 1968), pp. 204–61; Edgar A. Dryden, *Melville's Thematics of Form: The Great Art of Telling the Truth* (Baltimore: Johns Hopkins University Press, 1968); John Seelye, *Melville: The Ironic Diagram* (Evanston: Northwestern University Press, 1970); and Ann Douglas, *The Feminization of American Culture* (New York: Knopf, 1977), pp. 289–326.

2. Melville had nearly finished a first and apparently quite different version of *Moby-Dick* by August, 1850, which Evert Duyckinck, who later attacked the final version in the *Literary World,* described in a letter to his brother as "a romantic, fanciful & literal & most enjoyable presentment of the whale fishery" (quoted in Eleanor Melville Metcalf, *Herman Melville: Cycle and Epicycle* [Cambridge, Mass.: Harvard University Press, 1953], p. 84). For speculation on the process of composition and on the nature of the first version, see Howard P. Vincent, *The Trying-Out of Moby-Dick* (Carbondale: Southern Illinois University Press, 1949), pp. 13–49 (esp. p. 46, for speculation that "a conflict between two men, an officer and a common sailor," was the basis of the original plot); Leon Howard, *Herman Melville: A Biography* (Berkeley: University of California Press, 1951), pp. 162–79; George R. Stewart, "The Two *Moby-Dicks,*" *American Literature* 25 (1954): 417–48; James Barbour, "The Composition of *Moby-Dick,*" *American Literature* 47 (1975): 343–60; and Robert Milder, "The Composition of *Moby-Dick:* A Review and a Prospect," *ESQ* 23 (1977): 203–16.

3. Metcalf, *Herman Melville: Cycle and Epicycle,* p. 7.

4. White-Jacket's "long enough" especially recalls the passage, in Emerson's "American Scholar," that begins "We have listened too long to the courtly muses of Europe," and White-Jacket's whole peroration recalls Emerson's final sentence, "A nation of men will for the first time exist, because each believes himself inspired by the Divine Soul which also inspires all men" (*Selected Writings of Ralph Waldo Emerson,* Brooks Atkinson, ed. [New York: Modern Library, 1940], pp. 62, 63). Melville could have encountered such sentiments almost anywhere, but his letters

to Evert Duyckinck, in the spring of 1849, record his special excitement at discovering Emerson (see *Letters*, esp. pp. 78–80).

5. On American perceptions—and fears—of the similarities between Jackson and Napoleon, see, for instance, John William Ward, *Andrew Jackson: Symbol for an Age* (New York: Oxford University Press, 1962), esp. pp. 112–13, 182–85. For a fascinating account of one American's efforts to come to terms with Napoleon and Jackson (and, in this case, Goethe), see Perry Miller, "Emersonian Genius and the American Democracy," *Nature's Nation* (Cambridge, Mass.: Harvard University Press, 1967), pp. 163–74.

6. Melville's defiance of popular convention, in *Mardi*, came at a time when marriage (he had married Elizabeth Shaw in August, 1847) made commercial success far more imperative than it had been before. The association of marriage with confinement, in *Mardi*, thus intensifies one's perception of the perversity (in Poe's sense) of Melville's decision to "out with the Romance." The caricature of Anatoo, Samoa's "termagent wife," was written by a man recently married. The attack on Anatoo was of course thoroughly conventional: one thinks of Irving's Dame Van Winkle or of the shrewish wife of William the Testy in *Knickerbocker's History of New York*. But there is something perverse in Irving's handling of the theme, too; *Knickerbocker's History* was, after all, written in the midst, the first rush, of his bereavement at the death of his fiancée, Matilda Hoffman.

7. See Howard, *Herman Melville: A Biography*, pp. 115–16; Merrell R. Davis, *Melville's "Mardi": A Chartless Voyage* (New Haven: Yale University Press, 1952), pp. 45–99; and Elizabeth S. Foster, "Historical Note," in her edition of *Mardi: and A Voyage Thither* (Evanston and Chicago: Northwestern University Press and the Newberry Library, 1970), pp. 661–62.

8. Melville seems very close, here, to Freud's understanding of the interconnections between psychological and political repression in *Civilization and Its Discontents*. According to Ann Douglas (in *The Feminization of American Culture*, pp. 298–99), Melville "was perhaps the first major American author to sense that the essential question for the American writer and intellectual was whether he was going to subscribe to what would be the Freudian or what would be the Marxist analysis of his culture—whether he would focus on personality or on societal structures as causal agent." She then distinguishes between "Marxist" works (including *Typee, Omoo, Redburn, White-Jacket,* and *Moby-Dick*), in which "Melville is interested primarily in questions of class," and "Freudian" works (such as *Mardi, Pierre,* and *The Confidence-Man*), where the concern is "primarily psychological." This distinction—which Douglas admits to be "imprecise, since all the works show the influence of both kinds of thinking"—is important, especially as it illuminates Melville's relationship with the largely feminine American reading public of his day. But it seems to me even more important to stress the simultaneity and interpenetration of "Marxist" and "Freudian" concerns even in those early works that, in Douglas's view, focus on "the clash between employer and employed, master and slave, government and soldier." In his understanding of the psychological mechanism and function of "liberal" political power and oppression, Melville foreshadows the efforts of such thinkers as Herbert Marcuse to bridge the gap between Freudian and Marxist analyses (see Marcuse's *Eros and Civilization: A*

Philosophical Inquiry into Freud [New York: Random House, 1962], chaps. 3 and 4 and esp. pp. 82–84).

9. Charles Olson, *Call Me Ishmael* (San Francisco: City Lights, 1947), p. 82.

10. See, for instance, Newton Arvin's "mythic" reading of "the initiation of innocence into evil" in *Redburn* (in *Herman Melville: A Critical Biography*, p. 103). For objections to such readings, see James Schroeter, *"Redburn* and the Failure of Mythic Criticism," *American Literature* 39 (1967): 279–97, and Warner Berthoff, *The Example of Melville*, pp. 32–33.

11. Melville himself partly compensated for his lowly status as a mere sailor by exaggerating his importance on his own whaling voyages. In an 1850 letter to Richard Bentley, proposing *Moby-Dick* (then in progress) for British publication, he claimed "personal experience, of two years & more, as a harpooneer" (109). On the exaggeration of the claim, see Howard, *Herman Melville: A Biography*, pp. 63–64.

12. On Ishmael's projection of his own vision into the world and action of *Moby-Dick*, see, especially, Paul Brodtkorb, *Ishmael's White World*.

13. See, for instance, Marius Bewley, *The Eccentric Design: Form in the Classic American Novel* (New York: Columbia University Press, 1963), esp. pp. 210–11.

14. The classic account of this quality in our fiction is Richard Chase's discussion of the fascination, in the greatest American novels, with "the aesthetic possibilities of radical forms of alienation, contradiction, and disorder" (*The American Novel and Its Tradition* [Garden City, N.Y.: Doubleday, 1957], p. 2). On the importance of the tension between circular vision and linear action in Melville, see John Seelye, *Melville: The Ironic Diagram*.

15. That Bulkington's rebellion was possibly the crisis of the original version of *Moby-Dick* is suggested by Alan Heimert, *"Moby-Dick* and American Political Symbolism," *American Quarterly* 15 (1963): 530–31.

16. On the implications, for Melville, of nineteenth-century comparative mythology, see, especially, H. Bruce Franklin, *The Wake of the Gods: Melville's Mythology*, esp. chapter 1.

17. Charles Brockden Brown, "Journal Letters to Henrietta G.," in David Lee Clark, *Charles Brockden Brown: Pioneer Voice of America* (Durham, N.C.: Duke University Press, 1952), p. 102.

18. *Selected Writings of Ralph Waldo Emerson*, p. 336.

19. The phrase is F. O. Matthiessen's (*American Renaissance*, p. 119).

20. For suggestive speculation on Melville's original intentions in *Pierre*, see William Charvat, *The Profession of Authorship in America*, pp. 249–52. I am also indebted to Henry A. Murray's "Introduction" to *Pierre* (New York: Hendricks House, 1949).

21. See Michael Davitt Bell, "The Glendinning Heritage: Melville's Literary Borrowings in *Pierre*," *Studies in Romanticism* 12 (1973): 741–62.

22. Pierre's grandfather's baton, "this symbol of command," reemerges in "Benito Cereno" in Don Benito's "artificially stiffened" and "empty" scabbard, "apparent symbol of despotic command." Cereno, who ends in "melancholy" and "muteness" and who, at the last, "did, indeed, follow his leader," is yet another of Melville's enervated, paralytic victims, unable to face the implications, for his own

sense of his self, of the violence unleashed by Babo but also unable, on the other hand, to maintain Amasa Delano's obtuse equanimity (314–15).

23. See, for instance, Arvin, *Herman Melville*, pp. 229–31, and Matthiessen, *American Renaissance*, p. 486.

24. Not that Ishmael is totally immune to indulging in such calculatedly unfortunate similes. Hence, for instance, the account of man's hope of resurrection in "The Chapel": "But Faith, like a jackal, feeds among the tombs, and even from these dead doubts she gathers her most vital hope" (41). Poe might well have been thrilled.

25. For the contrary view, that the rhetorical surface of *The Confidence-Man* in fact testifies to the abiding energy of its own creation and that of its culture as well, see Warwick Wadlington, *The Confidence Game in American Literature* (Princeton: Princeton University Press, 1975), pp. 137–70. For my understanding of this difficult book I am indebted to the "Introduction" and notes in Elizabeth S. Foster's edition of *The Confidence-Man* (New York: Hendricks House, 1954). I am equally indebted to the notes in the editions of H. Bruce Franklin (New York: Bobbs-Merrill, 1967) and Hershel Parker (New York: Norton, 1971).

26. Paul Brodtkorb, *"The Confidence-Man:* the Con-Man as Hero," *Studies in the Novel* 1 (1969): 430. Also crucial is Brodtkorb's point that "the book's basic irony is not satirical: it is directed against neither the con-men, nor ordinary human hypocrisy which, presumably, could be changed into 'sincerity' by a cognitive act of will. Instead, it seems non-satirically to point out that, given the nature of selfhood, sincerity and consistency of belief are impossible" (ibid., p. 422).

27. Elizabeth Foster argues that the Confidence-Man represents the devil, not Christ (see the "Introduction" to her edition, pp. xlix–liii). More recently, H. Bruce Franklin has argued convincingly that the Confidence-Man is *both* Christ and Satan. Even if one finds unnecessarily limiting Franklin's claim that "Melville made the shape-shifting struggles and the ultimate identity of Vishnu and Siva into the central structural fact of *The Confidence-Man,*" his general point seems valid, namely, that in the universe of Melville's romance "man's Savior—Manco Capac, Vishnu, Christ, Apollo, the Buddhists' Buddha—is embodied by the Confidence-Man, who is also man's Destroyer—Satan, Siva, the Hindus' Buddha. Melville's mythology converts all gods into the Confidence Man" (*The Wake of the Gods*, p. 187). More recent criticism has also been increasingly aware of the relationship between the Confidence-Man's supernatural status (divine and/or satanic) and his status as a figure of the romancer. For instance, Carolyn Lury Karcher notes that the book "obscurely" links "the fictional representation of human 'reality' with the mythical representation of divine 'reality,'" and she goes on to argue that the Confidence-Man thus represents both Christ and the writer ("The Story of Charlemont: A Dramatization of Melville's Concepts of Fiction in *The Confidence-Man: His Masquerade,*" *Nineteenth-Century Fiction* 21 [1966]: 73–74). Joel Porte entitles his discussion of *The Confidence-Man*, in *The Romance in America* (Middletown, Conn.: Wesleyan University Press, 1969), "A Portrait of the Artist as Devil."

28. Compare Edgar Dryden's comments that "each newly discovered clue, each new operative pattern or allusion, leads not beneath the verbal surface but across it to another mystery," and, again, that *"The Confidence-Man* radically conflates the

supernatural, natural, and artistic realms, placing them all on one plane" (*Melville's Thematics of Form*, pp. 151–52, 153–54).

29. On the centrality of Moredock's story to the meaning of *The Confidence-Man*, see, for instance, William Ellery Sedgwick, *Herman Melville: The Tragedy of Mind*, p. 190, and Foster's "Introduction," p. xci. On Moredock as Melville's ideal, see John W. Schroeder, "Sources and Symbols for Melville's *Confidence-Man*," *PMLA* 66 (1951): 363–80. For the opposite view, see Roy Harvey Pearce, "Melville's Indian-hater: A Note on the Meaning of *The Confidence-Man*," *PMLA* 67 (1952): 942–48.

30. Hershel Parker, "The Metaphysics of Indian-hating," *Nineteenth-Century Fiction* 18 (1963): 169.

31. To cite another subverted distinction, Judge Hall speaks of the back-woodsman as "self-willed," as an exemplary instance of "self-reliance" as opposed to reliance on external forces or opinions (125); yet it is the ironic, deterministic point of his remarks that these "self-reliant" qualities derive from the *circumstances* of backwoods life. One recalls Hawthorne's comment about Hester, that "the tendency of her fate and fortunes had been to set her free" (199). Hawthorne's effect, however, is one of psychological and social complexity, while Melville's is one, simply, of ironic self-contradiction.

32. On Melville's (or Charlie's) distortion of Hall's *Sketches of History, Life, and Manners, in the West*, see Edwin Fussell, *Frontier: American Literature and the American West* (Princeton: Princeton University Press, 1965), pp. 320–24.

33. Michael Kammen, *People of Paradox: An Inquiry Concerning the Origins of American Civilization* (New York: Random House, 1973), pp. 3–4.

34. Edgar Dryden, *Melville's Thematics of Form*, p. 151.

35. On the many connections between the Confidence-Man and various sun gods see the notes to Franklin's edition and his discussion of *The Confidence-Man* in *The Wake of the Gods*, pp. 153–87. Also see Dryden, *Melville's Thematics of Form*, pp. 158–62, on the relationship of sun and sun-god images in *The Confidence-Man* to Ishmael's "colorless, all-color" of nihilism.

36. Melville had of course treated contemporary America allegorically in the Vivenza chapters of *Mardi* and briefly in the opening chapters of *Redburn*, but *Pierre* was his first work with a wholly contemporary American setting. Many of Hawthorne's sketches of the 1830s and 1840s also have a nominally contemporary setting, and analysis of contemporary American culture is the burden of such satires as "The Celestial Railroad" (1843); but *The House of the Seven Gables*, after the opening historical background, is his first extended contemporary American work. It is also worth noting that the mode of Hawthorne's contemporary satires resembles, in many respects, the mode of *The Confidence-Man*; "The Celestial Railroad," for instance, is reprinted in the "Backgrounds and Sources" section of Hershel Parker's Norton Critical Edition of *The Confidence-Man* (pp. 232–46).

37. Henry James, reprinted in Edmund Wilson, ed., *The Shock of Recognition* (New York: Modern Library, 1955), p. 465.

38. Hawthorne used this American "Master Genius" idea in "A Select Party." This story, collected in *Mosses from an Old Manse*, particularly struck Melville. In his review of *Mosses*, Melville noted the sketch's indication of "a parity of ideas, at least in this one point, between a man like Hawthorne and a man like me" (420).

BIBLIOGRAPHICAL APPENDIX

Parenthetical page references following quotations
in the text are to the editions listed below.

CHARLES BROCKDEN BROWN

Advertisement for *Sky Walk*. In Harry R. Warfel, ed., *"The Rhapsodist" and Other Uncollected Writings by Charles Brockden Brown*. New York: Scholars' Facsimiles and Reprints, 1943.

Arthur Mervyn, or Memoirs of the Year 1793. Edited by Warner Berthoff. New York: Rinehart, 1962.

Edgar Huntly, or Memoirs of a Sleep-Walker. Philadelphia: David McKay, 1887.

Ormond. Edited by Ernest Marchand. New York: Hafner, 1962.

The Rhapsodist. In *"The Rhapsodist" and Other Uncollected Writings*.

"Walstein's School of History." In *"The Rhapsodist" and Other Uncollected Writings*.

Wieland or The Transformation, together with Memoirs of Carwin the Biloquist, A Fragment. Edited by Fred Lewis Pattee. New York: Hafner, 1958.

NATHANIEL HAWTHORNE

The American Notebooks. Vol. 8 of the Centenary Edition of the Works of Nathaniel Hawthorne. Columbus: Ohio State University Press, 1962——.

"The Artist of the Beautiful." Centenary Edition, vol. 10.

"The Birth-mark." Centenary Edition, vol. 10.

The Blithedale Romance. Centenary Edition, vol. 3.

"The Custom-House." Centenary Edition, vol. 1.

"Endicott and the Red Cross." Centenary Edition, vol. 9.

The English Notebooks. Edited by Randall Stewart. New York: Russell & Russell, 1962.

"Ethan Brand." Centenary Edition, vol. 11.

"Fancy's Show Box." Centenary Edition, vol. 9.

"The Gentle Boy." Centenary Edition, vol. 9.
"The Gray Champion." Centenary Edition, vol. 9.
The House of the Seven Gables. Centenary Edition, vol. 2.
"Main Street." Centenary Edition, vol. 11.
The Marble Faun. Centenary Edition, vol. 4.
Our Old Home. Centenary Edition, vol. 5.
The Scarlet Letter. Centenary Edition, vol. 1.
Twice-Told Tales. Centenary Edition, vol. 9.
"Young Goodman Brown." Centenary Edition, vol. 10.

WASHINGTON IRVING

Bracebridge Hall. Edited by Herbert F. Smith. Boston: Twayne, 1977.
A History of New York . . . by Diedrich Knickerbocker. New York: Putnam, 1849.
"Robert Treat Paine." In *Biographies and Miscellanies,* edited by Pierre M. Irving. New York: Putnam, 1866.
The Sketch Book of Geoffrey Crayon, Gent. Edited by Haskell Springer. Boston: Twayne, 1978.
Tales of a Traveller. New York: Putnam, 1865.
"Thomas Campbell." In *Biographies and Miscellanies.*

HERMAN MELVILLE

"Bartleby, the Scrivener: A Story of Wall-Street." In *Great Short Works of Herman Melville,* edited by Warner Berthoff. New York: Harper & Row, 1966.
"Benito Cereno." In *Great Short Works.*
Billy Budd. In *Great Short Works.*
The Confidence-Man: His Masquerade. Edited by Hershel Parker. New York: Norton, 1971.
"Hawthorne and His *Mosses.*" In *The Portable Melville,* edited by Jay Leyda. New York: Viking, 1952.
Israel Potter: His Fifty Years of Exile. Edited by Lewis Leary. New York: Sagamore, 1957.
Journal of a Visit to London and the Continent (1849). Edited by Eleanor Melville Metcalf. Cambridge, Mass.: Harvard University Press, 1948.
The Letters of Herman Melville. Edited by Merrell R. Davis and William H. Gilman. New Haven: Yale University Press, 1960.
Mardi, and a Voyage Thither. Vol. 3 of *The Writings of Herman Melville.* Evanston and Chicago: Northwestern University Press and The Newberry Library, 1968——.
Moby-Dick. Edited by Harrison Hayford and Hershel Parker. New York: Norton, 1967.
Omoo: A Narrative of Adventures in the South Seas. Vol. 2 of *The Writings of Herman Melville.*
Pierre, or The Ambiguities. Vol. 7 of *The Writings of Herman Melville.*
Redburn: His First Voyage. Vol. 4 of *The Writings of Herman Melville.*
Typee: A Peep at Polynesian Life. Vol. 1 of *The Writings of Herman Melville.*

White-Jacket, or The World in a Man-of-War. Vol. 5 of *The Writings of Herman Melville.*

EDGAR ALLAN POE

The Complete Works of Edgar Allan Poe. 17 vols. Edited by James A. Harrison. New York: Thomas Y. Crowell, 1902.

The Letters of Edgar Allan Poe. Edited by John Ward Ostrom. Cambridge, Mass.: Harvard University Press, 1948.

INDEX

Abrams, M. H., 50
Aesthetics, associationist. *See* Associationist aesthetics
Ahlstrom, Sydney E., 249
Alison, Archibald, 53–54, 74, 249
Allegory: defined by Samuel Taylor Coleridge, 133, 134; dismissed by Poe, 87; distinction of, from symbolism rooted in sense of cultural malaise, 149–50; distinction of, as mode, from allegorical intention in Hawthorne, 133–36; in Hawthorne, 133–42; Hawthorne on, 131, 133; in Melville, 131; in Poe, 109–10; Poe on, 108; relationship of, to Common Sense philosophy, 142; relationship of, to symbolism in Hawthorne, 141–42; relevance of, to Hawthorne's portrayal of Puritan history, 136, 174, 176, 179
—distinguished from symbolism: to describe difference between Hawthorne and Melville, 130–31, 132–33; by Samuel Taylor Coleridge, 131–32
—relationship of, to romance, 136–37; in Hawthorne, 137–42, 148, 155
Allen, Hervey, 259
Alterton, Margaret, 260
Arabesque: as cultural condition in Hawthorne, 191; distinguished from

grotesque by Poe, 104–5; in Melville, 214, 219, 225; in Poe, 105–12. *See also* Irony, narrative; Phenomenal style
Arendt, Hannah, 270
Arvin, Newton, 271, 273, 274
Associationist aesthetics: importance of, to conservative theory of romance, 15, 18–22; in Irving, 73–77, 84; and literary nationalism, 16–18
Astor, John Jacob, 64
Austen, Jane, 82, 258

Bailey, J. O., 260
Bailyn, Bernard, 267
Barbour, James, 271
Baudelaire, Charles, 117
Baym, Nina, 262, 263
Becker, Howard S., 31–32
Bell, Michael Davitt, 250, 268, 273
Bentley, Richard, 273
Bernard, Kenneth, 254
Bernstein, John, 270
Berthoff, Warner, 253, 254, 271
Bewley, Marius, 270, 273
Blair, Hugh, 12–13, 124, 249
Bolwell, Robert W., 250
Bonaparte, Marie, 261, 262
Bone, Robert A., 256
Brackenridge, Hugh Henry: *Modern Chivalry*, 4

writiers to hostility toward fiction, 25, 28, 34, 35; clinical nature of, in Brown, 41–42; as logical consequence of conservative theory of romance, 19; as matter of effect in Poe, 87–88; as social norm, 30
Reed, Ishmael, 261
Reeve, Clara, 9, 249
Reid, Thomas, 74, 249
Relation, sacrifice of: centrality of, to nineteenth-century understanding of romance, 39, 142; conservative theory of romance as effort to evade or overcome, 29; as defining quality of romance for Henry James, 8; exacerbated by allegorical and symbolist strategies of Hawthorne and Melville, 133; as form of aesthetic suicide in Poe, 123, 125; in Irving, 64, 65, 76–77, 85; in Melville, 144, 242; in Poe, 87, 88, 102, 117; redefined by Poe as dissociation of effect from intention, 89–90; as repudiation of social normalcy by writer, 35. *See also* Romance; Vocation, literary, choice of
—between: allegorical mode and allegorical intention in Hawthorne, 140; effect and intention in Poe, 89–90; imagination and actuality, 10–11; promptings and utterance in Melville, 222; savagery and civilization in Melville, 216; sincerity and artifice, 242; sound and sense in Poe, 113
—as historical or cultural paradigm: in Hawthorne, 185, 192–93; in Hawthorne and Melville, 124, 155, 159–60, 243; in Melville, 239
—relevance of, to: crisis of Romantic spiritualism, 149, 153; narrative irony in Melville, 230; revolutionary ideology, 162
Revolution, ideology of: in Brown, 49, 51, 165; in Hawthorne, 169–71; Hawthorne on, 198; as ideal in Melville, 199, 201–2, 209, 213; in Irving,

166; in Melville, 169, 196–98, 199–216, 221–22, 226–28; Melville on, 198, 209; in Poe, 165–66
—relationship of, to: alienation of romancer in a hostile culture, 166–67; ideal of sincerity, 162–65, 177–78; romancer's understanding of the sources of his art, 165–67, 170–71, 172, 195–96, 197, 198, 200, 216–17; sacrifice of relation, 162
Richardson, Samuel, 11, 26, 28; *Clarissa*, 3, 4
Ringe, Donald A., 256
Romance: insufficiency of generic definitions of term, xi, xii, 9, 148–49; primacy of psychological or ethical implications of term, in nineteenth-century critical discourse, 9; relationship of, to Romanticism, 148–55; relevance of, to Hawthorne's portrayal of Puritan history, 174, 175–76; relevance of literary nationalism to its development in America, 160–62; relevance of romancers' understanding of its sources to their attitudes toward revolutionary ideology, 165–67, 195–96, 197, 198; sociological meaning of term, xiii; as spiritual mimesis, 50, 91–92, 148; as subjective mimesis, 50, 60. *See also* Relation, sacrifice of
—and allegory, 136–37; in Hawthorne, 137–42, 148, 155
—conservative theory of, 15–22, 29; breakdown of, in Irving, 76–77; in Hawthorne, 182, 187; realism as logical consequence of, 19; as response by fiction writers to hostility toward fiction, 25, 34, 36
—defined by: Hawthorne, 7; Henry James, 7–9
—distinguished from: fact or history, xii, 9–11, 22, 149; novel, as genre, xi, xii, 9
—as historical or cultural paradigm, xiii–xiv, 148; in Hawthorne, 181, 184–85; in Hawthorne and Melville,

Tate, Allen, 101, 260
Tenney, Tabitha: *Female Quixotism*, 25, 45–46
Tennyson, Alfred, 93, 103
Thompson, Lawrence, 271
Tompkins, J. M. S., 9, 249
Transcendentalism: and literary nationalsim, 164; and spiritualism, 91
Trilling, Lionel, xi, 59
Tudor, William, 16
Twain, Mark (Samuel L. Clemens), 66

Vincent, Howard P., 271
Vocation, literary: difficulties of, in pre–Civil War America, 3, 29, 32; Irving on difficulties of, 65–66; Irving's ambivalence toward, 66–67, 71, 73; Melville on difficulties of, 36; relevance of sociology of deviance to understanding of, 30–36
—choice of: by Brown, 3, 32, 43; by Hawthorne, 127–28; by Irving, 3, 32, 65–67, 71; by Melville, 10, 33, 128–29; by Poe, 117, 127; and sacrifice of relation, 10, 35

Wadlington, Warwick, 274
Ward, John William, 272
Warfel, Harry R., 253
Weber, Max, 192
Wellek, René, 259–60
Wells, H. G., 154
West, Nathanael, 185
Whipple, E. P., 133
White, Thomas W., 260
Whitman, Sarah Helen, 99
Whitman, Walt, 16
Wilbur, Richard, 262
Williams, Stanley T., 63, 78, 255, 257, 258
Willis, N. P., 94
Winters, Yvor, 102, 258
Witherington, Paul, 254
Wordsworth, William, 50

Zaller, Robert, 270
Ziff, Larzer, 253